THE
PROGRAMMER'S
ANSI
COBOL
REFERENCE
MANUAL

THE
PROGRAMMER'S
ANSI
COBOL
REFERENCE
MANUAL

DONALD A. SORDILLO

Met College, Boston University

PRENTICE-HALL, INC.
ENGLEWOOD CLIFFS, NEW JERSEY 07632

Library of Congress Cataloging in Publication Data

Sordillo, Donald A. (date)
   The programmer's ANSI COBOL reference manual.

   1. COBOL (Computer program language) I. Title.
QA76.73.C25S65   001.6'424   77-18999
ISBN 0-13-729491-3

© 1978 by Prentice-Hall, Inc., Englewood Cliffs, New Jersey 07632

COBOL is an industry language and is not the property of any company or group of companies, or of any organization or group of organizations.

No warranty, expressed or implied, is made by any contributor or by the CODASYL Programming Language Committee as to the accuracy and functioning of the programming system and language. Moreover, no responsibility is assumed by any contributor, or by the committee, in connection therewith.

The authors and copyright holders of the copyrighted material used herein

> FLOW-MATIC (trademark of Sperry Rand Corporation), Programming for the UNIVAC® I and II, Data Automation Systems copyrighted 1958, 1959, by Sperry Rand Corporation; IBM Commercial Translator Form No. F 28-8013, copyrighted 1959 by IBM; FACT, DSI 27A5260-2760, copyrighted 1960 by Minneapolis-Honeywell

have specifically authorized the use of this material in whole or in part, in the COBOL specifications. Such authorization extends to the reproduction and use of COBOL specifications in programming manuals or similar publications.

Printed in the United States of America

10 9 8 7 6 5 4 3 2

PRENTICE-HALL INTERNATIONAL, INC., *London*
PRENTICE-HALL OF AUSTRALIA PTY. LIMITED, *Sydney*
PRENTICE-HALL OF CANADA, LTD., *Toronto*
PRENTICE-HALL OF INDIA PRIVATE LIMITED, *New Delhi*
PRENTICE-HALL OF JAPAN, INC., *Tokyo*
PRENTICE-HALL OF SOUTHEAST ASIA PTE. LTD., *Singapore*
WHITEHALL BOOKS LIMITED, *Wellington, New Zealand*

TO THE READER

I know that you don't like to read introductions, but in this case you'd better make an exception or most of the potential benefits of this book will be lost to you.

This book is a COBOL reference book. It is for the programmer who knows COBOL but needs refreshing on a point or two in his daily work, in much the same way as an educated person still refers to a dictionary or encyclopedia. Consequently, it has neither a table of contents nor an index. Everything is in alphabetical order. If a reserved word and an ordinary word have the same spelling, the reserved word comes first. In the case of a hyphen it is treated as if it were not there and the two words concatenated. There has been one exception made to the alphabetical ordering of the entries: at the end of the book all the formats have been duplicated for easy reference.

In order to maximize this book's usefulness, the reader should read the entry 'notation in COBOL' before attempting to use the book, since the formats are presented in a simplified form.

Since all COBOLs are equal (but some more equal than others) I have made no attempt to tailor this book to a specific implementation of the language. Rather a 'pure' COBOL, that as defined by ANSI specification X3.23-1974, has been described. Since I have no control over the way in which this specification will be used by others, there can be no guarantee that the material in this book will conform to a specific implementation. In fact, this book contains no nonstandard or implementor-defined features at all. Rather, whenever a feature is implementor-specific, this fact is noted and the reader is directed to the appropriate literature.

Another feature of this book is that all substantive changes from 68 COBOL have been documented two times, collectively under the entry '68 COBOL', and individually under each affected entry. As with 74 COBOL, the 68 COBOL treated is the pure version, although it is recognized that some implementor-defined extensions to 68 COBOL may not be 'new' to 74 COBOL. This book should, then, be of considerable use to the programmer who is converting from 68 to 74 COBOL as well as to the one who wants to write programs with a view towards later movement to a different machine.

This book is heavily cross-referenced; there are almost 2000 of them. Explicit cross-references are indicated at the end of any entry by 'See...'. There are also implicit cross-references. Since every reserved word appears in its own entry, whenever one is encountered in the text it can be considered a cross-reference to that entry.

Some cross-references are intentionally cyclic since one never knows at which point in the cycle a given reader will enter.

The book is replete with redundancies; some features and restrictions are repeated more than once, even within the same entry. The hope is that if a reader looks in a certain place he will not be penalized because it isn't the 'logical' place to look.

As the reader probably knows, each module in COBOL has two non-null levels associated with it. In this book, whenever a feature is implemented only in level 2 of a module, this fact is noted in the description.

A word should be said about the phrase 'the results are undefined'. This does not necessarily mean that the program will abort and the OS crash to the eternal disgrace of the programmer. Operating Systems have a strong survival instinct; they may bail you out. On the other hand, they may not. It all depends on the charity of the systems programmer who, after all, is a human being like yourself.

In closing, I would like to give special thanks to my wife Jean who, foregoing innumerable trips, outings, and other entertainment, enabled me to complete the work. My debt to her is immeasurable. Of her I can only agree with Dante:

"Quand'i' vengo a veder voi, bella gioia;
E quand'io vi son presso, i'sento Amore."

DONALD A. SORDILLO

Medford, Massachusetts

A

abbreviated combined relation condition

An abbreviated combined relation condition is the combined condition that results from the explicit omission of a common subject or of a common subject and common relational operator in a consecutive sequence of relation conditions.

See combined condition, complex condition, relational operator, relation condition.

absolute line number

See LINE NUMBER.

ACCEPT

The ACCEPT verb is used to input low-volume data. The data is transferred according to the rules of the MOVE statement.

Format 1:

ACCEPT identifier-1 [FROM mnemonic-name]

This statement causes data to be transferred from a hardware device into identifier-1, replacing its previous contents. The size of the data transfer depends upon the input device accessed and is determined by the implementor.

Data is transferred as follows:

1. If the size of the data being transferred is identical to the size of identifier-1, the data is transferred and stored in identifier-1.

2. If the size of identifier-1 is less than the size of the data being transferred, the left-most characters of the data being transferred are stored in identifier-1, left-justified; characters to the right (for which there is no room in identifier-1) are ignored.

3. If the size of identifier-1 is greater than the size of the data being transferred, this data is stored left-justified and the remaining character positions in identifier-1 are space-filled or zero-filled.

Example: Assume the data being transferred is: ABCDEF

PIC of identifier-1	XXXXXXXX	XXXXXX	XXXXX
result in identifier-1	ABCDEF△△	ABCDEF	ABCDE

N.B. '△' represents a blank or space.

1

Level 2 Considerations

If level 2 of the Nucleus Module is implemented, whenever the size of the transferred data is less than the size of identifier-1, the data is stored left-justified and additional data is requested. For subsequent data transfers the 'size' of identifier-1 is taken to be equal to the as yet unfilled portion of it. These subsequent data transfers continue, following the previously stated rules, until the data being transferred either fits exactly or has excess characters (which will be truncated).

Programming note: Depending on the method of implementation, there is the possibility of the program hanging if sufficient data to fill identifier-1 is not made available. Note especially in the following example that the action is not complete until the third data transfer.

Example: Assume the input device has a transfer size of three characters and that the data being transferred is the alphabet, i.e., ABC, DEF, GHI, etc. Let MSG1 have a PICTURE of X(7).

ACCEPT MSG1

The first characters transferred will be ABC; MSG1 will contain

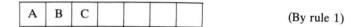

(By rule 1)

Since MSG1 is not filled, its new size is considered to be X(4), and more data is requested. This time DEF is sent. Now MSG1 contains

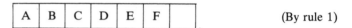

(By rule 1)

Now the effective size of identifier-1 is X. Since data is being transferred in three-character groups, rule 3 applies and the final contents of identifier-1 are

Note that the 'HI' has been dropped.

The From Option

The FROM option is part of level 2 of the Nucleus Module. If it is not implemented, the input device is defined by the implementor. If the FROM option is used, the mnemonic-name must be specified and associated with a hardware device in the SPECIAL-NAMES paragraph of the ENVIRONMENT DIVISION. Data is transferred from the designated device.

Format 2:

$$\text{\underline{ACCEPT} identifier-1 \underline{FROM}} \begin{Bmatrix} \text{\underline{DATE}} \\ \text{\underline{DAY}} \\ \text{\underline{TIME}} \end{Bmatrix}$$

This form of ACCEPT is a new feature of 74 COBOL, and is available only if level 2 of the Nucleus Module is implemented.

This statement causes the requested information to be transferred to identifier-1. DATE, DAY and TIME are special COBOL data items that must not be described by the user in his source program. They have implicit descriptions as follows:

DATE is implicitly described as an elementary item with a

PICTURE of: 999999V

The value of DATE represents the year of the century, the month of the year, and the day of the month, in that order from left to right. Thus August 27, 1978 would be represented as: 780827

DAY is implicitly described as an elementary item with a

PICTURE of: 99999V

The value of DAY represents the year of the century and the day of the year numbered from 1 to 366. August 27, 1976 would be represented as 76240. However, August 27, 1975 would be represented as 75239, because 1975 was not a Leap Year.

TIME is implicitly described as an elementary item with a

PICTURE of: 9(8)V

The value of TIME represents, in a 24-hour system, the number of elapsed hours, minutes, seconds, and hundredths of seconds after midnight (in that order, from left to right). The minimum value of TIME is 0, the maximum is 23595999. If the computer hardware does not have the capability to provide fractional parts of TIME, the closest decimal approximation is used. 9:03 A.M. would be expressed as 09030000; 9:03 P.M. as 21030000.

Format 3:

ACCEPT cd-name MESSAGE COUNT

This form of ACCEPT is available only if the Communication Module has been implemented. This statement causes the MESSAGE COUNT item for cd-name (data-name-11 in the communication description entry) to be set to a value that indicates the number of messages that currently exist in a queue or sub-queue.

When this statement is executed, the communication description specified by cd-name must contain the name of the queue to be tested. If a sub-queue is to be tested, both its name and its queue's name must be specified.

The Status Key item, data-name-10 of the communication description entry, is updated as follows:

Value	Meaning
00	No error detected. Action completed.
20	One or more queues or sub-queues unknown. No action taken.

This form of ACCEPT is new to 74 COBOL.

See cd-name, communication description entry, Communication Module, elementary item, FILE STATUS, mnemonic-name, Nucleus Module, queue, sub-queue.

ACCESS MODE

The ACCESS MODE clause specifies the manner in which records are accessed in a file. This clause is in the FILE-CONTROL paragraph.

Format:

$$\text{\underline{ACCESS} MODE IS} \begin{cases} \text{SEQUENTIAL} & \text{[\underline{RELATIVE} KEY IS data-name-1]} \\ \begin{Bmatrix} \text{\underline{RANDOM}} \\ \text{\underline{DYNAMIC}} \end{Bmatrix} & \text{\underline{RELATIVE} KEY IS data-name-1} \end{cases}$$

Sequential Access Mode

If the ACCESS MODE clause is not specified, SEQUENTIAL is implied. If the access mode is sequential, records are accessed in a certain sequence, depending upon the file's organization. If a file has sequential *organization*, records are accessed in the same sequence as they were written into the file when the file was created or extended.

If a file has relative organization, the sequence is the order of ascending relative record numbers of those records that currently exist in the file. The RELATIVE KEY clause can be specified only for files with relative organization. This clause is new to 74 COBOL.

If a file has indexed organization, the sequence is the order of ascending record key values within a given key of reference.

Random Access Mode

If the RANDOM access mode is specified, the file must have relative or indexed organization. For indexed files, the value of the record key data item indicates the record to be accessed. For relative files, the value of data-name-1 indicates the relative record number of the record to be accessed. The RELATIVE KEY clause can be specified only for files with relative organization. This clause is new to 74 COBOL.

Dynamic Access Mode

If the DYNAMIC access mode is specified, the file must have relative or indexed organization. In this mode, files can be accessed sequentially or randomly.

The RELATIVE KEY clause can be specified only for files with relative organization.

Both the DYNAMIC access mode and the RELATIVE KEY clause are new to 74 COBOL.

Relative Key Clause

The RELATIVE KEY clause can be specified only for files with relative organization. It must be specified if a file is to be referenced by a START statement. Data-name-1 must be an unsigned integer that is not defined in any record description entry associated with the file in whose file description the ACCESS MODE clause appears. Data-name-1 can be qualified.

See dynamic access, file description, indexed i-o, key of reference, random access, record description, record key, relative i-o, relative record number, SELECT, sequential access, sequential i-o, START.

actual decimal point

The actual decimal point is the physical representation of the decimal point position in a data item. It is usually indicated in the PICTURE clause by a period. However, if the DECIMAL-POINT IS COMMA option is specified in the SPECIAL-NAMES paragraph, a comma is used instead of a period to indicate the actual decimal point. The actual decimal point occupies one character position in the item.

Examples:

PICTURE IS 999.99
PICTURE IS 999,99

See character position.

ACTUAL KEY

ACTUAL KEY was formerly a clause in the FILE-CONTROL paragraph.

ADD

The ADD verb forms the sum of two or more data items and then sets one or more data items equal to the result. The composite of operands must not exceed 18 digits. In formats 1 and 2, the multiple receiving fields are a new feature of 74 COBOL, and are implemented only in level 2 of the Nucleus Module.

Format 1:

$$\underline{ADD} \begin{Bmatrix} \text{identifier-1} \\ \text{literal-1} \end{Bmatrix} \ldots \underline{TO} \; \{\text{identifier-m} \, [\underline{ROUNDED}],\} \ldots$$

[; ON <u>SIZE ERROR</u> imperative-statement-1]

All data items preceding TO are added together forming an intermediate sum. This intermediate sum is then added to the current value of each identifier following TO and the result of this addition becomes the new value of that identifier. Thus the new value of each identifier following TO is equal to its original value plus the sum of all the identifiers preceding TO. The composite of operands is determined by superimposing all the operands used, aligned by decimal point.

Examples: Assume as initial values: TAXES = 50
                                            BCBS = 10
                                            FICA = 15
                                            TOTAL = 30
                                            DEDUCTIONS = 0

1. ADD TAXES TO TOTAL
   After execution, the value of TOTAL is 80.
2. ADD TAXES,BCBS,FICA TO TOTAL
   After execution, the value of TOTAL is 105.
3. ADD TAXES TO TOTAL,DEDUCTIONS
   After execution, the value of TOTAL is 80; the value of DEDUCTIONS is 50.
4. ADD TAXES,BCBS,FICA TO TOTAL,DEDUCTIONS
   After execution, the value of TOTAL is 105; the value of DEDUCTIONS is 75.

In none of these examples is the value of TAXES, BCBS, or FICA changed.

Format 2:

$$\underline{ADD} \begin{Bmatrix} \text{identifier-1} \\ \text{literal-1} \end{Bmatrix}, \begin{Bmatrix} \text{identifier-2} \\ \text{literal-2} \end{Bmatrix} \ldots \underline{GIVING} \; \{\text{identifier-m} \, [\underline{ROUNDED}],\} \ldots$$

[; ON <u>SIZE ERROR</u> imperative-statement-1]

All data items preceding GIVING are added together. This sum is stored as the new value of each identifier following GIVING. Thus the new value of each identifier following GIVING is equal to the result of the addition. The composite of operands is determined by superimposing all of the operands preceding GIVING, aligned by decimal point. Note that the previous contents of identifiers following GIVING do not participate in the addition.

Examples: Assume as initial values: TAXES = 50
                                                           BCBS = 10
                                                           FICA = 15
                                                         TOTAL = 30
                                                         DEDUCTIONS = 0

1. ADD FICA,TAXES GIVING TOTAL
After execution, the value of TOTAL is 65.

2. ADD FICA,TAXES,BCBS GIVING TOTAL,DEDUCTIONS
After execution, the values of TOTAL and DEDUCTIONS are each 75.

In neither example is the value of TAXES, BCBS, or FICA changed.

Format 3:

$$\underline{ADD} \left\{ \begin{array}{l} \underline{CORRESPONDING} \\ \underline{CORR} \end{array} \right\} \text{identifier-1 } \underline{TO} \text{ identifier-2 [\underline{ROUNDED}]}$$

[; ON <u>SIZE</u> <u>ERROR</u> imperative-statement-1]

Every numeric data item in identifier-1 that has a *corresponding* data item in identifier-2 is added to its corresponding data item, the result being stored as the new value of the corresponding data item. Thus the new value of a data item in identifier-2 is its original value plus the value of the corresponding data item in identifier-1. Each identifier must be a group item. ROUNDED applies individually to each pair of operands that are added together. The composite of operands is determined by superimposing the two items aligned by decimal point.
This form of ADD is implemented only in level 2 of the Nucleus.

Example: Assume the following data structures with initial values in parentheses; all elementary items are numeric.

01 ABC	02 WXY	
02 DEF	05 DEF	
03 GHI (7)	06 GHI (10)	
03 JKL (20)	06 PDQ (10)	
02 MNO (40)	05 STU (10)	
02 PQR (15)	05 PQR (10)	

1. ADD CORRESPONDING ABC TO WXY
After execution, the values of WXY will be:

                                        02 WXY
                                            05 DEF
                                                06 GHI (17)
                                                      06 PDQ (10)
                                          05 STU (10)
                                          05 PQR (25)

Note that only the values of GHI and PQR have been changed.

Format 1

	Numeric
Literal-1	X
Identifier-1, -m	X

Format 2

	Numeric	Numeric-edited
Literal-1, -2	X	
Identifier-1, -2	X	
Identifier-m	X	X

See arithmetic statements, composite of operands, CORRESPONDING, multiple results in arithmetic statements, overlapping operands, ROUNDED, SIZE ERROR.

ADVANCING
See SEND, WRITE.

AFTER
See INSPECT, PERFORM, SEND, USE AFTER ERROR, WRITE.

alignment of data
See alignment rules, SYNCHRONIZED.

alignment rules
Alignment rules apply whenever data is moved to a receiving item that has no JUSTIFIED clause in its data description. These rules are listed by data category.

Numeric Items

The item being transferred and the receiving item are aligned by their decimal points. If no decimal point is specified for the receiving item, it is treated as if it had a decimal point following the right-most digit position. If the sizes of the sending and receiving items are different, there is the possibility of truncation or zero fill on either or both ends.

Examples: The following table shows the results for transferring various data into a receiving item. The symbol '‸' denotes the assumed decimal point.

PIC IS 999V99

Value	Result
1234.567	23456
123.456	12345
123.	12300
123.45	12345
12.3	1230

Numeric-Edited Items

The item is aligned and transferred according to the rules described above for numeric items. Any editing requirements affecting leading zeroes are also implemented.

Examples: The following table shows the results of transferring certain data into receiving items with various pictures.

PICTURE	Value	
	9876	98.76
99999	0 9876	000 98
ZZZZ9	9876	98
ZZZ.ZZ	876.00	98.76
$$$.$$	$76.00	$98.76

Alphanumeric, Alphabetic, or Alphanumeric-Edited Items

The data is transferred to the receiving item and aligned by the left-most character of each item. If the sizes of the sending and receiving items are different, there is the possibility of truncation or space fill on either or both ends.

Examples: The following table shows the results of transferring ABCDE into receiving items with various pictures.

PICTURE	Result
A(5) or X(5)	ABCDE
A(7) or X(7)	ABCDE△△
A(3) or X(3)	ABC

Special types of alignment may be provided by the implementor who will specify the appropriate rules.

See JUSTIFIED, receiving item, sending item, size, space fill, synchronization, SYNCHRONIZED, truncation, zero fill.

ALL

ALL is a figurative constant that is always used in conjunction with either a nonnumeric literal or another figurative constant except for ALL itself. When used with a nonnumeric literal it indicates one or more instances of the string that the literal represents. Used with a figurative constant, ALL is redundant and is employed only for readability.

For example, ALL "ABC" represents the continuous string

ABCABCABCABC...etc.

ALL ZEROES represents the continuous string

0000000000000...etc.

The exact length of each string is determined by the context in which it appears.

See figurative constant, INSPECT, nonnumeric literal, SEARCH, UNSTRING, USE.

ALPHABETIC

See class condition.

alphabetic character

An alphabetic character is any one of the following: A, B, C, D, E, F, G, H, I, J, K, L, M, N, O, P, Q, R, S, T, U, V, W, X, Y, Z and the space character.

alphabetic data item

An alphabetic data item is a data item which has a PICTURE clause containing only the characters A and B. An alphabetic data item can contain only alphabetic characters.

See alphabetic character, data item.

alphabet-name

An alphabet-name is a user-defined word that is used in the SPECIAL-NAMES paragraph to assign a name to a specific character set and/or collating sequence.

See character set, collating sequence, user-defined word.

alphanumeric character

An alphanumeric character is any character in the computer's character set. The range of characters available will vary depending upon the manufacturer of the computer.

See character set.

alphanumeric data item

An alphanumeric data item is a data item which has a PICTURE clause conforming to one of the following criteria:

1. It must contain at least one A *and* at least one 9.

2. It must contain at least one X, in which case occurrences of A or 9 are optional.

An alphanumeric data item is treated as if the PICTURE contained all X's; it can contain any character from the computer's character set.

alphanumeric-edited data item

An alphanumeric-edited data item is a data item which has a PICTURE clause fulfilling one or both of the following criteria:

1. It contains at least one X and at least one character from the set {0, B, /}.
2. It contains at least one A and at least one character from the set {0, /}.

An alphanumeric-edited data item can contain any character in the computer's character set.

ALSO

See SPECIAL-NAMES.

ALTER

The ALTER verb modifies the transfer location of a GO TO statement.

Format 1:

ALTER {procedure-name-1 TO [PROCEED TO] procedure-name-2}...

Procedure-name-1 must be the name of a paragraph that contains a single sentence consisting of a format 1 GO TO statement (i.e., one without the DEPENDING option). Procedure-name-2 must be the name of a paragraph or section in the PROCEDURE DIVISION.

Execution of the ALTER statement modifies the GO TO statement located in the paragraph designated by procedure-name-1, so that subsequent execution of the modified GO TO statement causes transfer of control to procedure-name-2 rather than to the original destination.

A procedure-name in a section with a segment-number greater than 49 can be referred to by an ALTER statement only if it is in a section with the same segment-number. In all other cases the ALTER statement is performed even if procedure-name-1 is in a fixed overlayable segment. A GO TO statement in an independent segment that is altered may, under some circumstances, be returned to its initial state. (See the entry on independent segments for details of these circumstances.)

Note that ALTER in and of itself does not cause a transfer of control. Rather it changes the location to which control is transferred when the associated GO TO is executed.

If level 2 of the Nucleus Module is implemented, then multiple instances of the material in braces can occur, otherwise only one instance can occur in a single ALTER statement.

Example: Assume that NORMAL-SEQUENCE and ERROR-HANDLING are paragraphs defined in the program.

```
DECISION-POINT.
     MOVE "BAD" TO RESULT. IF NO-ERROR-CONDITION MOVE
"GOOD" TO RESULT, ELSE ALTER SWITCH TO .PROCEED TO
ERROR-HANDLING.
SWITCH.
     GO TO NORMAL-SEQUENCE.
```

Upon execution of DECISION-POINT, if NO-ERROR-CONDITION is true, control is transferred to paragraph NORMAL-SEQUENCE upon executing SWITCH. If NO-ERROR-CONDITION is false, control is transferred to ERROR-HANDLING.

See fixed overlayable segment, independent segment, overlay, paragraph, section, segment-number, transfer of control.

ALTERNATE AREAS

Formerly a clause in the FILE-CONTROL paragraph, ALTERNATE AREAS has been replaced by RESERVE AREAS.

See RESERVE.

ALTERNATE RECORD KEY

See FILE-CONTROL, RECORD KEY, SELECT.

AND

AND is a logical binary operator that combines two operands in a manner such that the expression as a whole is true if and only if *both* of the operands are true.

An expression of more than two operands, all of which are connected by AND's, is true if and only if *all* of the constituent operands are true.

In the source program the word 'AND' must be preceded and followed by one or more spaces.

See binary operator, logical operations, operand, SEARCH.

ARE

See CONTROL, DATA RECORD, LABEL RECORD, PAGE, REPORT.

AREA, AREAS

See FILE-CONTROL, RESERVE, SELECT.

Area A

Area A is that part of a COBOL source line that occupies character positions 8, 9, 10, and 11. It is located between margin A and margin B.

See character position, margin, reference format.

Area B

Area B is that part of a COBOL source line that occupies those character positions from the position immediately to the right of margin B, i.e., position 12, to the position to the immediate left of margin R. The number of character positions in Area B is implementor-defined.

See character position, margin, reference format.

arithmetic expression

An arithmetic expression is a combination of identifiers, literals, and arithmetic operators that has a single numeric value. All identifiers and literals in an arithmetic expression must represent elementary numeric items or numeric literals. The order of evaluation of an arithmetic expression is

unary plus and minus	+ and −
exponentiation	**
multiplication and division	* and /
addition and subtraction	+ and −

(The admittance of the unary plus is a new feature of 74 COBOL.)

The symbols must have spaces on each side, except for the unary plus and minus. The exponentiation symbol cannot have a space between the two asterisks. If there is more than one instance of an operator with the same position in the order of evaluation, e.g., a multiplication and a division, evaluation is from left to right as the operators appear in the expression.

Parentheses can be used in arithmetic expressions to further specify the order in which elements are to be evaluated. Spaces can be used to separate parentheses from the various elements, if desired. When there is more than one level of nested (embedded) parentheses, the innermost set is evaluated first according to the order of evaluation described above. Then the next innermost set is evaluated, etc. For equal levels of parentheses, the order of evaluation is from left to right.

The following chart shows the ways in which operators, variables, and parentheses can be combined in an arithmetic expression.

		Second Symbol			
	Variable	Binary Operator	Unary Plus or Minus	(	)
Variable	X	P	X	X	P
Binary operator	P	X	P	P	X
Unary plus or minus	P	X	X	P	X
(	P	X	P	P	X
)	X	P	X	X	P

(First Symbol)

'P' indicates a permissible pair of symbols, and 'X' indicates an illegal pair of symbols.

See arithmetic operator, elementary item, identifier, literal.

arithmetic operator

An arithmetic operator is a symbol that represents an arithmetic operation. Arithmetic operators can have either one or two operands.

Binary Operators

A binary operator has two operands. The binary operators are

+	which denotes addition
−	which denotes subtraction
*	which denotes multiplication
/	which denotes division
**	which denotes exponentiation

Note. The symbol for exponentiation (**), although composed of two characters, is considered a single symbol.

Unary Operators

A unary operator has one operand. The unary operators are used to designate the algebraic sign of a number. The unary operators are

+	which denotes a positive number
−	which denotes a negative number

arithmetic statement

An arithmetic statement is one that causes an arithmetic operation to be performed. The verbs ADD, COMPUTE, DIVIDE, MULTIPLY, and SUB-TRACT are used to form arithmetic statements.

See composite of operands, entries for the individual verbs.

ASCENDING KEY

See MERGE, OCCURS, SORT.

ASCII Collating Sequence

The ASCII (American Standard Code for Information Interchange) collating sequence is:

△	space
"	quotation character.
$	dollar sign.
(	left parenthesis.
)	right parenthesis.
*	asterisk.
+	plus sign.
,	comma.
−	hyphen, minus sign.

. period.

/ slash.

0 through 9

; semi-colon.

< less than.

= equal sign.

> greater than.

A through Z

ASSIGN

See FILE-CONTROL, SELECT.

assumed decimal point

The assumed decimal point is a logical decimal point, which does not occupy a character position in the item and which has no physical representation. It must be kept track of by the programmer; it allows the programmer to interpret a data item. The assumed decimal point is denoted by the character 'P' or 'V' in the PICTURE clause.

Examples: Assume the content of the data item is 123

PICTURE	Value Represented
PP999	.00123
V999	.123
999V	123.
999PPP	123000.

See character position.

AT

See LINAGE, READ, RETURN, SEARCH, WRITE.

AT END

See READ, RETURN, SEARCH.

AT END Condition

The AT END condition occurs

1. When a READ is executed for a file being accessed sequentially and no next (logical) record exists in the file.

2. When, during execution of a format 1 SEARCH, the index-name used contains a value greater than the highest occurrence number for the identifier being searched.

3. When, during execution of a format 2 SEARCH, any condition specified in a WHEN clause cannot be satisfied for any valid setting of the index.

4. When in a SORT operation, during execution of a RETURN, no next (logical) record exists for a file.

See index-name, NEXT RECORD, occurrence number.

AUTHOR

The AUTHOR paragraph is an optional entry of the IDENTIFICATION DIVISION that is used only for documentation purposes. It does not affect the compilation of the program.

Format:

AUTHOR ● [comment-entry] . . .

The comment-entry cannot be continued by using a hyphen in the indicator area; however, the comment can be contained on more than one line. Any character in the computer's character set can appear in a comment-entry.

See comment-entry, comment line indicator area, indicator area.

B

BEFORE
> *See* INSPECT, SEND, USE, WRITE.

binary
> Binary refers to the property of having one or the other of two values, but not both. A binary digit is either 0 or 1; a condition is binary since it is either true or false.
>
> *See* condition.

binary operator
> A binary operator is one that requires two operands. A binary operator does not necessarily have anything to do with binary numbers.
>
> The symbols +, −, ×, and ÷ are arithmetic binary operators representing the operations of addition, subtraction, multiplication, and division, respectively. The COBOL reserved words AND and OR are logical binary operators representing the operations of conjunction and alternation, respectively.
>
> *See* operand, unary operator.

blank line
> A blank line is a line with no characters except spaces from margin C to margin R. A blank line can appear anywhere in the source program except immediately preceding a continuation line.
>
> *See* continuation of lines, margin.

BLANK WHEN ZERO
> The BLANK WHEN ZERO clause is used in the data description of an item to specify that, when the item has a value of zero, it is to contain blanks. Thus, if the item is printed when its value is zero, *nothing* appears on the line.
>
> The BLANK WHEN ZERO clause can be applied only to elementary items that are numeric or numeric-edited. If the item is numeric, addition of this clause causes the item to be considered numeric-edited.
>
> This clause cannot be used if an asterisk appears in the item's PICTURE clause. (This is a new restriction of 74 COBOL.)
>
> *Format:*
>
> BLANK <u>WHEN</u> <u>ZERO</u>
>
> *See* data description elementary item, numeric data item, numeric-edited data, report group description.

block
> The term 'block' is synonymous with 'physical record.' A block is a physical unit of data storage that can contain an entire logical record or many logical records.

For mass storage files a block can contain a portion of a logical record.

The size of a block has no direct relationship to the size of the file within which the block is contained or to the size of the logical record or records that are contained within the block or that overlap the block.

See logical record.

BLOCK CONTAINS

The BLOCK CONTAINS clause is a file description clause that specifies the size of a physical record.

Format:

$$\text{\underline{BLOCK} CONTAINS [integer-1 TO] integer-2} \begin{Bmatrix} \text{RECORDS} \\ \text{CHARACTERS} \end{Bmatrix}$$

The BLOCK CONTAINS clause is required except when (1) a physical record contains one and only one complete logical record, (2) the hardware device has only one physical record size, or (3) the hardware device has more than one physical record size but one size has been defined as standard by the implementor. In the latter case the absence of the BLOCK CONTAINS clause denotes the standard record size.

Records

If RECORDS is specified, the size of a block is defined in terms of logical records. This phrase cannot be used (1) in mass storage files where logical records can extend across blocks, (2) if the physical record contains padding, i.e., areas not contained in a logical record, or (3) if logical records are grouped in such a way that an inaccurate record size would be implied.

If logical records of differing sizes are grouped into one physical record, the technique for determining the size of each logical record is specified by the implementor.

Characters

If CHARACTERS is specified, the block size is defined in terms of the number of character positions required to store the physical record, regardless of the types of characters used to represent the items within the physical record.

If only integer-2 is used, it represents the exact size of the physical record. If both integer-1 and integer-2 are used, they refer to the minimum and maximum record sizes, respectively.

See block, file description, logical record, mass storage file.

body group

A body group is a report group with a TYPE of DETAIL, CONTROL HEADING, or CONTROL FOOTING.

See report group description.

BOTTOM

See file description, LINAGE.

braces

In formats, braces enclose two or more items from which one and only one must be chosen. For example, the format

$$\begin{Bmatrix} \text{identifier-1} \\ \text{literal-1} \end{Bmatrix}$$

indicates that either an identifier or a literal, but not both, must be chosen. Within braces, each line is defined as a single choice. Thus in

$$\begin{Bmatrix} \text{literal-1} \\ \text{identifier-1, identifier-2} \end{Bmatrix}$$

either a literal or two identifiers must be chosen.

An ellipsis can be applied to braces to indicate that the material in the braces can be repeated.

See ellipsis, notation in COBOL.

brackets

In formats, brackets denote an optional entry. For example, the format

$$\text{identifier-1 [identifier-2]}$$

indicates that either one or two identifiers could be selected. In the format

$$\begin{bmatrix} \text{literal-1} \\ \text{identifier-1, identifier-2} \end{bmatrix}$$

nothing, a literal, or two identifiers could be selected.

An ellipsis can be applied to brackets to indicate that the material in the brackets can be repeated.

See ellipsis, notation in COBOL.

BY

See communication description entry, COPY, DIVIDE, INSPECT, MULTIPLY, OCCURS, PERFORM, SET, STRING, UNSTRING.

C

CALL

The CALL verb causes control to be transferred from one program to another within a run unit.

Format:

$$\underline{CALL} \quad \begin{Bmatrix} \text{literal-1} \\ \text{identifier-1} \end{Bmatrix} \quad [\underline{USING} \ \{\text{data-name-1}\} \ldots]$$

$$[\ ; ON \ \underline{OVERFLOW} \ \text{imperative-statement-1}]$$

The program that contains the CALL statement is termed the *calling* program; the program whose name is specified by literal-1 or by identifier-1 is the *called* program. Both literal-1 and identifier-1 must have a program-name as their value. (The use of identifier-1 is permitted only if level 2 of the Inter-Program Communication Module is implemented.) When the CALL statement is executed, control passes from the calling program to the called program and a logical relationship is established between the two. The very first time a CALL statement is executed for a given program in the run unit, the called program is in its initial state. The called program is also in its initial state the first time it is called after a CANCEL statement has been applied to it. For all other callings the called program's state is the same as the state that existed the last time the called program was exited. During execution of a CALL statement, if there is no room for the called program in storage, then, imperative-statement-1 is executed if the ON OVERFLOW phrase is specified. If this phrase is not specified, the results are implementor-defined. (The ON OVERFLOW phrase is a new feature of 74 COBOL. It is part of level 2 of the Inter-Program Communication Module.)

If a program, A, calls another program, B; program B cannot, directly or indirectly, call program A. Program B can, however, call a third program, C, which, in turn, cannot call programs A or B, but can call another program, D, etc. Even though a program can be both a calling program and a called program, no program can call itself.

The Using Phrase

The USING phrase can be specified only if there is also a USING phrase in the Procedure Division header of the called program. There must be the same number of operands in each of these two USING phrases. Each of the operands in the USING phrase must have been defined as a data item in the FILE SECTION, WORKING-STORAGE SECTION, COMMUNICATION SECTION or LINKAGE SECTION of the DATA DIVISION and must have a level number of 01 or 77. Any data-name can be qualified if it references a data item in the FILE SECTION or the COMMUNICATION SECTION.

The data-names in the USING phrase designate those data items available to the calling program that can also be referred to by the called program. By this means common data is provided for the two programs. The ordering of these data-names is very important since (1) they are considered to be in a one-to-one correspondence with the data-names in the calling program's Procedure Division header USING phrase, and (2) a pair of corresponding names refers to a single set of data. This correspondence is strictly positional and not by name. No such correspondence is set up for index-names, however; index-names always refer to separate indices in the calling and called programs.

Leaving a Called Program

An EXIT PROGRAM statement is used to leave a called program. This statement returns control to the calling program at the statement following the CALL. The called program, including all data-fields, the status and position of all files, and all alterable switch settings, remains in the state it was in when the EXIT was executed. In particular, EXIT PROGRAM does *not* close files.

Segmentation Considerations

A CALL statement can appear anywhere within a segmented program. If a CALL statement is in an independent segment, when the EXIT PROGRAM statement returns control to the calling program, the segment containing the CALL statement is in its last-used state.

Example: Assume that the called program's name is PROC-ONE and that its Procedure Division header is

PROCEDURE DIVISION. USING DN-1,DN-2,DN-3.

Now, assume the calling program contains

CALL "PROC-ONE" USING ABC,RESULT,DN-2.
ADD 1 TO TABULATION.

When the CALL statement is executed a correspondence is set up between the two sets of data-names such that DN-1 and ABC refer to the same data item, DN-2 and RESULT refer to the same data item, and DN-3 in the called program and DN-2 in the calling program refer to the same data item. Thus if PROC-ONE modifies DN-1, DN-2, or DN-3, the new values of these data items are available to the calling program in ABC, RESULT, and DN-2, respectively. Note in particular that DN-2 of the calling program has no correspondence whatever with DN-2 of the called program. When PROC-ONE is exited, control returns to ADD 1 TO TABULATION.

	Nonnumeric	Alphanumeric
Literal-1	X	
Identifier-1		X

See CANCEL, EXIT, independent segment, program-name, run unit.

called program, calling program

Any program that contains a CALL statement is a calling program. The program whose name is specified in this CALL statement is the called program. A program can be both a calling and a called program.

CANCEL

The CANCEL verb releases the memory areas occupied by a program. This verb is new to 74 COBOL, and is part of level 2 of the Inter-Program Communication Module.

Format:

$$\text{CANCEL} \begin{Bmatrix} \text{identifier-1} \\ \text{literal-1} \end{Bmatrix} \dots$$

When the CANCEL statement is executed, the program that has been cancelled ceases to have a logical relationship to the run unit in which the CANCEL statement appears, and the memory areas occupied by the cancelled program are released. A subsequent CALL statement to that program will find the program in its initial state.

If a program named in a CANCEL statement has been called, it must have executed an EXIT PROGRAM statement prior to being cancelled or the results are undefined. A called program is cancelled either by execution of a CANCEL statement that specifies its name or by termination of its run unit.

If a program that has not been called or one that has been called and already cancelled is specified in the CANCEL statement, no action is taken and control passes to the statement following the CANCEL.

If a file has been opened in a called program and not closed in that program prior to execution of a CANCEL statement for the called program, the results are implementor-defined.

Literal-1 must be nonnumeric; identifier-1 must be alphanumeric and have a program-name as its value.

See CALL, EXIT, program-name.

category

The term 'category' is one way of describing a data item. Any data item is a member of one and only one category. The category to which a data item belongs depends on its PICTURE clause. The five categories are

- numeric
- numeric-edited
- alphabetic
- alphanumeric
- alphanumeric-edited

See the individual categories, class.

CD

See communication description entry.

cd-name

Cd-name stands for 'communication description name.' This is a user-defined word that names a Message Control System interface area, described in a communication description entry in the COMMUNICATION SECTION of the DATA DIVISION.

See communication description entry, communication description name, Message Control System.

CF

An abbreviation for CONTROL FOOTING.
See TYPE.

CH

An abbreviation for CONTROL HEADING.
See TYPE.

CHARACTER

See BLOCK CONTAINS, file description, INSPECT, MEMORY SIZE, OBJECT-COMPUTER, RECORD CONTAINS, SIGN IS, sort-merge file description.

character

The character is the basic indivisible unit of COBOL. Not all characters in the machine's character set are valid everywhere in the COBOL source program.
See character set.

character position

One character position is the amount of physical storage needed to hold a single standard data format character that has a usage of DISPLAY. The number of character positions in a data item determines its size.
See PICTURE, size, standard data format.

character set

> *See* COBOL character set.

character-string

> A character-string is one or more contiguous characters that form a word, literal, PICTURE entry, or comment-entry. A character-string is delimited by separators.
>
> For a word, numeric literal, PICTURE entry or comment-entry, the separators are spaces, commas, or semicolons. For a nonnumeric literal, the separators are quotation characters.
>
> *See* comma, comment-entry, literal, nonnumeric literal, numeric literal, PICTURE, quotation character, semicolon, space, word.

class

> One way of describing a data item is by its class. A data item belongs to one and only one of three classes: alphabetic, numeric, or alphanumeric. The concept of class is used in testing class conditions.
>
> For a group item, the class is considered alphanumeric, regardless of the categories of its constituent items. This is because a group item, per se, cannot be used in computations or be edited although its constituent parts can be.
>
> For an elementary item the three classes of data correspond to the five categories as shown in the table.

Class

	Alphabetic	Numeric	Alphanumeric
Category	alphabetic	numeric	alphanumeric alphanumeric-edited numeric-edited

> *See* alphabetic data item, alphanumeric data item, category, class condition, group item, numeric data item.

class condition

> The class condition is a determination of whether the contents of an item are numeric or alphanumeric.
>
> *Format:*
>
> $$\text{identifier-1 IS } [\underline{\text{NOT}}] \begin{Bmatrix} \text{NUMERIC} \\ \text{ALPHABETIC} \end{Bmatrix}$$
>
> Any item tested for a class condition must have a USAGE of DISPLAY. A numeric item is defined as one that consists entirely of the characters 0 through 9 and an optional operational sign. An alphabetic item is one composed entirely of the letters A through Z and the space character.

The test for numeric cannot be used with an item described as alphabetic or with a group item if it is composed of elementary items that have operational signs (this latter restriction is new to 74 COBOL). When a data item is described with a SIGN IS SEPARATE clause, the standard data format characters '+' and '−' are the only valid operational signs. If the data item does not have this clause, what constitutes a valid sign is implementor-defined. An item being tested is determined to be numeric if and only if the contents are numeric and, if an operational sign is specified in that item's data description, the operational sign is present in the item when tested, or if an operational sign is not specified for the item, one is not present in the item when tested.

The test for alphabetic cannot be used with an item that is described as numeric.

The following chart shows the valid tests for different classes of items.

Class	Test
Alphabetic	Alphabetic
Numeric	Numeric
Alphanumeric	Alphabetic, numeric

See operational sign, SIGN IS.

clause

A clause is a subdivision of a COBOL sentence. It is also used to specify an attribute of a data item (data clause), to qualify an entry in the ENVIRONMENT DIVISION (environment clause), or to specify an attribute of a file (file clause).

See data item, environment clause, file clause, sentence.

CLOCK-UNITS

See I-O-CONTROL, RERUN.

CLOSE

The CLOSE verb terminates the processing of files and, optionally, rewinds and/or locks them.

Format 1: Sequential files

$$\underline{\text{CLOSE}} \left\{ \text{file-name-1} \left[\begin{Bmatrix} \underline{\text{REEL}} \\ \underline{\text{UNIT}} \end{Bmatrix} \begin{bmatrix} \text{WITH } \underline{\text{NO}} \ \underline{\text{REWIND}} \\ \text{FOR } \underline{\text{REMOVAL}} \end{bmatrix} \right] \left[\text{WITH} \begin{Bmatrix} \underline{\text{NO}} \ \underline{\text{REWIND}} \\ \underline{\text{LOCK}} \end{Bmatrix} \right] \right\} \ldots$$

A format 1 CLOSE statement is used with files that have sequential organization. Following a successful execution of a CLOSE (without the REEL/UNIT phrase) on a file, the record area associated with that file is no longer available, and no other statement (except for a SORT or MERGE) that references the file explicitly or implicitly, can be executed unless an OPEN statement is first executed for the file. If the CLOSE is unsuccessful the availability of the record area is undefined. A CLOSE statement can be executed only for a file that is not a SORT or MERGE file and that is in an open mode. Files referenced in a given CLOSE statement need not have the same organization or access mode.

If a file that has been designated as optional in its FILE-CONTROL paragraph is not present, no processing takes place should an attempt be made to CLOSE that file.

In the following discussion, 'reel' will be used to represent 'reel/unit'; in the formats, REEL is logically equivalent to UNIT.

The action of a format 1 CLOSE is best described by considering a file as one of three types: nonreel, sequential single-reel, and sequential multireel. A nonreel file is one with an input or output medium such that one cannot meaningfully apply the terms 'rewind' and 'reel.' The forms of CLOSE applicable to nonreel files are CLOSE and CLOSE WITH LOCK.

A sequential single-reel file is one that is contained in its entirety on one reel. The forms of CLOSE that are applicable to sequential single-reel files are CLOSE, CLOSE WITH LOCK, and CLOSE WITH NO REWIND.

A sequential multireel file is one that is contained on more than one unit. The applicable forms of CLOSE are CLOSE, CLOSE WITH LOCK, CLOSE REEL, CLOSE REEL FOR REMOVAL, and CLOSE REEL WITH NO REWIND.

Nonreel Files

The action of CLOSE on nonreel files depends upon the mode in which the file is opened.

Input and Input-Output Files

If a file for which label records are specified is positioned at its end, i.e., the next READ would cause an AT END condition, the label records are processed according to the implementor's label processing procedures, and then the closing operations specified by the implementor are executed. If the file is positioned at its end and label records are not specified or if the file is not at its end, no label processing occurs, but the closing operations are executed. If label records are specified but not present or present but not specified, the action of CLOSE is undefined.

Output Files

If label records are specified, they are processed according to the implementor's label processing procedures, and the closing operations specified by the implementor are then executed. If label records are not specified, only the closing operations are executed. If label records are specified but not present or present but not specified, the action of CLOSE is undefined.

The Lock Option

If the WITH LOCK phrase is included in the CLOSE statement, in addition to the above procedures, an implementor-defined technique is invoked to insure that the file cannot be opened again during the current execution of the run unit. This phrase is supported only in level 2 of the Sequential I-O Module.

Sequential Single-Reel Files

The procedures specified above for nonreel files are executed. In addition, the device is positioned at its physical beginning unless the NO REWIND phrase is used, in which case the reel is left in its current position. This phrase is supported only in level 2 of the Sequential I-O Module.

Sequential Multireel File

If the REEL or UNIT phrase is not specified, all the processing specified above for single-reel files is executed. In addition, all reels in the file logically prior to the current reel are processed according to the implementor's standard reel swap procedures except for those reels affected by a prior CLOSE REEL statement. If the current reel is not the last reel of the file, any reels in the file logically following the current one are *not* processed.

If the REEL or UNIT phrase is specified, a reel swap takes place, and then the standard beginning reel procedures are implemented. The current reel is positioned at its physical beginning unless the NO REWIND phrase is specified, in which case the reel is left in its current position. Subsequent action depends on the mode in which the file is opened.

Input File

The next READ statement executed for the file makes the next data record on the new reel available.

Output File

The standard ending reel label procedure is executed. The next WRITE statement that is executed for the file directs the record to the next reel of the file.

Input-Output File

The next READ statement that is executed for the file makes the next data record on the next reel available.

For all modes, if FOR REMOVAL is specified, an implementor-defined technique is invoked to ensure that the current reel is rewound, when applicable, and that the reel is logically removed from the run unit. However, the reel can be accessed again if a CLOSE statement without the REEL or UNIT phrase is subsequently executed for the file, and this is followed by an OPEN statement for the file. (FOR REMOVAL is a new feature of 74 COBOL, and is supported only in level 2 of the Sequential I-O Module.)

Format 2: relative and indexed files

CLOSE {file-name-1 [WITH LOCK]} . . .

A format 2 CLOSE statement is used for files with relative or indexed organization. Following the successful execution of a CLOSE on a file, the record area associated with that file is no longer available, and no other statement that references the file explicitly or implicitly can be executed unless an OPEN statement is first executed for the file. If the CLOSE is unsuccessful, the availability of the record area is undefined. A CLOSE statement can be executed only for a file that is in an open mode. Files referenced in a given CLOSE statement need not have the same organization or access mode.

The action of a format 2 CLOSE depends upon the access mode and the mode in which the file is opened.

Input and Input-Output Files in Sequential Access Mode

If a file for which label records are specified is positioned at its end, i.e., the next READ would cause an AT END condition, the label records are processed according to the implementor's label-processing procedures, and then the closing operations specified by the implementor are executed. If the file is positioned at its end and label records are not specified or if the file is not at its end, no label processing occurs but the closing operations are executed. If label records are specified but not present, or present but not specified, the action of CLOSE is undefined.

Input and Input-Output Files in Random or Dynamic Access Mode; Output Files in Any Mode

If label records are specified they are processed according to the implementor's standard label processing procedures and the closing operations specified by the implementor are then executed. If label records are specified but not present, or present but not specified, the action of CLOSE is undefined.

The Lock Option

If the WITH LOCK phrase is specified, in addition to the above procedures, an implementor-defined technique is invoked to insure that the file cannot be opened again during the current execution of the run unit.

See FILE-CONTROL, indexed i-o, label record, merge file, record area, relative i-o, run unit, sequential i-o, sort file, sort-merge file description.

COBOL

COBOL is an acronym for COmmon Business Oriented Language.

COBOL character set

The COBOL character set consists of the 51 characters that are legal in COBOL. They are the uppercase letters A through Z, the digits 0 through 9, and the following special characters:

comma, decimal point	,
period, decimal point	.
semicolon	;
greater than sign	>
less than sign	<
equal sign	=
left parenthesis	(
right parenthesis	)
quotation character	"
currency sign	$
plus sign	+
minus sign, hyphen	-
asterisk	*
slash, stroke, virgule	/
blank, space	△

In nonnumeric literals characters other than the above can appear.

Note: In this book the symbol '△' is used when it is necessary to explicitly depict a space.

See nonnumeric literal.

CODE

The CODE clause specifies a literal that identifies each print line as belonging to a specific report.

Format:

CODE literal-1

When the CODE clause is specified, literal-1 is automatically placed in the first two character positions of each report writer logical record. If the CODE clause is specified for any report in a file, then it must be specified for all reports in the same file.

Literal-1 must be a two-character, nonnumeric literal. The two positions occupied by literal-1 are not included in the description of the print line but are included in the logical record size.

See report description, report writer logical record, Report Writer Module.

CODE-SET

The CODE-SET clause is used in a file description to specify the character code set used to represent data on external media.

Format:

CODE-SET IS alphabet-name

The CODE-SET clause can be specified only for files not in mass storage. If it is not specified, the native character code set is assumed.

If the CODE-SET clause is specified for a file, all data in the file must have a USAGE of DISPLAY, and any signed numeric data must have the SIGN IS SEPARATE clause in its description. Alphabet-name specifies the character code convention for converting the character codes on the external media to the native character codes. This code conversion occurs during the execution of input and output operations. This clause is a new feature of 74 COBOL.

See alphabet-name, file description, SPECIAL-NAMES USAGE.

COLLATING SEQUENCE

See MERGE, OBJECT-COMPUTER, SORT.

collating sequence

The collating sequence is the sequence in which characters are ordered for purposes of sorting, merging and comparing.

See MERGE, SORT.

column

On a printer, a column is one character position within a print line. The left-most column is column one, the next column two, etc.

On a card reader or punch, a column is any one of the 80 positions that corresponds to a column on a tab card.

COLUMN NUMBER

The COLUMN NUMBER clause identifies a printable item and specifies the column number position of the item on a print line.

Format:

COLUMN NUMBER IS integer-1

The COLUMN NUMBER clause indicates that the object of a SOURCE or VALUE clause or the sum counter defined by a SUM clause is to be presented on the print line. If this clause is not specified, the entry is not presented.

This clause can be specified only at the elementary level within a report group. If this clause is specified, it must appear in or be subordinate to an entry that contains a LINE NUMBER clause.

Within a given line, the printable items must be defined in ascending column number order such that each character defined occupies a unique position. The Report Writer Control System supplies space characters for all positions of a print line that are not occupied by printable items.

Integer-1 specifies the column number of the left-most character of the printable item. The left-most position of the print line is column 1.

See column, report group, Report Writer Control System.

combined condition

A combined condition is a condition that consists of two or more conditions connected by the logical operators AND or OR.

See complex condition, condition, logical operator.

COMMA

See DECIMAL-POINT IS COMMA, SPECIAL-NAMES.

comma

A comma is a connective that is used to separate consecutive operands. Although the presence of a comma in a statement is always optional, a comma cannot precede the first clause of an entry or paragraph. A comma must be followed by a space wherever it is used, except in a nonnumeric literal.

The comma is interchangeable with the semicolon; this is a new feature of 74 COBOL.

See connective, DECIMAL-POINT IS COMMA, nonnumeric literal, operand, SPECIAL-NAMES.

comment-entry

Comment-entries are used in the IDENTIFICATION DIVISION to document the program. A comment-entry can contain any combination of characters from the computer's character set. Comment-entries cannot be continued by using a hyphen in column 7. (This is a new restriction of 74 COBOL.) They can, however, be contained on more than one line.

Example:

DATE-WRITTEN. 27 August 1978

Here, '27 August 1978' is a comment-entry.

comment line

A comment line is included in the source program to annotate it. Thus it is not compiled and has no effect on the object program. Comment lines are designated by an asterisk in column 7. If a comment line is to be continued, the subsequent line or lines must have an asterisk in column 7, not a hyphen.

A special type of comment line is one with a slash (/) in column 7. This type of comment line causes the page currently in the printer to be ejected before the comment is printed.

In either form of the comment line, characters can appear in Area A of the line. The comment line, including the asterisk if used, appears in the output listing in exactly the same form as it appears in the source program.

The last line in the program can be a comment line; this is a new feature of 74 COBOL.

See Area A, object program, source program.

comment line indicator area

The comment line indicator area is the seventh character position in the line. It occupies the same physical position as the continuation line indicator. The asterisk, the symbol used to indicate comment lines, is placed in this area.

See comment line, continuation line indicator.

communication description entry

A communication description (CD) entry specifies the interface area between the Message Control System (MCS) and a COBOL program. This entry is new to 74 COBOL.

Format 1:

CD cd-name FOR [INITIAL] INPUT

```
⎡[[SYMBOLIC QUEUE IS data-name-1]                                          ⎤
⎢   [SYMBOLIC SUB-QUEUE-1 IS data-name-2]                                  ⎥
⎢   [SYMBOLIC SUB-QUEUE-2 IS data-name-3]                                  ⎥
⎢   [SYMBOLIC SUB-QUEUE-3 IS data-name-4]                                  ⎥
⎢   [MESSAGE DATE IS data-name-5]                                          ⎥
⎢   [MESSAGE TIME IS data-name-6]                                          ⎥
⎢   [SYMBOLIC SOURCE IS data-name-7]                                       ⎥
⎢   [TEXT LENGTH IS data-name-8]                                           ⎥
⎢   [END KEY IS data-name-9]                                               ⎥
⎢   [STATUS KEY IS data-name-10]                                           ⎥
⎢   [MESSAGE COUNT IS data-name-11]]                                       ⎥
⎢[data-name-1, data-name-2, data-name-3, data-name-4, data-name-5, data-name-6,⎥
⎣ data-name-7, data-name-8, data-name-9, data-name-10, data-name-11]        ⎦ •
```

A communication description entry (CD entry) is composed of the level-indicator, (CD), a cd-name, and a set of clauses as required. This is the highest level of organization in the COMMUNICATION SECTION, and it is only in this section that a CD entry can appear. The record areas defined in this section can be implicitly redefined by user-specified record description entries following the various communication description clauses. When used, the INITIAL clause must come first; the other clauses can be written in any order.

All data-names must be unique within the CD. If the option of writing only a series of data-names is chosen, any data-name that is omitted must be replaced with FILLER. This record cannot be accessed by the user at the 01 level unless it is redefined.

Each input CD defines a record area of 87 character positions with the following implicit description:

	Associated Clause	Character Positions
01 FILLER.		
02 data-name-1 PIC X(12).	Symbolic queue	1–12
02 data-name-2 PIC X(12).	Symbolic sub-queue-1	13–24
02 data-name-3 PIC X(12).	Symbolic sub-queue-2	25–36
02 data-name-4 PIC X(12).	Symbolic sub-queue-3	37–48
02 data-name-5 PIC 9(6).	Message date	49–54
02 data-name-6 PIC 9(8).	Message time	55–62
02 data-name-7 PIC X(12).	Symbolic source	63–74
02 data-name-8 PIC 9(4).	Text length	75–78
02 data-name-9 PIC X.	End key	79
02 data-name-10 PIC XX.	Status key	80–81
02 data-name-11 PIC 9(6).	Message count	82–87

Any record description following a CD implicitly redefines the record and so it must describe a record of exactly 87 characters. Multiple redefinitions of this record are permitted, but only the first redefinition can contain VALUE IS clauses. The Message Control System (MCS) always refers to the record according to the above description.

The input CD information is the communication between the MCS and the program. This information does not come from the terminal as part of the message.

Data-names -1, -2, -3, and -4 contain symbolic names designating queues and sub-queues. All symbolic names must follow the rules for system-names and have been previously defined to the MCS. When data-names -2, -3, and -4 are not used they must contain spaces.

The RECEIVE statement causes the serial return of the next message or portion of a message from the queue, as specified by the entries in the CD. If a message from a specific source is needed, data-names -2 through -4 can be used to specify the source. If a given level of the queue structure is specified, all higher levels must also be specified. If fewer than all of the levels of the queue hierarchy are specified, the MCS determines the 'next' message or portion of message according to an implementor-defined algorithm. After execution of a RECEIVE statement, data-name -1 through -4 will contain the symbolic names of all levels of the queue structure.

The Initial Clause

The INITIAL clause is implemented only in level 2 of the Communication Module; when a program is scheduled by the MCS to process a message, the symbolic names of the queue structure that demanded this activity will be placed in data-name-1 through data-name-4 of the CD with the INITIAL clause. Only one CD in a program can contain this clause, and it cannot be used in a program that specifies the USING phrase in its procedure division header.

In all other cases, data-names -1 through -4 of the CD with the INITIAL clause will contain spaces. The symbolic names or spaces are inserted prior to the execution of the first Procedure Division statement.

The execution of a subsequent RECEIVE statement, with the same contents of data-name-1 through data-name-4, will return the actual message that caused the program to be scheduled. At that time the remainder of the CD will be updated. If the MCS attempts to schedule a program without an INITIAL clause, the results are undefined.

Execution of a RECEIVE updates the following:

data-name-5 — has the format YYMMDD (year, month, day); its contents are the date on which the MCS recognizes that the message is complete.

data-name-6 — has the format HHMMSSHH (hours, minutes, seconds, hundredths of seconds); its contents are the time at which the MCS recognizes that the message is complete.

data-name-7 — receives the symbolic name of the communications terminal that is the source of the message being transferred. If the symbolic name of the communication terminal is not known to the MCS, data-name-7 will contain spaces.

data-name-8 — receives the number of character positions filled as a result of the execution of the RECEIVE statement.

data-name-9 — is set as follows:

A RECEIVE MESSAGE with an EGI	3
A RECEIVE MESSAGE with an EMI	2
A RECEIVE MESSAGE with less than a message	0
A RECEIVE SEGMENT with an EGI	3
A RECEIVE SEGMENT with an EMI	2
A RECEIVE SEGMENT with an ESI	1
A RECEIVE SEGMENT with less than a segment	0

When more than one of the above conditions is detected simultaneously, EGI takes precedence over EMI, and EMI takes precedence over ESI.

Execution of a RECEIVE, ACCEPT MESSAGE COUNT, ENABLE, or DISABLE statement updates the following:

data-name-10 — receives the status condition of the previously executed statement as shown by Table 1 on page 37.

Execution of an ACCEPT MESSAGE COUNT updates the following:

data-name-11 — receives the number of messages that exist in a queue, sub-queue, etc.

Format 2:

    CD cd-name FOR OUTPUT
        [DESTINATION COUNT IS data-name-1]
        [TEXT LENGTH IS data-name-2]
        [STATUS KEY IS data-name-3]
        [DESTINATION TABLE OCCURS integer-1 TIMES
            [INDEXED BY {index-name-1} ...]]
        [ERROR KEY IS data-name-4]
        [SYMBOLIC DESTINATION IS data-name-5]•

Each output CD defines a record area whose total size is 10 characters plus 13 times integer-1 characters long. This area is implicitly defined as

		Associated Clause	Character Positions
01	FILLER		
	02 data-name-1 PIC 9(4).	Destination count	1–4
	02 data-name-2 PIC 9(4).	Text length	5–8
	02 data-name-3 PIC XX.	Status key	9–10
	02 data-name-4 OCCURS integer-1 TIMES.		
	03 data-name-4 PIC X.	Error key	11
	03 data-name-5 PIC X(12).	Symbolic destination	12–23

This item cannot be referenced at the 01 level unless it is redefined. Any record description following a CD implicitly redefines the record and so it must describe a record of exactly the same number of characters. Multiple redefinitions are permitted, but only the first can contain the VALUE IS clause. The MCS always refers to this record as it was defined initially. All data-names must be unique within a CD.

If the OCCURS clause is not specified, one ERROR KEY and one SYMBOLIC DESTINATION are assumed. In this case, neither subscripting nor indexing is permitted when referencing these data items.

If the OCCURS clause is specified, data-names -4 and -5 can be referred to only by subscripting and indexing. If only level 1 of the Communication Module is implemented, data-name-1 and integer-1 must be 1.

The output CD information is the communication between the object program and the MCS. This information is not sent to the terminal.

During execution of SEND, ENABLE or DISABLE, the following are updated:

data-name-1 — is set to the number of symbolic destinations that are to be used from the area specified by data-name-5. The first symbolic destination is in the first occurrence of data-name-5, the second symbolic destination is in the second occurrence of data-name-5, etc.

If the value of data-name-1 is less than 1 or greater than integer-1, an error condition exists and execution of the statement is terminated.

data-name-3 — is set to indicate the status condition of the previously executed statement. Table 1 shows the values of data-name-3. If the MCS determines that any specified destination is unknown, data-name-3 and all occurrences of data-name-4 are updated.

data-name-4 — When data-name-1 is equal to 1, it indicates that the associated value in data-name-5 has not been previously defined to the MCS. Otherwise, data-name-4 is 0.

As part of the execution of a SEND statement, the following occurs:

data-name-2 — is interpreted to be the number of left-most character positions from which data is to be transferred.

data-name-5 — contains a symbolic destination previously known to the MCS. These symbolic destinations must follow the rules for system-names.

N.B. If none of the options is specified in a CD-entry (i.e., if the entry is either CD cd-name FOR INPUT• or CD cd-name FOR OUTPUT•), a level 01 data description must follow the entry.

See cd-name, Communication Module, COMMUNICATION SECTION, division header, indexing, level-indicator, Message Control System, queue, record description, sub-queue, subscripting, system-name.

communication description name

A communication description (CD) name is a user-defined word that names an area described in a communication description entry. This area is used to interface with the Message Control System (MCS).

See communication description entry, Message Control System, user-defined word.

communication device

A communication device is a mechanism (hardware or hardware/software) capable of sending and/or receiving data in conjunction with a queue. One or more programs containing communication description entries resident within a computer define one or more communication devices.

See communication description entry.

Communication Module

The Communication Module provides the ability to access, process, and create messages; and to communicate through the Message Control System (MCS) with local and remote communication devices. This module is new to 74 COBOL.

Table 1
Note: An 'X' indicates that the Status Key Code is applicable to the statement.

RECEIVE	SEND	ACCEPT MESSAGE COUNT	ENABLE INPUT	ENABLE INPUT TERMINAL*	ENABLE OUTPUT	DISABLE INPUT	DISABLE INPUT TERMINAL*	DISABLE OUTPUT*	STATUS KEY CODE	Meaning
X	X	X	X	X	X	X	X	X	00	No error detected. Action completed.
	X								10	One or more destinations are disabled. Action completed.
	X				X			X	20	One or more destinations unknown. Action completed for known destinations. No action taken for unknown destinations.
X		X	X			X			20	One or more queues or sub-queues unknown. No action taken.
				X			X		20	The source is unknown. No action taken.
	X				X			X	30	Content of data-name-1 invalid. No action taken.
			X	X	X	X	X	X	40	Password invalid. No enabling or disabling action taken.
	X								50	Character count greater than length of sending field. No action taken.
	X								60	Partial segment with either zero character count or no sending area specified. No action taken.

* Not in Level 1.

Level 1

Communication Level 1 provides limited capability for ENABLE, DISABLE, RECEIVE, and SEND, and a provision for determining the number of messages in an input queue.

Level 2

Communication Level 2 provides full communication capabilities for the communication verbs as well as the ability to handle partial messages, segmented messages, multiple destination messages and program invocation by the MCS.
   See message, Message Control System, queue.

COMMUNICATION SECTION

The COMMUNICATION SECTION is part of the DATA DIVISION wherein are described the interface areas between the Message Control System (MCS) and the program. It is composed of one or more communication description entries.
   See communication description entry, Message Control System.

COMP

See COMPUTATIONAL.

comparison rules

See relation condition.

compiler directing sentence

A compiler directing sentence is a single compiler directing statement, terminated by a period and space.

compiler directing statement

A compiler directing statement is a statement that begins with a compiler directing verb. It directs the compiler to take a certain action during compilation, as opposed to being compiled itself.

   Examples:

1. COPY TAPE-LIB-3.

2. ENTER FORTRAN.

compiler directing verb

The compiler directing verbs are COPY, ENTER, and USE.

compiler limits

Compiler limits are those restrictions that each implementor puts on the various operations which the compiler performs. The following chart can be filled in by consulting the appropriate reference manual.

Levels of qualification	_____
Size of alphanumeric literal	_____
Size of literal string	_____

Maximum number of PERFORM cycles   _____
Maximum occurrences of a repeated item in an OCCURS clause _____
Size of arithmetic temporary variables   _____
Number of lines per source program   _____
Number of identifiers per program   _____
Number of literals per program   _____
Number of procedure-names per program   _____
Nesting level of PERFORMs   _____
Number of GO TO DEPENDING entries   _____
Number of file descriptions   _____
Maximum size of an edited item   _____

compile time

Compile time is the time at which a COBOL source program is translated by a COBOL compiler into an object program.

See object program, object time, source program.

complex condition

A complex condition is two or more conditions combined by the logical operators AND and OR. The unary operator, NOT, can be applied to any and all conditions within a complex condition. Complex conditions are formatted as follows:

$$[NOT] \text{ condition-1} \left[\left\{ {AND \atop \underline{OR}} \right\} [NOT] \text{ condition-2} \right] \ldots$$

Condition-1 and condition-2 can be

- A simple condition, e.g., X < Y
- A negated simple condition, e.g., NOT (X < Y)
- A complex condition, e.g., X < Y OR X > Z
- A negated complex condition, e.g., NOT (X < Y OR X > Z)
- Any combination of the above conditions.

Evaluation of complex conditions takes place according to the following rules:

0. The innermost set of parentheses is considered first.

1. Arithmetic expressions are reduced to single numeric values.

2. All relation, class, condition-name, switch-status, and sign conditions, in that order, are evaluated for truth values.

3. All NOT's are evaluated from left to right.

4. All AND's are evaluated from left to right.

5. All OR's are evaluated from left to right.

6. The next innermost set of parentheses is then treated according to rules 1 through 5.

Abbreviated Form of Relation Conditions

When relation conditions are written consecutively in a complex condition, any condition except the first can be written in an abbreviated form by either omitting the subject or omitting both the subject and the binary relational operator. The 'subject' is defined as the term to the left of the relational operator.

When either of these abbreviated forms is used, the omitted subject or operator is considered to be identical to the last explicitly stated subject or operator. This implicit insertion of an omitted subject and/or relational operator ends with the next occurrence of a complete simple condition within the complex condition. (A complete simple condition is one with an expressed subject and operator.)

If any part of an abbreviated condition is enclosed in parentheses, all the subjects and operators necessary for the evaluation of that portion must be included in the same set of parentheses. Consequently, the first condition within any set of parentheses cannot be abbreviated. (This is a new restriction of 74 COBOL.)

The Operator NOT

In abbreviated complex conditions, NOT is interpreted as follows:

- If the word immediately following NOT is GREATER, LESS, EQUAL, $>$, $<$, or $=$, then the NOT is considered part of the relational operator.[1] That is, NOT $=$ is considered to be $\neq$; NOT $>$ is considered to be $\leq$, etc.

- In all other cases, NOT is considered a logical operator and goes with the preceding AND or OR, if present. The insertion of an implied subject or relational operator results in a negated condition. That is, NOT A $>$ B is interpreted as NOT (A $>$ B). In this case, NOT cannot be omitted.

   Examples:
1. A NOT $=$ B AND C
   NOT is considered part of the relational operator, $=$, and the statement is equivalent to (A NOT $=$ B) AND (A NOT $=$ C); i.e., A $\neq$ B AND A $\neq$ C
2. A NOT $=$ B AND C OR D
   Here, A is the subject and NOT is part of the equal sign. The statement is equivalent to A $\neq$ B AND A $\neq$ C OR A $\neq$ D
3. NOT A $=$ B OR C
   Here, NOT goes with A; since in this case NOT cannot be omitted, the implied subject is simply A, and the implied operator is the equal sign. The statement is equivalent to NOT (A $=$ B) OR (A $=$ C)

---
[1] In 68 COBOL, NOT was a logical operator.

4. A = B AND NOT > C OR D

   In this example, the NOT goes with the > sign. The statement is equivalent to (A = B) AND (A NOT > C) OR (A NOT > D)

5. NOT (A NOT = B AND C AND NOT D)

   This statement is equivalent to

   $$\text{NOT } ((A \neq B) \text{ AND } (A \neq C) \text{ AND NOT } (A \neq D))$$

   The implied subject and operator are 'A NOT = '; thus the NOT before the last term in the equivalent expression is the one that was in the original expression.

   The following chart shows the valid combinations of conditions, logical operators, and parentheses.

	First	Last	Simple Condition	OR and AND	NOT	Left Parenthesis	Right Parenthesis
Simple condition	Y	Y		PF	P	P	F
OR and AND	N	N	PF		F	F	P
NOT	Y	N	F	P		PF	
Left parenthesis	Y	N	F	P	PF	P	F
Right parenthesis	N	Y	P	F			PF

P means 'A can be preceded by B.'
F means 'A can be followed by B.'
Y means 'A can appear first/last in a combination.'
N means 'A cannot appear first/last in a combination.'

See condition, logical operator, relational operator, relation condition, unary operator.

composite of operands

The composite of operands is a hypothetical data item the size of which is determined by superimposing specified operands in a statement, aligned by their decimal points. The composite of operands cannot exceed 18 digits.

Example: With the operands

A PIC 9999999999V
B PIC V9999999999
C PIC 99999999V99999999

the composite of operands of C and B is determined by aligning C and B thus:

C   99999999V99999999
B   V9999999999
         99999999V9999999999   which contains 18 digits.

The composite of operands of C and A is determined by aligning C and A thus:

C   99999999V99999999
A   9999999999V
         9999999999V99999999   which contains 18 digits.

However, the composite of operands of A and B is 9999999999V9999999999, which contains 20 digits. Therefore if A and B were operands used in computing the composite of operands in a given statement, the composite of operands would exceed 18 digits and cause an error condition to occur.

In 74 COBOL, the composite of operands is limited to 18 digits for *all* arithmetic operations; previously, the limit was only for the ADD and SUBTRACT verbs.

See ADD, DIVIDE, MULTIPLY, SUBTRACT.

COMPUTATIONAL

COMPUTATIONAL indicates a type of USAGE of data. Computational data have values that are used in computations and, therefore, must be numeric items. If a group item is described as computational, all elementary items in the group are computational, but the group item, per se, is not computational since it cannot be used in computations as a group item.

The PICTURE of a computational item can contain only the characters 9, S, V, P, and parentheses. In USAGE clauses, COMP is a valid abbreviation for COMPUTATIONAL.

Most manufacturers provide for different types of computational data. These different types are generally indicated by COMP-1, COMP-2, etc. Consult the appropriate manuals for details of these data types.

COMPUTE

The COMPUTE verb sets one or more data items equal to the value of an arithmetic expression. It enables the user to combine arithmetic operations without the restrictions on the composite of operands and/or receiving items which are imposed by ADD, SUBTRACT, MULTIPLY, and DIVIDE. This verb is implemented only in level 2 of the Nucleus.

Format 1:

COMPUTE {identifier-1 [<u>ROUNDED</u>]}... = arithmetic-expression
[; ON <u>SIZE</u> <u>ERROR</u> imperative-statement-1]

The value of the arithmetic expression is determined. This value then replaces the contents of each identifier to the left of the equal sign. (The equal sign is required.)

An arithmetic expression that consists of a single identifier or literal provides a means of setting each identifier to the left of the equal sign to the value of the single identifier or literal. Although this could be done with a MOVE statement, COMPUTE permits rounding and/or size error operations to be used.

Examples. Assume that XYZ = 12.

1. COMPUTE ABC = 6 * XYZ + 10/2
   After execution, ABC has the value 77.

2. COMPUTE ABC,DEF = 6 * XYZ − 30
   After execution, ABC and DEF each have the value 42.

3. COMPUTE ABC,DEF,XYZ = 0
   After execution, all three items have the value 0.

	Numeric	Numeric-edited
Identifier-1	X	X

N.B. The presence of multiple fields is a new feature of 74 COBOL.

See arithmetic expression, arithmetic statements, composite of operands, overlapping operands, multiple results in arithmetic statements, receiving item, ROUNDED, SIZE ERROR.

computer-name

A computer-name is a system-name that appears in the SOURCE-COMPUTER and OBJECT-COMPUTER entries of the ENVIRONMENT DIVISION. It identifies the computer on which the program is to be compiled or run.

Computer-names are assigned by the implementor. The computer-name may also provide a means of identifying a particular equipment configuration. In this case both the computer-name and its implied configuration are specified by the implementor.

See system-name.

condition

A condition is a circumstance to which a truth value can be assigned. There are five kinds of conditions used in conditional expressions.

1. Relation condition: whether or not a specified relationship exists between two operands, e.g., X > Y

2. Class condition: whether or not a data item is composed entirely of characters of a certain category, e.g., ABC IS NUMERIC

3. Condition-name condition: whether or not a conditional variable has a value corresponding to an associated condition-name, e.g., IF OVER-PAY . . .

4. Sign condition: whether a data item or expression has a value less than, greater than, or equal to zero, e.g., ABC IS NEGATIVE

5. Switch-status condition: whether a switch is 'on' or 'off.'

When 'condition' appears in a format it represents any simple or complex condition for which a truth value is determinable. The truth value of a complex condition is determined by evaluating the truth values of its constituent parts. Any condition, simple or complex, can be enclosed in parentheses without affecting its truth value.

See class condition, complex condition, conditional expression, condition-name condition, relation condition, sign condition, switch-status condition.

condition-name (level 88)

A condition-name is a word that is associated with a data item by being assigned to one or more values that the data item can assume.

Format:

$$88 \text{ condition-name } \left\{ \begin{array}{l} \underline{\text{VALUE}} \text{ IS} \\ \underline{\text{VALUES}} \text{ ARE} \end{array} \right\} \left\{ \text{literal-1} \left[\left\{ \begin{array}{l} \underline{\text{THROUGH}} \\ \underline{\text{THRU}} \end{array} \right\} \text{literal-2} \right] \right\} \ldots$$

When a data item has one or more condition-names associated with it, it is called a conditional variable. Condition-names are defined in the DATA DIVISION as level 88 entries. The condition-name entries for a conditional variable must immediately follow the entry that describes the item. In the data description, only the condition-name and the VALUE IS clause are allowed, the VALUE IS being mandatory. The characteristics of a condition-name are implicitly those of its conditional variable.

A condition-name cannot be used with an item that

1. Is a level 66 (redefines) item.

2. Is an index data item.

3. Is a group item containing items that are JUSTIFIED, SYNCHRONIZED, or have a USAGE other than DISPLAY.

Example:

```
02  ABC  PIC IS 99.
    88  OVER-PAY VALUE IS 60 THROUGH 99.
    88  ILLEGAL-PAY VALUES ARE 3, 6, 9.
    88  RE-ORDER VALUE IS 23.
```

In this example the value of ABC is limited by its picture clause to the range of 0 through 99. OVER-PAY is the condition-name assigned to the values from 60 through and including 99. ILLEGAL-PAY is the condition-name assigned to the three values 3, 6, and 9. RE-ORDER is the condition-name assigned to the single value 23.

Condition-names are used in place of relation conditions. With the above example the statement 'IF OVER-PAY THEN . . .' is equivalent to the statement 'IF ABC IS GREATER THAN 59 . . .'; the statement 'IF ILLEGAL-PAY THEN . . .' is equivalent to the statement 'IF ABC = 3 OR ABC = 6 OR ABC = 9 THEN . . .'; the statement 'IF RE-ORDER THEN . . .' is equivalent to the statement 'IF ABC EQUALS 23 THEN . . .'.

A condition-name must be unique or be made unique through qualification, indexing, or subscripting. The conditional variable with which the condition-name is associated can be used in qualifying it. If a reference to a conditional variable must be subscripted or indexed, then any reference to a condition-name associated with that variable must also be subscripted or indexed.

Example:

```
02  ABC  PIC IS 99 OCCURS 10 TIMES.
    88  CUT-OFF VALUE IS 27.
```

One would refer to ABC via subscripting; e.g., ADD ABC(5) TO TEMP. To refer to CUT-OFF one would also have to use subscripting:

IF CUT-OFF(5) THEN . . .

This statement is equivalent to writing IF ABC(5) IS EQUAL TO 27 THEN . . .'

See conditional variable, group item, index data item, indexing, level 88, level 66, qualification, subscripting.

condition-name condition

A condition-name condition is one in which a conditional variable is tested to determine whether or not its value is equal to the value(s) associated with the specified condition-name. It appears in an IF statement in this way:

IF condition-name

The result of the test is true if any one of the values corresponding to the condition-name equals the value of the associated conditional variable. If the condition-name is associated with a range of values, the test is true if the conditional variable's value falls within this range, including the end values.

Example: If the DATA DIVISION contains

    02 ABC PIC IS 99.
        88   TOO-BIG VALUE IS 65 THRU 99.
        88   O-K-SIZE VALUE IS 30.

The statement 'IF O-K-SIZE ...' is equivalent to 'IF ABC EQUALS 30 ...'.
The statement 'IF TOO-BIG ...' is equivalent to 'IF ABC > 64 ...'. In this
example, ABC is the conditional variable and TOO-BIG and O-K-SIZE are the
condition-names. The rules for comparison are the same as those specified for
relation conditions.

See condition-name, conditional variable, relation condition.

conditional expression

A conditional expression is a simple condition or a complex condition that is
specified in an IF, PERFORM, or SEARCH statement.

A conditional expression identifies one or more conditions that are tested to
enable the program to select between alternate program paths depending upon
the truth value of the condition.

See complex condition, condition, truth value.

conditional sentence

A conditional sentence is composed of a conditional statement, optionally preceded by an imperative statement, and terminated by a period and space. A
conditional sentence specifies that the truth value of a condition is to be
determined; the subsequent action of the program depends upon this truth value.

Example:

IF A > B ADD 2 TO C ELSE ADD 3 TO D.

The condition to be evaluated is: A > B. If this condition is true the
program then executes: ADD 2 TO C; if the condition is false, ADD 2 TO C is
not executed but ADD 3 TO D is.

See conditional statement, imperative statement.

conditional statement

A conditional statement is one in which the action taken is based upon whether a
specified condition is true or false. The conditional statements are

IF and SEARCH.

ADD, COMPUTE, DIVIDE, MULTIPLY, and SUBTRACT, when they have
the SIZE ERROR phrase.

DELETE, READ, REWRITE, START, and WRITE, when they have the
INVALID KEY phrase.

CALL, STRING, and UNSTRING, when they have the ON OVERFLOW phrase.

READ and RETURN, when they have the AT END phrase.

RECEIVE, when it has the NO DATA phrase.

WRITE when it has the END-OF-PAGE phrase.

For details, see the individual entries for each verb.

conditional variable

A conditional variable is a data item that has one or more condition-names (level 88) assigned to it.

For example, with the data description:

```
01  RPQ.
    02   ABC   PIC IS 99.
         88   TOO-BIG VALUE IS 67.
         88   TOO-SMALL VALUE IS 20, 21, 22, 23.
         88   O-K-SIZE VALUES ARE 24 THRU 66.
    02   DEF   PIC IS 99.
```

ABC is a conditional variable, while DEF is not.

See condition-name, condition-name condition.

CONFIGURATION SECTION

The CONFIGURATION SECTION is part of the ENVIRONMENT DIVISION. In it are described the characteristics of the source computer and the object computer; furthermore, any implementor-names used by the compiler are related to the mnemonic-names used by the source program.

Format:

> <u>CONFIGURATION SECTION</u>.
> <u>SOURCE-COMPUTER</u>. source-computer entry
> <u>OBJECT-COMPUTER</u>. object-computer entry
> [<u>SPECIAL-NAMES</u>. special-names entry]

See the individual entries for details; also mnemonic-name, source program.

connective

A connective is a reserved word or symbol that qualifies a data item, separates consecutive operands, or forms complex conditions.

1. OF and IN are used to qualify data items.

2. The comma and semicolon are used to separate consecutive operands.

3. AND and OR are used to form complex conditions.

See logical operations, complex conditions, qualification, reserved word.

CONTAINS

See MULTIPLE FILE TAPE, I-O-CONTROL.

contiguous item

Contiguous items are those that bear a definite hierarchical relationship to one another. They must be described by consecutive entries in the DATA DIVISION. However, two consecutive entries are not necessarily contiguous items, since they may not be related.

continuation line indicator area

The continuation line indicator area is the seventh character position in a line. It has the same physical location as the comment line indicator area.

See comment line indicator area, continuation of lines.

continuation of lines

Any sentence or entry that requires more than one line can be continued simply by writing as many complete words on one line as desired and starting the rest of the entry on the next line in Area B. Sometimes it happens that one wishes to split a word or literal across two lines. In this case the subsequent lines are called 'continuation lines,' and the line being continued is the 'continued line.' Any word or literal except the pseudo-text delimiter (= =) can be split in such a manner that part of it appears on a continuation line. If only Level 1 of the nucleus is implemented, a word or numeric literal cannot be split across two lines.

A continuation line is indicated by a hyphen in the continuation area, character position 7, of the line. This indicates that the first nonblank character in Area B of the line is considered as being adjacent to the last nonblank character of the continued line. If a line containing a nonnumeric literal is to be continued, and it does not have the closing quotation character on the continued line, then the first nonblank character in Area B of the continuation line must be a quotation character. This quotation character is not part of the nonnumeric literal, and the continuation starts with the character immediately after the quotation character. Also, all spaces at the end of the continued line are considered part of the literal. Area A of the continuation line must always be blank.

Any line without a hyphen in column 7 causes the compiler to assume that the last character in the preceding line is followed by a space—even though there may not be an explicit space on the line. Comment lines cannot be continued by means of the hyphen, since each comment line must have an asterisk in column 7.

The most frequent use for continuation lines is to continue the VALUE IS entry for a nonnumeric literal. For example:

Column 7   02   FILLER PIC X(120) VALUE "PAYROLL NUMBER

     -      " GROSS PAY   FICA   STATE TAX

     -      " FED. TAX   MISC. DED.   NET PAY".

See Area A, Area B, continuation line indicator area.

CONTROL

The CONTROL clause establishes the levels of the control hierarchy for a report.

Format:

$$\begin{Bmatrix} \underline{CONTROL} \text{ IS} \\ \underline{CONTROLS} \text{ ARE} \end{Bmatrix} \begin{Bmatrix} \{\text{data-name-1}\}\dots \\ \underline{FINAL} \text{ [data-name-1]}\dots \end{Bmatrix}$$

The CONTROL clause is part of a report description (RD) entry. The data-names and FINAL specify the levels of the control hierarchy. FINAL, if specified, is the highest control. Data-name-1 is the major control, the second and following data-names specify intermediate controls, and the last data-name is the minor control.

The first GENERATE statement that is executed for a report causes the Report Writer Control System (RWCS) to save the values of all control data items associated with that report. On subsequent executions of GENERATE statements for that report, the RWCS tests these control data items to see if their values have changed. Whenever a control item's value is different from the one saved, a control break occurs. The control break is always associated with the highest level control item for which a change of value is noted. Then, these current values are saved to be used in the next comparison, etc.

The RWCS applies the IS NOT EQUAL TO test, as described under 'relation condition,' as follows:

- If the control data item is a numeric data item, the test is for the comparison of two numeric operands.
- If the control data item is an index data item, the test is for the comparison of two index data items, i.e., the actual values are compared without conversion.
- If the control data item is anything but a numeric data item or an index data item, the test is for the comparison of two nonnumeric operands.

Each data-name must identify a different data item. No data-name can have subordinate to it a data item whose size is variable. A data-name can be qualified, but cannot be subscripted or indexed. No data-name can be defined in the REPORT SECTION.

See control break, control data item, indexed data-name, relation condition, report description, Report Writer Control System, size, subscripted data-name, TYPE.

control break

A control break is caused by a change in the value of a data item that has been specified in a CONTROL clause. This change of value is used to control the hierarchical structure of a report.

control break level

A control break can occur at any number of levels within a designated hierarchy. To speak of the 'control break level' is to refer to the position within the hierarchy at which the most major (i.e., highest) control break occurred.

control data item

A control data item is a data item that is specified in a CONTROL clause. A change in the value of a control data item produces a control break.

See control break.

control data-name

A control data-name is a data-name that appears in a CONTROL clause. A control data-name specifies a control data item, that is, a data item that may cause a control break when its contents are changed.

See control data item.

Control Footing

A Control Footing is a report group that is presented at the end of the Control Group to which it belongs.

See Control Group, report group, report group description, TYPE.

Control Group

A Control Group is a set of body groups that is presented for a given value of a control data item or for the word FINAL. A control group can begin with a Control Heading, end with a Control Footing, and contain one or more Detail report groups.

See body group, Control Footing, Control Heading.

Control Heading

A Control Heading is a report group that is presented at the beginning of the Control Group to which it belongs.

See Control Group, report group, report group description, TYPE.

control hierarchy

The control hierarchy is a designated sequence of a report subdivisions that is defined by the positional order of the word FINAL and of data-names within a CONTROL clause.

COPY

The COPY verb allows a library-text to be inserted into a source program at compile time. This text is then treated as part of the source program.

Format:

$$\underline{COPY} \text{ text-name} \left[\left\{ \begin{matrix} \underline{OF} \\ \underline{IN} \end{matrix} \right\} \text{library-name} \right]$$

$$\left[\underline{REPLACING} \left\{ \left\{ \begin{matrix} = = \text{pseudo-text-1} = = \\ \text{identifier-1} \\ \text{literal-1} \\ \text{word-1} \end{matrix} \right\} \underline{BY} \left\{ \begin{matrix} = = \text{pseudo-text-2} = = \\ \text{identifier-2} \\ \text{literal-2} \\ \text{word-2} \end{matrix} \right\} \right\} \dots \right]$$

Compilation of a program containing COPY statements proceeds as if all COPY statements are first processed and the resultant source program is then compiled. The effect of a COPY statement is that the text referenced by text-name is copied into the source program, logically replacing the entire COPY statement from the word COPY to the period that terminates the sentence. If the REPLACING phrase is not specified, the library-text is copied unchanged.

The text being copied cannot itself contain a COPY statement. The syntactic correctness of library-text usually cannot be determined independently of the program in which it is incorporated; also, the syntactic correctness of a COBOL program containing any COPY statement cannot be determined until all COPY statements have been processed.

A COPY statement can appear anywhere within a program where a character-string or separator can occur. The only exception, mentioned above, is that a COPY statement cannot appear within another COPY statement. (N.B. 68 COBOL permitted COPY statements only in specified places.)

Qualification of Texts

If more than one COBOL library is available during compilation,[1] the text-name must be qualified by the name of the library to which it belongs. This must be done even if the text-name is unique. Qualification is done using the OF/IN phrase. Within any one library, all text-names must be unique. If only level 1 of the Library Module is implemented, qualification is not allowed and all text-names must be unique.

Debugging Lines

If the COPY statement appears in a debugging line, all text included as a result of that COPY will be treated as if it were specified on debugging lines, except for comment lines which are still treated as comment lines. Debugging lines are not permitted in pseudo-text-1 but are allowed in pseudo-text-2 and in the library-text.

---

[1] The fact that more than one library can exist is new to 74 COBOL.

Continuation of Lines

Character-strings within any pseudo-text can be continued; however, the pseudo-text delimiter (= =) cannot be split across two lines.

The Replacing Phrase

The REPLACING phrase permits modification of the text that is copied into the source program. Pseudo-text-1 cannot be null, cannot consist solely of comment-lines or solely of spaces, and cannot contain debugging lines. Pseudo-text-2 can be null. Any comment-lines in pseudo-text-2 are copied into the source program unchanged. Word-1 and word-2 can be any single COBOL word. (N.B. 68 COBOL did not permit groups of words to be replaced.)

Text to be changed is identified by being matched with an item before the word BY. Once the text is matched, the item following the BY is inserted into the source program in place of the original text that was matched. No changes are ever made to the text in the library.

The comparison to determine whether or not text is to be replaced proceeds according to the following rules:

1. Words within a debugging line are treated as if the 'D' did not appear in that line's continuation-indicator area.

2. Any comment line in either the library-text or pseudo-text-1 is considered a single space. A comment line in pseudo-text-2 is copied into the program unchanged.

3. Each occurrence of a comma or a semicolon in pseudo-text-1 or in the library-text is considered a single space unless pseudo-text-1 consists solely of a comma or a semicolon; in this case these characters participate in the match as text-words.

4. Each sequence of one or more spaces is considered a single space.

5. Identifier-1, word-1, and literal-1 are treated as pseudo-text; that is, their values are not considered, only their names.

A match is defined as follows. The item before the word BY is said to match the library-text if and only if the two sequences of text words are identical, character for character, subject to the above rules.

The process of matching takes place in the following way:

1. Any comma, semicolon, or space preceding the left-most word in the library-text is copied into the source program.

2. The item to the left of the first BY in the REPLACING clause is compared to an equal number of consecutive words of library-text, beginning with the left-most word of that text.

3. If no match occurs, the comparison is repeated with the item before the next BY phrase in the REPLACING clause. This continues until either a match is made or there are no more BY phrases with which to compare.

4. When there are no more BY phrases left, the left-most library word is copied into the source program, the word immediately following the one just copied is now considered the left-most word, and the comparison process starts again as in step 1.

5. When a match occurs, the item following the BY phrase that corresponds to the word that matched is copied into the source program. The library-text word that immediately follows the right-most word that participated in the successful match is now considered the left-most word, and the comparison process starts again with step 1.

6. This process continues until the right-most word in the library-text has either participated in a successful match or has been considered in the left-most word and has participated in a complete cycle of comparison against the items preceding all the BY phrases in the REPLACING clause.

See character-string, comment line, compile time, continuation line indicator area, debugging line, library-text, qualification, separator, source program.

CORRESPONDING, CORR

The CORRESPONDING phrase is used with the ADD, SUBTRACT, and MOVE verbs. It allows 'corresponding' data items to be used as operands without explicitly specifying each one.

Consider a pair of data items: d_1 from group item G_1; and d_2 from group item G_2. The two data items, d_1 and d_2, are 'corresponding' when all of the following conditions hold:

1. Neither d_1 nor d_2 is a FILLER item.

2. d_1 and d_2 have the same data-name and qualifiers up to, but not including, G_1 and G_2.

3. Neither d_1 nor d_2 contains level-number 66, 77 or 88, or the USAGE IS INDEX phrase in its data description.

4. For the MOVE statement, d_1 and/or d_2 must be an elementary item.

5. For the ADD and SUBTRACT statements, both d_1 and d_2 must be elementary numeric items.

Any item in G_1 or G_2 that contains a REDEFINES, RENAMES, OCCURS, or USAGE IS INDEX clause or that is subordinate to an item containing one of these clauses is ignored during execution of a statement with the corresponding phrase. However, G_1 or G_2 can have a REDEFINES or OCCURS clause or be subordinate to an item with one of these clauses.

Example: Consider the two group items:

02	MASTER-RECORD		02	DETAIL-RECORD	
	03	R-HOURS		05	R-HOURS
	03	O-T		05	O-T
		04 TIME-HALF			06 TIME-HALF
		04 DBL-TIME			06 TPL-TIME
	03	RATE-PAY		05	RATE-PAY
		04 REG-RATE			
		04 SPEC-RATE			

An ADD or SUBTRACT CORRESPONDING would affect R-HOURS and TIME-HALF. A MOVE CORRESPONDING would affect R-HOURS, TIME-HALF, and RATE-PAY.

See elementary item, group item, numeric data item, qualifier.

COUNT

See ACCEPT, communication description entry, MESSAGE COUNT, UN-STRING.

counter

A counter is a data item that is used for storing a value in such a way that the value can be increased or decreased by the value of another number and can be reset to an arbitrary value.

crossfooting

See SUM, TYPE.

CURRENCY SIGN

See SPECIAL-NAMES.

currency sign

The currency sign is the character: $.

currency symbol

The currency symbol is that character defined in the CURRENCY SIGN clause in the SPECIAL-NAMES paragraph. If this clause is not specified, the currency symbol is the currency sign ($).

See currency sign.

current record

The current record for a file is the record that is presently available in the file's record area. A file may not always have a current record defined.

current-record pointer

The current-record pointer is a conceptual entity that specifies the next record to be accessed in a file. This term has no meaning when used with output files. The setting of the current-record pointer is affected by the OPEN, START, and READ verbs.

See output mode.

D

DATA

> *See* DATA DIVISION, DATA RECORD, RECEIVE.

data alignment

> *See* alignment rules, SYNCHRONIZED.

data clause

> A data clause is a clause that appears in a data description entry in the DATA DIVISION; it describes some attribute of a data item.
>
> PICTURE, VALUE IS, and BLANK WHEN ZERO are examples of data clauses.
>
> *See* data description entry.

data description

> *See* record description.

data description entry

> A data description entry is an entry in the DATA DIVISION that begins with a level-number and is followed by a data-name or the reserved word FILLER and optional data clauses. Any entry that begins with 01 or 77 must have the level-number in area A, followed by a space, and the data-name in area B.
>
> *Format 1:*

$$\text{level-number} \begin{Bmatrix} \text{data-name-1} \\ \underline{\text{FILLER}} \end{Bmatrix}$$

$$[\underline{\text{REDEFINES}} \text{ data-name-2}]$$

$$\left[\begin{Bmatrix} \underline{\text{PICTURE}} \\ \underline{\text{PIC}} \end{Bmatrix} \text{IS character-string} \right]$$

$$\left[\underline{\text{USAGE}} \text{ IS} \begin{Bmatrix} \underline{\text{COMPUTATIONAL}} \\ \underline{\text{COMP}} \\ \underline{\text{DISPLAY}} \\ \underline{\text{INDEX}} \end{Bmatrix} \right]$$

$$\left[\underline{\text{SIGN}} \text{ IS} \begin{Bmatrix} \underline{\text{LEADING}} \\ \underline{\text{TRAILING}} \end{Bmatrix} [\underline{\text{SEPARATE}} \text{ CHARACTER}] \right]$$

$$\left[\begin{Bmatrix} \underline{\text{SYNCHRONIZED}} \\ \underline{\text{SYNC}} \end{Bmatrix} \begin{bmatrix} \underline{\text{LEFT}} \\ \underline{\text{RIGHT}} \end{bmatrix} \right]$$

$$\left[\begin{Bmatrix} \underline{\text{JUSTIFIED}} \\ \underline{\text{JUST}} \end{Bmatrix} \text{RIGHT} \right]$$

$$[\underline{\text{BLANK}} \text{ WHEN } \underline{\text{ZERO}}]$$

$$[\underline{\text{VALUE}} \text{ IS literal}].$$

A format 1 entry can have a level-number from 01 to 49 or 77. If only level 1 of the Nucleus module is implemented, the value of level-number must be from 01 through 10 or 77.

The clauses can be written in any order except that data-name-1 or FILLER must immediately follow the level-number and REDEFINES, if used, must immediately follow data-name-1.

The SYNCHRONIZED, PICTURE, JUSTIFIED, and BLANK WHEN ZERO clauses can be specified only for elementary items. Every elementary item except an index data-item must have a PICTURE clause.

Report Section Considerations

In the REPORT SECTION a data-name need not appear; furthermore, FILLER is not allowed. A data-name must be specified when

- The data-name represents a report group that is referenced by a GENERATE or USE statement.
- The sum counter is referenced in either the PROCEDURE DIVISION or the REPORT SECTION.
- A DETAIL report group is referenced in the UPON phrase of the SUM clause.
- The data-name is needed to qualify a sum counter.

Format 2:

$$66 \quad \text{data-name-1 } \underline{\text{RENAMES}} \text{ data-name-2 } \left[\left\{ \begin{matrix} \underline{\text{THROUGH}} \\ \underline{\text{THRU}} \end{matrix} \right\} \text{data-name-3} \right].$$

Format 3:

$$88 \quad \text{condition-name} \left\{ \begin{matrix} \underline{\text{VALUE}} \text{ IS} \\ \underline{\text{VALUES}} \text{ ARE} \end{matrix} \right\} \left\{ \text{literal-1} \left[\left\{ \begin{matrix} \underline{\text{THROUGH}} \\ \underline{\text{THRU}} \end{matrix} \right\} \text{literal-2} \right] \right\} \dots.$$

See area A, area B, condition-name, elementary item, index data item, level-number, OCCURS, RENAMES.

DATA DIVISION

The DATA DIVISION of a COBOL program is that division in which the characteristics of all the data used by that program, the hierarchical relationships among data, and condition-names are defined.

Format:

```
DATA DIVISION.
[FILE SECTION. file description entry]
[WORKING-STORAGE SECTION. data description entry]
[LINKAGE SECTION. data description entry]
[COMMUNICATION SECTION. communication description entry]
[REPORT SECTION. report description entry]
```

The division header and each section header must start in area A and be terminated by a period and space. Except within the PICTURE character-string, commas and semicolons can be used in this division wherever necessary to improve readability.

See the individual entries for details of the various sections; also area A, character-string, communication description entry, condition-name, data description entry, division header, file description entry, report description entry, section header.

data item

A data item is a character or set of contiguous characters defined as a unit of data in a COBOL program. Literals are not considered data items.

data-movement verbs

The data-movement verbs are ACCEPT, ACCEPT MESSAGE COUNT, INSPECT . . . REPLACING, MOVE, STRING, and UNSTRING.

data-name

A data-name is a user-defined word of up to 30 characters of which at least one is alphabetic. A data-name names an entry described in the DATA DIVISION. In the formats, 'data-name' represents a word that can neither be subscripted, indexed, nor qualified, unless specifically permitted by the rules for that format.

See alphabetic character, identifier, indexing, qualification, subscripting, user-defined word.

DATA RECORD

The DATA RECORD clause is used in a file description to document the names of the data records in the file.

Format:

$$\underline{DATA} \left\{ \begin{array}{l} \underline{RECORDS} \ ARE \\ \underline{RECORD} \ IS \end{array} \right\} \{data\text{-}name\text{-}1\} \ldots$$

The presence of more than one data-name indicates that more than one type of record is in the file. All data records in a file occupy the same storage area; the presence of more than one type of data record within the file in no way alters this fact. The order in which the data-names are listed is immaterial.

All data-names are the names of data records and must be named in an 01 level entry in the file's record description.

See file description, record description.

DATE

See ACCEPT, communication description entry.

DATE-COMPILED

The DATE-COMPILED paragraph is part of the IDENTIFICATION DIVISION. It is implemented in level 2 of the Nucleus Module. It provides a means of inserting the compilation date in the source program listing.

Format:

DATE-COMPILED. [comment-entry] . . .

The DATE-COMPILED paragraph is optional. If it is included, during compilation the entire paragraph is replaced in the output listing by

DATE-COMPILED. current-date

DATE-WRITTEN

The DATE-WRITTEN paragraph is an optional entry in the IDENTIFICATION DIVISION used only for documentation purposes. It does not affect the compilation of the program.

Format:

DATE-WRITTEN. [comment-entry] . . .

The comment-entry cannot be continued by using a hyphen in the comment line indicator area; however, the comment can be contained on more than one line. Any character in the computer's character set can appear in a comment-entry.

See comment line indicator area.

DAY

See ACCEPT.

DE

An abbreviation for DETAIL.

See report group description, TYPE.

DEBUG-CONTENTS

See USE FOR DEBUGGING.

DEBUGGING

See SOURCE-COMPUTER, USE FOR DEBUGGING.

debugging line

A debugging line is any line that contains a D in the continuation area,[1] column 7. Debugging lines can appear anywhere in the program after the OBJECT-COMPUTER paragraph.

A program containing debugging lines must be syntactically and logically correct whether the debugging lines are compiled or not. Successive debugging

---

[1] This means of identifying debugging lines is new to 74 COBOL.

lines are allowed. If a debugging line is to be continued, each continuation line must contain a D in the continuation area. A character-string cannot be broken across two debugging lines. A debugging line consisting solely of spaces from margin A to margin R is considered to be a blank line.

If the WITH DEBUGGING MODE clause is specified in the SOURCE-COMPUTER paragraph, all debugging lines are compiled. If this clause does not appear, all debugging lines are treated as comment lines during compilation.

See margin.

DEBUGGING MODE

See SOURCE-COMPUTER.

debugging section

A debugging section is a section that contains a USE FOR DEBUGGING statement.

DEBUG-ITEM

DEBUG-ITEM is a special register generated when the debug facility is used. Only one DEBUG-ITEM is allocated per program. DEBUG-ITEM has the implicit description:

```
01  DEBUG-ITEM.
    02  DEBUG-LINE          PIC X(6).
    02  FILLER              PIC X VALUE SPACE.
    02  DEBUG-NAME          PIC X(30).
    02  FILLER              PIC X VALUE SPACE.
    02  DEBUG-SUB-1         PIC S9999 SIGN IS LEADING SEPARATE CHARACTER.
    02  FILLER              PIC X VALUE SPACE.
    02  DEBUG-SUB-2         PIC S9999 SIGN LEADING SEPARATE CHARACTER.
    02  FILLER              PIC X VALUE SPACE.
    02  DEBUG-SUB-3         PIC S9999 SIGN LEADING SEPARATE CHARACTER.
    02  FILLER              PIC X VALUE SPACE.
    02  DEBUG-CONTENTS      PIC X(n)
```

Where 'n' denotes a size large enough to hold different contents depending on the use of DEBUG-ITEM.

See USE FOR DEBUGGING, special register.

DEBUG-LINE

See USE FOR DEBUGGING.

Debug Module

The Debug Module provides a means for the user to monitor data items or procedures during execution of the program. This module is new to 74 COBOL.

Level 1

Debug level 1 provides a basic debug capability, including the ability to specify selective or full monitoring of procedures, and debugging statements that are compiled at the user's option.

Level 2

Debug level 2 provides the additional capability of monitoring identifiers and file operations.

See USE FOR DEBUGGING.

DEBUG-NAME

See USE FOR DEBUGGING.

DEBUG-SUB-1, DEBUG-SUB-2, DEBUG-SUB-3

See USE FOR DEBUGGING.

DECIMAL-POINT IS COMMA

The DECIMAL-POINT IS COMMA clause is used in the SPECIAL-NAMES paragraph to interchange the function of the decimal point and the comma in the PICTURE clause and in numeric literals. This is used in continental European applications where these characters are employed differently than in the United States.

For example, in the United States the amount twelve dollars and thirty-five cents would be written as $12.35; if the DECIMAL-POINT IS COMMA clause is used, the amount would be written $12,35. Similarly for stateside operations a PICTURE string would be 999,999.99 ; for European operations the PICTURE string would be written 999.999,99 .

See numeric literal.

DECLARATIVES

DECLARATIVES are a group of one or more special purpose sections, the first of which is preceded by the reserved word DECLARATIVES and the last of which is followed by the reserved words END DECLARATIVES. Each of these must be on a line by itself, beginning in area A and followed by a period and space. A declarative is composed of a section header, a USE statement, and optionally, one or more paragraphs. Declaratives must appear at the beginning of the Procedure Division.

Format:

```
PROCEDURE DIVISION [USING {identifier-1}...].
[DECLARATIVES.
{section-name SECTION [segment-number]. declarative sentence
[paragraph-name. [sentence]...]...}...
END DECLARATIVES.]
```

The declarative sections contain USE statements and their associated procedures. After END DECLARATIVES, no text can appear prior to the next section header. If a declarative section has a segment-number, the number must be less than 50. The fact that segment-numbers are allowed is new to 74 COBOL.

See area A, section header.

declarative sentence

A declarative sentence is a compiler-directing sentence consisting of a single USE statement terminated by a period.

See compiler directing sentence.

default

Sometimes, when a programmer has to make a selection from a number of options, he need not choose anything. The *default* is that option that the compiler assumes when the programmer does not explicitly make a choice. For example, if the USAGE clause is not specified, the compiler assumes a usage of DISPLAY.

DELETE

The DELETE verb logically removes a record from a mass storage file. This is a new feature of 74 COBOL.

Format:

DELETE file-name RECORD [INVALID KEY imperative-statement-1]

The DELETE statement cannot be used with a SORT or MERGE file or with a sequential file. The file must be open in the input-output mode when the DELETE is executed. When a DELETE has been successfully executed, the record that was deleted is logically removed from the file and cannot subsequently be accessed. The current-record pointer and the file's record area are not affected by the DELETE.

Files with Sequential Access

When a DELETE statement is applied to a file that is being sequentially accessed, the last successful input-output statement executed for the file must have been a format 1 READ. The record that was accessed by that READ is the one that is deleted. The INVALID KEY phrase cannot be specified for the file in the sequential access mode.

Files with Random or Dynamic Access

When a DELETE statement is applied to a file that is being accessed in the random or dynamic mode, if the file is relative, the record identified by the Relative Key data item is deleted; if the file is indexed, the record identified by the prime record key is deleted. If the file does not contain the record specified by the key, the Invalid Key condition exists.

Invalid Key Phrase

The INVALID KEY phrase must be specified if the file is in random or dynamic access mode, unless a format 1 USE procedure is specified.

When the Invalid Key condition occurs, if the INVALID KEY phrase is specified, imperative-statement-1 is executed. If the INVALID KEY phrase is not specified, then the applicable format 1 USE procedure is executed. If both the INVALID KEY phrase and a USE procedure are specified, only imperative-statement-1 is executed.

File Status

If a File Status data item is specified, it is updated as follows:

Status Key 1	Status Key 2	Meaning
0	0	Successful completion
2	2	Duplicate key
2	3	No record found
2	4	Boundary violation
3	0	Permanent error
9	–	Implementor-defined

See dynamic access, indexed i-o, input-output mode, prime record, key, random access, relative i-o, sequential access, sequential i-o.

DELIMITED BY

The DELIMITED BY phrase is used in the STRING and UNSTRING verbs to specify the character or characters that are the delimiters.

See delimiter.

DELIMITER

See UNSTRING.

delimiter

A delimiter is a symbol(s) that defines the boundaries of an item. For a nonnumeric literal the quotation character (") is the delimiter; for pseudo-text in the COPY statement, two equal signs (==) are the delimiter.

The delimiter is never part of the string that it delimits. In the case of nonnumeric literals, the delimiter is also termed a separator.

See nonnumeric literal, pseudo-text.

DEPENDING

See GO TO, OCCURS.

DESCENDING KEY

See MERGE, OCCURS, SORT.

DESTINATION

See communication description entry.

destination

A destination is the symbolic identification of the receiver of a transmission from a queue.

See queue.

DETAIL

See PAGE, report group, report group description, TYPE.

digit position

A digit position is the amount of storage needed to hold a single digit. This amount of storage varies as a function of the USAGE of the data item. Refer to the computer manufacturer's manual for details for a particular machine.

DISABLE

The DISABLE verb notifies the Message Control System (MCS) to inhibit data transfer between specified queues and sources or destinations. This verb is new to 74 COBOL.

Format:

$$\text{DISABLE} \left\{ \begin{array}{l} \underline{\text{INPUT}} \ [\underline{\text{TERMINAL}}] \\ \underline{\text{OUTPUT}} \end{array} \right\} \text{cd-name WITH } \underline{\text{KEY}} \left\{ \begin{array}{l} \text{identifier-1} \\ \text{literal-1} \end{array} \right\}$$

This statement logically disconnects the MCS and the specified sources or destinations. If this disconnection already exists, or is handled by means outside of the object program, the DISABLE statement is not required. This statement does not affect the logical path for the transfer of data between the MCS and the object program; it only notifies the MCS to inhibit data transfers.

The MCS will never execute a DISABLE so that a portion of a message already in transit will be cut off and not transmitted. The logical disconnection will occur at the earliest time after the source or destination becomes inactive.

The Input Phrase

When the INPUT phrase is specified, cd-name must refer to an input communication description. If TERMINAL is not specified, the logical paths for all of the sources associated with the queues and sub-queues specified by the SYMBOLIC QUEUE (data-name-1 in the description of cd-name) through SYMBOLIC SUB-QUEUE-3 (data-name-4 in the description of cd-name) are deactivated. If TERMINAL is specified, only the SYMBOLIC SOURCE is used by the MCS. All paths between this source and the associated queues and sub-queues are deactivated.

The Output Phrase

When the OUTPUT phrase is specified, cd-name must refer to an output communication description. The logical path for all destinations, as specified by SYMBOLIC DESTINATION (data-name-5 in the description of cd-name) through SYMBOLIC SUB-QUEUE-3 (data-name-4 in the description of cd-name) are deactivated.

The Key Phrase

The KEY phrase provides a password facility. The data, which must be alphanumeric, specified by literal-1 or identifier-1, will be compared with a password built into the system. The DISABLE statement is honored only if this data matches the system password. If they do not match, the STATUS KEY item in the cd-name definition is set to 40. The size of a password can be from 1 to 10 characters, inclusive, and it is entered into the system by means outside COBOL.

See cd-name, communication description entry, destination, Message Control System, queue, source, sub-queue.

DISPLAY

DISPLAY is a type of USAGE of data that specifies that the predominant use of the data is for output rather than computation. If no USAGE is specified, a usage of DISPLAY is assumed.

DISPLAY items are stored in standard data format.

See data description, report group description.

DISPLAY

The DISPLAY statement is used to output low-volume data.

$$\underline{\text{DISPLAY}} \left\{ \begin{array}{l} \text{identifier-1} \\ \text{literal-1} \end{array} \right\} \dots [\underline{\text{UPON}} \text{ mnemonic-name}]$$

This statement causes the contents of each identifier (or literal) to be transferred to a hardware device. The size of data that each device can receive, as well as the standard device for the display statement, are implementor-defined. Multiple operands are transferred in the order listed in the statement, from left to right.

The size of the data being transferred is considered equal to the sum of the sizes of all the operands. If the size of the data being transferred is equal to that of the hardware device, the data is transferred. If the size of the data being transferred is less than the size of the hardware device, the data is transferred left-aligned. If the size of the data being transferred is greater than the size of the hardware device, transfer begins with the left-most character of the data and continues until the hardware device is filled. If level 2 of the Nucleus is implemented, additional data is transferred until the transfer is complete.

The UPON Phrase

The UPON phrase is implemented in level 2 of the Nucleus. If the UPON phrase is specified, the mnemonic-name must be associated with a hardware device in the SPECIAL-NAMES paragraph in the ENVIRONMENT DIVISION.

Example: Assume that the output device has a size of 5 and that TEMP1 and TEMP2 have contents as shown:

TEMP1 | A | B | C | D | E | TEMP2 | F | G | H | I | J | K | L | M |

1. DISPLAY TEMP1
   This statement causes the following to be output:

   A B C D E

2. DISPLAY TEMP2
   This statement causes the following to be output:

   F G H I J   if only level 1 of the Nucleus is implemented.

   F G H I J
   K L M   if level 2 of the Nucleus is implemented.

3. DISPLAY TEMP1,SPACE,TEMP2,QUOTE
   This statement causes the following to be output:

   A   B   C   D   E
   △   F   G   H   I
   J   K   L   M   "   assuming level 2 of the Nucleus.

	Numeric	Numeric-edited	Alphanumeric	Alphanumeric-edited	Alphabetic
Identifier-1	X	X	X	X	X
Literal-1	X[1]	X	X	X	X

---

[1] If literal-1 is numeric, it must be an unsigned integer. This is a new restriction of 74 COBOL.

Literal-1 can be any figurative constant except ALL. In the DISPLAY statement a figurative constant stands for a single instance of the character.

See figurative constant, mnemonic-name.

DIVIDE

The DIVIDE verb divides one data item into one or more data items and then sets one or more data items equal to the quotient and, optionally, the remainder. The composite of operands, determined by superimposing all receiving items except the remainder aligned by decimal point, must not exceed 18 digits. The multiple receiving fields of formats 1, 2, and 3 is a new feature of 74 COBOL, and is implemented in level 2 of the Nucleus.

Format 1:

$$\underline{\text{DIVIDE}} \left\{ \begin{array}{l} \text{identifier-1} \\ \text{literal-1} \end{array} \right\} \underline{\text{INTO}} \ \{\text{identifier-2} \ [\underline{\text{ROUNDED}}]\} \ldots$$

[; ON $\underline{\text{SIZE}}$ $\underline{\text{ERROR}}$ imperative-statement-1]

Identifier-1 (or literal-1) is the divisor. The divisor is divided into identifier-2, the quotient replacing the original contents of identifier-2. If there is more than one identifier after INTO, each of them, in turn, is divided by the divisor with the quotient replacing each identifier's original contents. Thus, the new value of each identifier following INTO is the quotient of its original value, divided by the divisor.

Example: Assume as initial values: TEMP1 = 100
                                          UNITS = 10
                                          TEMP2 = 200

1. DIVIDE 5 INTO TEMP1.
   After execution, the new value of TEMP1 is 20.

2. DIVIDE UNITS INTO TEMP1, TEMP2.
   After execution, the new value of TEMP1 is 10, and the new value of TEMP2 is 20.

Format 2:

$$\underline{\text{DIVIDE}} \left\{ \begin{array}{l} \text{identifier-1} \\ \text{literal-1} \end{array} \right\} \underline{\text{INTO}} \left\{ \begin{array}{l} \text{identifier-2} \\ \text{literal-2} \end{array} \right\} \underline{\text{GIVING}} \ \{\text{identifier-3} \ [\underline{\text{ROUNDED}}]\} \ldots$$

[; ON $\underline{\text{SIZE}}$ $\underline{\text{ERROR}}$ imperative-statement-1]

Format 3:

$$\underline{\text{DIVIDE}} \left\{ \begin{array}{l} \text{identifier-1} \\ \text{literal-1} \end{array} \right\} \underline{\text{BY}} \left\{ \begin{array}{l} \text{identifier-2} \\ \text{literal-2} \end{array} \right\} \underline{\text{GIVING}} \ \{\text{identifier-3} \ [\underline{\text{ROUNDED}}]\} \ldots$$

[; ON $\underline{\text{SIZE}}$ $\underline{\text{ERROR}}$ imperative-statement-1]

In format 2, identifier-1 or literal-1 is the divisor; identifier-2 or literal-2 is the dividend. In format 3, identifier-2 or literal-2 is the divisor; identifier-1 or literal-1, the dividend. Except for this distinction, the two formats operate identically.

The dividend is divided by the divisor, and the quotient is placed in each data item following GIVING. Thus, the new value of each identifier following GIVING is equal to the quotient. Note that the previous contents of identifiers following GIVING do not participate in the division.

Example: Assume as initial values: COST = 100
UNITS = 10
RESULT1 = 100
RESULT2 = 0

1. DIVIDE COST BY UNITS GIVING RESULT1.
2. DIVIDE UNITS INTO COST GIVING RESULT1.
After execution, the new value of RESULT1 is 10.
3. DIVIDE COST BY 10 GIVING RESULT1, RESULT2.
4. DIVIDE 10 INTO COST GIVING RESULT1, RESULT2.
5. DIVIDE COST BY UNITS GIVING RESULT1, RESULT2.
6. DIVIDE UNITS INTO COST GIVING RESULT1, RESULT2.
After execution the new values of RESULT1 and RESULT2 are each 10.

Format 4:

$$\underline{\text{DIVIDE}} \left\{ \begin{array}{l} \text{identifier-1} \\ \text{literal-1} \end{array} \right\} \underline{\text{INTO}} \left\{ \begin{array}{l} \text{identifier-2} \\ \text{literal-2} \end{array} \right\} \underline{\text{GIVING}} \text{ identifier-3 [\underline{ROUNDED}]}$$

$$\underline{\text{REMAINDER}} \text{ identifier-4 [; ON } \underline{\text{SIZE}} \ \underline{\text{ERROR}} \text{ imperative-statement-1]}$$

Format 5:

$$\underline{\text{DIVIDE}} \left\{ \begin{array}{l} \text{identifier-1} \\ \text{literal-1} \end{array} \right\} \underline{\text{BY}} \left\{ \begin{array}{l} \text{identifier-2} \\ \text{literal-2} \end{array} \right\} \underline{\text{GIVING}} \text{ identifier-3 [\underline{ROUNDED}]}$$

$$\underline{\text{REMAINDER}} \text{ identifier-4 [; ON } \underline{\text{SIZE}} \ \underline{\text{ERROR}} \text{ imperative-statement-1]}$$

Formats 4 and 5 are implemented in level 2 of the Nucleus. In format 4, identifier-1 or literal-1 is the divisor; identifier-2 or literal-2 the dividend. In format 5, identifier-2 or literal-2 is the divisor; identifier-1 or literal-1, the dividend. Except for this distinction the two formats operate identically.

The dividend is divided by the divisor, and the quotient is placed into identifier-3; the remainder, into identifier-4. In COBOL the remainder is defined as the result of subtracting the product of the quotient and divisor from the dividend. Decimal point alignment and truncation, if needed, are then performed on the remainder. For example, if 22 is divided by 6, the quotient is 3.666 ... If the PICTURE of the receiving item is 9V9, the remainder is computed thus:

1. Multiply the quotient and divisor, $3.6 \times 6 = 21.6$

2. Subtract the result from the dividend, $22 - 21.6 = .4$

3. The result, .4, is the remainder.

Observe that if the PICTURE of the receiving item were 9V99, the remainder would have been .04.

If the quotient is in a numeric-edited item, the unedited quotient is used to calculate the remainder. If ROUNDED is applied to the quotient, the truncated value of the quotient, rather than the rounded one, is used to calculate the remainder. In the above example, if rounding were specified, the remainder would still have been .4, but the quotient would have been 3.7.

When the SIZE ERROR phrase is applied, if a size error occurs on the quotient, neither identifier-3 nor identifier-4 is changed. If the size error occurs only on the remainder, identifier-4 is unchanged. No indication of which of these two conditions has occurred is given, however, and the user must perform his own analysis.

Examples: Assume as initial values: OVER = .12 PIC V99
RESULT = 5 PIC 99V9
RESULT1 = 5 PIC 9V9
RESULT2 = 5 PIC 99
UNITS = 7
COST = 72

1. DIVIDE UNITS INTO COST GIVING RESULT REMAINDER OVER.

2. DIVIDE COST BY UNITS GIVING RESULT REMAINDER OVER.
   After execution, the value of RESULT is 10.2; the value of OVER is .60.

3. DIVIDE UNITS INTO COST GIVING RESULT1 REMAINDER OVER ON SIZE ERROR ADD 1 TO COST.
   After execution the values of RESULT1 and OVER are unchanged and the value of COST is 73, since there was a size error on the quotient.

4. DIVIDE UNITS INTO COST GIVING RESULT2 REMAINDER OVER ON SIZE ERROR ADD 1 TO COST.
   After execution the value of RESULT2 is 10, the value of OVER is unchanged and the value of COST is 73. Since the calculated remainder was 2 but OVER could not contain this value, there was a size error on the remainder.

	Format 1						Format 2 / Format 3						Format 4 / Format 5				
	Numeric	Numeric-edited	Alphanumeric	Alphanumeric-edited	Alphabetic		Numeric	Numeric-edited	Alphanumeric	Alphanumeric-edited	Alphabetic		Numeric	Numeric-edited	Alphanumeric	Alphanumeric-edited	Alphabetic
Literal-1, -2	X						X						X				
Identifier-1, -2	X						X						X				
Identifier-3							X	X					X	X			
Identifier-4													X	X			

See arithmetic statements, composite of operands, CORRESPONDING, multiple results in arithmetic statements, overlapping operands, ROUNDED, SIZE ERROR, truncation.

division

A division is the most inclusive grouping of a COBOL program. It consists of zero, one, or more sections or paragraphs called the division body. Every COBOL program must include the four divisions IDENTIFICATION, ENVIRONMENT, DATA, and PROCEDURE, in that order.

See paragraph, section.

division header

A division header is a series of one or more words followed by a period and space that indicates the beginning of a division. The division header must begin in area A. The division headers are

        IDENTIFICATION DIVISION.
        ENVIRONMENT DIVISION.
        DATA DIVISION.
        PROCEDURE DIVISION [USING {data-name-1}...].

See area A, margin.

documentation-entry

A documentation-entry contains information which, although part of the source program, is not compiled. It serves only to annotate the program.

DOWN BY
> *See* SET.

DUPLICATES
> *See* FILE-CONTROL, RECORD KEY, SELECT.

DYNAMIC
> *See* ACCESS MODE, FILE-CONTROL, SELECT.

dynamic access
> Dynamic access is an access mode in which records in a mass storage file can be accessed either randomly or sequentially during the scope of the same OPEN statement. This mode is new to 74 COBOL.
>
> *See* FILE-CONTROL, random access, sequential access.

E

editing character

An editing character is a single character or a special two-character combination. The editing characters are

B	$
0	,
+	.
−	/
Z	CR
*	DB

See PICTURE.

EGI

EGI is an abbreviation for 'End of Group Indicator.'
See message indicator, SEND.

elementary item

An elementary item is a data item that is not further subdivided into other data items. In the DATA DIVISION, any item with a level-number of 49 (or if only level 1 of the Nucleus is implemented, a level-number of 10) is automatically an elementary item. For entries with any other level-numbers, an item is elementary if the item immediately following it has a level-number that is not numerically greater than it has.

Example:

```
01  ABC
    02  DEF
        03  GHI
        03  JKL
    02  MNO
    02  PQR
        49  RST
```

In this example, GHI, JKL, MNO, and RST are elementary items.
See level-number, unstructured data item.

ellipsis

The ellipsis (...) is used in formats to indicate that the preceding material in brackets or braces can be repeated as often as necessary. This book adopts the convention that if an ellipsis is applied to a set of braces, at least *one* instance of the material in the braces must appear, and subsequent instances of it are optional. If applied to a set of brackets, ellipses indicate that zero, one, or more instances of the material in the brackets can appear.

See braces, brackets, notation in COBOL.

ELSE

See IF.

embedded conditional

See IF.

EMI

EMI is an abbreviation for 'End of Message Indicator.'

See message indicator, SEND.

ENABLE

The ENABLE verb notifies the Message Control System (MCS) to allow data transfers between specified queues and specified sources and destinations. This verb is new to 74 COBOL.

Format:

$$\text{ENABLE} \left\{ \begin{array}{l} \underline{\text{INPUT}} \, [\text{TERMINAL}] \\ \underline{\text{OUTPUT}} \end{array} \right\} \text{cd-name WITH } \underline{\text{KEY}} \left\{ \begin{array}{l} \text{identifier-1} \\ \text{literal-1} \end{array} \right\}$$

The ENABLE statement logically connects the MCS and the specified sources or destinations. If this connection already exists or is handled by means outside of the object program, the ENABLE statement is not required. The ENABLE statement does not affect the logical path for the transfer of data between the MCS and the object program; it merely notifies the MCS to allow data transfers.

The Input Phrase

When the INPUT phrase is specified, cd-name must refer to an input communication description. If TERMINAL is not specified, the logical paths for all sources associated with the queues and sub-queues specified by SYMBOLIC QUEUE (data-name-1 in the description of cd-name) through SYMBOLIC SUB-QUEUE-3 (data-name-4 in the description of cd-name) are activated.

If TERMINAL is specified, only the SYMBOLIC SOURCE (data-name-7 in the description of cd-name) is used by the MCS. All paths between this source and all associated queues and sub-queues already enabled are activated. TER-MINAL is supported only in level 2 of the Communication Module.

The Output Phrase

When the OUTPUT phrase is specified, cd-name must refer to an output communication description. The logical paths for all destinations, as specified by the SYMBOLIC DESTINATION (data-name-5 in the description of cd-name), are activated.

The Key Phrase

The KEY phrase provides a password facility. The data that is specified by literal-1 or identifier-1 will be compared with a password built into the system. The ENABLE statement is honored only if this data matches the system's password. If it does not match, the STATUS KEY (data-name-10 in the description of cd-name) is set to 40. The size of a password can be from 1 to 10 characters, inclusive. It is entered into the system by means outside COBOL.

	Alphanumeric
Literal-1	X
Identifier-1	X

> *See* cd-name, communication description name, destination, Message Control System, queue, source.

END
> *See* communication description entry, READ, RERUN, RETURN, SEARCH.

END DECLARATIVES
> *See* DECLARATIVES.

ending statement
> The statement STOP RUN is the ending statement.

End of Group Indicator
> *See* message indicator.

End of Message Indicator
> *See* message indicator.

END-OF-PAGE
> *See* WRITE.

end of page condition
> *See* WRITE.

end of Procedure Division

The end of the Procedure Division is that point in a COBOL source program after which no more Procedure Division statements appear.

See source program.

End of Segment Indicator

See message indicator.

ENTER

The ENTER verb allows more than one language to be used in a COBOL source program.

Format 1:

<u>ENTER</u> language-name [routine-name]•

Language-name is a system-name that can refer to any programming language that the implementor allows to be entered through COBOL. The spelling of the language-name, as well as details on how the other language is to be written, are defined by the implementor for each language.

Following the ENTER statement are the various statements in the other language. These are executed as if they were compiled into the object program following the ENTER statement. The sentence ENTER COBOL• must follow the last statement in the other language to effect a return to the COBOL source language.

Routine-name is a COBOL word that can be referred to only in an ENTER statement. It is used when the other language statements cannot be written in-line. Routine-name identifies the other language statements to be executed when the ENTER statement is reached during execution of the object program.

Example:

(1)   PAR-1•
      ENTER FORTRAN•
      $X = Y * (Z * X) ** .5$
      ENTER COBOL• ADD 1 TO TEMP•

(2)   PAR-1•
      ENTER FORTRAN PAR-5•
      PAR-2•
      ADD 1 TO TEMP•
          ⋮
      PAR-5•
      $X = Y * (Z * X) ** .5$
      ENTER COBOL PAR-2•

N.B. As this verb need not be implemented in order for a COBOL compiler to conform to ANSI specifications, the reader is advised to consult the appropriate manual for his system.

See source program, system-name.

entry

An entry is any set of one or more consecutive clauses terminated by a period and written in the Identification, Environment, or Data Divisions of a COBOL source program.

See clause, DATA DIVISION, ENVIRONMENT DIVISION, IDENTIFICATION DIVISION, source program.

environment clause

An environment clause is a clause that appears as part of an entry in the ENVIRONMENT DIVISION.

See clause.

ENVIRONMENT DIVISION

The ENVIRONMENT DIVISION is that division of the COBOL source program in which those aspects of a program that depend upon the particular hardware to be used are defined.

Format:

```
ENVIRONMENT DIVISION.
CONFIGURATION SECTION.
SOURCE-COMPUTER. source-computer-entry.
OBJECT-COMPUTER. object-computer-entry.
[SPECIAL-NAMES. special-names-entry.]
[INPUT-OUTPUT SECTION.
FILE-CONTROL. {file-control-entry}... .
[I-O-CONTROL. [input-output-control-entry]...]].
```

The ENVIRONMENT DIVISION, the presence of which is mandatory in every COBOL source program, must begin with the division header in area A, followed by a period and space. The order of presentation of entries, even optional ones, must conform to the format shown above. Commas and semicolons can be used to improve readability.

See the individual entries for details; also area A, source program.

EOP

See WRITE.

EQUAL

See IF, relation condition, SEARCH, START.

ERROR

See communication description entry, SIZE ERROR, USE.

ESI

ESI is an abbreviation for 'End of Segment Indicator.'

See message indicator, SEND.

EVERY

See RERUN.

EXAMINE

Formerly a verb, EXAMINE has been replaced by INSPECT.

EXCEPTION

See USE.

execution of object program

Execution of an object program begins with the first statement of the PRO-CEDURE DIVISION after the DECLARATIVES. Statements are then executed in the order in which they appear in the source program, except where the rules for the verb involved indicate otherwise.

See object program.

execution time

See object time.

EXIT

The EXIT verb provides a common ending point for a group of procedures or indicates the logical end of a called program.

Format 1:

EXIT.

The EXIT statement is used to assign a procedure-name to a point in the program so that control can be transferred to that point. Usually when one wishes to leave a procedure before it is completely executed, one transfers control to the paragraph following the procedure. However, this technique will not work if the procedure is in the range of a PERFORM or USE statement. For example, assume the following structure in the program:

PAR-1.

.
.
.

IF TEST-A . . .

.
.
.

PAR-2.

.
.
.

PAR-3.

.
.
.

Now assume that PERFORM PAR-1 THROUGH PAR-3 is executed. First, control is transferred to PAR-1. If, as a result of TEST-A, the rest of PAR-1 through PAR-3 is *not* to be performed, there is no convenient way to break out of the range, since one cannot transfer control to the end of a paragraph. Furthermore, one cannot use a GO TO to return to the statement following the PERFORM, since there may be several such statements referencing PAR-1 and there is no way of knowing which statement transferred control nor the current range of the PERFORM.

However, by adding a fourth paragraph that contains the EXIT statement and changing the PERFORM to: PERFORM PAR-1 THROUGH PAR-4, one can now execute a GO TO as a function of TEST-A and subsequently return to the statement following whichever PERFORM transferred control. The structure is

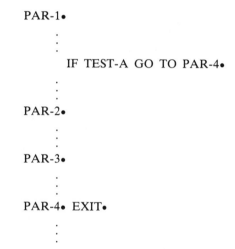

If no associated PERFORM or USE statement is active when an EXIT statement is encountered, control passes to the first sentence of the next paragraph.

Format 2:

<u>EXIT PROGRAM</u>●

This form of the EXIT statement is available only if the Inter-Program Communication Module is implemented. It indicates the logical end of a called program. The EXIT PROGRAM statement must appear in a sentence by itself, and that sentence must be the only sentence in the paragraph.

If the EXIT PROGRAM statement is met in a called program, control returns to the calling program. If the program is not called, control passes through the EXIT PROGRAM statement to the first sentence of the next paragraph. This statement is a new feature of 74 COBOL.

See CALL, called program, Inter-Program Communication Module, procedure-name.

explicit attribute

An explicit attribute is an attribute that has been expressly stated in the source program. This is in distinction to an implicit attribute, which is assumed as the default case. For instance, if USAGE IS COMP is specified, the usage of the data item is explicitly specified as computational; thus, the usage is an explicit attribute. If no USAGE is specified, a usage of DISPLAY is assumed. In this case, the item is said to have an implicit usage of DISPLAY.

See implicit attribute.

explicit reference

An explicit reference to a data item in the Procedure Division occurs if the name of the item referenced has been written in a statement or if it has been copied into the source program by a COPY statement.

See implicit reference.

explicit transfer

See transfer of control.

exponentiation

Exponentiation is the operation of raising an arithmetic expression to a power. In COBOL, it is indicated by the symbol: ∗∗. It is used as follows:

arithmetic-expression ∗∗ exponent

Note that spaces must appear on each side of the exponentiation symbol.

Examples:

$$
\begin{array}{ll}
\text{RADIUS} \ast\ast \text{ 2 is equivalent to:} & R^2 \\
\text{2} \ast\ast \text{ 5 is equivalent to:} & 2^5 \\
\text{RADIUS} \ast\ast \text{ RADIUS is equivalent to:} & R^R
\end{array}
$$

See arithmetic expression.

EXTEND

See OPEN, USE.

extend mode

Extend mode is that state of a file from the time after an OPEN statement with the EXTEND phrase is executed for the file to the time before a CLOSE statement is executed for the file.

F

FD

FD is a level-indicator indicating 'file description.'

See file description, level-indicator.

figurative constant

A figurative constant is a constant with a name which represents its value. This is an exception to the rule that the name of the item and its value are not necessarily related.

The figurative constants and the values they represent are

ZERO, ZEROES, ZEROS	the value zero, or one, or more instances of the character '0,' depending on context.
SPACE, SPACES	one or more instances of the space character.
HIGH-VALUE, HIGH-VALUES	one or more instances of the character that has the highest ordinal position in the collating sequence
LOW-VALUE, LOW-VALUES	one or more instances of the character that has the lowest ordinal position in the collating sequence.
QUOTE, QUOTES	one or more instances of the quotation character.
ALL	when used with a literal, one or more instances of the literal. When used with a figurative constant, its purpose is only to improve readability.

A figurative constant can represent one or more instances of the character it represents. When it represents a string of characters, the length is determined by the context in which it appears.

If a figurative constant appears in a DISPLAY, STRING, STOP, or UN-STRING statement, the length of the string is one character. The figurative constant ALL cannot be used in any of these statements.

If a figurative constant is taken in conjunction with another data item, such as in a move or compare situation, the string of characters which it represents is considered equal in value to the size of the associated data item. This determination of the data item's size is done prior to and independently of the application of any JUSTIFIED clause that may be associated with the data item.

Generally, a figurative constant can be used wherever 'literal' appears in a format. However, if the literal is limited to being numeric, the only figurative constant permitted is ZERO.

For all figurative constants, the singular and plural forms are considered to be identical and may be used interchangeably. The choice is usually made for readability. If only level 1 of the Nucleus is implemented, only the singular forms can be used.

See collating sequence, Nucleus Module, ordinal position.

file

A file is a collection of records of one or more different types. A file is a logical grouping and does not depend upon the physical characteristics of the medium which contains it. Files are described by file description (FD) entries in the DATA DIVISION.

See file description.

file clause

A file clause is any clause that appears as part of a file description (FD), a sort-merge file description (SD), or a communication description (CD).

See communication description entry, file description, sort-merge file description.

FILE-CONTROL

The FILE-CONTROL paragraph names each file and specifies other file-related information. It is part of the ENVIRONMENT DIVISION.

Format 1:

FILE-CONTROL•
    SELECT [OPTIONAL] file-name ASSIGN TO {implementor-name-1} . . .

$$\left[\text{RESERVE integer-1} \begin{bmatrix} \text{AREAS} \\ \text{AREA} \end{bmatrix}\right]$$

    [ORGANIZATION IS SEQUENTIAL]
    [ACCESS MODE IS SEQUENTIAL]
    [FILE STATUS IS data-name-1]•

A format 1 FILE-CONTROL entry is used for files that have sequential organization.

Format 2:

FILE-CONTROL•
    SELECT file-name ASSIGN TO {implementor-name-1} . . .

$$\left[\text{RESERVE integer-1} \begin{bmatrix} \text{AREAS} \\ \text{AREA} \end{bmatrix}\right]$$

    ORGANIZATION IS RELATIVE

$$\left[\text{ACCESS MODE IS} \left\{ \begin{array}{l} \text{SEQUENTIAL [RELATIVE KEY IS data-name-2]} \\ \begin{Bmatrix} \text{RANDOM} \\ \text{DYNAMIC} \end{Bmatrix} \text{RELATIVE KEY IS data-name-2} \end{array} \right\}\right]$$

    [FILE STATUS IS data-name-1]•

A format 2 FILE-CONTROL entry is used for files that have relative organization. This form of SELECT is new to 74 COBOL.

Format 3:

FILE-CONTROL.
    SELECT file-name ASSIGN TO {implementor-name-1} . . .
    $\left[\underline{\text{RESERVE}} \text{ integer-1} \begin{bmatrix} \text{AREAS} \\ \text{AREA} \end{bmatrix} \right]$
    ORGANIZATION IS INDEXED
    $\left[\underline{\text{ACCESS}} \text{ MODE IS} \left\{ \begin{array}{l} \text{SEQUENTIAL} \\ \underline{\text{RANDOM}} \\ \underline{\text{DYNAMIC}} \end{array} \right\} \right]$
    RECORD KEY IS data-name-2
    [ALTERNATE RECORD KEY IS data-name-3 [WITH DUPLICATES]] . . .
    [FILE STATUS IS data-name-1].

A format 3 FILE-CONTROL entry is used for files that have indexed organization. This form of SELECT is new to 74 COBOL.

Format 4:

    FILE-CONTROL.
        SELECT file-name ASSIGN TO {implementor-name-1} . . .

A format 4 FILE-CONTROL entry is used for sort-merge files.

All Formats: Except for the ASSIGN clause, all other clauses can appear in any order; this is new to 74 COBOL. The RESERVE integer AREAS clause is also new to 74 COBOL.

Each file described in the DATA DIVISION must be named once and only once in the FILE-CONTROL paragraph. Each file specified in the FILE-CONTROL paragraph must have a file description in the DATA DIVISION.

Note that DYNAMIC access mode is new to 74 COBOL.

See file descriptions.

file description

The file description (FD) appears in the FILE SECTION of the DATA DIVISION. It contains information about the physical structure, identification, and record-names of a given file. A file description is the highest level of organization within the FILE SECTION.

Format:

FD file-name $\left[\underline{\text{BLOCK}} \text{ CONTAINS [integer-1 } \underline{\text{TO}} \text{] integer-2} \left\{ \begin{array}{l} \text{RECORDS} \\ \text{CHARACTERS} \end{array} \right\} \right]$
    [RECORD CONTAINS [integer-3 TO] integer-4 CHARACTERS]
    $\underline{\text{LABEL}} \left\{ \begin{array}{l} \underline{\text{RECORDS}} \text{ ARE} \\ \underline{\text{RECORD}} \text{ IS} \end{array} \right\} \left\{ \begin{array}{l} \text{STANDARD} \\ \text{OMITTED} \end{array} \right\}$
    $\left[\underline{\text{VALUE}} \text{ } \underline{\text{OF}} \left\{ \text{implementor-name-1 IS} \left\{ \begin{array}{l} \text{data-name-1} \\ \text{literal-1} \end{array} \right\} \right\} \dots \right]$

$$\left[\text{DATA} \begin{Bmatrix} \underline{\text{RECORDS}} \text{ ARE} \\ \underline{\text{RECORD}} \text{ IS} \end{Bmatrix} \{\text{data-name-2}\} \ldots \right]$$

$$\left[\underline{\text{LINAGE}} \text{ IS} \begin{Bmatrix} \text{data-name-3} \\ \text{integer-5} \end{Bmatrix} \text{LINES} \left[\text{WITH} \underline{\text{FOOTING}} \text{ AT} \begin{Bmatrix} \text{data-name-4} \\ \text{integer-6} \end{Bmatrix} \right] \right]$$

$$\left[\text{LINES AT } \underline{\text{TOP}} \begin{Bmatrix} \text{data-name-5} \\ \text{integer-7} \end{Bmatrix} \right] \left[\text{LINES AT } \underline{\text{BOTTOM}} \begin{Bmatrix} \text{data-name-6} \\ \text{integer-8} \end{Bmatrix} \right]$$

[CODE-SET IS alphabet-name]

$$\left[\begin{Bmatrix} \underline{\text{REPORT}} \text{ IS} \\ \underline{\text{REPORTS}} \text{ ARE} \end{Bmatrix} \{\text{report-name-1}\} \ldots \right] \bullet$$

[record-description-entry] . . .

The level-indicator, FD, must precede the file-name. It must begin in area A and be followed by a space. The clauses, which begin in area B, can follow the file-name in any order. One or more record descriptions must follow the file description.

See area A, area B, level indicator, record description.

file description entry

A file description entry is an entry in the FILE SECTION that is composed of the level-indicator, FD, a file-name, and a set of one or more file clauses.

See BLOCK CONTAINS, CODE-SET, DATA RECORD, file-name, LABEL RECORD, level-indicator, LINAGE, RECORD CONTAINS, REPORT, VALUE IS.

FILE-LIMIT

FILE-LIMIT was formerly a clause in the FILE-CONTROL paragraph.

file-name

A file-name names a file that is described in a file description entry or a sort-merge file description entry in the FILE SECTION of the DATA DIVISION. A file-name is selected by the user and must conform to the rules for a user-defined word.

See file description entry, sort-merge file description, user-defined word.

file organization

The file organization is the logical file structure that was established at the time the file was created. The three classes of organization are sequential, relative, and indexed.

See indexed i-o, relative i-o, sequential i-o.

FILE SECTION

The FILE SECTION is part of the DATA DIVISION. It defines the structure of files. Each file in the program must be defined by a file description (FD) entry or a sort-merge file description (SD) entry, and by one or more record description clauses.

See file description entry, record description entry, sort-merge file description.

FILE STATUS

The FILE STATUS clause defines a data item as a File Status item. It appears in the FILE-CONTROL entry.

Format:

FILE <u>STATUS</u> IS date-name-1

If the FILE STATUS clause is used, a value is placed into the File Status item after every statement that references the file, implicitly or explicitly. This value indicates the status of the statement. The updating of data-name-1 is a new feature of 74 COBOL.

Data-name-1 must be a two-character alphanumeric data item. The left character is Status Key 1; the right character is Status Key 2. Data-name-1, which can be qualified, cannot be defined in the File, Report, or Communication Sections.

The values of the File Status Keys are

Status Key 1	Status Key 2	Meaning
0	0	Successful completion
0	2	Successful completion, duplicate key
1	0	At end
2	1	Sequence error
2	2	Invalid key, duplicate key
2	3	No record found
2	4	Boundary violation
3	0	Permanent error
3	4	Boundary violation
9	–	Implementor-defined

See the individual verbs and indexed i-o, relative i-o, sequential i-o.

FILLER

The reserved word FILLER specifies an elementary item of a record that cannot be referenced directly. FILLER can appear in the FILE, WORKING-STORAGE, COMMUNICATION and LINKAGE SECTIONS of the DATA DIVISION. FILLER can appear at any level and can have a VALUE clause associated with it. A data-name or the word FILLER must be the first word following the level-number in each data description entry.

If level 2 of the Nucleus is implemented, a FILLER item can be a conditional variable, since in this case, there is no explicit reference to the item but only to its value. For example, one can have

```
03  FILLER PIC XX.
88  OUT-SIDE VALUE IS "BY".
```

In the Procedure Division, one could write IF OUT-SIDE THEN . . . , which is equivalent to 'if the value of FILLER is 'BY,' then . . . .'

Example: An implicit reference of a FILLER item can come about as follows:

```
02  GROUP-ITEM
    03  SUB-ITEM-1
        04  SUB-1
        04  SUB-2
    03  FILLER
    03  SUB-ITEM-2
```

Although one could not write MOVE FILLER TO AREA-A, one could write MOVE GROUP-ITEM TO AREA-A and thereby implicitly reference the FILLER item. A FILLER item can also have its value altered by a group move. In the above structure, if one executed MOVE ABC TO GROUP-ITEM, depending on the size of ABC, the FILLER item could be given a new value.

A use of FILLER in a program that prints a report is

```
01  HEADER-1.
    02  FILLER PIC X(59) VALUE SPACES.
    02  FILLER PIC X(14) VALUE "WEEKLY PAYROLL".
01  DETAIL-1.
    02  FILLER PIC X(10) VALUE SPACES.
    02  DEPT-NO PIC 9999.
    02  FILLER PIC X(10) VALUE SPACES.
    02  MANPOWER PIC 9999.
```

See conditional variable, data description entry, elementary item, level-number, reserved word.

FINAL

See CONTROL, Control Footing, Control Heading, report group, SUM, TYPE.

FIRST

See INSPECT, PAGE, report description.

fixed overlayable segment

A fixed overlayable segment is a segment in the fixed portion of storage that, although logically always in main storage, can be overlaid by another segment to optimize storage utilization. Usually, sections that need not be available at all times but are still referred to frequently are in fixed overlayable segments. Fixed overlayable segments are always made available in their last-used state.

The number of fixed overlayable segments can be varied by using the SEGMENT-LIMIT clause.

See fixed permanent segment, independent segment, overlay, SEGMENT-LIMIT, Segmentation Module.

fixed permanent segment

A fixed permanent segment is a segment in the fixed portion of storage that is logically always in main storage. It cannot be overlaid by any other part of the program. Usually, sections that must be available at all times or that are referred to very frequently are in fixed permanent segments. Fixed permanent segments are always left in their last-used state, i.e., they are not initialized.

The number of fixed permanent segments can be varied by using the SEGMENT-LIMIT clause.

See fixed overlayable segment, independent segment, overlay, SEGMENT-LIMIT, Segmentation Module.

fixed portion

The fixed portion of the program is the part that is logically always in main storage. Segments with segment-numbers 0 through 49 belong to the fixed portion of the program. The fixed portion is composed of fixed permanent segments and fixed overlayable segments.

See fixed overlayable segments, fixed permanent segments, overlay, segmentation, SEGMENT-LIMIT.

FOOTING

See File Description, LINAGE, PAGE, Report Description, TYPE.

FOR

See CLOSE, SAME AREA.

format

A format indicates the specific ordering of a clause or statement. When more than one ordering is allowed, numbered formats are used to indicate the alternatives. Clauses generally must be written in the same order as shown in the formats, even if optional. Exceptions to this rule are indicated in the discussions associated with the formats.

A list of all the formats used in ANSI 74 COBOL is located at the end of this book. The reader should be familiar with the material discussed in the entry, 'notation in COBOL' before attempting to interpret formats.

FROM

See PERFORM, REWRITE, SEND, SUBTRACT, WRITE.

G

GENERATE

The GENERATE verb directs the Report Writer Control System (RWCS) to produce a report.

Format:

$$\underline{\text{GENERATE}} \begin{Bmatrix} \text{data-name} \\ \text{report-name} \end{Bmatrix}$$

The GENERATE statement produces a report in accordance with the report description that was specified in the REPORT SECTION of the DATA DIVISION. A GENERATE statement can be executed for a report only after an INITIATE statement has been executed for that report and before any TERMINATE statement has been executed.

When the first GENERATE statement for a report is executed, the RWCS saves the values of the control data items. These values are then used during subsequent execution of GENERATE statements to determine whether a control break has occurred. When a control break occurs, the current values of the control data items are saved and used to sense the next control break, etc.

Also during processing of the first GENERATE statement for a record, the RWCS processes all specified Report Heading, Page Heading, and Control Heading report groups from major to minor. Then, the processing for the Detail report group is performed, if one is specified. Page Heading and Page Footing report groups are processed as needed.

When any GENERATE statement but the first is executed for a report, the RWCS will sense for a control break and, if one has occurred, will

- Enable the Control Footing USE procedures and SOURCE clauses to access the values of the control data items involved.

- Process the Control Footing report group from minor to major up to the level at which the control break occurred.

- Process the Control Heading report group from major to minor, starting with the level at which the control break occurred.

Then, the designated Detail report group processing is performed. Any Page Heading or Page Footing report groups that are required are processed.

data-name

If a GENERATE data-name is executed, the RWCS will perform detail processing for the Detail report group specified. Data-name must be a TYPE Detail report group and can be qualified by a report-name.

report-name

If a GENERATE report-name is executed, the RWCS performs summary processing. Detail, Control Heading and Control Footing groups may be processed. If all of the GENERATE statements that are executed for a report are of the GENERATE report-name type, the report is called a 'summary report'—i.e., one in which no Detail report group is presented.

See control break, control data item, CONTROL HEADING, DETAIL, PAGE FOOTING, PAGE HEADING, presentation rules, report description, REPORT HEADING, REPORT SECTION, TYPE.

GIVING

See ADD, DIVIDE, MERGE, MULTIPLY, SORT, SUBTRACT.

GO TO

The GO TO verb provides a means of overriding the normal, sequential execution of statements in the Procedure Division by transferring control to a designated paragraph or section.

Format 1:

GO TO [procedure-name-1]

When a GO TO statement is executed, control is transferred to the paragraph or section designated by procedure-name-1. If the GO TO statement appears in a consecutive sequence of imperative statements within a sentence, it must appear as the last statement in that sentence.

A format 1 GO TO without a procedure-name can be used only if level 2 of the Nucleus is implemented. It must be the only statement in the paragraph in which it appears. An ALTER statement referencing this paragraph must be executed prior to the execution of the GO TO.

Examples:

(1) GO TO PAR-A.

After execution, control is transferred to the paragraph or section whose name is PAR-A.

(2) ALTER PAR-1 TO PAR-A. *or* ALTER PAR-1 TO PROCEED TO PAR-A.
     PAR-1.
        GO TO.

When PAR-1 is executed, control passes to PAR-A.

Format 2:

GO TO procedure-name-1{procedure-name-2}... DEPENDING ON identifier-1

A format 2 GO TO statement transfers control to the procedure-name whose ordinal position in the list following GO TO corresponds to the value of identifier-1. If identifier-1 is zero or negative, or if the list position corresponding to its value contains no procedure-name, no transfer occurs and control passes to the next statement in the normal sequence. Identifier-1 must be a numeric integer data item.

Example:

PAR-1•
    GO TO PAR-A, PAR-B, PAR-C, PAR-D DEPENDING ON PAR-A
PAR-2•

If PTR-A is zero, negative, or greater than four, control passes to PAR-2. If PTR-A is one, control passes to PAR-A; if it is two, control passes to PAR-B, etc.

Note that the word TO is no longer required; this is new to 74 COBOL.

See ALTER, ordinal position.

GREATER

See IF, relation condition, START.

GROUP INDICATE

The GROUP INDICATE clause specifies that the associated printable item is presented only on the first occurrence of its report group after a control break or page advance.

Format:

GROUP INDICATE

The GROUP INDICATE clause can appear only in a DETAIL report group entry that defines a printable item. If this clause is specified it causes the SOURCE or VALUE clause to be ignored and supplies spaces for the associated item except

1. On the first presentation of the Detail report group in the report.

2. On the first presentation after every page advance.

3. On the first presentation after every control break.

If the report description entry does not specify a PAGE or CONTROL clause, then an item with the GROUP INDICATE clause is presented the first time its DETAIL is presented after the INITIATE statement is executed. Thereafter, spaces are supplied for those items with SOURCE or VALUE clauses.

See control break, printable item, report group.

group item

A group item is a contiguous set of elementary items and/or other group items
that has a name.

Example:

```
02  ITEM-A
    03  ITEM-B
        04  ITEM-C
        04  ITEM-D
            05  ITEM-E
            05  ITEM-F
        04  ITEM-G
```

In this structure, ITEM-A, ITEM-B and ITEM-D are group items.

A group item includes all groups and elementary items following it until a
level-number numerically less than or equal to the group's level-number is
encountered. Any item in a group must have a level-number numerically greater
than that of the group to which it belongs. All items immediately subordinate to a
group item must have the same level-number. All group items are considered of
class alphanumeric.

In the above example:

ITEM-A includes all the other items.

ITEM-B includes items C, D, E, F, and G.

ITEM-D includes items E and F.

See class, level-number.

H

HEADING

See PAGE, report description, TYPE.

high-order character

The high-order character or position is the left-most character position in a data item, regardless of whether this position holds a character or not.

Example: In a numeric data item with a PICTURE of 99V99 the hundred's position is the high-order position. If the contents of this item are 12.34, the '1' is in the high-order position. If the contents of the item were 2.34, the high-order position would be empty.

In an item with a PICTURE of XXXX the left-most X defines the high-order position. If this item contained ABCD, 'A' would be in the high-order position. If the contents were △ABC, a blank would be in the high-order position.

Note that the high-order position is not necessarily the same as the most significant digit or the left-most character of the contents.

Note: '△' denotes a blank.

See numeric data item.

HIGH-VALUE

HIGH-VALUE is a figurative constant that represents one or more occurrences of the character that has the highest ordinal position in the program's collating sequence. The character represented by HIGH-VALUE may change as a function of the collating sequence currently being used by the program.

The form HIGH-VALUES can be used if level 2 of the Nucleus is implemented. In this case, the singular and plural forms are identical, and the choice is generally made for readability.

See COLLATING SEQUENCE, figurative constant, Nucleus Module, ordinal position.

I

IDENTIFICATION DIVISION

The IDENTIFICATION DIVISION is one of the four divisions in a COBOL source program. It contains the name of the program and optional documentation.

Format:

> IDENTIFICATION DIVISION•
> PROGRAM-ID• program-name•
> [AUTHOR• [comment-entry]...]
> [INSTALLATION• [comment-entry]...]
> [DATE-WRITTEN• [comment-entry]...]
> [DATE-COMPILED• [comment-entry]...]
> [SECURITY• [comment-entry]...]

The IDENTIFICATION DIVISION must appear first in the source program. The words IDENTIFICATION DIVISION• must begin in area A, followed by a period and space. Comment-entries can be any combination of characters from the computer's character set.

See the individual entries for further information; also area A, comment entry, source program.

identifier

An identifier is a data-name followed by any qualifiers, subscripts, or indices necessary to make a unique reference to a data item.

Format 1:

$$\text{data-name-1} \left[\left\{ \frac{OF}{IN} \right\} \text{data-name-2} \right] \ldots \left[\left\{ \frac{OF}{IN} \right\} \left\{ \begin{array}{l} \text{file-name} \\ \text{cd-name} \end{array} \right\} \right]$$
$$[(\text{subscript-1} [, \text{subscript-2}][, \text{subscript-3}])]$$

Format 2:

$$\text{data-name-1} \left[\left\{ \frac{OF}{IN} \right\} \text{data-name-2} \right] \ldots \left[\left\{ \frac{OF}{IN} \right\} \left\{ \begin{array}{l} \text{file-name} \\ \text{cd-name} \end{array} \right\} \right]$$
$$\left[\left(\left\{ \begin{array}{l} \text{index-name-1}[\pm\text{literal-2}] \\ \text{literal-1} \end{array} \right\} \left[\left\{ \begin{array}{l} \text{index-name-2}[\pm\text{literal-4}] \\ \text{literal-3} \end{array} \right\} \left\{ \begin{array}{l} \text{index-name-3}[\pm\text{literal-6}] \\ \text{literal-5} \end{array} \right\} \right] \right) \right]$$

When a data-name is used as an index, subscript, or qualifier, it must not itself be subscripted or indexed. Up to three subscripts or indices are permitted for any one item. If subscripting is not permitted in a particular context, then indexing is not permitted in that context. When using subscripts or indices, the parentheses are required. Commas may be used to separate qualifiers, subscripts, or indices. An index can be modified only by the SET, SEARCH, and PERFORM statements.

Examples: Consider the structure:

```
01  ABC
    02  DEF
        03  GHI
        03  JKL
    02  MNO
    02  PQR   OCCURS 10 TIMES INDEXED BY XYZ
    02  STU   OCCURS 10 TIMES
```

JKL OF DEF IN ABC and GHI IN DEF OF ABC are examples of qualification.

STU(5) and STU(NUMBR) are examples of subscripting.

PQR(XYZ), PQR(XYZ-2) and PQR(5) are examples of indexing.

PQR OF ABC (NUMBR) is an example of qualification and subscripting.

	Positive integer	Unsigned numeric integer
Literal-1, -3, -5	X	
Literal-2, -4, -6		X

See data-name indexing, qualification, subscripting.

IF

The IF verb evaluates a condition. Subsequent program action depends on whether this condition is true or false.

Format 1:

$$\underline{\text{IF}}\ \text{condition-1} \begin{Bmatrix} \text{statement-1} \\ \underline{\text{NEXT SENTENCE}} \end{Bmatrix} \begin{Bmatrix} ; \underline{\text{ELSE}}\ \text{statement-2} \\ ; \underline{\text{ELSE}}\ \underline{\text{NEXT SENTENCE}} \end{Bmatrix}$$

True Condition

When condition-1 is true, the ELSE clause is ignored. If NEXT SENTENCE is specified, control passes to the sentence immediately following the IF sentence. If statement-1 is specified it is executed. Then, unless statement-1 contains a procedure branching or conditional statement, control passes to the sentence immediately after the IF. If statement-1 does contain a procedure branching or conditional statement, control is explicitly transferred in accordance with the rules for that statement.

False Condition

When condition-1 is false, *only* the ELSE clause is considered. If NEXT SENTENCE is specified control passes to the sentence immediately following the IF sentence. If statement-2 is specified, it is executed. Then, unless statement-2 contains a procedure branching or conditional statement, control passes to the sentence immediately after the IF. If statement-2 does contain a procedure branching or conditional statement, control is explicitly transferred in accordance with the rules for that statement.

Statement-1 and statement-2 must be imperative statements. The ELSE NEXT SENTENCE phrase can be omitted if it is the last statement in the IF sentence.

Level-2 Nucleus

If level 2 of the Nucleus is implemented, statement-1 and statement-2 can be imperative or conditional statements and can be followed by a conditional statement. Furthermore, either statement can contain an IF statement. In this case, the IF statement is said to be *nested*. Nested IF statements can be considered as paired IF and ELSE combinations proceeding from left to right. Thus, an ELSE is considered to be paired with the immediately preceding IF that has not already been paired with an ELSE.

Examples: Assume that TCOND is true and FCOND is false and that the value of TEMP is 10.

1. IF TCOND ADD 1 TO TEMP ELSE SUBTRACT 1 FROM TEMP
   After execution the value of TEMP is 11.

2. IF FCOND ADD 1 TO TEMP ELSE SUBTRACT 1 FROM TEMP
   After execution the value of TEMP is 9.

3. IF TCOND NEXT SENTENCE ELSE ADD 1 TO TEMP
   After execution the value of TEMP is 10.

4. IF FCOND SUBTRACT 1 FROM TEMP ELSE NEXT SENTENCE
   After execution the value of TEMP is 10.

5. IF FCOND SUBTRACT 1 FROM TEMP
   After execution the value of TEMP is 10.

   See condition, conditional statement, imperative statement, procedure branching statement.

imperative sentence

An imperative sentence is an imperative statement followed by a period and space.

imperative statement

An imperative statement specifies an action that is to be undertaken unconditionally by the program. An imperative statement is any statement that is neither a conditional statement nor a compiler directing statement. An imperative statement can consist of a series of imperative statements separated from each other by means of commas, spaces, or semicolons.

Whenever 'imperative-statement' appears in a format, it signifies a sequence of imperative statements that ends with a period, with an ELSE phrase and period (IF), or with a WHEN phrase and period (SEARCH).

The imperative verbs are

ACCEPT	DIVIDE (1)	PERFORM	STRING (2)
ADD (1)	ENABLE	READ (5)	STRING (3)
ALTER	EXIT	RECEIVE (4)	SUBTRACT (1)
CALL (3)	GENERATE	RELEASE	SUPPRESS
CANCEL	GO	REWRITE (2)	TERMINATE
CLOSE	INITIATE	SEND	UNSTRING (3)
COMPUTE (1)	INSPECT	SET	WRITE (6)
DELETE (2)	MOVE	SORT	
DISABLE	MULTIPLY (1)	START (2)	
DISPLAY	OPEN	STOP	

1. Without the SIZE ERROR phrase.

2. Without the INVALID KEY phrase.

3. Without the ON OVERFLOW phrase.

4. Without the NO DATA phrase.

5. Without the AT END phrase or INVALID KEY phrase.

6. Without the INVALID KEY phrase or END-OF-PAGE phrase.

   See compiler directing statement, conditional statement.

implementor-defined

When a feature is said to be 'implementor-defined,' it means that the supplier of the COBOL compiler is responsible for the specifics of the feature and his literature must be consulted in order to understand the feature.

The elements with a syntax which is partly implementor-defined are

Element	Implementor-Defined Aspect
SOURCE-COMPUTER paragraph	computer-name
OBJECT-COMPUTER paragraph	computer-name
MEMORY SIZE clause	integer
alphabet-name	implementor-name; whether implementor-names are provided
SPECIAL-NAMES paragraph	implementor-name
ASSIGN clause	implementor-name
VALUE OF clause	implementor-name; whether implementor-names are provided
RERUN clause	implementor-name and the form; the implementor provides at least one of seven specified forms
CALL and CANCEL statements	Relationship between operand and the referenced program
COPY statement	Relationship between library-name, text-name, and the library
ENTER statement	language-name
Margin R	Location
Area B	Number of character positions
Qualification	Number of qualifiers; at least five levels must be supported

The elements whose effect is partly implementor-defined are

Element	Implementor-Defined Aspect
alphabet-name	Correspondence between native and foreign character sets
implementor-name switches	Whether setting can change during execution
USAGE IS COMPUTATIONAL clause	Representation and whether automatic alignment occurs
USAGE IS INDEX clause	Representation and whether automatic alignment occurs
SYNCHRONIZED clause	Whether implicit FILLER positions are generated; their effect on the size of group items and redefining items
ACCEPT statement	Maximum size of one transfer of data in level 1 Nucleus
DISPLAY statement	Maximum size of one transfer of data in level 1 Nucleus
Numeric test	Representation of valid sign in the absence of the SIGN IS SEPARATE clause
Comparison of nonnumeric items	Collating sequence, where NATIVE or implementor-name collating sequence is implicitly or explicitly specified
Arithmetic expressions	Number of places carried for intermediate results

implementor-name

An implementor-name is a system-name that refers to a particular feature available on that implementor's system.

See system-name.

implicit attribute

If an attribute is not expressly specified for an item, the item is frequently assigned the default value for that attribute. This type of attribute is called an implicit attribute.

For example, since the usage of a data item need not be specified, if no USAGE clause exists for an item, its USAGE is assumed to be DISPLAY. Thus, the item is implicitly specified as DISPLAY, and DISPLAY is an implicit attribute.

implicit reference

An implicit reference to a data item in the PROCEDURE DIVISION occurs when the item is referred to by a statement without that item's name having been written in the statement. An implicit reference also occurs during the execution of a PERFORM statement when an item referenced by the index-name or identifier which is specified in the VARYING, AFTER, or UNTIL phrase is initialized, modified, or evaluated by the PERFORM. This implicit reference occurs if and only if the data item is accessed during the execution of the statement. This distinction is important in considering the operation of the debug facility.

A FILLER item is implicitly referenced when the group item containing it is referenced.

See Debug Module.

implicit transfer

See transfer of control.

IN

See COPY, qualification, UNSTRING.

incompatible data

Except for the class condition test, when the contents of a data item referenced in the PROCEDURE DIVISION are not compatible with the class as specified by the item's PICTURE clause, the result is termed incompatible data. Any operation using incompatible data is undefined.

independent segment

An independent segment is that part of the object program that can overlay, and be overlaid by, either a fixed overlayable segment or another independent segment. An independent segment has a segment-number of from 50 to 99. Usually, statements that are referred to infrequently are placed in independent segments.

An independent segment is in its initial state whenever control is transferred to it, explicitly or implicitly, for the first time during execution of the program. On subsequent transfers of control, the segment is in its initial state whenever

• Control is explicitly transferred to that segment from a segment with a different segment-number.

- Control is transferred to that segment by the implicit transfer of control between consecutive statements and their transfer comes from a segment with a different segment-number.

- Control is transferred to that segment by the implicit transfer of control between a SORT or MERGE statement that is in a segment with a different segment-number but whose associated input or output procedure is in that independent segment.

An independent segment is in its last-used state whenever control is implicitly transferred to that segment from a segment with a different segment-number, unless this implicit transfer of control is between consecutive statements. It is also in the last-used state when control is transferred to that segment by an EXIT PROGRAM statement.

See CALL, fixed overlayable statement, fixed permanent segment, overlay, SEGMENT-LIMIT, transfer of control.

INDEX

INDEX is a type of USAGE of data. An item described as USAGE IS INDEX is called an index data item.

See index data item.

index data item

An index data item is a data item that contains a USAGE IS INDEX phrase in its description. A value associated with an index-name can be stored in an index data item. An index data item cannot have a SYNCHRONIZED, JUSTIFIED, PICTURE, VALUE, or BLANK WHEN ZERO clause in its data description.

See data description.

INDEXED

See communication description entry, FILE-CONTROL, OCCURS, ORGANIZATION, SELECT.

indexed data-name

An indexed data-name is an identifier consisting of a data-name, followed by one or more index-names enclosed in parentheses.

Example: Assume that TABLE-A has an INDEXED BY phrase in its OCCURS clause and the NAME-1 and NAME-2 are the index-names associated with TABLE-A. The following are all indexed data-names:

TABLE-A (NAME-1)
TABLE-A (NAME-1 – 3)
TABLE-A (3)
TABLE-A (NAME-1, NAME-2)

See index-name.

indexed file

An indexed file is a file with indexed organization.

See indexed i-o.

indexed i-o

Indexed i-o can be used only with mass storage files. In an indexed file, each record is uniquely identified by one of its constituent data items, called the prime record key. The prime record key is defined in the RECORD KEY clause in the FILE-CONTROL paragraph. The prime record key provides a logical path to every data record in the file, and so it must have a unique value in each record of the file and must not be changed when updating a record.

For example: Suppose a file's record description contains

```
01  MASTER-FILE
    02  ABC PIC X(5)
    02  DEF PIC 9(5)
```

If the clause RECORD KEY IS ABC appears in the file's FILE-CONTROL paragraph, ABC is the prime record key. This being the case, each record in the file must have a value for ABC that is unique and defined. Thus, if some record has the value SMITH for ABC, no other record can have this value.

Level 2 of the indexed i-o module provides for alternate keys. The value of an alternate key need not be unique in the file if the DUPLICATES phrase is used. Alternate keys provide alternate access paths for retrieval of records.

Sequential Access of Indexed Files

In the sequential access mode, records must be written so that the prime record key values are in strictly monotonically ascending order. (Note that although the values must be ascending, they need not be consecutive.) If some record in the file already has the same value of the prime record key as the record being written, the write is unsuccessful. If records are being retrieved, for the initial access the prime record key item in the file's record area must have been set equal to the value of some record's prime record key by the OPEN or START verb. The record retrieved is the one with a prime record key value which matches the one in the record area. For subsequent retrievals the next record accessed will be the one whose key has the next higher value than the record last accessed.

Random Access of Indexed Files

In the random access mode, when records are being written, the data to be written (including a value for the prime record key) are moved into the record area and the WRITE, or REWRITE, is issued. If any record in the file has the same value for its prime record key as the record being written, the write is unsuccessful.

If records are being retrieved, the prime record key must have been set to point to some record in the file by the START or OPEN verb. If that record is not the desired one, the user must move a value equal to the value of the prime record key item of the desired record into the prime record key item in the file's record area.

Dynamic Access of Indexed Files

In the dynamic access mode the user can change back and forth between sequential and random access modes by using the appropriate verbs.

Level 1

Level 1 provides partial facilities for FILE-CONTROL, I-O CONTROL, and FD entries, as well as partial capabilities for READ and USE. Full capabilities are provided for CLOSE, DELETE, OPEN, REWRITE, and WRITE.

Level 2

Level 2 provides full facilities for all indexed i-o functions, including RESERVE, SAME RECORD AREA, READ NEXT, dynamic access, and alternate key features.

Current-Record Pointer

In indexed i-o the current-record pointer is affected by OPEN, READ, and START statements.

File Status

The file status item, if specified, is updated by indexed i-o verbs. Valid combinations are

Status Key 1	Status Key 2	Meaning
0	0	Successful completion
0	2	Successful completion, duplicate key
1	0	At end
2	1	Sequence error
2	2	Duplicate key
2	3	No record found
2	4	Boundary violation
3	4	Permanent error
9	–	Implementor-defined

The verbs CLOSE, OPEN, READ, REWRITE, START, USE, and WRITE can be used with indexed files.

See current-record pointer, file description entry, FILE STATUS, monotonically, prime record key, record description.

Indexed I-O Module

See indexed i-o.

indexing

Indexing is one way of manipulating tables, the other being subscripting. The following discussion deals with one-dimensional tables and is intended to be an overview of the subject. For detailed explanations of the various elements and operations, consult the appropriate entries. In the following exposition, assume the clauses:

```
02  XYZ USAGE IS INDEX.
02  TABLE-A OCCURS 10 TIMES, PIC XXX, INDEXED BY ABC,DEF.
```

The second entry describes a table, named TABLE-A, which consists of 10 elements each element 3 character positions long.

Index-name

An index-name is specified in the INDEXED BY phrase of the OCCURS clause. In the example, ABC and DEF are indices for TABLE-A. ABC is termed the *primary* index since it appears first in the INDEXED BY phrase.

Index Data Item

An index data item is specified by having the USAGE IS INDEX phrase in its data description. In the above example, XYZ is an index data item. Unlike an index-name, an index data item is not bound to a particular table.

Occurrence Number

To the user, an element of a table is designated by its occurrence number. The occurrence number of a table element is its ordinal position in the table, i.e., the first element has an occurrence number of 1, the second element has an occurrence number of 2, etc. The maximum valid occurrence number for a table is the value specified in the OCCURS clause. In the case of TABLE-A, this value is 10. An index-name can never have a value less than 1 or greater than the highest occurrence number for its table.

Format:

$$
\begin{Bmatrix} \text{data-name-1} \\ \text{condition-name} \end{Bmatrix} \left(\begin{cases} \text{index-name-1} \left[\begin{Bmatrix} + \\ - \end{Bmatrix} \text{literal-2} \right] \\ \text{literal-1} \end{cases} \right.
$$

$$
\left. \begin{bmatrix} \text{index-name-2} \left[\begin{Bmatrix} + \\ - \end{Bmatrix} \text{literal-4} \right] \\ \text{literal-3} \end{bmatrix} \begin{bmatrix} \text{index-name-3} \left[\begin{Bmatrix} + \\ - \end{Bmatrix} \text{literal-6} \right] \\ \text{literal-5} \end{bmatrix} \right)
$$

Accessing Table Elements

Table elements are accessed by writing the table name, followed by the index-name in parentheses. There are two types of indexing, direct and relative.

Direct Indexing

Direct indexing, referred to simply as 'indexing,' consists of the table name, followed by the index-name in parentheses. For example, TABLE-A(ABC) and TABLE-A(DEF) each reference an element in TABLE-A. The specific element is determined by the current value of ABC and DEF.

Relative Indexing

Relative indexing consists of the table name followed, in parentheses, by an index-name and a displacement consisting of a plus or minus sign and an integer. For example, if ABC currently designates the fourth element of TABLE-A, then TABLE-A(ABC + 2) and TABLE-A(ABC − 3) illustrate relative indexing and, respectively, designate the sixth and first elements of TABLE-A.

When relative indexing is used, the value formed by combining the current value of the index-name with the displacement must be at least 1 and not greater than the highest valid occurrence number of the table. The use of relative indexing does not, however, change the value of the index-name.

For example: With ABC and DEF having values representing occurrence numbers 3 and 4, respectively,

TABLE-A(ABC − 3) is invalid, since the resulting occurrence number is less than 1.

TABLE-A(ABC + 7) is valid, since it references the 10th table element.

TABLE-A(DEF + 7) is invalid, since the resulting occurrence number is 11.

Searching Tables

Index-names and index data items are used with the SEARCH verb to search tables for a particular element that satisfies certain specified criteria. There are serial searches and nonserial searches.

Multidimensional Tables

The concepts presented here can readily be extended to two- and three-dimensional tables. For such tables, commas are not necessary between indices, and literals and index-names can be mixed in a multidimensional table reference. These are new features of 74 COBOL.

See index data item, index-name, occurrence number, ordinal position, primary index, subscripting, SET, table.

index-name

An index-name is specified for a table by an OCCURS clause with the INDEXED BY phrase. Index-names are not data items themselves and are not defined in the DATA DIVISION.

Index-names can be used in relation conditions and can be modified and examined only by the SEARCH, SET, and PERFORM statements. Since an index-name is not a data item, it cannot be manipulated by the program, except as noted above.

Index-names must be initialized before they can be used to refer to table elements. SET, SEARCH ALL, and PERFORM initialize index-names. More than one index-name can be associated with a given table, but no index-name can be associated with more than one table.

INDICATE

See GROUP INDICATE.

indicator area

The indicator area is the seventh character position of a line. The characters that can appear in the indicator area and their meanings are listed in the table.

Character	Meaning
D	Debugging line
-	Continuation line
*	Comment line
/	Page eject

See comment line, continuation line indicator area, debugging line.

INITIAL

See communication description entry, INSPECT.

initialized

Initialized refers to the state of a program or subprogram before it has begun to execute. Variables have a user-defined initial value; program flags are set to an initial state; etc.

When a program has been executed, many of these values and settings will have been changed. If the program were to be re-entered, the results might be unpredictable. Consequently, it is necessary to restore a program to its initial state before executing it another time. This is done automatically by the reloading of a program from mass storage; it may also be accomplished by user-written housekeeping routines.

Programs in independent segments can be restored to their initial state during program execution under certain conditions.

See independent segment.

INITIATE

The INITIATE verb causes the Report Writer Control System (RWCS) to begin processing a report.

Format:

INITIATE {report-name-1} . . .

Each report-name must be defined by a report description entry in the REPORT SECTION of the DATA DIVISION. The INITIATE statement sets all the report sum counters and the report's LINE-COUNTER to zero and sets the report's PAGE-COUNTER to 1.

The INITIATE statement does not open the report's file. Therefore, prior to execution of this statement, the file must be opened with the OUTPUT or EXTEND phrase.

After an INITIATE has been executed for a report-name, a subsequent INITIATE statement cannot be executed unless a TERMINATE statement for that report-name is issued first.

See report description, report-name, Report Writer Control System, sum counter.

INPUT

See communication description entry, DISABLE, ENABLE, OPEN, SORT, USE.

input file

An input file is a file that is opened in input mode.

input mode

Input mode is that state of a file from the time after an OPEN statement with the INPUT phrase is executed for the file to the time before a CLOSE statement is executed for the file.

input-output file

An input-output file is a file that is opened in the input-output mode.

input-output mode

Input-output mode is that state of a file from the time after an OPEN statement with the I-O phrase is executed for the file to the time before a CLOSE statement is executed for the file.

INPUT-OUTPUT SECTION

The INPUT-OUTPUT SECTION is an optional part of the ENVIRONMENT DIVISION which contains the FILE-CONTROL and I-O-CONTROL entries.

Format:

<u>INPUT-OUTPUT SECTION</u>•
<u>FILE-CONTROL</u>• {file-control-entry} . . .
[<u>I-O-CONTROL</u>• [input-output-control-entry] . . .]

The INPUT-OUTPUT SECTION contains information needed to control the transmission and handling of data between external media and the object program.

See object program.

input-output statements

Input-output statements are those statements that cause data to be transferred between internal storage and external media. The are ACCEPT, CLOSE, DELETE, DISABLE, DISPLAY, ENABLE, OPEN, READ, RECEIVE, REWRITE, SEND, START, STOP literal, and WRITE.

input procedure

An input procedure is a set of statements that is executed each time a record is released to a sort file.

See SORT.

INSPECT

The INSPECT verb counts and/or replaces occurrences of a character or group[1] of characters in a data item.

Introduction

The complete formats for INSPECT will be shown with their respective descriptions later. To better explain the operation of INSPECT, a general discussion, appropriate to all forms of INSPECT, will first be given. The INSPECT statement takes the form:

$$\underline{\text{INSPECT}}\ \text{identifier-1} \left\{ \text{tallying-or-replacing-phrase} \left[\left\{ \frac{\text{BEFORE}}{\text{AFTER}} \right\} \text{literal-2} \right] \right\} \dots$$

The INSPECT statement operates on identifier-1, the process of inspection always proceeding from left to right within the range of inspection.

Range of Inspection

If neither the BEFORE nor AFTER phrase is specified, the range of inspection is all of identifier-1. If either the BEFORE or AFTER phrase is specified, literal-2 is termed the *delimiting item* and the range of inspection is modified as follows.

---

[1] The ability to manipulate groups of characters is new to 74 COBOL and is implemented in level 2 of the Nucleus.

The Before Phrase

The BEFORE phrase alters the range of inspection so that it begins with the left-most character of identifier-1 and terminates with that character that is to the immediate left of the first instance of the deliming item that is encountered in identifier-1. Thus, the delimiting item is not part of the range of inspection. If no instance of the delimiting item appears in identifier-1, the range of inspection is all of identifier-1.

Examples: Assume that identifier-1 contains the alphabet, A through Z.

Phrase	Range of Inspection
None	A through Z
BEFORE "M"	A through L
BEFORE "QRS"	A through P
BEFORE "PDQ"	A through Z
BEFORE "A"	Null

The After Phrase

The AFTER phrase alters the range of inspection so that it begins with the character that is to the immediate right of the first instance of the delimiting item that is encountered in identifier-1. If no instance of the delimiting item appears in identifier-1, inspection of identifier-1 does not take place.

Examples: Assume that identifier-1 contains the alphabet, A through Z.

Phrase	Range of Inspection
None	A through Z
AFTER "M"	N through Z
AFTER "QRS"	T through Z
AFTER "PDQ"	Null
AFTER "Z"	Null

It is important to recognize that, within the same INSPECT statement, each phrase that is specified can designate a different range of inspection than the others.

Classes of Data Items

For purposes of the INSPECT statement, all identifiers that are used in the comparison operation are treated as follows:

- If the identifier is alphanumeric or alphabetic the contents are treated as a character-string.

- If the identifier is unsigned numeric, alphanumeric-edited, or numeric-edited, the contents are treated as if they had first been redefined as alphanumeric.

This redefinition is only for purposes of the INSPECT; the actual identifier is not redefined.

- If the identifier is signed numeric, the contents are treated as if they had first been moved, according to the rules for a MOVE statement, to an unsigned numeric item of the same length, and then redefined as alphanumeric (see rules for unsigned numeric items under MOVE).

Definition of a Match

A match takes place when the two character-strings being compared are identical, character for character.

Format 1:

INSPECT identifier-1

$$\text{TALLYING} \left\{ \text{identifier-2} \; \underline{\text{FOR}} \; \left\{ \left\{ \begin{matrix} \underline{\text{ALL}} \\ \underline{\text{LEADING}} \\ \\ \text{CHARACTERS} \end{matrix} \right\} \left\{ \begin{matrix} \text{identifier-3} \\ \text{literal-1} \end{matrix} \right\} \right\} \left[\left\{ \underline{\text{BEFORE}} \atop \underline{\text{AFTER}} \right\} \text{INITIAL} \left\{ \begin{matrix} \text{literal-2} \\ \text{identifier-4} \end{matrix} \right\} \right] \right\} \cdots \right\} \cdots$$

A format 1 INSPECT is used to tally (count) occurrences of a given item or items within identifier-1. Identifier-2 is incremented by 1 for every occurrence of each literal[1] in its phrase that matches. In the format the two sets of ellipses are applicable only if level 2 of the Nucleus is implemented. Thus if only level 1 of the Nucleus is implemented, only one TALLY phrase can appear in an INSPECT statement. Within this phrase only one FOR clause can appear. However, more than one identifier can be incremented by a single INSPECT TALLYING statement if level 2 of the Nucleus Module is implemented.

Rules for Tallying

- Identifier-2 is *not* initialized by the INSPECT statement.

- Once a character in identifier-1 has participated in a successful match, that character no longer participates in the subsequent action of that INSPECT statement.

- The operands of the TALLYING phrase are taken in the same left-to-right order in which they appear in the INSPECT statement, irrespective of whether or not they are associated with the same identifier-2.

- If the CHARACTERS phrase is specified, no comparison takes place. Rather, identifier-2 is incremented by 1 for each character within the range of inspection. This is a way of counting the number of characters in a data item.

---

[1] In this and subsequent discussions of INSPECT, any reference to, or constraint on, a literal also applies to the corresponding identifier.

- If the ALL phrase is specified, identifier-2 is incremented by 1 for each nonoverlapping occurrence of literal-1 that occurs in identifier-1.
- If the LEADING phrase is specified, only leading instances of literal-1 that are within the range of inspection will be counted. Again, it is important to recognize that each literal compared with identifier-1 may have a different set of limits and, therefore, a different 'leading' character, since the leading character for a certain set of limits is not necessarily the same as the leading character of identifier-1. For example, if identifier-1 contains the alphabet, and a clause in the INSPECT statement contains the phrase, AFTER "HI", then as far as that clause is concerned the leading character is "J". However, the leading character of identifier-1 is still "A".

Examples:

1. INSPECT ID-1 TALLYING CTR-1 FOR CHARACTERS.

ID-1	CTR-1
12△XZA,B△△	10
ADJECTIVE	9
COBOL△PROGRAM	13

2. INSPECT ID-1 TALLYING CTR-1 FOR ALL "AA".

ID-1	CTR-1
AAAABC	2
ABAAAAA	2

Note that the prohibition against a character being matched more than once prevents the tallying from proceeding.

$$\begin{matrix} & 2 \\ & \overbrace{} \\ A\underbrace{\overbrace{AA}}ABC \\ 1\quad 3 \end{matrix}$$

3. INSPECT ID-1 TALLYING CTR-1 FOR ALL "A" BEFORE INITIAL "L".

ID-1	CTR-1
LARGE	0
ANALYST	2

4. INSPECT ID-1 TALLYING CTR-1 FOR LEADING "L" BEFORE INITIAL "A", CTR-2 FOR LEADING "A" BEFORE INITIAL "L".

ID-1	CTR-1	CTR-2
LARGE	1	0
ANALYST	0	1

The count in CTR-2 is 1, not 2, since *leading* was specified.

5. INSPECT ID-1 TALLYING CTR-1 FOR CHARACTERS BEFORE INITIAL "A", CTR-2 FOR CHARACTERS AFTER INITIAL "J".

ID-1	CTR-1	CTR-2
123XZAYJED	5	2
XYZAJPDQ	3	3

Format 2:

INSPECT identifier-1

$$\text{REPLACING} \left\{ \begin{array}{l} \text{CHARACTERS } \underline{\text{BY}} \left\{ \begin{array}{l} \text{identifier-6} \\ \text{literal-4} \end{array} \right\} \left[\left\{ \begin{array}{l} \underline{\text{BEFORE}} \\ \underline{\text{AFTER}} \end{array} \right\} \text{INITIAL} \left\{ \begin{array}{l} \text{identifier-7} \\ \text{literal-5} \end{array} \right\} \right] \\ \left\{ \left\{ \begin{array}{l} \underline{\text{ALL}} \\ \underline{\text{LEADING}} \\ \underline{\text{FIRST}} \end{array} \right\} \left\{ \left\{ \begin{array}{l} \text{identifier-5} \\ \text{literal-3} \end{array} \right\} \underline{\text{BY}} \left\{ \begin{array}{l} \text{identifier-6} \\ \text{literal-4} \end{array} \right\} \left[\left\{ \begin{array}{l} \underline{\text{BEFORE}} \\ \underline{\text{AFTER}} \end{array} \right\} \text{INITIAL} \left\{ \begin{array}{l} \text{identifier-7} \\ \text{literal-5} \end{array} \right\} \right] \right\} \cdots \right\} \cdots \end{array} \right\}$$

A format 2 INSPECT is used to replace occurrences of a given item or items within identifier-1 by a specified item or items. In the format, the two sets of ellipses are applicable only if level 2 of the Nucleus Module is implemented.

Rules for Replacing

- The clauses of the REPLACING phrase(s) are taken in the same left-to-right order in which they appear in the INSPECT statement.

- Once a character in identifier-1 has been replaced, that character position no longer participates in the action of that INSPECT statement.

- If the CHARACTERS phrase is specified, no comparison takes place. Each character in identifier-1 is replaced by literal-4.

- If the ALL phrase is specified, each occurrence of literal-3 that is within the limits of the clause is replaced by literal-4.

- If the LEADING phrase is specified, only leading instances of literal-3 within the limits of the clause are replaced by literal-4.

- If the FIRST phrase is specified, only the left-most occurrence of literal-3 within the limits of the clause is replaced by literal-4.

- The words ALL, LEADING, and FIRST are adjectives that apply to each succeeding BY phrase until the next adjective appears.

Examples:

1. INSPECT ID-1 REPLACING ALL "A" BY "B".

ID-1 before	ID-1 after
ADJECTIVE	BDJECTIVE
JACKANDJILL	JBCKBNDJILL
PADACA	PBDBCB

2. INSPECT ID-1 REPLACING ALL "A" BY "G" BEFORE INITIAL "X".

ID-1 before	ID-1 after
ARXAX	GRXAX
HANDAX	HGNDGX

3. INSPECT ID-1 REPLACING LEADING "A" BY "E" AFTER INITIAL "L".

ID-1 before	ID-1 after
CALLAR	CALLAR
LATTER	LETTER
AXLAAALA	AXLEEELA

4. INSPECT ID-1 REPLACING CHARACTERS BY "B".

ID-1 before	ID-1 after
123XYZABCD	BBBBBBBBBB
HANDAX	BBBBBB

5. INSPECT ID-1 REPLACING CHARACTERS BY "B" BEFORE INITIAL "A".

ID-1 before	ID-1 after
123XYZABCD	BBBBBBABCD
HANDAX	BANDAX

Format 3:

$$
\begin{aligned}
&\underline{\text{INSPECT}}\ \text{identifier-1} \\
&\underline{\text{TALLYING}} \left\{ \text{identifier-2}\ \underline{\text{FOR}} \left\{ \left\{ \begin{matrix} \underline{\text{ALL}} \\ \underline{\text{LEADING}} \\ \underline{\text{CHARACTERS}} \end{matrix} \right\} \left\{ \begin{matrix} \text{identifier-3} \\ \text{literal-1} \end{matrix} \right\} \left[\left\{ \begin{matrix} \underline{\text{BEFORE}} \\ \underline{\text{AFTER}} \end{matrix} \right\} \text{INITIAL} \left\{ \begin{matrix} \text{identifier-4} \\ \text{literal-2} \end{matrix} \right\} \right] \right\} \cdots \right\} \cdots
\end{aligned}
$$

$$
\begin{aligned}
&\underline{\text{REPLACING}} \left\{ \begin{matrix} \underline{\text{CHARACTERS}}\ \underline{\text{BY}} \left\{ \begin{matrix} \text{identifier-6} \\ \text{literal-4} \end{matrix} \right\} \left[\left\{ \begin{matrix} \underline{\text{BEFORE}} \\ \underline{\text{AFTER}} \end{matrix} \right\} \text{INITIAL} \left\{ \begin{matrix} \text{identifier-7} \\ \text{literal-5} \end{matrix} \right\} \right] \\ \left\{ \begin{matrix} \underline{\text{ALL}} \\ \underline{\text{LEADING}} \\ \underline{\text{FIRST}} \end{matrix} \right\} \left\{ \left\{ \begin{matrix} \text{identifier-5} \\ \text{literal-3} \end{matrix} \right\} \underline{\text{BY}} \left\{ \begin{matrix} \text{identifier-6} \\ \text{literal-4} \end{matrix} \right\} \left[\left\{ \begin{matrix} \underline{\text{BEFORE}} \\ \underline{\text{AFTER}} \end{matrix} \right\} \text{INITIAL} \left\{ \begin{matrix} \text{identifier-7} \\ \text{literal-5} \end{matrix} \right\} \right] \right\} \cdots \end{matrix} \right\} \cdots
\end{aligned}
$$

A format 3 INSPECT combines the actions of tallying and replacing. It operates as if two INSPECT statements had been written specifying the same identifier-1; the first a format 1 INSPECT, the second a format 2 INSPECT. All the rules for a format 1 and a format 2 INSPECT apply to the respective parts of the format 3 INSPECT.

Example:

INSPECT ID-1 TALLYING CTR-1 FOR ALL "L"; REPLACING LEADING
"A" BY "E" AFTER INITIAL "L"•

ID-1 before	CTR-1	ID-1 after
CALLAR	2	CALLAR
SALAMI	1	SALEMI
LATTER	1	LETTER

Formats 1 and 3

	Elementary item	Numeric	Usage DISPLAY	Figurative constant	Nonnumeric	Alphabetic	Alphanumeric	Numeric
Identifier-1			X					
Identifier-2	X	X						
Identifier-3 to -n	X		X			X	X	X
All literals				X	X			

Formats 2 and 3

	Usage DISPLAY	Alphabetic	Alphanumeric	Numeric	Figurative constant	Nonnumeric
Identifier-1	X					
Identifier-3 to -n	X	X	X	X		
All literals					X	X

If literal-1 or literal-2 is a figurative constant, it implies a one-character item.

If literal-4 is a figurative constant, the size is equal to the size of literal-3 or identifier-5.
If literal-3 is a figurative constant, then literal-4 or identifier-6 must be one character.
The size of literal-4/identifier-6 must be equal to the size of literal-1/identifier-5.
If CHARACTERS is used, literal-4, literal-5, identifier-6, identifier-7 must be one character in length.

If only level 1 of the Nucleus is implemented, then *all literals must be one character in length.*

Operation of the INSPECT Statement

Note that this description is conceptual and does not necessarily reflect how the verb is actually implemented by a manufacturer.

The INSPECT statement operates as follows:

1. The limits for each phrase in the statement are established with respect to the original contents of identifier-1, taking into account any BEFORE or AFTER clauses. These limits are defined for each clause in the INSPECT by character

position, and once established, these limits are not altered by any subsequent modification of identifier-1 by the INSPECT statement.

2. The range of inspection is established as beginning with the left-most character of identifier-1.

3. The first clause in the INSPECT is considered. If its limits are not within the current range of inspection, then the next clause is considered. If its limits are within the current range of inspection, then the clause's literal is compared with the same number of left-most characters of the range. If the two do not match, the next clause is considered.

4. If at any time no more clauses remain to be compared with the current range, the range of inspection is modified so that the left-most character is now excluded from the range. If there are still characters in the range, action proceeds as in 3 above.

5. If the two character-strings match, tallying or replacing takes place as specified in the statement. Then, the range of inspection is modified so that *all* of the characters of identifier-1 that matched are now excluded from the range of inspection, the new range beginning with the character to the immediate right of the right-most character that matched. If characters still remain in the range of inspection, subsequent action proceeds by again considering the first clause in the INSPECT as in step 3 above. If no characters remain, the statement ends.

The previous description of INSPECT is modified when FIRST or LEADING is applied to a clause.

First

The following description applies to an INSPECT statement of the form

INSPECT ID-1 REPLACING FIRST literal-1 BY literal-2.

Inspection begins by comparing literal-1 with the same number of left-most characters in the range of inspection of ID-1. If there is no match, the left-most character in the range of inspection is no longer considered part of the range, and if the range is not null, inspection begins anew comparing literal-1 with the left-most character(s) of the new range. When a match occurs, replacement of the matched characters by literal-2 is effected, and the INSPECT terminates. Whenever the range is null, the INSPECT terminates.

Leading

The following description applies to an INSPECT statement of the form

INSPECT ID-1 REPLACING LEADING literal-1 BY literal-2.

Literal-1 is compared with the same number of left-most characters in the range of execution. If they do not match, inspection terminates. If they do match, the matched character(s) in ID-1 are replaced by literal-2, and the range of inspection is decreased by no longer considering the characters that matched as part of the range. If there are still characters in the range, the new range is compared with literal-1 again. This process continues until either there are no more characters in the range or until there is no match.

Examples: The following examples are designed to show the interaction of the adjectives FIRST, ALL, and LEADING. Assume that the INSPECT statement is of the form

       INSPECT ID-1 REPLACING clause-1, clause-2, clause-3•

Also, assume that ID-1 contains

                     A A A B A A

	Clause	ID-1 after
1.	ALL "A" BY "Y"	
2.	FIRST "A" BY "X"	Y Y Y B Y Y
3.	LEADING "A" BY "Z"	
1.	ALL "A" BY "Y"	
2.	LEADING "A" BY "Z"	Y Y Y B Y Y
3.	FIRST "A" BY "X"	
1.	LEADING "A" BY "Z"	
2.	ALL "A" BY "Y"	Z Z Z B Y Y
3.	FIRST "A" BY "X"	
1.	LEADING "A" BY "Z"	
2.	FIRST "A" BY "X"	Z Z Z B X Y
3.	ALL "A" BY "Y"	

                            since the first time that clause 2 matched was here.

1.	FIRST "A" BY "X"	
2.	ALL "A" BY "Y"	X Y Y B Y Y
3.	LEADING "A" BY "Z"	
1.	FIRST "A" BY "X"	
2.	LEADING "A" BY "Z"	X Y Y B Y Y
3.	ALL "A" BY "Y"	

                          since as soon as the first character matched, clause 2 was no longer eligible to participate.

Example: Following is a detailed example of the operation of an INSPECT statement with the replacing phrase. If the tallying phrase were to have been specified, then the appropriate identifier would have been incremented by one wherever a replacement occurred.

Consider the statement

INSPECT ID-1 REPLACING
        ALL "A" BY "E"
        ALL "BC" BY "WX" AFTER INITIAL "C"
        FIRST "E" BY "Y"
        ALL "FGH" BY "ZAP" AFTER INITIAL "A"
        LEADING "BCDE" BY "XXXX" AFTER INITIAL "B".

Assume that ID-1 has the contents:

A	B	C	D	E	F	G

Step 1. The limits for each phrase are established. For the first and third phrases, the limits are the entire item—the first through seventh characters. For the second phrase, the limits are the fourth through seventh characters only. For the fourth phrase, the limits are the second through seventh characters. For the fifth phrase, the limits are the third through seventh characters.

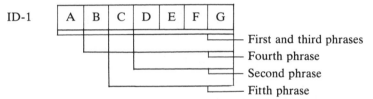

Step 2. The range of inspection is now set up to include the first through seventh characters of identifier-1.

Step 3. The first clause is now considered. Since it contains a literal of one character, it is compared with the left-most character of the current range, viz., character one.

Step 4. The two characters match, so the A is replaced by E. The new contents of ID-1 are

E	B	D	C	E	F	G

The range of inspection is now amended to be only the second through seventh characters. New range:

B	C	D	E	F	G

Step 5. Now, with this new range, the first clause is again considered. This time the 'A' in the clause does not match the left-most character of the range which is 'B.'

Step 6. Clause two is not considered at this point, since its limits begin with the fourth character and the range currently begins with the second.

Step 7. The third clause is considered; the 'B' does not match the 'E' in the clause.

Step 8. The fourth clause is considered. Note that even though the initial 'A' in identifier-1 is now an 'E,' this clause is still eligible, its limits having been established at the start of the inspection to begin with the second character. The 'BCD' does not match the 'FGH,' however.

Step 9. Since the new range is outside the limits of the fifth clause, it is not considered at this time.

Step 10. At this point all the eligible clauses have been considered, and none of them has matched. The range of inspection is now changed by deleting the left-most character, position two, from the range. The new range is from the third through seventh characters. New range:

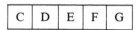

Step 11. The first clause is again considered and compared with the left-most character of the range, viz., 'C,' which does not match 'A.'

Step 12. The second clause is still ineligible.

Step 13. The third clause is compared, and 'E' does not match 'C.'

Step 14. The fourth clause is compared; 'FGH' does not match 'CDE.'

Step 15. The fifth clause is compared. 'BCDE' does not match 'CDEF.' Since this clause had LEADING specified, and there was no match the first time that the clause became eligible, this clause will no longer be considered by the INSPECT statement.

Step 16. Since all eligible clauses have been considered, the range of inspection is now decreased by dropping the left-most character once again. The new range consists of the fourth through seventh characters. New range:

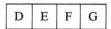

Step 17. The first clause is considered. It is compared with the left-most character of the new range, viz., 'D.' There is no match.

Step 18. The second clause is now eligible to participate. It is compared with the two left-most characters of the range, 'DE.' They do not match.

Step 19. The third clause is now compared, and there is no match.

Step 20. The fourth clause is considered. 'FGH' does not match 'DEF.'

Step 21. As mentioned, the fifth clause is no longer considered. Since no more clauses remain, the range is decreased by one character again. New range:

Step 22. The first clause is compared; there is no match.

Step 23. The second clause is compared. 'BC' does not match 'EF.'

Step 24. The third clause is considered. There is a match and the replacement of 'E' by 'Y' occurs.

ID-1 | E | B | C | D | Y | F | G |

Step 25. The matching character's position is now excluded from the range. New range:

Step 26. The first clause is considered. There is no match.

Step 27. The second clause is considered; again, there is no match.

Step 28. The third clause is no longer considered since it had the FIRST adjective and it had already matched.

Step 29. The fourth clause is not considered since there are only two characters in the range and there are three in the clause.

Step 30. Since all eligible clauses have been considered, the range is decreased by one character.

Step 31. The first clause is considered; there is no match.

Step 32. The second clause is not considered since it has two characters and there is only one character left in the range.

Step 33. The third clause is not considered for the same reason given in step 28.

Step 34. The fourth clause is not considered since it contains three characters.

Step 35. The range is now decreased by one character again. Since no more characters are in the range, the INSPECT terminates. Final contents of ID-1:

| E | B | C | D | Y | F | G |

See alphabetic data item, alphanumeric data item, alphanumeric-edited data item, category, class, delimiter, figurative constant, leading character, numeric data item, numeric-edited data.

INSTALLATION

The INSTALLATION paragraph is an optional entry in the IDENTIFICATION DIVISION, used only for documentation purposes. It does not affect the compilation of the program.

Format:

INSTALLATION• [comment-entry] . . .

The comment-entry cannot be continued by using a hyphen in the indicator area. However, the comment can be contained on more than one line. Any character in the computer's character set can appear in a comment-entry.

See character set, comment-entry, indicator area.

integer

An integer is a natural number, or the negative of a natural number. In COBOL, an integer refers to a numeric item that contains no positions to the right of the decimal point in its PICTURE clause. A numeric literal is an integer if it does not contain a decimal point.

When 'integer' appears in a format, it must not be signed, nor have the value zero, unless specifically allowed by the rules of that format.

See numeric literal.

Inter-Program Communication Module

The Inter-Program Communication Module allows a given program to communicate with one or more programs by providing the capacity to transfer control from one program to another in a given run unit, and for two or more programs to have access to the same data items. This module is new to 74 COBOL.

Level 1

Inter-Program Communication Level 1 provides the capability of transferring control to one or more programs whose names are known at compile time and of sharing data among programs.

Level 2

Inter-Program Communication Level 2 provides the additional capability of transferring control to one or more programs whose names are not known at compile time, as well as the ability to determine at run time the availability of main storage for the program to which control is being passed.

See CALL, CANCEL.

inter-program communication statement

The inter-program communication statements are the CALL and CANCEL statements. They enable a program to transfer control to another program within the same run unit.

See run unit.

INTO

See DIVIDE, READ, RECEIVE, RETURN, STRING, UNSTRING.

INVALID KEY

The INVALID KEY phrase can be specified in a START, READ, WRITE, REWRITE, or DELETE statement for relative or indexed files.

See indexed i-o, relative i-o.

Invalid Key condition

The Invalid Key condition can occur as a result of executing a START, READ, WRITE, REWRITE, or DELETE. For the specific causes of this condition consult each verb.

When the Invalid Key condition occurs, the statement whose execution is responsible for it is considered unsuccessful, and the file is not affected. When the Invalid Key condition is recognized, the following actions are taken in the order listed:

1. If a File Status item has been specified, it is set to a value to indicate the condition.

2. If the INVALID KEY phrase is specified, the associated imperative statement is executed. Any format 1 USE procedure specified is not executed.

3. If the INVALID KEY phrase is not specified, but a format 1 USE procedure is specified for that file, explicitly or implicitly, that USE procedure is executed.

4. If neither the INVALID KEY nor an applicable format 1 USE procedure is specified, the results are undefined.

See imperative statement.

I-O

I-O specifies input-output mode in the OPEN statement. 'I-O' is not a valid substitution for 'INPUT-OUTPUT' in any other context in COBOL.

When a file is opened in the input-output mode, records can be both retrieved from and written to it. The input-output mode assumes a pre-existing file and cannot be used when the file is being created.

See input-output mode, USE.

I-O-CONTROL

The I-O-CONTROL paragraph, in the INPUT-OUTPUT SECTION of the ENVIRONMENT DIVISION, specifies the points at which rerun is to be established, the memory area that is to be shared by different files, and the location of files on multiple file tapes.

Format:

$$\left[\underline{RERUN} \left[\underline{ON} \left\{ \begin{array}{l} \text{file-name-1} \\ \text{implementor-name} \end{array} \right\} \right] \text{EVERY} \left\{ \begin{array}{l} \left\{ \begin{array}{l} [\underline{END} \ OF] \left\{ \begin{array}{l} \underline{REEL} \\ \underline{UNIT} \end{array} \right\} \\ \text{integer-1} \ \underline{RECORDS} \end{array} \right\} OF \ \text{file-name-2} \\ \text{integer-2} \ \underline{CLOCK\text{-}UNITS} \\ \text{condition-name} \end{array} \right\} \right] \ldots$$

$$\left[\underline{SAME} \left[\begin{array}{l} \underline{RECORD} \\ \underline{SORT} \\ \underline{SORT\text{-}MERGE} \end{array} \right] AREA \ FOR \ \{\text{file-name-3}\} \ldots \right] \ldots$$

[$\underline{MULTIPLE}$ $\underline{FILE}$ TAPE CONTAINS {file-name-4 [$\underline{POSITION}$ integer-3]} ...] ...•

See the individual entries for details.

I-O mode

See input-output mode.

IS

See ASCENDING KEY, cd-entry, CODE-SET, COLLATING SEQUENCE, condition, CONTROL, DATA RECORD, LABEL RECORD, LINAGE, LINE NUMBER, MERGE, NEXT GROUP, PAGE, PICTURE, READ, RECORD KEY, REPORT, SEARCH, SEGMENT-LIMIT, SIGN, SORT, SOURCE, SPECIAL-NAMES, START, TYPE, USAGE, VALUE.

J

JUSTIFIED, JUST

JUSTIFIED is a clause in a data description that describes the positioning of data within a receiving data item.

Format:

$$\left\{ \begin{array}{l} \underline{\text{JUSTIFIED}} \\ \underline{\text{JUST}} \end{array} \right\} \text{RIGHT}$$

The JUSTIFIED clause can be specified only for an elementary item. When a receiving item is described as JUSTIFIED, the right-most character of the sending item is aligned with the right-most position of the receiving item. If the sending item is larger than the receiving item, the left-most characters of the sending item are truncated. If the sending item is smaller than the receiving item, space-filling occurs in the receiving item from the left.

The JUSTIFIED clause can be specified only for alphabetic, alphanumeric, or alphanumeric-edited items. If this clause is omitted, the standard rules for aligning data within an elementary item apply.

When used on an item that has an OCCURS clause in its description, the JUSTIFIED clause applies to all of the items in the table so defined.

JUST is equivalent to JUSTIFIED.

Example:

77   REC-ITEM PIC XXXXXX JUST RIGHT

Sending Item	Receiving Item
ABCDEF	ABCDEF
ABCDEFG	BCDEFG
ABC	△△△ABC

Note: '△' denotes a space.

See alignment rules, data description, elementary item, receiving item, space fill, truncation.

K

KEY

See ACCESS MODE, cd-entry, DELETE, DISABLE, ENABLE, READ, REWRITE, SORT, START, WRITE.

key

1. A key is an element of a table, with the property that each occurrence of the key element is in monotonically ascending or descending order. *See* MERGE, monotonically, OCCURS, SEARCH, SORT, table.

2. A key is a data item that identifies the location of a record in a relative or indexed file. *See* FILE-CONTROL, indexed i-o, relative i-o.

3. A key is an entry in the ENABLE and DISABLE statements.

key of reference

The key of reference is the key that is currently being used to access records within an indexed file.

See indexed i-o, OPEN, prime record key, START.

keyword

A keyword is a reserved word whose presence is required when the format in which the word appears is used in writing a source program.

See format, reserved word, source program.

L

LABEL RECORD

The LABEL RECORD clause is the only mandatory clause in a file description. It indicates the presence or absence of label records.

Format:

$$\text{\underline{LABEL}} \begin{Bmatrix} \text{\underline{RECORD}} \text{ IS} \\ \text{\underline{RECORDS}} \text{ ARE} \end{Bmatrix} \begin{Bmatrix} \text{\underline{STANDARD}} \\ \text{\underline{OMITTED}} \end{Bmatrix}$$

STANDARD indicates that the labels for this file exist and conform to the implementor's label specifications.

OMITTED indicates that no labels exist for this file.

There is no difference between the singular and plural forms; the choice is generally made for readability.

In 74 COBOL, the data-name option has been deleted.

See file description.

label records

Label records are records that contain information about a file but are not part of the file's data. They are analogous to labels on a file drawer.

The ability of a user to define and access his own labels has been dropped from COBOL for the present.

language-name

A language-name is a system-name that specifies a particular programming language other than COBOL.

See system-name.

LAST

See PAGE, report description.

LEADING

See INSPECT, SIGN IS.

leading character

To say that a character is 'leading' means that it is the left-most character in a string. For example, in the string ABCDEFG, the leading character is A. For any string, there is only one leading character, but there may be more than one *instance* of that character, since any other instance of the leading character that is contiguous to the leading character is also considered 'leading.' For example, in the string AAABACDE the three left-most A's are all leading. The A following the B is not leading since it is not contiguous to the leading A's.

The concept of leading can readily be extended to more than one character. For example, in the string ABCABCDABC, there is one leading A, one leading AB, and two leading ABC's. In the string AAAABC, there are two leading AA's, one leading AAA, and one leading AAAA.

LEFT

See SYNCHRONIZED.

LENGTH

See communication description entry.

LESS

See IF, relation condition, START.

level 88

See condition-name.

level-indicator

A level-indicator consists of two alphabetic characters that identify a specific type of file or a position in a hierarchy.

The level-indicators are:

FD File Description
SD Sort-Merge File Description
RD Report Description
CD Communication Description

The level-indicator must appear in area A, followed by a space; the associated data-name and descriptive information must begin in area B.

See area A, area B, communication description entry, file description, report description, sort-merge file description.

level-number

Level-numbers indicate the hierarchical relationships that exist between elementary items and group items in a record. They are also used for condition-names, working-storage items, linkage items and in the RENAMES clause. When a specific level-number appears in a format, e.g., 01, 66, 77, or 88, only that number can be used.

Level-numbers are taken from the set '01, 02, 03 . . . 49, 66, 77, 88.' If only level 1 of the Nucleus is implemented, level-numbers are taken from the set '01, 02 . . . 10, 77.' Level numbers from one to nine may be written with or without the leading zero. A level-number must be the first element in a data description entry and must be followed by at least one space. In a record description the level-numbers from 01 to 49 (or 01 to 10) are used to indicate the hierarchical relationships that exist between various elementary items and group items. Level-number 01 is reserved for the entire record. All items immediately subordinate to a specified group item are given level-numbers that are identical to one another and numerically greater than the level-number of the group item.

A group item includes all group and elementary items following up to the point at which a level-number numerically less than or equal to its own is encountered in the data description.

Level-numbers 66, 77, and 88 are used with RENAMES, WORKING-STORAGE, and condition-names, respectively, although a true concept of level does not exist for them.

Level-numbers 01 and 77 must begin in area A. All other level numbers must begin anywhere to the right of margin A. (This is a new feature of 74 COBOL.) If a level-number is in area A, the associated clauses must begin in area B.

Multiple 01 entries subordinate to a given level-indicator represent implicit redefinitions of the same area, but they do not have to all represent records of the same size.

Examples:

```
02  A
    03  B
    03  C
        04  D
        04  E
    03  F
02  G
```

A includes B, C, D, E, and F; C includes D and E. There are no other inclusions.

```
FD
    01  A
        02  B
        02  C
    01  D
        02  E
        02  F
```

In this structure, A and D refer to the same area.

See area A, area B, condition-name, data description entry, elementary item, group item, LINKAGE SECTION, margin.

level 77

See data description, WORKING-STORAGE.

level 66

> *See* RENAMES.

library

> A library contains texts that are available to the compiler. Library-texts are copied into the source program at compile time by the compiler. Once this is done, the copied text is then treated as part of the source program, and the latter is compiled.
>
> Generation and updating of library texts is performed independently of COBOL.
>
> *See* compile time, library-text, source program.

Library Module

> The Library Module provides a capability for specifying text that is to be copied from a library. COBOL libraries contain library-texts that are available to the compiler for copying at compile time.
>
> Text is placed in a library as a function independent of a COBOL program and is done according to implementor-defined techniques.

> Level 1

> Library level 1 provides the facility for copying text, unchanged, from a single library into the source program.

> Level 2

> Library level 2 provides the additional capability of replacing all occurrences of a given word, literal, identifier, or group of words in the library text with alternate text during the copying process. Level 2 also provides for the availability of more than one library at compile time.
>
> *See* compile time, library-text, source program.

library-name

> A library-name is a user-defined word that names a COBOL library that will be accessed by the compiler during a source program compilation. A library-name can be used to qualify a text-name in a COPY statement. The fact that library-name is a user-defined word is new to 74 COBOL.
>
> *See* text-name, user-defined word.

library-text

> A library-text is a text that is contained in a library.
>
> *See* library.

LIMIT

> *See* PAGE.

LINAGE

The LINAGE clause is part of a file description entry. It specifies the size of a logical page in terms of numbers of lines. It also specifies the size of top and bottom margins and the line number at which the footing area begins. This clause is a new feature of 74 COBOL, and is implemented in level 2 of the Sequential I-O Module.

Format:

$$\underline{\text{LINAGE}} \ \text{IS} \begin{Bmatrix} \text{data-name-1} \\ \text{integer-1} \end{Bmatrix} \text{LINES} \left[\text{WITH} \ \underline{\text{FOOTING}} \ \text{AT} \begin{Bmatrix} \text{data-name-2} \\ \text{integer-2} \end{Bmatrix} \right]$$

$$\left[\text{LINES} \ \text{AT} \ \underline{\text{TOP}} \begin{Bmatrix} \text{data-name-3} \\ \text{integer-3} \end{Bmatrix} \right] \left[\text{LINES} \ \text{AT} \ \underline{\text{BOTTOM}} \begin{Bmatrix} \text{data-name-4} \\ \text{integer-4} \end{Bmatrix} \right]$$

Page Size

The logical page size is the sum of the values specified in all of the clauses except FOOTING. If TOP and BOTTOM values are not specified, zero is assumed. If FOOTING is not specified, its value is taken to be equal to the value specified in the LINAGE phrase. The size of a logical page is not necessarily the same as the size of a physical page. Each logical page is considered contiguous to the next page, with no additional spacing provided between pages.

The item in the LINAGE phrase specifies the number of lines that can be written and/or spaced. This value must be greater than zero. This area is called the *page body*.

The values in the TOP and BOTTOM phrases specify, respectively, the number of lines in the top and bottom margins. Either or both of these can be zero.

The value in the FOOTING phrase specifies the line number at which the footing area begins. This value must be greater than zero and less than or equal to the value of the LINAGE phrase. The footing area is between the line number specified in FOOTING and the line number specified in LINAGE and includes both of these lines.

If integers are specified in any phrase, when the file is opened these values specify the number of lines comprising each section of the page. The values hold for all logical pages written during execution of the program.

If data-names are specified, when the file is opened the current values of these data-names are used to define the lines comprising each section for the first logical page printed. Then, whenever a WRITE statement with the ADVANC-ING PAGE phrase is executed or a page overflow condition exists, the current values of these data-items specify the number of lines that comprise each of the sections for the next logical page.

Linage-counter

The presence of a LINAGE clause generates a special register called LINAGE-COUNTER. The value in LINAGE-COUNTER represents the line number at which the output device is currently positioned within the page body.

A separate LINAGE-COUNTER is supplied for each file whose file description contains the LINAGE clause. LINAGE-COUNTER can be referenced by Procedure Division statements but not modified by them. If more than one LINAGE-COUNTER exists, it must be qualified by the associated file-name when referenced.

Whenever a WRITE statement is executed for the file, LINAGE-COUNTER is automatically modified as follows:

- If ADVANCING PAGE is specified, LINAGE-COUNTER is set to a value of one.
- If no ADVANCING phrase is specified, LINAGE-COUNTER is incremented by one.
- If ADVANCING identifier/integer is specified, LINAGE-COUNTER is incremented by the value of the identifier or integer.
- When the output device is repositioned to the first line of a new logical page, LINAGE-COUNTER is set to a value of one.
- LINAGE-COUNTER is automatically reset to one whenever an OPEN statement is executed for the file.

	Greater than zero	Greater than or equal to zero	Elementary item	Unsigned numeric integer
All data-names			X	X
Integer-1, -2	X			
Integer-3, -4		X		

Integer-2 must be $\leq$ integer-1.

See file description, qualification, sequential i-o.

LINAGE-COUNTER

LINAGE-COUNTER is a special register used in conjunction with the writing of records. This is not the same as LINE-COUNTER.

See LINAGE, special register, WRITE.

LINE, LINES

See file description, LINAGE, PAGE, report description, SEND, WRITE.

line

See report line.

LINE-COUNTER

LINE-COUNTER is a special register that is generated for each report description entry in the REPORT SECTION of the DATA DIVISION. The implicit description is PICTURE 999999 with the USAGE implementor-defined. Note that LINE-COUNTER is not the same as LINAGE-COUNTER.

The value of LINE-COUNTER is maintained by the Report Writer Control System (RWCS) and is used to determine the vertical positioning of a report. Although LINE-COUNTER can be accessed by Procedure Division statements, only the RWCS can initialize or modify it.

Within the REPORT SECTION, LINE-COUNTER can be referenced only in a SOURCE clause. Outside of the REPORT SECTION, LINE-COUNTER can appear in any context in which an integer data-name can appear, with the constraint that only the RWCS can alter the value of LINE-COUNTER.

If more than one LINE-COUNTER exists in a program, reference to LINE-COUNTER in the Procedure Division must be qualified by a report-name. In the REPORT SECTION, an unqualified reference refers to the LINE-COUNTER of the report in which the reference is made. If only level 1 of the Nucleus is implemented, qualification is not allowed.

Execution of an INITIATE statement for a report causes the RWCS to set that report's LINE-COUNTER to zero. The RWCS automatically sets the LINE-COUNTER to zero each time it executes a page advance for that report.

The value of LINE-COUNTER is not affected by the processing of non-printable report groups nor by the processing of a printable report group whose printing was suppressed. At the time that a print line is presented, the value of LINE-COUNTER represents the line number on which the print line is presented. The value of LINE-COUNTER after the presentation of a report group is governed by the presentation rules for that report group.

See LINAGE-COUNTER, Presentation Rules, report description, Report Writer Control System, special register.

LINE NUMBER

The LINE NUMBER clause specifies vertical positioning information for a report group.

Format:

$$\text{\underline{LINE} NUMBER IS } \begin{Bmatrix} \text{integer-1 [ON \underline{NEXT} \underline{PAGE}]} \\ \text{\underline{PLUS} integer-2} \end{Bmatrix}$$

The LINE NUMBER clause is part of a report group description entry. It must be specified to establish each print line of a report group. Every entry that defines a printable item must either contain a LINE NUMBER clause or be subordinate to an entry that contains a LINE NUMBER clause. The Report Writer Control System (RWCS) effects the vertical positioning specified by the LINE NUMBER clause before presenting the associated print line.

If integer-1 is specified, it denotes an absolute line number; that is, it specifies the actual line number on which the print line is presented.

If PLUS integer-2 is specified, it denotes a relative line number; that is, if the LINE NUMBER clause is not the first LINE NUMBER clause in the report group description entry, then the print line is presented on that line whose number is equal to the sum of integer-2 and the line number on which the previous print line of the report group was presented. If the LINE NUMBER clause is the first LINE NUMBER clause in the report group description entry, then the line number on which its print line is presented is determined in accordance with the Presentation Rules tables.

Neither integer-1 nor integer-2 can exceed 999, nor can either be specified in such a way as to cause a line of a report group to be presented outside of the appropriate subdivision of the page designated for the report group type as specified in the PAGE clause.

The following rules govern the LINE NUMBER clause:

- An entry that contains a LINE NUMBER clause cannot contain a subordinate entry that also contains a LINE NUMBER clause.

- All absolute line numbers must precede all relative line numbers.

- Successive absolute LINE NUMBER clauses must specify integers that are in strictly ascending, but not necessarily consecutive, order.

- If the PAGE clause is omitted from a report group description entry, only relative LINE NUMBER clauses can be specified within that report.

- The first LINE NUMBER clause specified in a Page Footing group must be an absolute LINE NUMBER clause.

The Next Page Phrase

The NEXT PAGE phrase specifies that the report group is to be presented on a new page at the indicated line number. This phrase can appear only in descriptions of body groups and Report Footing groups. Within a given report group description entry, only one NEXT PAGE phrase can be specified, and it must be in the first LINE NUMBER clause in that entry.

See Presentation Rules, report group, report group description, Report Writer Control System.

LINKAGE SECTION

The LINKAGE SECTION is an optional part of the DATA DIVISION. It is used when the object program is to be a called program and the CALL statement in the calling program contains the USING phrase. This section is new to 74 COBOL.

Format:

LINKAGE SECTION.

$$\begin{bmatrix} \text{77-level description-entry} \\ \text{record-description-entry} \end{bmatrix} \dots$$

The LINKAGE SECTION describes data that is part of the calling program but is to be referred to by both the calling and the called program. No space is allocated in the program for data described in this section; Procedure Division references to such data are resolved at object time by equating the reference in the called program to the location as defined by the calling program. However, since index-names refer to separate indices, no such correspondence is set up for them. Index-names in the called and calling program always refer to separate indices.

Data items defined in the LINKAGE SECTION of the called program can be referenced in that program's Procedure Division only if they are specified in the USING phrase of that Procedure Division header, or are subordinate to items specified in this phrase and the called program is under control of a CALL statement that contains a USING phrase.

The structure and rules for data in the LINKAGE SECTION are the same as for data in the WORKING STORAGE Section, but each LINKAGE SECTION record-name and unstructured data item must be unique within the called program since it cannot be qualified.

Data items specified in the LINKAGE SECTION of the program cannot be associated with data items defined in the REPORT SECTION of the calling program.

Unstructured Data

Unstructured data must have in their data description entries level-number 77, a data-name, and either a PICTURE clause or a USAGE IS INDEX clause. Any other data description clause is optional, except for the VALUE IS clause, which cannot be specified for any item in the LINKAGE SECTION with the exception of condition-name (level 88) entries, for which it is mandatory.

Records

Data items that have a hierarchical relationship to one another must be grouped into records according to the rules for record descriptions. Any clause that is used in a record description can be used in a LINKAGE SECTION except for the VALUE IS clause, as noted above.

See CALL, called program, calling program, condition-name (level 88), index-name, object program, object time, record description, record-name, unstructured data item.

literal

A literal is a word with a value expressed by the characters that make up the word. A literal is either numeric or nonnumeric.

See figurative constant, nonnumeric literal, numeric literal.

LOCK

See CLOSE.

logical connective

The words AND, OR, AND NOT, and OR NOT are logical connectives.

See logical operations.

logical operations

In COBOL, logical operations are indicated by three operators: AND, OR, and NOT. AND and OR are binary operators, that is, they require two operands. NOT is a unary operator, requiring only one operand.

The operands in logical operations are variables that, instead of having a numerical value, have a *truth value*. Thus, the condition 'NET-PAY IS LESS THAN 100' is a logical operand, since it can be either true or false. On the other hand, 'NET-PAY' by itself cannot be a logical operand, since it is neither true nor false, but has only a numerical value.

The term 'condition' will be used to indicate a logical operand that can always be reduced to a value of true or false.

The operators AND and OR combine two or more conditions. The combination of two conditions is also a condition—called a complex condition—since it also has a truth value. To facilitate this discussion, we will call the condition that is the result of combining two or more conditions, the 'AND' (or the 'OR') of the conditions. For example, if A and B are conditions, the expression 'A AND B' is called 'the AND of A and B' or 'the AND function of A and B.' The expression 'A OR B' is called 'the OR of A and B' or 'the OR function of A and B.'

The AND Function

The AND function of two conditions is true if and only if both conditions are true. With two conditions, there are four possible combinations of their truth values as shown in the chart, which is called a 'truth table.'

Cond-1	Cond-2	Cond-1 AND Cond-2
F	F	F
F	T	F
T	F	F
T	T	T

It can be seen that the AND of two conditions is true in the last case and false in the other three. For example, the condition '$X > 0$ AND $Y < 0$' is true if and only if it is true that X is positive and Y is negative. Note that one part of the AND condition can be true, but the condition as a whole false. This would be the case if both X and Y were positive in the above example.

If more than two conditions are joined by AND, as in 'condition-1 AND condition-2 AND condition-3,' they could be segmented in either of two ways:

(condition-1 AND condition-2) AND condition-3
condition-1 AND (condition-2 AND condition-3)

In a fashion similar to arithmetic processes, the condition within the innermost set of parentheses is evaluated first and then evaluation proceeds outward. For three variables there are eight possibilities:

Cond-1	Cond-2	Cond-3
F	F	F
F	F	T
F	T	F
F	T	T
T	F	F
T	F	T
T	T	F
T	T	T

To evaluate this function a table is constructed for condition-1 AND condition-2.

Cond-1	Cond-2	Cond-1 AND Cond-2
F	F	F
F	F	F
F	T	F
F	T	F
T	F	F
T	F	F
T	T	T
T	T	T

The final result is determined by evaluating the 'condition-1 AND condition-2' column with the condition-3 column.

Cond-1 AND Cond-2	Cond-3	(Cond-1 AND Cond-2) AND Cond-3
F	F	F
F	T	F
F	F	F
F	T	F
F	F	F
F	T	F
T	F	F
T	T	T

Thus in evaluating the condition '(condition-1 AND condition-2) AND condition-3,' the result is true when and only when all three conditions are true. The condition 'condition-1 AND (condition-2 AND condition-3)' can be shown to yield the same conclusion.

The definition of AND can now be extended to include any number of conditions: The AND of any number of conditions is true if and only if each and every one of the conditions is true. The AND is false if any one of the conditions is false.

The OR Function

The OR function of two conditions is true if either or both of the conditions is true; it is false when and only when both conditions are false.

Cond-1	Cond-2	Cond-1 OR Cond-2
F	F	F
F	T	T
T	F	T
T	T	T

By an analysis similar to the treatment of the AND function, one can prove that, the OR of any number of conditions is true if at least one of the conditions is true. The OR is false if and only if all of the conditions are false.

Expressions with both AND and OR

When AND and OR functions are mixed in a condition, the use of parentheses is required to define the condition unambiguously. This segmentation is critical to the value of the result. Consider the following two conditions.

Condition-1 OR (Condition-2 AND Condition-3)
(Condition-1 OR Condition-2) AND Condition-3

The truth table for each of these follows.

	Cond-1	Cond-2	Cond-3	Cond-1 OR Cond-2	Cond-2 AND Cond-3	Cond-1 OR (Cond-2 AND Cond-3)	(Cond-1 OR Cond-2) AND Cond-3
a	F	F	F	F	F	F	F
b	F	F	T	F	F	F	F
c	F	T	F	T	F	F	F
d	F	T	T	T	T	T	T
e	T	F	F	T	F	T	F
f	T	F	T	T	F	T	T
g	T	T	F	T	F	T	F
h	T	T	T	T	T	T	T

From the truth table, it can readily be seen that the two groupings are not equivalent, since cases 'e' and 'g' yield different results for the same values of the three conditions.

If parentheses are not used, complex conditions are evaluated by the rules:

1. All AND's from left to right.

2. All OR's from left to right.

For example, the condition 'A OR B AND C OR D AND E AND F' is evaluated as follows (the underlining shows the grouping that is evaluated at each step; parentheses and brackets are used to enclose groupings once they have been evaluated):

Step 1. A OR B AND C OR D AND E AND F

Step 2. A OR (B AND C) OR D AND E AND F

Step 3. A OR (B AND C) OR (D AND E) AND F

Step 4. A OR (B AND C) OR [(D AND E) AND F]

Step 5. [A OR (B AND C)] OR [(D AND E) AND F]

The same expression would be evaluated differently if parentheses were used. Consider '(A OR B AND C) OR D AND E AND F.' Evaluation proceeds:

Step 1. (A OR B AND C) OR D AND E AND F

Step 2. (A OR [B AND C]) OR D AND E AND F

Step 3. (A OR [B AND C]) OR D AND E AND F

Step 4. (A OR [B AND C]) OR (D AND E) AND F

Step 5. (A OR [B AND C]) OR [(D AND E) AND F]

The NOT Operator

The NOT operator has the effect of changing a true value to a false one and a false value to a true one. This process is called *negation*. For example, the condition $9 > 6$ is true. The negation of this condition is the condition 'NOT $(9 > 6)$.' It is read 'it is not true that nine is greater than 6.' Since 9 *is* greater than 6, the condition 'NOT $(9 > 6)$' is false. Similarly, the condition $5 > 9$ is false. The negation of this condition is 'NOT $(5 > 9)$,' read 'it is not the case that 5 is greater than 9.' Since 9 is indeed greater than 5, the negation is true.

NOT can be applied to any condition. In a complex condition, all NOT's are evaluated before AND's and OR's. The complete evaluation rules are:

1. The innermost set of parentheses.

2. Within this set of parentheses, all NOT's from left to right.

3. Next, all AND's from left to right.

4. Finally, all OR's from left to right.

5. The next set of parentheses is then considered subject to the above rules.

If one or more sets of parentheses tie for being the 'innermost,' they are evaluated from left to right.

In any combination of conditions, when NOT applies to an element, one uses the negation of that condition's truth value and proceeds, as described, to evaluate the condition. If NOT applies to a parenthetical condition, that entire condition is first evaluated, and then negation takes place. Consider the two conditions:

NOT (A AND B)   and   NOT A AND B

	A	B	A AND B	NOT (A AND B)	NOT A	B	NOT A AND B
a	F	F	F	T	T	F	F
b	T	F	F	T	F	F	F
c	F	T	F	T	T	T	T
d	T	T	T	F	F	T	F

It can be seen that in cases a and b the two expressions yield different results for the same values of A and B.

logical operator

Logical operator is another term for logical connective.

See logical connective.

logical record

> A logical record is a record considered from a functional viewpoint, without regard to how it is physically stored. A logical record is the most inclusive data item and has a level-number of 01. A logical record may be contained in one, more than one, or a partial physical record area.

low-order character

> The low-order character or position in a data item is the right-most position in that item, whether or not this position currently contains a character.

> *Examples:* In an item with a PICTURE of XXXX and contents of ABCD, D is the low-order character. If the contents were ABC△, the low-order character would be △.

> In an item with a PICTURE of 99V99 and contents of 1234, 4 is the low-order character. If the contents were 1230, the low-order character would be zero.

> *See* high-order character.

LOW-VALUE

> LOW-VALUE is a figurative constant that represents one or more occurrences of the character that has the lowest ordinal position in the program's collating sequence. The character represented by LOW-VALUE may change as a function of the collating sequence currently being used by the program.

> The form LOW-VALUES can be used if level 2 of the Nucleus is implemented. In this case, the singular and plural forms are identical, and the choice is generally made for readability.

> *See* COLLATING SEQUENCE, figurative constant, Nucleus Module, ordinal position.

M

margin

A margin is a conceptual entity that is used to segment a line of the source program. There are five margins:

	L					C	A			B				R
1	2	3	4	5	6	7	8	9	10	11	12	13	...	

Margin L is to the immediate left of the left-most character position of a line.

Margin R is to the immediate right of the right-most character position of a line.

Margin C is between the 6th and 7th character positions.

Margin A is between the 7th and 8th character positions.

Margin B is between the 11th and 12th character positions.

Margins are used to define locations on a source line where different entries can begin. For example, a file description must have the level header, FD, begin at margin A; in a record description, certain entries must begin to the right of margin B.

See area A, area B.

mass storage

Mass storage refers to a device that is capable of storing many times more data than main storage and that can organize data both sequentially and nonsequentially.

Mass Storage Control System

The Mass Storage Control System (MSCS) is an input-output control system that controls the processing of mass storage files.

See mass storage file.

mass storage file

A mass storage file is a file that is contained in a mass storage device.

MCS

See message control system.

MEMORY SIZE

The MEMORY SIZE clause is part of the OBJECT-COMPUTER paragraph in the CONFIGURATION SECTION of the ENVIRONMENT DIVISION.

MERGE

The MERGE verb combines two or more files according to a set of specified keys and makes records available, in merged order, to an output procedure or to an output file. MERGE is implemented only in level 2 of the Sort-Merge Module and is a new feature of 74 COBOL.

Format:

$$\underline{\text{MERGE}} \text{ file-name-1} \left\{ \text{ON} \left\{ \begin{array}{l} \underline{\text{ASCENDING}} \\ \underline{\text{DESCENDING}} \end{array} \right\} \text{KEY } \{\text{data-name-1}\} \dots \right\} \dots$$

[COLLATING $\underline{\text{SEQUENCE}}$ IS alphabet-name]

$\underline{\text{USING}}$ file-name-2 {file-name-3} . . .

$$\left\{ \begin{array}{l} \underline{\text{OUTPUT}} \ \underline{\text{PROCEDURE}} \text{ IS section-name-1} \left[\left\{ \begin{array}{l} \underline{\text{THROUGH}} \\ \underline{\text{THRU}} \end{array} \right\} \text{section-name-2} \right] \\ \underline{\text{GIVING}} \text{ file-name-4} \end{array} \right\}$$

A MERGE statement has three phases:

1. Records are obtained from input files.

2. The records are merged.

3. Records are returned by the MERGE so that they can be processed by the program.

MERGE statements can appear anywhere in the Procedure Division except in the DECLARATIVES portion or in the input or output procedures associated with a SORT or MERGE statement.

File-name-1 must be described in a sort-merge file description in the Data Division. File-name-2, file-name-3, and file-name-4 must be described in a file description entry; none of these can be a sort-merge file. A given file can be named only once in a MERGE statement. Also, no more than one file from a MULTIPLE FILE reel can be specified.

When ASCENDING is specified, the sorted sequence will be from the lowest value of the data items specified in the KEY clause to the highest value defined by the rules for comparison of operands in a relation condition.

When DESCENDING is specified, the sorted sequence will be from the highest value of the data item specified in the KEY clause to the lowest value defined by the rules for comparison of operands in a relation condition.

The data-names following KEY are listed from left to right in order of decreasing significance. If there is more than one key phrase, the way in which the data-names are divided among the KEY phrases does not affect this order. The data-names specified in the KEY clause must conform to these rules:

1. They must be described in records associated with file-name-1.

2. They cannot be variable length items, their data description cannot contain an OCCURS clause, and they cannot be subordinate to an entry with an OCCURS clause.

3. If file-name-1 has more than one record description, the data items need be described in only one of the record descriptions.

4. They can be qualified.

If two records that are compared are equal, they are written into file-name-4 or returned to the output procedure in the order in which the input files are specified in the MERGE statement. The results of the MERGE operation are predictable only when the records in file-name-2 and file-name-3 are ordered by values of the data-name(s) described in the KEY clause specified in the MERGE statement.

The Using Phrase

All of the records in file-names-2 and -3 are transferred to file-name-1. File-names-2 and -3 must have sequential organization and must *not* be open at the time that the MERGE is executed. The MERGE statement uses these files in such a way that any associated USE procedures are executed. When the MERGE statement is through with these files, the terminating function that is performed on them is equivalent to a CLOSE statement with no optional phrases.

The actual size of the records for file-names-2, -3, and -4 must be equal to the actual size of the records of file-name-1. If the data descriptions are not identical, it is up to the user to describe the records so that an equal number of character positions will be allocated for corresponding records.

Output Procedure

If only section-name-1 is specified, it defines the output procedure. If section-name-2 is also specified, the output procedure is from the first statement in section-name-1 to the last statement in section-name-2. The statements comprising the output procedure must be contiguous in the program and not be a part of any input procedure.

The output procedure can include any statements needed to select, copy, or modify records except

- A SORT or MERGE statement.

- Any statement that causes an explicit transfer of control to points outside the input procedure, e.g., ALTER, GO TO, or PERFORM.

Control cannot be transferred into the input procedure from points outside of it. Control can, however, be transferred implicitly to declaratives.

If an output procedure is specified, control passes to it when the MERGE is at a point where it can select the next record in merged order when requested. In order to make merged records available for subsequent processing by other parts of the program, the output procedure must include at least one RETURN statement.

A return mechanism is inserted at the end of the last section of the output procedure. When control passes from the last statement of this procedure, the return mechanism terminates the MERGE and passes control to the statement following the MERGE.

The Giving Phrase

If the GIVING phrase is specified, all the merged records in file-name-1 are written to file-name-4. This is the implied output procedure. File-name-4 must have sequential organization and must not be open at the time the MERGE is executed. The MERGE statement uses file-name-4 in such a way that any associated USE procedures are executed. When the MERGE statement is through with file-name-4, the terminating function that is performed is equivalent to a CLOSE statement with no optional phrases.

The actual size of the records for file-name-4 must be equal to the actual size of the records of file-name-1. If the data descriptions are not identical, it is up to the user to describe the records in such a way that an equal number of character positions will be allocated for corresponding records.

The Collating Sequence Phrase

If the COLLATING SEQUENCE phrase is specified, the collating sequence specified by alphabet-name is used in the merge operation. If this phrase is not specified the sequence that has been established as the program collating sequence in the OBJECT-COMPUTER paragraph is used.

Segmentation Considerations

If a MERGE statement appears in an independent segment, any output procedure referred to by that MERGE statement must be wholly within the same independent segment as the MERGE statement itself, or be contained wholly within nonindependent segments.

If a MERGE statement appears in a nonindependent segment, any input or output procedure referred to by that MERGE must be wholly within a single independent segment or be wholly contained within nonindependent segments.

See ·independent segment, input procedure, OBJECT-COMPUTER, ORGANIZATION, relation condition, SORT, transfer of control, variable.

merge file

A merge file is a collection of records to be merged. It is created when the

MERGE statement transfers records from two or more files. A merge file can be accessed only by the MERGE statement.

MESSAGE

See ACCEPT, communication description entry, RECEIVE.

message

A message is data that has an end-of-message indicator or an end-of-group indicator ánd that is processed by the message control system.

message control system

The message control system (MCS) is a communications control system that supports the processing of messages.

See communication description entry, SEND, RECEIVE.

MESSAGE COUNT

MESSAGE COUNT is data-name-11 of a communication description entry.

The message count of a queue or sub-queue is the number of complete messages that exists in the designated queue or sub-queue.

See ACCEPT, communication description entry.

message indicators

The three types of message indicators are EGI, end-of-group indicator; EMI, end-of-message indicator; and ESI, end-of-segment indicator. Message indicators notify the message control system (MCS) that a specified condition exists.

Within the hierarchy of EGI, EMI, and ESI, an EGI is conceptually equivalent to an ESI and to an EMI. Thus a message *segment* can be terminated by an ESI, EMI, or EGI. A message can be terminated by an EMI or EGI.

See message control system, message segment.

message segment

A message segment is data that forms a logical subdivision of a message; it usually is terminated by an end-of-segment indicator (ESI) but may also be terminated by an end-of-message indicator (EMI) or an end-of-group indicator (EGI).

mnemonic-name

A mnemonic-name is a user-defined word, containing at least one alphabetic character. The SPECIAL-NAMES paragraph associates a mnemonic-name with an implementor-name. The requirement of having at least one alphabetic character is new to 74 COBOL.

See implementor-name, user-defined word.

MODE

See SOURCE-COMPUTER.

MODULES

See MEMORY SIZE, OBJECT-COMPUTER.

monotonically

A sequence is said to be monotonically ascending (or increasing) when the second member of the sequence is greater than or equal to the first member, the third member is greater than or equal to the second, etc., for all members of the sequence.

In mathematical notation a sequence is monotonically increasing if, for every element E of the sequence $E_{n-1} \leq E_n$ (where n represents the element's ordinal position in the sequence).

A sequence is *strictly* monotonically ascending (or increasing) when the second member of the sequence is greater than the first, the third member is greater than the second, etc., for all members of the sequence.

In mathematical notation a sequence is strictly monotonically increasing if, for every element E of the sequence, $E_{n-1} < E_n$.

Examples: The following sequences are monotonically ascending:

1. A, B, B, C, D, E, H, W, Y, Z
2. A, B, C, H, K, P, S, V, Z
3. 1, 2, 3, 3, 4, 4, 5, 5, 5, 6
4. 1, 2, 4, 6, 8, 9

Sequences 2 and 4 are strictly monotonically ascending.

A sequence is said to be monotonically descending (or decreasing) when the second member of the sequence is less than or equal to the first member, the third member is less than or equal to the second, etc., for all members of the sequence.

In mathematical notation a sequence is monotonically decreasing if, for every element E of the sequence, $E_{n-1} \geq E_n$ (where 'n' represents the element's ordinal position in the sequence).

A sequence is strictly monotonically descending (or decreasing) when the second member of the sequence is less than the first, the third member is less than the second, etc., for all members of the sequence.

In mathematical notation a sequence is strictly monotonically decreasing if, for every element E of the sequence, $E_{n-1} > E_n$.

Examples: The following sequences are monotonically descending:

1. Z, Y, W, S, Q, Q, D, B
2. Z, Y, W, S, Q, D, B
3. 8, 8, 7, 7, 7, 6, 5, 4, 3, 3, 2
4. 9, 8, 7, 6, 5, 4, 3, 2, 1

Sequences 2 and 4 are strictly monotonically descending.

See ordinal position.

MOVE

The MOVE verb transfers data to one or more data items in accordance with editing rules.

Format 1:

$$\text{\underline{MOVE}} \begin{Bmatrix} \text{identifier-1} \\ \text{literal-1} \end{Bmatrix} \text{\underline{TO}} \ \{\text{identifier-2}\}\ldots$$

Identifier-1 or literal-1 represents the sending item; identifier-2, the receiving item. The sending item is moved to each receiving item in the statement. Any subscripting or indexing associated with identifier-1 is evaluated once, immediately prior to moving data to the first receiving item. Any subscripting or indexing associated with identifier-2 is evaluated immediately before the data is moved into it. An index data item cannot be the operand of a MOVE statement.

For example, the statement

MOVE A(B) TO B, C(B)

is equivalent to the sequence

MOVE A(B) TO temp

MOVE temp TO B

MOVE temp TO C(B)

It is the *new* value to B that is used in evaluating the subscript in C(B).

There are two sets of rules for the MOVE statement, alphanumeric and numeric. All moves are subject to one or the other set of rules; however, the sending item is *never* altered by action of the MOVE statement.

Alphanumeric Rules

The alphanumeric rules apply when the receiving item is alphabetic, alphanumeric or alphanumeric-edited and does not contain a JUSTIFIED clause in its description.

1. The left-most character of the sending item is moved into the left-most character position of the receiving item. Then additional characters are moved, from left to right, until the end of one item is reached.

2. If the receiving item is longer than the sending item, the portion of the receiving item that did not receive any characters is filled with spaces.

3. If the receiving item is shorter than the sending item, the MOVE stops when the receiving item is filled. The surplus characters in the sending item are not moved.

4. If the sending item is signed numeric, the operational sign is not moved even if it occupies a separate position. If the sign does occupy a separate position, the size of the sending item is considered to be one less than its actual size.

5. Any editing required by the receiving item is performed.

6. An integer item with a right-most character of P can be moved to an alphanumeric or alphanumeric-edited item. This is new to 74 COBOL. Positions described by P are considered to contain zeroes.

7. If the receiving item contains a JUSTIFIED clause in its description, rules are as described for that clause.

Numeric Rules

The numeric rules apply when the receiving item is numeric or numeric-edited.

1. The numeric value is preserved by aligning the two items by decimal points. Any item without a decimal point is assumed to have a decimal point to the immediate right of its low-order digit.

2. The sending item is then moved to the receiving item. Digits in the sending item, on either side of the decimal point, that have no corresponding position in the receiving item are *lost*. If there are extra positions in the receiving item, they are filled with zeroes.

3. If the sending is alphanumeric, data is moved as if the sending item were an unsigned numeric integer.

4. The sign is moved. If the receiving item is signed and the sending item is unsigned, a *positive* (+) sign will be created. If the receiving item is unsigned, the absolute value of the sending item is moved, and no operational sign is generated for the receiving item.

Elementary MOVE

An elementary MOVE is one in which the sending item and the receiving item are both elementary. (A level 01 item that has a PICTURE clause is treated as an elementary item.) An elementary MOVE can follow either set of rules. During an elementary move any necessary conversion of data from one form to another is performed, as well as any editing associated with the receiving item.

Group MOVE

Any move that is not an elementary move is a group move. All group moves are treated as alphanumeric to alphanumeric moves with *no* conversion of data taking place. A group move is a straight character by character move with no attempt made to preserve the boundaries of the individual or group items contained within either the sending item or the receiving item. However, if an item has a format 2 OCCURS clause in its description, only that part of the item that is currently defined is moved.

The following table shows the legal moves and the rules that the moves follow by category of sending and receiving item.

		Category of Receiving Item		
Category of Sending Item		Numeric, Numeric- Edited	Alphabetic	Alphanumeric, Alphanumeric- Edited
Alphabetic Alphanumeric-edited SPACE		X	AN	AN
Alphanumeric Nonnumeric literals All other figurative constants		AN	AN	AN
Numeric-edited		X	X	AN
Numeric, ZERO	Integer	N	X	AN
Numeric literals	Non-integer	N	X	X

Note. 'AN' indicates a move that follows the alphanumeric rules.
'N' indicates a move that follows the numeric rules.
'X' indicates an illegal move, the results of which are undefined.

Examples: Following is a summary of various elementary moves. All moves are the result of executing

MOVE ITEM-A TO ITEM-B.

The abbreviations used are

A	alphabetic
AN	alphanumeric
AN-ed	alphanumeric-edited
N	numeric (integer or non-integer)
NI	numeric integer
NF	numeric non-integer
N-ed	numeric-edited
△	blank or space

Moves by Alphanumeric Rules

Category of MOVE	Contents of ITEM-A	PICTURE of ITEM-B	Result in ITEM-B
A to A or to AN	A B C D E	A(6) or X(6) A(5) or X(5) A(2) or X(2)	A B C D E △ A B C D E A B
A to AN-ed	A B C D E	XXBXX XXBXXX	A B △ C D A B △ C D E
AN to A or to AN	A B C D E	A(6) or X(6) A(5) or X(5) A(4) or X(4)	A B C D E △ A B C D E A B C D
AN to AN-ed	A B C D E	XXBXXX XXBXX	A B △ C D E A B △ C D
AN to N-ed	1976	99.99 $$$$9	76.00 $1976
AN to N	1976	99V99 9999	7600 1976
N-ed to AN	$19.76	X(7) X(6) X(5)	$ 1 9 . 7 6 △ $ 1 9 . 7 6 $ 1 9 . 7
N-ed to AN-ed	$19.76	XXXBXXXX XXXBXXX XXXBX	$ 1 9 △ . 7 6 △ $ 1 9 △ . 7 6 $ 1 9 △ .
NI to AN	1976	X(5) X(4) X(3)	1 9 7 6 △ 1 9 7 6 1 9 7
NI to AN-ed	1976	XBXXXX XBXXX XBXX	1 △ 9 7 6 △ 1 △ 9 7 6 1 △ 9 7
AN-ed to AN-ed	PIC = XXBXXX A B △ C D E	XX/XXXX XX/XX X/XXXX	A B / △ C D E A B / △ C A / B △ C D
AN-ed to A or to AN	PIC = XXBXXX A B △ C D E	A(6) or X(6) A(5) or X(5) A(7) or X(7)	A B △ C D E A B △ C D A B △ C D E △

Moves by Numeric Rules

NI to N	1976	9999 99V99 V9999	1976 7600 0000
NI to N-ed	1976	99.99 $$$99	76.00 $1976
NF to N	19.76	9999 99V99 V9999	0019 1976 7600
NF to N-ed	19.76	$99.99 $$.9	$19.76 $9.7

	PICTURE of ITEM-B	Result in ITEM-B
MOVE SPACE TO ITEM-B	A(4) or X(4) XX/XX	△ △ △ △ △ △ / △ △
MOVE ZERO TO ITEM-B	X(4) XXBXX	0 0 0 0 0 0 △ 0 0
MOVE "ABC" TO ITEM-B	A(6) or X(6) XXBXXXX XXBXXX	A B C A B C A B △ C A B C A B △ C A B
MOVE QUOTE TO ITEM-B	A(6) or X(6) XXBXXXX XB/XX	" " " " " " " " △ " " " " " △ / " "
MOVE 12 TO ITEM-B	XXX X/X	1 2 △ 1 / 2
MOVE ZERO TO ITEM-B	XXX X/X	0 0 0 0 / 0

(The following are numeric moves.)

MOVE ZERO TO ITEM-B	99V99 $$9	0000 $0
MOVE 12 TO ITEM-B	99V99 9V9 $$9 $9	1200 20 $12 $2

Example: The operation of a group move is shown as follows. For purposes of illustration, assume that the records have layouts as given and that unused character positions are a result of the way in which the SYNCHRONIZED clause is implemented.

```
01  Z-1.
    02  A PIC X(3) VALUE "PDQ".
    02  B.
        03  C PIC X(2) VALUE "QR".
        03  D PIC X(6) VALUE "STVWXY".
```

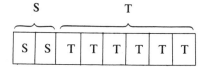

A				B								
P	D	Q		Q	R	α	β	S	T	V	W	X	Y
A	A	A	u	C	C	u	u	D	D	D	D	D	D

Contents

```
02  Z-2.
    03  S  PIC X(2).
    03  T  PIC X(6).
```

S			T				
S	S	T	T	T	T	T	T

Executing a MOVE B TO Z-2. results in the following:

Q	R	α	β	S	T	V	W
S	S	T	T	T	T	T	T

Contents

A subsequent reference to T with the expectation of finding 'STVWXY' will not work, since T now contains $\alpha\beta$STVW. The group move precluded any attempt to preserve the boundries of C and T.

Format 2:

$$\text{MOVE}\left\{\begin{array}{l}\underline{\text{CORRESPONDING}}\\\underline{\text{CORR}}\end{array}\right\}\text{ identifier-1 }\underline{\text{TO}}\text{ identifier-2}$$

In a format 2 MOVE both identifiers must be group items. Items in identifier-1 that have corresponding items in identifier-2 are moved to identifier-2. The rules that apply to the moves depend upon the categories of each pair of corresponding items and whether the move is an elementary or a group move. The result of a MOVE CORRESPONDING is the same as if each corresponding item had been referred to in a separate MOVE statement.

MOVE CORRESPONDING is implemented in level 2 of the Nucleus.

Example: Consider the two group items:

02	MAS-RECORD		02	DET-RECORD
	03	REG-HOURS		05	REG-HOURS
	03	O-T-HOURS		05	O-T-HOURS
		04	TIME-HALF			06	TIME-HALF
		04	DBL-TIME			06	TRIP-TIME
	03	RATE-OF-PAY		05	RATE-OF-PAY
		04	REG-RATE
		04	SPEC-RATE

For purposes of the MOVE, the corresponding items are REG-HOURS, TIME-HALF, and RATE-OF-PAY.

Executing the statement

MOVE CORRESPONDING MAS-RECORD TO DET-RECORD

is equivalent to executing the three statements

MOVE REG-HOURS IN MAS-RECORD TO REG-HOURS IN DET-RECORD
MOVE TIME-HALF IN MAS-RECORD TO TIME-HALF IN DET-RECORD
MOVE RATE-OF-PAY IN MAS-RECORD TO RATE-OF-PAY IN DET-RECORD

The first two moves are elementary moves since both the sending and receiving items are elementary. The third move is a group move, since the sending item is a group item. This move is an alphanumeric to alphanumeric move. Thus, the rules that apply are determined by the category of each pair of items.

See alphabetic data item, alphanumeric data item, alphanumeric-edited data item, CORRESPONDING, elementary item, indexing, JUSTIFIED, numeric data item, numeric-edited data, subscripting.

MSCS

See Mass Storage Control System.

MULTIPLE FILE

The MULTIPLE FILE clause is an optional entry in the I-O-CONTROL paragraph of the ENVIRONMENT DIVISION. It is required when more than one file share the same physical reel of tape.

Format:

MULTIPLE FILE TAPE CONTAINS {file-name-1 [POSITION integer-1]}...

Regardless of the number of files on a reel of tape, only those files that are used in the object program need be specified. At most, one file on a multiple reel tape can be open at any one time. If the file names as listed are in consecutive order on the tape, the POSITION phrase need not be specified. If any file in the sequence on tape is not named in this clause, the position relative to the beginning of the tape must be specified for *all* files.

Example: Assume that the tape contains five files named FILE-A through FILE-E. One could write MULTIPLE FILE TAPE CONTAINS FILE-A, FILE-B, FILE-C• or MULTIPLE FILE TAPE CONTAINS FILE-A POSITION 1, FILE-B POSITION 2, FILE-C POSITION 3•. However, if only FILE-A and FILE-C were to be used one would *have* to write MULTIPLE FILE TAPE CONTAINS FILE-A POSITION 1, FILE-C POSITION 3•

MULTIPLE REEL (UNIT)

MULTIPLE REEL (UNIT) was formerly a clause in the FILE-CONTROL paragraph.

multiple results in arithmetic statements

The ADD, COMPUTE, DIVIDE, MULTIPLY, and SUBTRACT statements may have more than one receiving item. Such statements act as if they are executed as follows:

First, a statement that performs all the arithmetic necessary to arrive at the result is executed, and this result is put in a temporary storage location.

Then, a sequence of statements is executed, each one of which transfers or combines this result with a single receiving item. These statements are considered to be written in the same left-to-right sequence as the multiple receiving items in the statement.

Example: Assume the initial values are:

$$A = 3 \quad D(1) = 5$$
$$B = 2 \quad D(6) = 5$$
$$C = 1 \quad D(7) = 5$$
$$E = 10$$

ADD A, B, C TO C, D(C), E

This statement is executed as if it were the following sequence:

ADD A, B, C GIVING temp
ADD temp TO C
ADD temp TO D(C)
ADD temp TO E

During execution, temp has the value 6. After execution, C has the value 7; E, the value 16; and D(7), the value 11. All other variables are unchanged.

See receiving item.

MULTIPLY

The MULTIPLY verb forms the product of two data items and stores this product in one or more data items. The composite of operands, determined by superimposing all receiving items, aligned by decimal point, must not exceed 18 digits. Multiple receiving items are permitted only if level 2 of the Nucleus is implemented.

Format 1:

MULTIPLY $\begin{Bmatrix} \text{identifier-1} \\ \text{literal-1} \end{Bmatrix}$ BY {identifier-2 [ROUNDED]} ...
[; ON SIZE ERROR imperative-statement-1]

The product of identifier-1 (or literal-1) and identifier-2 is formed. It then replaces the original contents of identifier-2. If there is more than one identifier after BY, identifier-1 (or literal-1) is multiplied by each identifier in turn, the product replacing each identifier's previous contents. Thus the new value of each identifier following BY is the product of its old value times identifier-1 (or literal-1).

Examples: Assume as initial values: BASE = 50
                                          RATE1 = .1
                                          RATE2 = .2

1. MULTIPLY BASE BY RATE1
After execution, the new value of RATE1 is 5.0.

2. MULTIPLY 10 BY RATE1, RATE2
After execution, the new value of RATE1 is 1.0, the new value of RATE2 is 2.0.

3. MULTIPLY BASE BY RATE1, RATE2
After execution, the new value of RATE1 is 5.0, of RATE2 is 10.0.

Format 2:

MULTIPLY $\begin{Bmatrix} \text{identifier-1} \\ \text{literal-1} \end{Bmatrix}$ BY $\begin{Bmatrix} \text{identifier-2} \\ \text{literal-2} \end{Bmatrix}$ GIVING {identifier-3 [ROUNDED]} ...

[; ON SIZE ERROR imperative-statement-1]

The product of the item before BY and the item after BY is formed. This product is then moved into each data item following GIVING. Thus the new value of each identifier following GIVING is equal to the result of the multiplication. Note that the previous contents of identifiers following GIVING do not participate in the multiply.

Examples: Assume as initial values: BASE = 50
                                          RATE1 = .1
                                          RATE2 = .2
                                          RESULT = 0
                                          PERCENTAGE = 10

1. MULTIPLY BASE BY RATE1 GIVING PERCENTAGE
   After execution, the new value of PERCENTAGE is 5.
2. MULTIPLY BASE BY RATE2 GIVING RESULT, PERCENTAGE
   After execution, the new values of RESULT and PERCENTAGE are each
   10.

Format 1:

	Numeric
Identifier-1, -2	X
Literal-1, -2	X

Format 2:

	Numeric	Numeric-edited
Identifier-1, -2	X	
Literal-1, -2	X	
Identifier-3	X	X

See arithmetic statements, composite of operands, multiple results in arithmetic statements, Nucleus Module, overlapping operands, receiving item, ROUNDED, SIZE ERROR.

N

NATIVE

    See SPECIAL-NAMES.

native character set

    The native character set is the implementor-defined character set that is associated with the computer specified in the OBJECT-COMPUTER paragraph.

native collating sequence

    The native collating sequence is the collating sequence that is associated with the computer specified in the OBJECT-COMPUTER paragraph.

    See collating sequence.

negated combined condition

    A negated combined condition is a condition composed of the word 'NOT,' followed by a combined condition in parentheses.

    See combined condition, condition.

negated simple condition

    A negated simple condition is a condition composed of the word 'NOT,' followed by a simple condition.

    See condition, simple condition.

negation

    Negation is the process of changing a condition into one which has the opposite truth value. If a condition is true, its negation is false. If a condition is false, its negation is true.

Condition	Truth Value	
condition-1	T	F
NOT condition-1	F	T

    Example: The condition '10 is greater than 3' is true. The negation of this condition, 'NOT (10 is greater than 3)' or 'it is not the case that 10 is greater than 3' is false.

    The condition '10 is greater than 15' is false. The negation of this condition, 'NOT (10 is greater than 15)' or 'it is not the case that 10 is greater than 15,' is true.

    See condition.

NEGATIVE

See sign condition.

NEXT

See IF, READ, SEARCH.

next executable sentence

If a certain statement is being executed, the 'next executable sentence' is the sentence to which control is transferred when execution of the current statement is completed.

The next executable sentence may be the sentence that immediately follows a given statement, or in the case of a statement being executed under control of a PERFORM statement, the next executable sentence may be the sentence following the PERFORM.

See transfer of control.

next executable statement

If a certain statement is being executed, the 'next executable statement' is the statement to which control is transferred when execution of the current statement is completed.

The next executable statement may be the statement that immediately follows a given statement, or in the case of a statement being executed under control of a PERFORM statement, the next executable statement may be the statement following the PERFORM.

See transfer of control.

NEXT GROUP

The NEXT GROUP clause specifies information for vertical positioning of a page following the presentation of the last line of a report group.

Format:

$$\underline{\text{NEXT}} \ \underline{\text{GROUP}} \ \text{IS} \ \begin{Bmatrix} \text{integer-1} \\ \underline{\text{PLUS}} \ \text{integer-2} \\ \underline{\text{NEXT}} \ \underline{\text{PAGE}} \end{Bmatrix}$$

The NEXT GROUP clause is used by the Report Writer Control System (RWCS) in conjunction with information from the TYPE and PAGE clauses and the value of LINE-COUNTER to determine a new value for LINE-COUNTER. Any positioning of the page specified by this clause is effected after the presentation of the clause's report group.

If this clause is specified in a Control Footing report group which is at any level other than the highest one at which a control break occurred, it is ignored.

The NEXT GROUP clause of a body group refers to the next body group to be presented. The NEXT GROUP clause of a REPORT HEADING report group can affect the location at which the Page Heading group is presented. The NEXT GROUP clause of a Page Footing report group can affect the location at which the REPORT FOOTING report group is presented.

If integer-1 is specified, the clause is an absolute NEXT GROUP clause. If PLUS integer-2 or NEXT PAGE is specified, the clause is a relative NEXT GROUP clause.

- This clause must not be specified in a Report Footing or Page Heading report group. NEXT PAGE cannot be specified in a Page Footing report group.
- A report group cannot contain a NEXT GROUP clause unless the description of that report group contains at least one LINE NUMBER clause.
- If the PAGE clause is not specified in the report description entry, only a relative NEXT GROUP clause can be specified in any report group description entry within that report.
- Integer-1 and integer-2 must not exceed 999.

For details of the effects of this clause see the Presentation Rules entry.

See body group, control break, Control Footing, Presentation Rules, report group description, REPORT HEADING.

NEXT PAGE

See LINE NUMBER, NEXT GROUP, report group description.

next record

The next record is the record that *logically* follows the current record of a file. This is not necessarily the next sequential nor the next physical record of the file.
See READ.

NEXT SENTENCE

See IF, SEARCH.

NO

See CLOSE, OPEN, RECEIVE

NO DATA

See RECEIVE.

noncontiguous item

A noncontiguous item is an item that bears no hierarchical relationship to other data items. It must be described with level-number 77 in either the WORKING-STORAGE or LINKAGE SECTION.

nonnumeric data item

A nonnumeric data item is a data item that can be composed of any combination of characters from the computer's character set. Sometimes a nonnumeric data item is formed from a more restricted character set.

See character set.

nonnumeric literal

A nonnumeric literal is a character-string delimited by quotation characters. The character-string can include any character in the machine's character set. To represent a quotation character (″) inside a nonnumeric literal, two contiguous quotation characters are used. These represent one quotation character and do not delimit the nonnumeric literal.

The value of a nonnumeric literal is that of its characters, excluding the delimiting quotation characters. All punctuation characters inside a nonnumeric literal are part of the literal and are not considered separators.

Nonnumeric literals can be up to 120 characters long and are considered to be of category alphanumeric.

Examples:

Character-string	How it would appear as a nonnumeric literal
DON	″DON″
GRADE△″A″△EGGS	″GRADE△″″A″″△EGGS″
△△MONTH△△	″△△MONTH△△″

See alphanumeric character, category, character-string, character set, delimiter, separator.

NO REWIND

See CLOSE, OPEN.

NOT

NOT is a logical unary operator that negates the operand with which it is associated. For example, if condition-1 is true, then NOT condition-1 is false. Likewise, if condition-1 is false, then NOT condition-1 is true.

In the source program, NOT must be preceded and followed by one or more spaces.

See logical operations, negation, unary operator.

notation in COBOL

A general representation of a COBOL statement or entry is called a *format*. This discussion defines the way in which formats are presented in this book. It is not the way that the source program deck appears.

Uppercase Letters

A word entirely in uppercase letters is a *reserved word*. A reserved word is one that is already defined in COBOL; the programmer cannot redefine it or use it in any other way than the one specified.

Key Words and Optional Words

Reserved words are frequently used in groups. In many cases, some words are unessential and included only for readability, while other words are required. The essential words are called *key words*. They are underlined in the formats. The nonessential words are called *optional words*. They are not underlined in the formats. It is important to remember that both key words and optional words are reserved. Thus, if an optional word is used, it must be spelled exactly the same way as in the formats and appear only where indicated in the formats.

  Examples:

RECORDS ARE STANDARD

In this format all three words are reserved words. RECORDS and STANDARD are key words; ARE is an optional word. A correct interpretation of this format is

RECORDS STANDARD   · or
RECORDS ARE STANDARD

However, the following two interpretations are erroneous:

RECORDS STANDARD ARE
RECORDS AR STANDARD

Lowercase Letters

A word in lowercase letters indicates an item to be filled in by the programmer. For example, if 'literal' appears in a format, the programmer must substitute for it some literal such as 6.7 or 'ABC'; 'literal' is called a *dummy variable*, that is, it does not appear in the statement but merely saves a place for something else. Another dummy variable is 'data-name.' Whenever 'data-name' is encountered in a format, the programmer is expected to supply a data-name. A full list of dummy variables appears later in this discussion.

Sometimes more than one of a particular dummy variable is required in a format. In this case the dummy variables are qualified by a numerical postfix. For example, data-name-1, data-name-2, etc. In some formats, 'data-name-m' and the like, appear. This indicates that an unspecified number of data-names can appear before data-name-m. Within a given format, all instances of a given-data-name refer to the *same* data item.

Braces

Braces { } enclose two or more items from which one and only one must be chosen. The items are listed vertically, with each line considered a single choice. For example, in

$$\begin{Bmatrix} \text{data-name} \\ \text{literal} \end{Bmatrix}$$

the user must select either a data-name or literal, but not both. In the format

$$\begin{Bmatrix} \text{literal} \\ \text{data-name-1 data-name-2} \end{Bmatrix}$$

one must select either a literal or *two* data names. Braces do not, however, necessarily mean that the item chosen will be written in the statement. For example, in

$$\underline{\text{BLOCK}} \ \underline{\text{CONTAINS}} \begin{Bmatrix} \underline{\text{RECORDS}} \\ \underline{\text{CHARACTERS}} \end{Bmatrix}$$

BLOCK and CONTAINS are key words and must appear. Applying the rule for braces, the user selects one of the alternatives. If he chooses RECORDS, it must also be written since it too is a key word. However, if CHARACTERS is chosen from the braces, one need not include it. Valid interpretations of the format are

```
BLOCK CONTAINS RECORDS
BLOCK CONTAINS CHARACTERS
BLOCK CONTAINS
```

Brackets

Brackets [ ] indicate an option to be used or not as the situation demands. However, once an option is selected, all rules for key words, etc., must be followed. For example, in

$$\underline{\text{BLOCK}} \ \text{literal-1} \begin{bmatrix} \underline{\text{RECORDS}} \\ \text{CHARACTERS} \end{bmatrix}$$

one can write:

```
BLOCK 5
BLOCK 5 RECORDS
BLOCK 5 CHARACTERS
```

Ellipses

The ellipsis is a symbol consisting of three dots (...); it indicates that the preceding group can be repeated as often as necessary. In this book, if ellipses are applied to a set of braces, the meaning is that at least one instance of the material in braces must appear and that subsequent instances are optional. If ellipses are applied to a set of brackets, the meaning is that the material in the brackets can appear one or more times or need not appear at all. For example, consider the format

$$\underline{\text{ADD}} \begin{Bmatrix} \text{data-name-1} \\ \text{literal-1} \end{Bmatrix} \ldots \underline{\text{TO}}$$

Valid instances are

    ADD NET-PAY TO
    ADD 5 TO
    ADD NET-PAY, DEDUCTIONS, FICA TO
    ADD 5, 6.7, 3 TO
    ADD 5, NET-PAY, FICA, 6.7 TO

Note that, as shown by the last example, subsequent instances need not be the same choice as the first.

A single choice within braces can develop if an ellipsis is applied to the braces. For example, there is only one choice in the format

$$\{\text{literal-1, data-name-1}\} \ldots$$

But the ellipsis indicates that one can write as many literal/data-name pairs as desired. If the format were

$$\{\text{literal-1}\} \ldots \{\text{data-name-1}\} \ldots$$

it would mean that first one wrote as many literals as desired and then as many data names.

Punctuation

COBOL has three punctuation marks—the period (.), the comma (,), and the semicolon (;). The comma and semicolon are always optional in statements and can be used interchangeably where desired. Sometimes, to avoid clutter they are not shown in the formats; however, since they improve readability, their use is recommended.

The period, on the other hand, is absolutely essential wherever indicated and can only be used where explicitly shown in the formats. To prevent the period from being confused with a dot in an ellipsis, etc., it will be indicated in the formats by a bullet (•).

Dummy Variables

The remaining group of components found in formats are dummy variables. In the formats, most dummy variables are self-explanatory. They are indicated, as mentioned, by being expressed entirely in lowercase letters. They are

arithmetic-expression — a combination of data-names, literals and arithmetic-operators that has a single numeric value.

character-string — a sequence of contiguous characters.

comment-entry — an entry used to annotate the program.

condition — an event, status, or statement that has a determinable truth value, either true or false.

condition-name — a word assigned to a status or to a set of values of a variable.

data-name — a word that conforms to certain rules and which is the name of a variable defined in the Data Division.

figurative-constant — a reserved word that represents a numeric value, a character, or a string of characters.

file-name — a name that is associated with a file in the Data Division.

imperative-statement — a statement containing a verb and specifying an unconditional action.

index-name — a word that names an index associated with a table.

literal — a word that stands for itself. The context determines whether it must be numeric or nonnumeric.

mnemonic-name — a word assigned by the programmer to denote a piece of hardware.

paragraph-name — a word that identifies a paragraph in the Procedure Division.

procedure-name — a word that identifies a paragraph or section in the Procedure Division.

program-name — the name of the program being compiled.

record-name — a name that identifies a record defined in the Data Division.

section-name — the name of a section.

sentence — one or more statements terminated by a period and space. The comma and semicolon may be used within a sentence to separate the various statements.

Special Characters

Whenever any special character ($+$, $-$, $<$, $>$, $=$) appears in a format, it is to be considered a key word. The special characters are not underlined in the formats so as to avoid confusion.

Equivalent Words

In all formats, THROUGH and THRU, CORRESPONDING and CORR, and COMPUTATIONAL and COMP are considered identical.

For a more detailed discussion of each of these items, see the individual entries.

NOTE

Formerly a verb indicating that the rest of the statement was a comment, NOTE has been replaced by a general comment facility.

See comment line.

NOT LESS

See START.

Nucleus Module

The Nucleus Module provides the basic language capability for the processing of data.

Level 1

Nucleus Level 1 provides limited facilities as follows:

- The separators—comma and semicolon—are not included.
- All data-names must begin with an alphabetic character.
- All data-names, paragraph-names, and text-names must be unique.
- Qualification is not included.
- The only figurative constants are ZERO, SPACE, HIGH-VALUE, LOW-VALUE, and QUOTE.
- A word or numeric literal cannot be broken in such a way that part of it appears on a continuation line.

Level 2

Nucleus Level 2 provides full COBOL facilities.

null

Null, when applied to a collection of objects, means that there are no members in the group. A null character-string is a string that contains no characters. When applied to a character, the null character is the one that represents nothing. This is not the same as the character that represents a space or the one that represents a zero.

NUMERIC

See class condition.

numeric character

A numeric character is one of the digits 0 through 9.

numeric data item

A numeric data item is a data item that is composed entirely of numeric characters and an optional plus or minus sign. The maximum size of a numeric field is 18 digits; this is a new restriction of 74 COBOL.

numeric-edited data

Numeric-edited data is numeric data that has been subjected to an editing process.

numeric literal

A numeric literal is a literal that is composed of one or more numeric characters and of an optional decimal point and/or algebraic sign. The decimal point cannot be the right-most character. If a sign is present, it must be the left-most character.

See literal, numeric character.

O

OBJECT-COMPUTER

The OBJECT-COMPUTER paragraph is in the CONFIGURATION SECTION of the ENVIRONMENT DIVISION. It defines the hardware on which the object program is to be run.

Format:

$$
\text{OBJECT-COMPUTER.}\ \text{computer-name}\ \left[\text{MEMORY SIZE integer} \left\{ \begin{array}{l} \underline{\text{WORDS}} \\ \underline{\text{CHARACTERS}} \\ \underline{\text{MODULES}} \end{array} \right\} \right]
$$

[PROGRAM COLLATING SEQUENCE IS alphabet-name]
[SEGMENT-LIMIT IS segment-number].

The computer-name is specified by the implementor.

Memory Size Clause

The MEMORY SIZE clause, if specified, defines the size of the memory of the computer on which the object program is to be run. If the specified size is less than the minimum required for running the object program, the results are implementor-defined.

Collating Sequence Clause

If the COLLATING SEQUENCE clause is not specified, the native collating sequence is used. If this clause is specified, 'alphabet-name' defines the collating sequence that will be used in nonnumeric comparisons involving relation conditions, condition-name conditions, and those comparisons implicitly specified by the presence of a CONTROL clause in a report description entry. The specified collating sequence is also applied to nonnumeric merge or sort keys unless the COLLATING SEQUENCE phrase is specified in a SORT or MERGE statement. The alphabet-name used is associated with a sequence of characters in the SPECIAL-NAMES paragraph. This clause is a new feature of 74 COBOL.

Segment-Limit Clause

If the SEGMENT-LIMIT clause is not specified, segments with segment-numbers from 0 through 49 are considered fixed permanent segments. If this clause is specified, segments with numbers from 0 up to, but not including, the value of the specified segment-number are considered fixed permanent segments. Segments with values ranging from that of the specified segment-number up to 49 are considered fixed overlayable segments. 'Segment-number' must have a value of from 1 to 49.

See alphabet-name, collating sequence, condition-name, fixed overlayable segment, fixed permanent segment, report description entry.

object of condition

The 'object' of a relation condition is the operand that follows the operator.

See relational operator, relation condition, subject of condition.

object of entry

The object of an entry is a set of operands and/or reserved words that immediately follows the subject of a DATA DIVISION entry.

See subject of entry.

object program

An object program is the result of having compiled a source program. It is a set of executable instructions, designed to operate on data for the purpose of providing a solution to a data-processing task.

See source program.

object time

Object time is the time at which an object program is executed.

See compile time, object program.

object time switch

The Debug Module provides a means by which the user can monitor data items or procedures during execution of the object program. Included is an object time switch that dynamically activates the debugging code that was inserted by the compiler. This switch, which cannot be accessed by the program, is controlled outside of the COBOL environment.

If the switch is 'on,' all of the effects of the debugging language statements in the program are permitted. If the switch is 'off,' these effects are inhibited. Recompilation of the source program is not necessary to provide or remove the debugging capability. The object time switch has no effect on the execution of the program if the WITH DEBUGGING MODE clause was not specified in the source program at compile time.

See compile time, object program.

occurrence number

The occurrence number of a table element is that element's ordinal position within the table. An occurrence number can never be less than one, nor greater than the maximum number of elements in the table, as defined by that table's OCCURS clause.

See ordinal position, table.

OCCURS

The OCCURS clause eliminates the need for separate entries for repeated data items and supplies information required to use subscripts or indices.

Format 1:

$$\underline{OCCURS}\ integer\text{-}2\ TIMES\left[\left\{\begin{array}{l}\underline{ASCENDING}\\\underline{DESCENDING}\end{array}\right\}KEY\ IS\ \{data\text{-}name\text{-}2\}\dots\right]\dots$$

[INDEXED BY {index-name-1} . . .]

Format 2:

$$\underline{OCCURS}\ integer\text{-}1\ \underline{TO}\ integer\text{-}2\ TIMES\ \underline{DEPENDING}\ ON\ data\text{-}name\text{-}1$$
$$\left[\left\{\begin{array}{l}\underline{ASCENDING}\\\underline{DESCENDING}\end{array}\right\}KEY\ IS\ \{data\text{-}name\text{-}2\}\dots\right]\dots$$

[INDEXED BY {index-name-1} . . .]

The OCCURS clause appears in an item's data description. It is used in defining tables and sets of repeated data items. The subject of an entry containing an OCCURS clause must be either subscripted or indexed whenever it is referred to other than in a SEARCH or USE FOR DEBUGGING statement. Furthermore, if the data-name containing an OCCURS clause is the name of a group item, then all data-names in this group must be subscripted or indexed wherever they are used as operands, unless they appear as the object of a REDEFINES clause.

Except for the OCCURS clause itself, all data description clauses associated with an item which is described with an OCCURS clause apply to each occurrence of the item. The VALUE clause cannot be used with an item that has an OCCURS clause.

If SYNC is specified any implicit FILLER generated is generated for *each* occurrence of the item. This is new to 74 COBOL.

The KEY IS Phrase

The KEY IS phrase designates one or more data items as keys for the entry. The data-names are listed in order of decreasing significance. Any data item specified in the KEY IS phrase must have strictly increasing or decreasing values from the beginning to the end of the table. The order is determined by the rules for comparison of operands, that is, for ASCENDING KEY items, the values must be strictly monotonically increasing. This means that the first occurrence of the element must have a smaller value than the second occurrence, the second occurrence must have a smaller value than the third, etc. It does not mean that the values are necessarily consecutive although they may be. For example, the sequences

```
1  3  13  97  101
1  2  3   4   5   6
A  B  D   F   T
```

are all valid for an ASCENDING KEY item. The sequences

```
1  2   2   3   4
1  5   19  16  27
A  B   B   C   D   E
```

are invalid, since the first and third have two values that are the same and the second has a value out of order.

For DESCENDING KEY items the values must be strictly monotonically decreasing. This means that the first occurrence must have a higher value than the second, the second occurrence must have a higher value than the third, etc. It does not mean that the values are necessarily consecutive although they may be.

The first data-name in the KEY IS phrase must either be the item that is the subject of the OCCURS clause or an item subordinate to this item. If more than one key is specified, the second through last items must be subordinate to the group item that is the subject of the entry. If the first item in the KEY IS phrase is subordinate to the subject of the entry, then

1. Any other item in the KEY IS phrase must be subordinate to the group item that is the subject of the OCCURS clause.

2. No item in the KEY IS phrase can contain an OCCURS clause.

3. No item that contains an OCCURS clause can exist between the subject of the entry and any item specified in the KEY IS phrase.

Example: Consider the structure

```
02  A  OCCURS 10 TIMES KEY IS———
    03  B
    03  C
    03  E OCCURS 10 TIMES
        04  F
        04  G
02  J
```

The KEY IS phrase can name A, B, or C. It cannot name (1) J, since J is not within the group item, A; (2) E, since E contains an OCCURS clause; (3) F, G, or H since an intervening item contains an OCCURS clause, viz., E. Observe that the phrases KEY IS A, B, C or KEY IS B, C are valid, but that KEY IS B, C, A is not.

The INDEXED BY Phrase

The INDEXED BY phrase is required if the subject of this entry, or an entry subordinate to the subject of this entry, is to be referred to by indexing. Index-name-1 is not defined elsewhere since its allocation and format depend on hardware considerations, and since it is not data, it cannot be associated with any data hierarchy. All index-names must be unique within a program.

Size of Entry—DEPENDING ON Phrase

The number of occurrences of the entry depends upon the format of the OCCURS clause. In format 1, integer-2 specifies the exact number of occurrences. In format 2, integer-1 specifies the minimum number of occurrences, integer-2 specifies the maximum number.[1] At any point during execution of the program, the number of valid occurrences is determined by the current value of data-name-1. Note that this does not mean that the length of an item is variable, only that the number of its occurrences is. The value of data-name-1 must be within the range of integer-1 to integer-2. If data-name-1 has a value less than that of integer-2, those data items having an occurrence number greater than the current value of data-name-1 will have unpredictable contents. When reference is made to a group item that has a subordinate entry specifying a format 2 OCCURS clause, only that part of the table whose occurrence numbers have a value less than or equal to the current value of data-name-1 will be used in the operation.

No part of data-name-1 can overlap any part of the entry defined by the OCCURS clause. That is, since the size of the entry depends upon data-name-1, data-name-1 cannot be part of the entry. A data description entry that contains a format 2 OCCURS clause can be followed, within that record description, only by data description entries that are subordinate to it.

The OCCURS clause must not be specified in a data description entry that has a level-number of 01, 66, 77, or 88 nor in one that describes an item with a variable size. In other words, an element subordinate to the data description entry with an OCCURS clause cannot contain a format 2 OCCURS clause.

Any data-name used in the OCCURS clause can be qualified.

	Non-negative	Positive
Integer-1		X
Integer-2	X	
Data-name-1		X

Integer-2 must be greater than integer-1.

---

[1] The fact that DEPENDING ON is mandatory is new to 74 COBOL.

N.B. The fact that integer-1 cannot be zero is new to 74 COBOL.

See comparison rules, communication description entry, data description, group item, indexing, monotonically, qualified data-name, subject of entry, subscripting, SYNCHRONIZED, synchronization, table.

OF

See COPY, qualification, RERUN, USE, VALUE.

OFF

See SPECIAL-NAMES.

OMITTED

See file description, LABEL RECORDS.

ON

See GO TO, I-O-CONTROL, LINE NUMBER, MERGE, OCCURS, SORT, SUM, UNSTRING, USE.

ON OVERFLOW

See CALL, STRING, UNSTRING.

ON SIZE ERROR

See ADD, COMPUTE, DIVIDE, MULTIPLY, SUBTRACT.

OPEN

The OPEN verb makes files available for processing, checks and writes labels, and performs other input-output operations.

Format:

$$\underline{\text{OPEN}} \begin{Bmatrix} \underline{\text{INPUT}} \begin{Bmatrix} \text{file-name-1} \begin{bmatrix} \underline{\text{REVERSED}} \\ \text{WITH } \underline{\text{NO}} \underline{\text{REWIND}} \end{bmatrix} \end{Bmatrix} \dots \\ \underline{\text{OUTPUT}} \{\text{file-name-2} [\text{WITH } \underline{\text{NO}} \underline{\text{REWIND}}]\} \dots \\ \underline{\text{I-O}} \{\text{file-name-3}\} \dots \\ \underline{\text{EXTEND}} \{\text{file-name-4}\} \dots \end{Bmatrix} \dots$$

An OPEN statement must be executed for a file before any statement references the file explicitly or implicitly, except for a SORT or MERGE statement with the USING or GIVING phrase. After the OPEN statement is successfully executed, the file is placed in the open mode and its associated record area(s) made available to the program. (The INPUT and I-O options are new features of 74 COBOL.) OPEN does not obtain or release the first data record. The OPEN statement cannot reference a SORT or MERGE file. Files referenced by a given OPEN statement need not all have the same organization or access mode. If label records are specified and not present, or not specified and present, the action of OPEN is undefined.

For sequential files, if only level 1 of the sequential i-o module is implemented only one file-name can appear in an OPEN statement. That is, the above format is interpreted as if no ellipses appeared in it. Furthermore, the REVERSED and NO REWIND clauses are not supported.

A file can have the various options—INPUT, OUTPUT, I-O, and EXTEND—applied to it by OPEN statements throughout execution of a program. Depending on the option chosen, one says that the file is open in the input mode, output mode, I-O mode, or extend mode. However, a file that has been opened must be closed by a CLOSE statement without the REEL, UNIT, or LOCK phrase before a subsequent OPEN can be executed for that file. If a file is opened in any mode except output, its file description must be identical to the file description that it had when it was created. (This is a new feature of 74 COBOL.)

Input Mode

When a file is opened in the input mode, the current-record pointer is positioned to the first record of the file. If no records exist in the file, then the current-record pointer is positioned so that the next format 1 READ executed for the file will cause the AT END condition. If a file is designated as optional in its SELECT clause and is not present when opened, the first format 1 READ for this file will cause the AT END condition to occur. For indexed files, the prime record key is the key of reference and is used to determine the first record of the file. If label records are specified, the beginning labels are checked in accordance with the implementor's conventions for input label checking.

The No Rewind Phrase

NO REWIND can be used only with sequentially organized single-reel/unit files. It is implemented in level 2 of the sequential i-o module. If NO REWIND does not apply to the medium containing the file, this phrase is ignored. (Previously, the application of this phrase was more restricted.) When this phrase is specified, no repositioning occurs and the file must have already been positioned at its beginning before executing the OPEN STATEMENT. If this phrase is not specified, the file is positioned at the first data record.

The Reversed Phrase

REVERSED can be used only with sequentially organized single-reel/unit files. If REVERSED is specified, the file is positioned at its last data record and subsequent READ statements make the data records available in reverse order, starting at the last and proceeding to the first. The feature of positioning the file at its end point is new to 74 COBOL, and is implemented in level 2 of the sequential i-o module.

Output Mode

Opening a file in the output mode creates the file. At the time of its creation a file has *no* data records. If label records are specified, they are written in accordance with the implementor's conventions for output label writing.

The No Rewind Phrase

The same considerations as listed under NO REWIND for input mode files apply if the NO REWIND phrase is specified.

I-O Mode

When a file is opened with the I-O phrase, the current-record pointer is positioned at the first record of the file. If no records exist in the file, then the current-record pointer is set so that the next READ for the file causes an AT END condition. For indexed files the prime record key is the key of reference and is used to determine the first record of the file.

The I-O phrase can be used only with mass storage files. It allows the file to be used for both input and output operations. The file must already exist, that is, the I-O phrase cannot be used to create a file. If label records are present, they are checked in accordance with the implementor's conventions for input-output label checking.

Extend Mode

The EXTEND phrase can only be used with sequentially organized files. It cannot be specified for a multiple file reel. When a file is opened in the extend mode, subsequent WRITE statements will add records to the file, beginning after the last data record in the file, as though the file had been opened with the OUTPUT phrase. If the file contains label records, then:

If the file is on a single reel/unit, the beginning file label records are processed.

If the file is on multiple reels, *file* label records are not processed. The beginning *reel* labels on the last reel of the file are processed as if the file were opened with the INPUT phrase. The currently existing end *file* labels are first processed as if the file were opened with the INPUT phrase and these labels are deleted. Processing then continues as if the file were opened with the OUTPUT phrase.

The EXTEND phrase is a new feature of 74 COBOL and is implemented in level 2 of the sequential i-o module.

Status Keys

If status keys are specified for the file they are updated as follows:

SK1	SK2	Meaning
0	0	Successful completion
3	0	Permanent error
9	—	Implementor-defined conditions

Following are charts showing the permissible open modes for files accessed by the various verbs. The first two charts are by file organization, the second two by access mode.

Files with Sequential Organization

Access Mode	VERB		
	Read	Write	Rewrite
Sequential	Input I-O	Output Extend	I-O

Files with Relative or Indexed Organization

Access Mode	VERB				
	Read	Write	Rewrite	Start	Delete
Sequential	Input I-O	Output	I-O	Input I-O	I-O
Random	Input I-O	Output I-O	I-O		I-O
Dynamic	Input I-O	Output I-O	I-O	Input I-O	I-O

Files with Sequential Access

File Organization	Read	Write	Rewrite	Start	Delete
Sequential	Input I-O	Output Extend	I-O		
Relative or indexed	Input I-O	Output Extend	I-O	Input I-O	I-O

Files with Random or Dynamic Access

File Organization	Read	Write	Rewrite	Start	Delete
Relative or indexed	Input I-O	Output I-O	I-O		I-O

See ACCESS MODE, current-record pointer, indexed i-o, key of reference, label records, MULTIPLE FILE, ORGANIZATION, prime record key, relative i-o, sequential i-o.

open mode

Open mode is that state of a file from the time after an OPEN statement is executed for the file to the time before a CLOSE statement is executed for that file. The particular open mode is specified in the OPEN statement as input, output, input-output, or extend.

See extend mode, input mode, input-output mode, output mode.

operand

An operand is an item that is operated on. In the Procedure Division, operands are indicated by lowercase words.

operational sign

The operational sign is an algebraic sign that is associated with signed numeric data items and signed numeric literals. It indicates whether the item's value is greater or less than zero. The sign of an item with a value of zero is defined as positive.

The SIGN clause can be used to explicitly specify the location of the operational sign. If this clause is not used, operational signs are specified by the implementor.

operator, arithmetic

See arithmetic operator.

OPTIONAL

See FILE-CONTROL, SELECT.

optional word

An optional word is a reserved word that is included in a format only to improve readability. As such, its presence is optional when the format is used in writing a source program. If used, however, it must be spelled exactly as in the formats and appear only where indicated in the formats.

See notation in COBOL, reserved word, source program.

OR

OR is a logical connective that combines two operands in such a way that the entire expression is true whenever either one or both of the operands is true. When a series of operands are combined by OR's, the entire expression is true whenever at least one of the operands is true.

Any instance of the word 'OR' must be preceded and followed by a space.

See logical operations, UNSTRING.

ordering statement

An ordering statement causes records to be arranged in a certain order. The ordering statements are MERGE, RELEASE, RETURN, and SORT.

ordinal position

The ordinal position of an item is its position in a well-defined sequence of items—first, second, third, etc. Note that no two items can have the same ordinal position, since the ordinal position of an item is unique.

ORGANIZATION

The ORGANIZATION clause specifies whether a file has sequential, relative, or indexed organization. It is specified in the FILE-CONTROL paragraph.

Format:

$$\text{ORGANIZATION IS} \begin{Bmatrix} \underline{\text{SEQUENTIAL}} \\ \underline{\text{RELATIVE}} \\ \underline{\text{INDEXED}} \end{Bmatrix}$$

The ORGANIZATION clause specifies the logical structure of a file. A file's organization is established at the time the file is created and cannot be subsequently changed. If this clause is omitted, SEQUENTIAL is assumed. This clause is new to 74 COBOL.

See indexed i-o, relative i-o, sequential i-o.

OUTPUT

See communication description entry, DISABLE, ENABLE, MERGE, OPEN, SORT, USE.

output file

An output file is a file that is opened in the output mode.

See OPEN, output mode.

output mode

Output mode is that state of a file from the time after an OPEN statement with the OUTPUT phrase is executed for the file to the time before a CLOSE statement is executed for that file.

See OPEN.

output procedure

An output procedure is a set of statements to which control passes either during execution of a SORT statement after the sort function is completed or during execution of a MERGE statement after the merge function has selected the next record in merged order.

See MERGE, SORT.

OVERFLOW

See STRING, UNSTRING, CALL.

overflow condition

The overflow condition can occur as a result of executing a CALL, STRING, or UNSTRING statement.

In a CALL statement the overflow condition occurs when the available portion of memory is incapable of accommodating the program specified in the statement.

In a STRING statement the overflow condition occurs when the receiving item is unable to accommodate all the characters from the sending item.

In an UNSTRING statement the overflow condition occurs when the pointer item is less than one or greater than the number of characters in the sending item or if all the receiving items are filled and the sending item still contains characters that have not been acted upon.

overlapping operand

Two operands in a statement, one a sending item and one a receiving item, are said to be 'overlapping' if they do not refer to the identical storage area, yet there is a part of storage that is part of both operands.

In an INSPECT, MOVE, SET, STRING, UNSTRING, or an arithmetic statement, when a sending and receiving item are overlapping, the result of the execution of the statement is undefined.

See receiving item, sending item.

overlay

Overlay is the process of calling a program segment into main storage in such a way that part or all of a resident program segment is destroyed.

Assume that a program is made up of three segments—A, B, and C. Assume that main storage can contain, at most, two of these segments at a time. If A and B are residing in main storage and it is desired to load C, then C must overlay A or B, or both. That is, C must use some or all of A's or B's storage. When C is loaded, either A or B or both no longer exist in main storage.

When overlaying is used, the Procedure Division must be divided into sections. All sections are in one of two classes—fixed or independent. The fixed segments are those that are logically always in main storage. Independent segments may or may not be in storage at any given time. Although the process of overlaying does not affect the logical operation of the program, it may affect object program efficiency.

When overlaying is used, fixed segments are of two types: fixed permanent and fixed overlayable. A fixed permanent segment is one located in the fixed portion of the program that cannot be overlaid by any other part of the program. A fixed overlayable segment is one located in the fixed portion of the program that, although logically treated as if it were always present in storage, can in actuality be overlaid by another segment to optimize utilization of storage.

The number of fixed permanent versus fixed overlayable segments can be varied by the SEGMENT-LIMIT clause. Any fixed segment that is moved in and out of storage is always made available in its last-used state. Fixed segments have segment-numbers from 1 through 49.

An independent segment is one that can overlay and be overlaid by either a fixed overlayable segment or another independent segment. Independent segments have segment-numbers from 50 through 99.

See fixed overlayable segment, fixed permanent segment, independent segment.

P

PAGE

The PAGE clause defines the length of a page and of the vertical subdivisions of a page within which the report groups are presented.

Format:

$$\underline{PAGE}\begin{bmatrix} LIMIT\ IS \\ LIMITS\ ARE \end{bmatrix} integer\text{-}1 \begin{bmatrix} LINE \\ LINES \end{bmatrix}$$

$$[\underline{HEADING}\ integer\text{-}2][\underline{FIRST}\ \underline{DETAIL}\ integer\text{-}3]$$

$$[\underline{LAST}\ \underline{DETAIL}\ integer\text{-}4][\underline{FOOTING}\ integer\text{-}5]$$

The PAGE clause is part of a report description (RD) entry; it establishes the vertical format of a report page. The four optional clauses can be written in any order.

Integer-1 — specifies the number of lines available on each page.

Integer-2 — specifies the first line on which a Report Heading or Page Heading report group can be presented.

Integer-3 — specifies the first line on which a body group, i.e., a Detail, Control Heading or Control Footing report group, can be presented. Report Heading or Page Heading groups cannot be presented on or beyond the line number specified by integer-3.

Integer-4 — specifies the last line on which a Control Heading or Detail group can be presented.

Integer-5 — specifies the last line on which a Control Footing group can be presented. Page Footing and Report Footing groups must be presented beyond the line specified by integer-5.

The values of integer-1 through integer-5 must conform to the following:

Integer-	Range of Values
1	$\geq$ integer-5 and $<$ 999
2	$\geq$ 1
3	$\geq$ integer-2
4	$\geq$ integer-3
5	$\geq$ integer-4

If the PAGE clause is specified, the following values are assumed for any omitted phrases:

Integer	Assumed Value
2	1
3	integer-2
4	integer-5, if specified; otherwise integer-1
5	integer-4, if specified; otherwise integer-1

If the PAGE clause is omitted, the report consists of a single page of indefinite length.

Specifying the PAGE clause establishes five regions in a page. The following chart shows the limits for each region and the report groups that can be presented within each region:

First Line Number of Region	Last Line Number of Region	Report Groups That Can Be Presented Within the Region
integer-2	integer-1	Report Heading with NEXT GROUP NEXT PAGE clause. Report Footing with LINE integer-1 NEXT PAGE clause.
integer-2	integer-3 − 1	Report Heading without NEXT GROUP NEXT PAGE clause. Page Heading
integer-3	integer-4	Control Heading Detail
integer-3	integer-5	Control Footing
integer-5 + 1	integer-1	Page Footing Report Footing without LINE integer-1 NEXT PAGE clause.

All report groups must be described so that they can be presented on one page since the Report Writer Control System will not split a multiline report group across page boundaries.

See Control Footing, Control Heading, DETAIL, LINE NUMBER, NEXT GROUP, page, Page Heading, report description, report group, Report Heading, Report Writer Control System, SEND, TYPE, WRITE.

page

A page is a vertical division of a report that represents a physical separation of report data, based on internal reporting requirements and/or external characteristics of the reporting medium.

See PAGE.

page body

The page body is that part of the logical page in which lines can be written and/or spaced.

See LINAGE, PAGE.

PAGE-COUNTER

PAGE-COUNTER is a special register that is generated for each report description entry in the REPORT SECTION of the DATA DIVISION. The implicit description is PICTURE 999999, with the USAGE being implementor-defined. Although the value of PAGE-COUNTER is maintained by the Report Writer Control System (RWCS), it can be altered by Procedure Division statements. It is used as a means of numbering pages within a report.

Within the REPORT SECTION, PAGE-COUNTER can be referenced only in a SOURCE clause. Outside of the REPORT SECTION, PAGE-COUNTER can appear in any context in which an integer data-name can appear.

If more than one PAGE-COUNTER exists in a program, PAGE-COUNTER must be qualified by a report-name if it is referenced in the Procedure Division. In the REPORT SECTION, an unqualified reference refers to that report's PAGE-COUNTER. If only level 1 of the Nucleus is implemented, qualification is not allowed.

Execution of the INITIATE statement for a report causes the RWCS to set that report's PAGE-COUNTER to one. PAGE-COUNTER is incremented by one each time the RWCS executes a page advance for that report.

See report description, report-name, special register.

Page Footing

A Page Footing is a report group that is presented at the end of each report by the Report Writer Control System.

See report group, Report Writer Control System.

Page Heading

A Page Heading is a report group that is presented at the top of each page in a report by the Report Writer Control System.

See report group, Report Writer Control System.

page overflow condition

See WRITE.

paragraph

A paragraph is a subdivision of a Section or a Division. In the Identification and Environment Divisions a paragraph consists of a paragraph header, followed by one or more entries. In the Procedure Division a paragraph consists of a paragraph-name, followed by a period and space, and by zero,[1] one, or more entries.

The first sentence or entry in a paragraph can begin either on the same line as the paragraph header or paragraph-name, or in area B of the next nonblank line

---

[1] The fact that a paragraph can consist of no entries is a new feature of 74 COBOL.

that is not a comment line. Successive entries begin in either area B of the line containing the previous entry or in area B of the next nonblank line that is not a comment line.

A paragraph ends immediately before the next paragraph-name, section-name or division header or at the end of the Procedure Division. If the paragraph is in the declaratives part of the Procedure Division, it ends immediately before the next paragraph-name or section-name, or at the words END DECLARA-TIVES.

If an entry in a paragraph requires more than one line, it can be continued.

See area B, comment line, continuation of lines, division header, paragraph header, paragraph-name, section.

paragraph header

A paragraph header is a reserved word followed by a period and space that starts in area A and that indicates the beginning of a paragraph in the Identification and Environment Divisions.

Identification Division Paragraph Headers

PROGRAM-ID.

AUTHOR.

INSTALLATION.

DATE-WRITTEN.

DATE-COMPILED.

SECURITY.

Environment Division Paragraph Headers

SOURCE-COMPUTER.

OBJECT-COMPUTER.

SPECIAL-NAMES.

FILE-CONTROL.

I-O-CONTROL.

See Area A.

paragraph-name

A paragraph-name is a user-defined word that identifies a paragraph in the Procedure Division. A paragraph-name can consist entirely of numeric characters. A paragraph-name must begin in area A and be followed by a period and space. The first entry in the paragraph can begin in area B of this line or in area B of a subsequent line that is not a comment line.

Two paragraph-names are considered equal if and only if they contain the same number of characters in the same positions. For example, as paragraph-names, 007 and 7 are not equal.

See Area A, Area B, comment line, paragraph, user-defined word.

parentheses

Parentheses are used in subscripts, indices, arithmetic expressions, and conditions. Parentheses must always be in balanced pairs of left and right parentheses.

See arithmetic expression, condition, indexed data-name, subscript.

parity

Parity refers to control data that is associated with, but is not part of, information data. The value of this control data is determined by the configuration of the information data. Usually 'parity' is synonymous with 'parity bit,' and it refers to a single bit that is associated with a byte of data.

If a parity bit possesses the property that when the number of '1' bits in the associated byte is odd, the parity bit is a '1,' and when the number of '1' bits in the byte is even, the parity bit is a '0,' the parity is termed 'even parity'; that is, the value of the parity bit is such that the total number of '1' bits in the aggregate of the data bits and parity bit is always even. Similarly, if the value of the parity bit is chosen so as to always give an odd number of '1' bits, the parity is termed 'odd parity.'

PERFORM

The PERFORM verb transfers control to and executes one or more procedures; control is then returned to the PERFORM. The basic statement is

PERFORM procedure-name-1 THROUGH procedure-name-2

Procedure-name-1 and procedure-name-2 must each name a section or paragraph in the Procedure Division. The only relationship that need hold between these names is that the program logic must allow some path between them. In particular, GO TO and PERFORM statements can occur between procedure-name-1 and procedure-name-2. If there are two or more logical paths to the return point, procedure-name-2 may have to be a paragraph consisting only of the EXIT statement.

When the PERFORM is executed, control is transferred to the first statement in procedure-name-1.[1] This transfer occurs only once for each execution of the PERFORM statement. Control returns to the first statement following the PERFORM, as defined in the table. However, if control passes to any of these procedures by means other than a PERFORM, control passes from the last

---

[1] If action of the PERFORM is contingent upon a condition, as is the case in a format 2, 3 or 4 PERFORM, a transfer of control may not take place.

statement in the paragraph or section to the next sequential statement, as if no PERFORM accessed these procedures.

If procedure-name-1 is	And procedure-name-2 is	Control returns after execution of
A paragraph-name	not specified	the last statement in procedure-name-1
A section-name	not specified	the last statement in the last paragraph of procedure-name-1
Either a paragraph-name or a section-name	a paragraph-name	the last statement in procedure-name-2
	a section-name	the last statement in the last paragraph of procedure-name-2

The Range of the Perform

The *range* of the PERFORM is defined as consisting of all the statements from the first statement executed through the last statement, inclusively, as defined in the preceding table. Barring any anomalous conditions, such as an abort, unless the program logic indicates the contrary, the range of the PERFORM will be executed in its entirety an integral number of times.

Segmentation Considerations

A PERFORM in a nonindependent segment must have its range wholly contained either in one or more nonindependent segments or in a single independent segment, but not in both. A PERFORM in an independent segment can have its range wholly contained either in one or more nonindependent segments or in the same independent segment as the PERFORM. (N.B. 68 COBOL had restrictions on the range of PERFORMs involving fixed overlayable segments.)

Nested Perform Statements

If a PERFORM is contained within the range of another PERFORM, they are said to be *nested*. In this case, certain formalities must be observed with respect to their ranges. First, one PERFORM must be wholly included in or wholly excluded from the range of the other. Furthermore, they cannot have a common exit. The reason for this restriction is that the PERFORM statement uses a return mechanism at the end of its range. If this return mechanism is encountered by a

PERFORM that is different from the one that inserted it, the results are undefined.

Declarative Sections

If both procedure-names are specified, either both must be in the same Declarative section or neither can be in a Declarative section.

Examples of Ranges of Perform

For simplicity, 'Pn' is used as an abbreviation for 'PERFORM range n.' Since the details of the return mechanism are dependent upon the implementor, these examples are only to give a conceptual description of the processes.

Examples: The following are examples of *valid* nesting of PERFORMs:

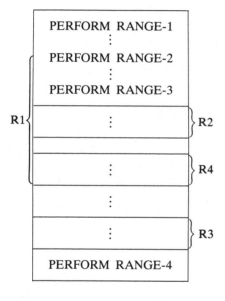

P1 establishes a return mechanism inside range 1. P2, which is within range 1, establishes a return mechanism inside range 2. Once P2 has finished, its return mechanism is removed so that when control reaches the end of range 2 under the influence of P1, execution continues as normal. P3, since it has a range outside of range 1, should present no conceptual difficulties. P4 establishes a return mechanism that would coincide with that set up by P1. However, since P1 is not active at the same time as P4, there is no confusion as to which PERFORM is in control.

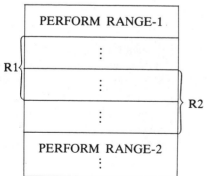

P1 establishes a return mechanism inside range 2. Range 2 is not executed until P1 is finished so there is no confusion as to which PERFORM is in control.

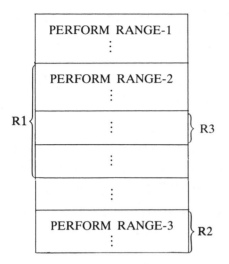

P1 establishes a return mechanism inside range 1. Within range 1, P2 establishes a return mechanism and executes range 2. P3 establishes a return mechanism within range 1, just after range 3. When P3 is finished, its return mechanism is removed so that when the point just after range 3 is encountered under control of P1, there is no confusion.

Examples: The following are examples of *invalid* nesting of PERFORMs:

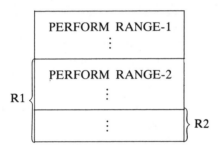

P1 will establish a return mechanism inside range 1. While P1 is still active, P2 also tries to establish a return mechanism at the same place inside range 1. Thus when the end of range 2 is reached, it is unclear as to which PERFORM is in control. Consequently, an error results.

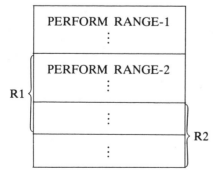

P1 establishes a return mechanism at the end of range 1, which is in the middle of range 2. Then, while P1 is still active, P2 sets up a return mechanism at the end of range 2. While range 2 is being executed, the return established by P1 is encountered, and the results are undefined.

Format 1:

$$\underline{\text{PERFORM}}\ \text{procedure-name-1}\left[\left\{\begin{array}{l}\underline{\text{THROUGH}}\\\underline{\text{THRU}}\end{array}\right\}\text{procedure-name-2}\right]$$

A format 1 PERFORM executes the range only once. Control then returns to the statement following the PERFORM.

Examples: Assume the following procedures, and that TEMP has a value of 1:

```
PAR-1.
    ADD 1 TO TEMP.
PAR-2.
    ADD 1 TO TEMP.
PAR-3.
    ADD 1 TO TEMP.
```

1. PERFORM PAR-1
   After execution, TEMP has a value of 1.
2. PERFORM PAR-1 THRU PAR-3
   After execution, TEMP has a value of 3.

Format 2:

$$\underline{\text{PERFORM}}\ \text{procedure-name-1}\left[\left\{\begin{array}{l}\underline{\text{THROUGH}}\\\underline{\text{THRU}}\end{array}\right\}\text{procedure-name-2}\right]\left\{\begin{array}{l}\text{identifier-1}\\\text{integer-1}\end{array}\right\}\underline{\text{TIMES}}$$

A format 2 PERFORM causes the range to be executed the number of times indicated by integer-1 or by the initial value of identifier-1. Control is passed to the range only once; therefore a procedure in an independent segment will be made available in its initial state only once for each execution of the PERFORM. This is a new feature of 74 COBOL. If either of these items is less than one, control immediately passes to the statement following the PERFORM without the range having been performed. Once execution of the PERFORM has begun, changing the value of identifier-1 does not alter the number of times the range is executed. When the range has been executed the requisite number of times, control returns to the statement following the PERFORM. Identifier-1 must be a numeric integer.

Examples: Assume as initial values for each example, TEMP = 0 and ID-1 = 2.

```
PAR-1.
    ADD 1 TO TEMP.
PAR-2.
    ADD 1 TO TEMP.
PAR-3.
    ADD 1 TO TEMP.
```

1. PERFORM PAR-1 ID-1 TIMES
   After execution, TEMP has a value of 2.

2. PERFORM PAR-1 TO PAR-3 ID-1 TIMES
   After execution, TEMP has a value of 6.

3. PERFORM PAR-1 TO PAR-3 TEMP TIMES
   After execution, TEMP has a value of 0 since the range was *not* performed.

   Format 3:

   $$\underline{\text{PERFORM}} \text{ procedure-name-1} \left[\left\{ \begin{array}{l} \underline{\text{THROUGH}} \\ \underline{\text{THRU}} \end{array} \right\} \text{procedure-name-2} \right] \underline{\text{UNTIL}} \text{ condition-1}$$

   In a format 3 PERFORM, condition-1, which can be any conditional expression, is first tested. If condition-1 is true, no transfer of control takes place, the range is not performed, and control immediately passes to the next statement after the PERFORM. If condition-1 is false, the range is executed and condition-1 is tested again. This cycle of testing and execution continues until condition-1 is true, at which time control returns to the statement following the PERFORM. Obviously, if condition-1 never becomes true, the program will be in an infinite loop. During execution of the PERFORM, any changes to variables referenced in condition-1 will be reflected in subsequent evaluations of the truth value of condition-1.

   This form of the PERFORM is implemented only in level 2 of the Nucleus.

   Examples: Assume in each example that the initial value of TEMP is 0:

```
                    PAR-1•
                        ADD 2 TO TEMP•
                    PAR-2•
                        ADD 1 TO TEMP•
                    PAR-3•
                        ADD 1 TO TEMP•
```

1. PERFORM PAR-1 UNTIL TEMP = 6
   PAR-1 is executed three times; after execution, TEMP = 6.

2. PERFORM PAR-1 UNTIL TEMP = 5
   This is an infinite loop since TEMP will take on the values 2, 4, 6, . . . and so will never be equal to 5. Better: UNTIL TEMP > 5.

3. PERFORM PAR-1 TO PAR-3 UNTIL TEMP > 13
   The range is executed four times; the final value of TEMP is 16 since TEMP is evaluated only before executing the entire range.

4. PERFORM PAR-1 TO PAR-3 UNTIL TEMP NOT < 0
   The range is not executed since TEMP is in fact not less than 0 at the outset.

Format 4:

$$\underline{PERFORM}\ procedure\text{-}name\text{-}1\left[\left\{\begin{array}{l}\underline{THROUGH}\\ \underline{THRU}\end{array}\right\}procedure\text{-}name\text{-}2\right]$$

$$\underline{VARYING}\left\{\begin{array}{l}identifier\text{-}1\\ index\text{-}name\text{-}1\end{array}\right\}\underline{FROM}\left\{\begin{array}{l}identifier\text{-}2\\ index\text{-}name\text{-}2\\ literal\text{-}1\end{array}\right\}\underline{BY}\left\{\begin{array}{l}identifier\text{-}3\\ literal\text{-}2\end{array}\right\}\underline{UNTIL}\ condition\text{-}1$$

$$\left[\underline{AFTER}\left\{\begin{array}{l}identifier\text{-}4\\ index\text{-}name\text{-}3\end{array}\right\}\underline{FROM}\left\{\begin{array}{l}identifier\text{-}5\\ index\text{-}name\text{-}4\\ literal\text{-}3\end{array}\right\}\underline{BY}\left\{\begin{array}{l}identifier\text{-}6\\ literal\text{-}4\end{array}\right\}\underline{UNTIL}\ condition\text{-}2\right]$$

$$\left[\underline{AFTER}\left\{\begin{array}{l}identifier\text{-}7\\ index\text{-}name\text{-}5\end{array}\right\}\underline{FROM}\left\{\begin{array}{l}identifier\text{-}8\\ index\text{-}name\text{-}6\\ literal\text{-}5\end{array}\right\}\underline{BY}\left\{\begin{array}{l}identifier\text{-}9\\ literal\text{-}6\end{array}\right\}\underline{UNTIL}\ condition\text{-}3\right]$$

This form of the PERFORM is implemented only in level 2 of the Nucleus.

A format 4 PERFORM can specify one, two, or three conditions. However, only condition-1 being true causes the PERFORM to terminate. The only effect of condition-2 and condition-3 is on how many times the range is executed. The three conditions can be any conditional expression. If the procedures executed by the PERFORM cause a change in any of the variables in these conditions the new values are used in evaluating the conditions.

The *initial value* of an identifier or index-name is the current value of the item specified in the associated FROM phrase. The *augment* of an identifier or index-name is the current value of the item specified in the associated BY phrase. The augment can be positive or negative. In other words, the value used as the augment and initial value may not be the same during execution of a PERFORM. If an index-name appears in a VARYING or AFTER phrase, it is initialized and augmented according to the rules of the SET statement. If an index-name appears in a FROM phrase, any identifier in the associated VARYING or AFTER phrase is initialized according to the rules of the SET statement.

Changing the FROM variable during execution might affect the number of times the range is executed if more than one AFTER phrase is specified. This is new to 74 COBOL.

In the following exposition, any reference to an identifier also applies to the corresponding index-name if there is one. Presumably the identifiers that are varied are also used in the associated condition, although this need not be so. If not, however, it is the programmer's responsibility to ensure that control will ultimately leave the PERFORM.

One Item Varied

Identifier-1 is set to its initial value. Then condition-1 is tested. If it is true, control returns to the statement following the PERFORM and the range is not executed. If condition-1 is false, the range is executed once. Then the augment is added to identifier-1, and condition-1 is tested again. This sequence of testing, executing the range, and augmenting identifier-1 continues until condition-1 is true, at which time control leaves the PERFORM.

Two Items Varied

Identifier-1 and identifier-4 are set to their initial values. Then condition-1 is tested. If it is true, control passes to the statement following the PERFORM. If condition-1 is false, condition-2 is tested; if it is false, the range is executed once, identifier-4 is augmented, and condition-2 is tested again. This sequence of testing condition-2, executing the range, and augmenting identifier-4 is continued until condition-2 is true. When this happens, identifier-4 is again set to its initial value, identifier-1 is augmented, and condition-1 is tested with subsequent action proceeding as described above. Condition-1 is the only criterion for leaving the PERFORM.

At the end of the PERFORM, identifier-4 has the current value of identifier-5. The value of identifier-1 exceeds the last-used value by one augment value unless condition-1 was true when the PERFORM was entered. In this case, identifier-1 contains the current value of identifier-2.

Three Items Varied

Identifier-1, identifier-4, and identifier-7 are all set to their respective initial values. Condition-1 is tested; if it is true, control passes to the statement following the PERFORM; if false, then condition-2 is tested. If condition-2 is false, condition-3 is tested. If condition-3 is false, the range is executed, identifier-7 is augmented, and condition-3 is tested again. This sequence of testing condition-3, executing the range, and augmenting identifier-7 is continued until condition-3 becomes true. At this time, identifier-7 is set to its initial value, identifier-4 is augmented, and condition-2 is tested again. This sequence continues until condition-2 is true at which time identifier-4 is set to its initial value, identifier-1 is augmented, and condition-1 is tested again.

At the end of the PERFORM, identifier-4 has the current value of identifier-5; identifier-7 has the current value of identifier-8. The value of identifier-1 exceeds the last-used value by one augment value unless condition-1 was true when the PERFORM was entered. In this case, identifier-1 contains the current value of identifier-2.

All Formats:

	Numeric	Non-zero
Literal-2, -4, -6	X	X
Literal-1, -3, -5	X	
Identifier-1, -2, -4, -5, -7, -8	X	
Identifier-3, -6, -9	X	X

N.B. The fact that identifiers in a format 4 PERFORM need not be integers is new to 74 COBOL.

Format 5: The following apply if an index-name is in a VARYING or AFTER clause. They are in addition to the constraints listed under 'all formats.'

	Integer data item	Positive integer	Non-zero integer
Identifier-3, -6, -9	X		
Identifier-2, -5, -8	X	X	
Literal-2, -4, -6			X
Literal-1, -3, -5		X	

The following apply in addition to the constraints listed under 'all formats' if an index-name is in a FROM phrase.

	Integer data item	Integer
Identifier-1, -3, -4, -6, -7, -9	X	
Literal-2, -4, -6		X

Logic Flow Charts

The following are logic flow charts for a format 4 PERFORM with one, two, or three items varied.

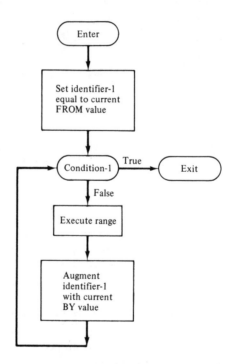

One item varied.

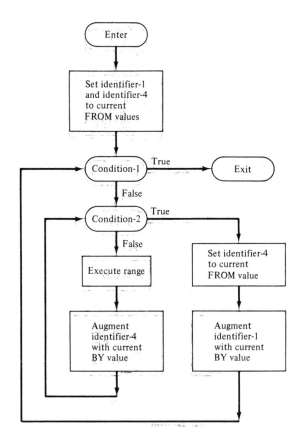

Two items varied.

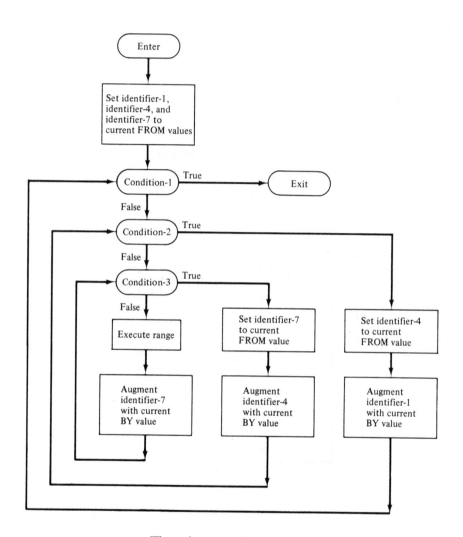

Three items varied.

General Flow Chart for the PERFORM

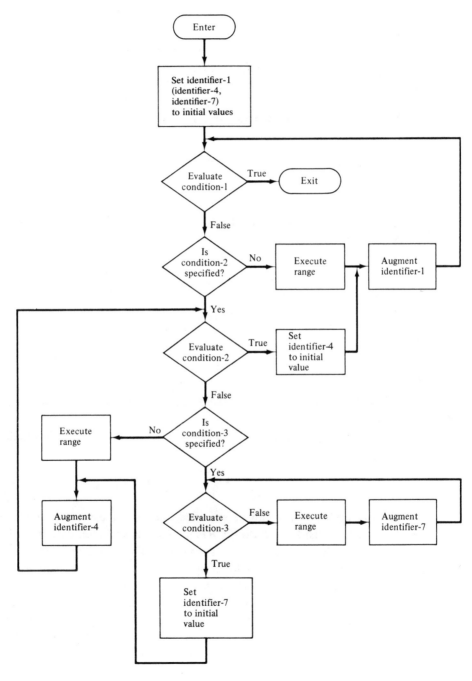

period

The period is a punctuation character that is used as a terminator for sentences, paragraph and section names, and entries in the ENVIRONMENT and DATA DIVISIONS.

It is indicated in the formats by a bullet (•) and its use is mandatory where shown. Furthermore, it can appear in the formats only where shown.

The period can also appear in a PICTURE clause. In this case, it represents the decimal point unless the DECIMAL-POINT IS COMMA clause is used in the SPECIAL-NAMES paragraph.

See punctuation character, separator.

PF

An abbreviation for PAGE FOOTING.
See TYPE.

PH

An abbreviation for PAGE HEADING.
See TYPE.

phrase

A phrase is a set of one or more consecutive character-strings that forms a portion of a clause or statement.

See character-string, clause, statement.

physical record

See block.

PICTURE, PIC

The PICTURE clause describes an elementary data item and specifies any editing to be performed on the item. Each elementary item in the program has to be described by a PICTURE since there is no default case for an item's makeup.

Format:

$$\left\{ \begin{array}{l} \underline{PICTURE} \\ \underline{PIC} \end{array} \right\} \text{IS character-string}$$

The PICTURE clause can be specified only for elementary items, and each elementary item must have a PICTURE unless it is an index data item, in which case use of the PICTURE clause is forbidden. The character-string consists of combinations of characters as defined by the rules that follow. Any punctuation character that appears in the character-string takes on a special meaning, as described below, and is not considered a punctuation character proper.

There are two ways to write symbols in a PICTURE clause. One can explicitly write one character for each occurrence, viz., XXXXXXXXXX, or one can write one instance of the character, followed by a number in parentheses that indicates the number of times the character is to appear, viz., X(10), which is equivalent to the string of ten X's above. This latter feature is important since there is a limit of 30 characters[1] in the character-string; however, the string can represent an item greater than 30 characters long. For example, the string X(40) contains only 5 characters but represents an item 40 characters long.

There are three classes of PICTURE characters: data-type, operational, and editing.

Data-Type Characters

A data-type character indicates whether the data is alphabetic, numeric, or alphanumeric. The three characters are A, 9, and X, respectively.

A   Represents a character position that can be occupied only by the characters A through Z or space. Each 'A' in a PICTURE is counted in determining the size of an item.

9   Represents a character position that can be occupied only by the characters 0 through 9. Each '9' in a PICTURE is counted in determining the size of an item.

X   Represents a character position that can be occupied by any member of the computer's character set. Each 'X' in a PICTURE is counted in determining the size of an item.

Operational Characters

Operational characters are used with numeric items to indicate the sign, the position of the decimal point, and if the number is scaled by the implicit presence of an exponent, the assumed scaling factor.

S   Indicates the presence, but neither the representation nor necessarily the position, of the operational sign. Only one S can appear in a PICTURE. If used, S must be the left-most character in the string. To represent a field of four digits that is signed, S9999 would be used. The S is not included in the size of an item unless the SEPARATE CHARACTER phrase is included in the SIGN IS clause, in which case it is included in determining the item's size.

V   Represents an assumed decimal point within a data item. Only one V can appear in a string. The string 9999V99 represents a six-digit item with an assumed decimal point between the second and third least significant digits. If the contents of the field were 48250, the value used in computations would be 482.50. If the string were 9V99999, the same contents would represent the value 4.8250. The V is not counted in determining the size of an item. When the assumed decimal point is to the immediate right of the right-most 9 in the string, V is redundant. That is, 999V and 999 are equivalent.

---

[1] This is a new feature of 74 COBOL. Previously, the character-string was limited to 30 symbols in which a symbol could have been two characters.

P   Represents an assumed decimal point located outside of a data item. One P is used for each assumed position that precedes or follows the decimal point. P's are not counted in determining the size of an item. However, the positions implied by P's are counted in determining the maximum number of digits in a numeric or numeric-edited item, viz., 18. P's can appear only at the left or right of a string, and all P's in a string must be adjacent. In a string containing P's the use of V is redundant. A P cannot occur in a string that contains the insertion character, 'period,' or if the decimal-point and comma functions are interchanged, in a string that contains the insertion character, 'comma.' For example, a string of PPPPP99999 would mean that 5 implied zeroes are to the left of the number. If the contents were 12345, the value represented would be .0000012345. If the string were 99999PPPPP, the same contents would represent 1234500000. If the PICTURE of a data item that is being converted from one form of internal representation to another contains a P, each position so described is considered to contain a zero, and the size of the item is considered to include the positions so described.

Editing Characters

Editing characters indicate that editing operations are to be performed on the item. These characters can be divided into four nonmutually-exclusive classes.

1. Simple suppression—those that cause suppression of data to occur.
2. Suppression with replacement—those that cause suppression of data to occur and also substitute characters for the suppressed data.
3. Floating replacement—those that cause a single instance of a character to be inserted.
4. Fixed insertion—those that cause a character to be inserted in the item.

    In COBOL, 'editing' refers to the replacing and/or suppressing of data in a numeric-edited or alphanumeric-edited item in storage. Thus, whenever data is transferred to these items, the editing takes place. If one of these items is output, e.g., to the printer, it is the edited version that is printed, not the unedited one.

Simple Suppression

Simple suppression is accomplished by the character Z. Z is used to suppress leading zeroes. A leading zero is one that comes to the left of the most significant digit in the integer portion of a number and thus contributes nothing to the value of the number. Any leading zero occurring in an item whose PICTURE contains a Z in the corresponding character position is replaced by a blank. Each Z is included in the size of the item. If Z's appear only to the left of the decimal point, suppression within the string of Z's terminates at the first non-zero digit to the left of the decimal point or at the decimal point itself, whichever comes first. If a Z appears to the right of the decimal point, then *all* numeric positions in the item must be represented by Z's. In this case, if the value of the item is zero, the entire item, including the decimal point, is suppressed. If the item has a value other than zero, suppression occurs as if only the positions to the left of the decimal point contained Z's. In a PICTURE, all Z's must be contiguous except for insertion characters. Any fixed insertion characters in a suppressed string will also be suppressed.

The following chart shows the edited results for different combinations of data and PICTURE strings.

Data	PICTURE						
	9999	Z999	ZZ99	ZZZ9	ZZZZ	ZZ.ZZ	Z,ZZZ
0	0000	000	00	0			
1.01	0001	001	01	1	1	1.01	1
217.	0217	217	217	217	217	17.00	217
1010.20	1010	1010	1010	1010	1010	10.20	1,010
.01	0000	000	00	0		.01	

Suppression with Replacement

Suppression with replacement is accomplished by the character *. Many applications require that leading zeroes be suppressed without leaving the vacated positions blank. The asterisk accomplishes this by suppressing leading zeroes and placing an asterisk in any position that was suppressed. Thus any insertion character that was located in the string being suppressed is replaced by an asterisk. Asterisks are counted in determining the size of an item. If an asterisk appears to the right of a decimal point, then all numeric positions in the number must contain asterisks. All asterisks in a character-string must be contiguous, except for fixed insertion characters. An asterisk cannot appear in a picture with Z, A, X, or S. If the BLANK WHEN ZERO clause is applied to an item, the asterisk cannot be used as a suppression symbol.

The following chart shows the edited results for different combinations of data and PICTURE strings.

	PICTURE				
Data	*999	**99	***9	**.**	*,***.**
0	*000	**00	***0	**.**	*****.**[1]
13	*013	**13	**13	13.00	13.00
123	*123	*123	*123	23.00	**123.00
2010	2010	2010	2010	10.00	2,010.00
1010.2	1010	1010	1010	10.20	1,010.20
.01	*000	**00	***0	**.01	*****.01[1]

[1] Note that the comma position was filled by an asterisk, but the decimal point was not.

Floating Replacement

Three characters can serve as floating replacement symbols: the currency symbol, the plus sign, and the minus sign.

Currency Symbol. The currency symbol is represented either by the currency sign or by the single character specified in the CURRENCY SIGN IS clause in the SPECIAL-NAMES paragraph. It is both a replacement character and a fixed insertion character.

When more than one currency sign appears in the character-string, it is a replacement symbol. (For the rest of this discussion we will use the character '$' for the currency sign.) The $'s are counted in determining the size of the item. Except for + and −, no character that is counted in the size of the item can appear to the left of the $.

When the $ is used as a replacement symbol, only the last position suppressed is filled with the symbol. This is called *floating* the character. I.e., one instance of the character is allowed to float as far to the right in the item as it can until it abuts the first nonsuppressed character.

In the PICTURE string the left-most occurrence of the $ represents the left-most limit of the floating symbol in the edited data. This position *cannot* be filled by a digit; the second $ from the left represents the left-most limit of the numeric data that can be placed in the item. The right-most $ represents the right-most limit of the floating symbol in the item.

The following chart shows the edited results for different combinations of data and PICTURE strings.

	PICTURE			
Data	$$99	$$$$9	$$$$$.99	$$,$$$.$$
0	$00	$0	$.00	
.02	$00	$0	$.02	$.02
12	$12	$12	$12.00	$12.00
12.34	$12	$12	$12.34	$12.34
1234	$234	$1234	$1234.00	$1,234.00
1234.56	$234	$1234	$1234.56	$1,234.56

Sign Control Symbols. The plus and minus signs can be used as either fixed or replacement characters. If a minus sign is used, it is inserted whenever the number is negative; if the number is positive or zero, no sign appears.

If the plus sign is used, it is inserted if the number is positive or unsigned, and a minus sign is inserted if the number is negative.

The plus and minus signs are mutually exclusive in a given PICTURE string and are counted in the size of an item. The limits of data in an item with a plus or minus sign in its PICTURE are the same as described for the $.

The following chart shows the edited results for different combinations of data and PICTURE strings.

Data	PICTURE							
	+9999	−9999	++++9	----9	+++++	-----	+++++.++	--,---.--
0	+0000	0000	+0	0				
12	+0012	0012	+12	12	+12	12	+12.00	12.00
−12	−0012	−0012	−12	−12	−12	−12	−12.00	−12.00
123	+0123	0123	+123	123	+123	123	+123.00	123.00
−123	−0123	−0123	−123	−123	−123	−123	−123.00	−123.00
1234	+1234	1234	+1234	1234	+1234	1234	+1234.00	1,234.00
−1234	−1234	−1234	−1234	−1234	−1234	−1234	−1234.00	−1,234.00
12.34	+0012	0012	+12	12	+12	12	+12.34	12.34
−12.34	−0012	−0012	−12	−12	−12	−12	−12.34	−12.34

Fixed Insertion

The characters used for fixed insertion[1] are the comma, 0, /, B, CR, and DB, and if only one instance appears in a PICTURE string, the characters $, +, and −. Whenever any fixed insertion character appears in a string the appropriate character is inserted in the corresponding position. However, any fixed insertion character is suppressed if it is embedded in a string being suppressed or if it is to the immediate right of a character that is suppressed.

All simple insertion characters are counted in the size of an item. CR and DB count as *two* characters in determining the size. The comma cannot be the last symbol in the character-string.

The following chart shows the edited results for different combinations of data and PICTURE strings.

---

[1] In 68 COBOL, the stroke (/) was not an editing character.

	PICTURE					
Data	99B99	9,999	99/909	**,***	9B9/900	99,99
0	00 00	0,000	00/000	******	0 0/000	00,00
12	00 12	0,012	00/102	****12	0 1/200	00,12
123	01 23	0,123	01/203	***123	1 2/300	01,23
1234	12 34	1,234	12/304	*1,234	2 3/400	12,34

CR and DB, which represent credit and debit, respectively, must be the right-most characters of a picture string. They are inserted in the same position as they occupy in the string whenever the item is negative. Neither CR nor DB can be used in a string that contains A, X, −, +, or S. CR and DB are mutually exclusive in a given string, and only one instance of either can appear.

The following chart shows the edited results for different combinations of data and PICTURE strings.

	PICTURE					
Data	$9999CR	$9999DB	$$,$$$CR	$$,$$$DB	ZZZZCR	ZZZZDB
0	$0000	$0000				
12	$0012	$0012	$12	$12	12	12
−12	$0012CR	$0012DB	$12CR	$12DB	12CR	12DB
1234	$1234	$1234	$1,234	$1,234	1234	1234
−1234	$1234CR	$1234DB	$1,234CR	$1,234DB	1234CR	1234DB

Observe that there is no way, using a single PICTURE string, to cause one of 'CR, DB' to be inserted if the item is positive and the other to be inserted if it is negative.

The characters +, −, and $ are simple insertion characters when only one appears in a string. The characters + and − are mutually exclusive in a given string. When used as fixed insertion symbols, they must be at the right-most or left-most character of the string. When the $ is used as a fixed insertion symbol, the only character that can appear to the left of it is a single plus or minus sign. However, any character that is not counted in the size of the item can be to the left of +, −, and $.

The following chart shows the edited results for different combinations of data and PICTURE strings.

Data	PICTURE							
	+999	−999	999+	999−	+$999	−$999	$****CR	$ZZZZCR
0	+000	000	000+	000	+$000	$000	$****	
12	+012	012	012+	012	+$012	$012	$**12	$ 12
−12	−012	−012	012−	012−	−$012	−$012	$**12CR	$ 12CR
123	+123	123	123+	123	+$123	$123	$*123	$ 123
−123	−123	−123	123−	123−	−$123	−$123	$*123CR	$ 123CR

The following table summarizes the results of using CR, DB, + , and − as fixed insertion characters

Symbol	Positive or Zero	Negative
+	+	−
−	space	−
CR	2 spaces	CR
DB	2 spaces	DB

The Explicit Decimal Point

One editing character remains—the period. It does not fit conveniently in any of the above categories since it is not only a fixed insertion character, but also denotes the actual decimal point of the item. Only one period can appear in a string, and if it is used, A, X, P, and V cannot be used. Since it is a fixed insertion character, a period will be inserted in the item unless some character to its right has been suppressed. (This usually happens only when the entire item is suppressed.) The period specifies the decimal point for alignment, just as V or P does. The period is counted in the size of the item and cannot be the last symbol in the string.

If the DECIMAL-POINT IS COMMA phrase appears in the SPECIAL-NAMES paragraph, the function and rules governing the decimal point and comma are interchanged for all PICTURE strings. Uses of the period in PICTURE strings have been shown in the previous charts.

Categories of Data

The PICTURE clause is used to define the five categories of data: alphabetic, alphanumeric, alphanumeric-edited, numeric, and numeric-edited. The rules for defining each category follow.

Alphabetic

An alphabetic data item's PICTURE clause can contain only the symbols A and B. An alphabetic data item can contain only a letter of the alphabet or a space.

Alphanumeric

An alphanumeric data item's PICTURE clause can contain only certain combinations of A, X, and 9. The data item is treated as if the PICTURE were all X's. The combinations are (1) at least one A and one 9, or (2) any number of X's and optional A's and 9's. An alphanumeric data item can contain any character in the computer's character set. If the contents of an alphanumeric data item are all alphabetic characters or all digits, the item is still alphanumeric; the contents cannot change the category of the data item.

Alphanumeric-Edited

An alphanumeric-edited data item's PICTURE clause can contain certain combinations of A, X, 9, B, 0, and /. At least one X or one A must appear in the clause. If an X appears, at least one item from the group B, 0, / must also appear. If an A appears, at least one item from the group 0, / must appear. (If the clause contains all A's or all 9's, the item is not alphanumeric-edited.) An alphanumeric-edited data item can contain any character in the computer's character set.

Numeric

A numeric data item's PICTURE clause can contain only the symbols 9, P, S, and V. The number of digit positions cannot exceed 18. A numeric data item can contain only the characters 0 through 9, and if signed, a plus sign, minus sign, or other representation of an operational sign.

Numeric-Edited

A numeric-edited data item's PICTURE clause can contain only the symbols: B, /, P, V, Z, 0, 9, *, +, −, CR, DB, comma, period, and the currency symbol, herein represented as $. The number of digits that can be represented is at most 18. The string must contain at least one character from the set {0, B, /, Z, *, −, +, CR, DB, $, period, comma}. A numeric-edited data item can contain only the digits 0 through 9.

Editing by Category

The following table summarizes the types of editing that can be performed on a data item.

Category of Data Item	Editing
Alphabetic	Fixed insertion of B
Alphanumeric	None
Alphanumeric-edited	Fixed insertion of 0, B, /
Numeric	None
Numeric-edited	All as described in the rules

Size of a Data Item

The size of a data item is determined by adding the number of symbols that represent character positions. In the case of an integer in parentheses following a symbol, the integer defines the number to be used in the count.

The items that are counted in determining the size of a data item are

A 9 X Z * $ + − B 0 / , .	which all count as 1
CR and DB	which count as 2
S	which counts as 1 if and only if the SEPARATE CHARACTER phrase is used in the data description.

The items not counted in determining the size of the item are V, P, and if the SEPARATE CHARACTER phrase is not used in the data description, S. To avoid truncation, the size of a receiving item's picture must be at least equal to the sum of the number of characters in the sending item plus the number of nonfloating characters being inserted plus 1 if a floating character is used.

The chart overleaf defines the precedence rules for all characters in the PICTURE clause.

See alignment rules, currency sign.

PLUS
See LINE NUMBER, NEXT GROUP, report group description.

POINTER
See STRING, UNSTRING.

POSITION
See MULTIPLE FILE, I-O-CONTROL.

POSITIVE
See sign condition.

Presentation Rules

The Presentation Rules govern the presenting of report groups. Each type of report group has a set of rules governing it. The term 'body group' is used to denote Detail, Control Heading, and Control Footing groups, as these three types are governed by a common set of rules.

Column groups — **Nonfloating Insertion Symbols:** B, 0, /, ",", ".", $\{+/-\}^1$, $\{+/-\}^2$, $\{CR/DB\}$, cs · **Floating Insertion Symbols:** $\{Z/*\}^1$, $\{Z/*\}^2$, $\{+/-\}^1$, $\{+/-\}^2$, cs^1, cs^2 · **Other Symbols:** 9, A/X, S, V, P^1, P^2

Second Symbol \ First Symbol	B	0	/	,	.	$\{+/-\}^1$	$\{+/-\}^2$	$\{CR/DB\}$	cs	$\{Z/*\}^1$	$\{Z/*\}^2$	$\{+/-\}^1$	$\{+/-\}^2$	cs^1	cs^2	9	A/X	S	V	P^1	P^2
B	x	x	x	x	x	x			x	x	x	x	x	x	x	x	x		x		x
0	x	x	x	x	x	x			x	x	x	x	x	x	x	x	x		x		x
/	x	x	x	x	x	x			x	x	x	x	x	x	x	x	x		x		x
,	x	x	x	x	x	x			x	x	x	x	x	x	x	x			x		x
.	x	x	x	x		x			x	x			x			x					
$\{+/-\}^1$																					
$\{+/-\}^2$	x	x	x	x	x				x	x	x			x	x	x			x	x	x
$\{CR/DB\}$	x	x	x	x	x				x	x	x			x	x	x			x	x	x
cs						x															
$\{Z/*\}^1$	x	x	x	x		x			x	x											
$\{Z/*\}^2$	x	x	x	x	x	x			x	x	x								x		x
$\{+/-\}^1$	x	x	x	x					x			x									
$\{+/-\}^2$	x	x	x	x	x				x			x	x						x		x
cs^1	x	x	x	x		x								x							
cs^2	x	x	x	x	x	x								x	x				x		x
9	x	x	x	x	x	x			x	x		x		x		x	x	x	x		x
A/X	x	x	x													x	x				
S																					
V	x	x	x	x		x			x	x		x		x		x		x		x	
P^1	x	x	x	x		x			x	x		x		x		x		x		x	
P^2					x				x									x	x		x

[1] When character is to left of decimal point.

[2] When character is to right of decimal point.

The rules that apply in a given case vary depending on which type of LINE NUMBER and NEXT GROUP clauses are specified in the report group description, and whether the report group description contains a PAGE clause or not.

The headings of the various tables are defined as follows:

Upper Limit—the first line on which the group can be presented.

Lower Limit—the last line on which the group can be presented.

First Print Line Position—the line on which the first print line of the given report will be presented.

Next Group—the restrictions on the NEXT GROUP clause.

Final Line-Counter Value—the value that will be in special register, LINE-COUNTER, after the group has been presented.

The *saved next group integer* is a data item that is accessible only by the Report Writer Control System (RWCS). When an absolute NEXT GROUP clause specifies a vertical positioning value that cannot be accommodated on the current page, the RWCS stores that value in the saved next group integer.

After page advancing processing has been done, the next body group is presented using the stored value.

The values referred to in the tables are those of the PAGE clause:

PAGE LIMITS ARE integer-1 LINES, HEADING integer-2, FIRST DETAIL integer-3, LAST DETAIL integer-4, FOOTING integer-5

Note: In the charts the following abbreviations are used:

RH	Report Heading
PH	Page Heading
PF	Page Footing
RF	Report Footing
L-C	LINE-COUNTER

REPORT HEADING Presentation Rules

	LINE NUMBER and PAGE Clauses Specified			
	No NEXT GROUP Clause	Absolute NEXT GROUP Clause	Relative NEXT GROUP Clause	Next Page
Upper Limit is	integer-2			
Lower Limit is	integer-3 minus 1			integer-1
First Print Line Position is	If the first print line description contains an absolute LINE NUMBER clause, the first line is presented on the line designated by the integer in that clause. If the first print line description contains a relative LINE NUMBER clause, the first print line is presented on integer-2 minus 1 plus the integer specified in the LINE NUMBER clause.			
Next Group		The Next Group integer must be greater than the line number on which the final line of the group is presented and less than integer-3.	The sum of the Next Group integer and the line number of the final print line must be less than integer-3.	The Report Heading is presented by itself on the first page of the report.
Final LINE-COUNTER Value is	The line number on which the final print line was presented.	The value of the Next Group integer.	The sum of the Next Group integer and the line number on which the final print line was presented.	The line number on which the final print line was presented.

REPORT HEADING Presentation Rules

	LINE NUMBER, but No PAGE Clause Specified		No LINE NUMBER Clause Specified
	Relative NEXT GROUP clause	No NEXT GROUP clause	
First Print Line Position is	integer of LINE NUMBER clause		Group is not presented.
Final LINE-COUNTER Value is	Sum of the Next Group integer and the line number on which the final print line was presented.	The line number on which the final print line was presented.	The setting of LINE-COUNTER is not affected.

PAGE HEADING Presentation Rules

	PAGE Clause Specified in Report Description Entry	No LINE NUMBER Clause
	LINE NUMBER Clause Specified	
Upper Limit is	If a RH group has been presented on the page, 1 greater than the final LINE-COUNTER setting for the RH group. If no RH group has been presented on the page, the value of integer-2.	
Lower Limit is	integer-3 minus 1	

First Print Line Position is	If the first print line has an absolute LINE NUMBER clause, the integer specified in the clause.
	  If not, and there has been an RH group presented on the page, the sum of LINE-COUNTER setting for the RH group and the integer of the LINE NUMBER clause.
	  If no RH group has been presented, integer-2 minus 1 plus the integer of the LINE NUMBER clause.
		The group is not presented.

Final LINE-COUNTER Value is	The line number on which the last print line of the group was presented.	LINE-COUNTER is unaffected.

Body Group Presentation Rules if PAGE Clause Specified

	LINE NUMBER Clause Specified			
	No NEXT GROUP Clause	Absolute NEXT GROUP Clause	Relative NEXT GROUP Clause	Next Page
Upper Limit is	integer-3			
Lower Limit is	For CH or DE integer-4, for CF integer-5.			
First Print Line Position is	If LINE-COUNTER is less than integer-3, on integer-3. If an absolute LINE NUMBER clause, on the integer specified in the LINE NUMBER clause. If a relative LINE NUMBER clause, then if LINE-COUNTER is not less than integer-3 and if no body group has been presented on the current page, the first print line is the one following the value in LINE-COUNTER. If a body group has been presented, the first print line is on the line designated by the sum of the value of LINE-COUNTER plus the integer in the first LINE NUMBER clause of the current group.			
Next Group		The integer of the Next Group clause must be not less than integer-3 and not greater than integer-5.		
Final LINE-COUNTER Value is	The line number on which the final print line was presented.	If a CF that is not for the highest control break detected, the final print line of the group is the final value of LINE-COUNTER.		
		Otherwise, if the Next Group integer is not less than the final print line, this integer. If the integer is less than the final print line, the value is integer-5. Also the integer goes to saved next group integer.	Otherwise, a trial sum is made by adding Next Group integer to the final line number of the group. If the sum is less than integer-5, the sum is the value of LINE-COUNTER. Otherwise, integer-5 is the value.	Otherwise, integer-5 is the value.

Body Group Presentation Rules if PAGE Clause Is Omitted

	Relative LINE NUMBER Clause without Next Page		Relative Line Number Clause with Next Page and without NEXT GROUP
	No NEXT GROUP	Relative NEXT GROUP	
First Print Line Position is	Sum of LINE-COUNTER and the integer of the first LINE NUMBER clause.		The group is not presented.
Final LINE-COUNTER Value is	The line number on which the final print line of the group was presented.	If a CF group that is not associated with the highest level break, the number on which the final line was presented. Otherwise, the sum of the final line and the Next Group integer.	LINE-COUNTER is not affected.

A body group is also subjected to a set of rules to see if it will fit on the page. These rules are as follows:

• If the LINE NUMBER clause is absolute and does not specify Next Page

If the value of LINE-COUNTER is less than the integer in the first LINE NUMBER clause, the body group is presented on the current page. Otherwise, a page advance is executed and, if specified, a Page Heading group is processed. Then, if the saved next group integer was set when the final body group was presented on the preceding page, this integer is first moved to LINE-COUNTER and then reset to zero, and this rule is reapplied. If the saved next group integer was not set, the body group is presented on the current page.

• If the LINE NUMBER clause is relative

If a body group has been presented on the current page, a trial sum is computed by adding LINE-COUNTER to the integers of all the report group's LINE NUMBER clauses. If this trial sum is not greater than the lower limit of the group, the group is presented on the current page. If the trial sum exceeds this lower limit, a page advance is executed and, if specified, a Page Heading group is processed. This rule is then reapplied.

• If the LINE NUMBER clause is absolute and specifies Next Page

If a body group has been presented on the current page, a page advance is executed and, if specified, a Page Heading group is processed. This rule is then reapplied.

If no body group has been presented on the current page, then if the saved next group integer was not set, the body group is presented on the current page. If the saved next group integer was set, it is first moved to LINE-COUNTER and then set to zero. Then, if the value in LINE-COUNTER is less than the integer of the first LINE NUMBER clause, the body group is presented on the current page.

Otherwise, a page advance is executed and, if specified, a Page Heading group is processed. Then the body group is presented on that page.

PAGE FOOTING Presentation Rules

	LINE NUMBER Clause is Specified			
	No NEXT GROUP Clause	Absolute NEXT GROUP Clause	Relative NEXT GROUP Clause	No LINE NUMBER Clause
Upper Limit is	integer-5 plus 1			
Lower Limit is	integer-1			
First Print Line Position is	The line specified by the integer in the LINE NUMBER clause.			Group is not presented
Next Group		Next Group integer must be greater than the line number on which the final print line is presented, and not greater than integer-1.	The sum of the Next Group integer and the line number on which the final print line is presented must be less than or equal to integer-1.	
Final LINE-COUNTER Value is	The line number on which the final print line was presented.	The value of the Next Group integer.	Sum of the Next Group integer and the line number on which the final print line was presented.	LINE-COUNTER is not affected.

REPORT FOOTING Presentation Rules

| | A PAGE clause is specified | | | | No PAGE clause | |
	No LINE NUMBER Clause	Absolute LINE NUMBER Clause	Relative LINE NUMBER Clause	NEXT PAGE	Relative LINE NUMBER Clause	No LINE NUMBER Clause
Upper Limit is		If a PF has been presented, 1 greater than the final LINE-COUNTER setting of the PF group. If not, integer-5 plus 1.		integer-2		
Lower Limit is		integer-1				
First Print Line Position	Group is not presented.	The integer of the LINE NUMBER clause.	If a PF has been presented, the final LINE-COUNTER setting plus the integer of the first LINE NUMBER clause. Else, the sum of that integer and integer-5.	On the next page by itself as specified by the integer of its LINE NUMBER clause.	The sum of LINE-COUNTER and the integer of the first LINE NUMBER clause.	Group is not presented.
Final LINE-COUNTER Value is	LINE-COUNTER is not affected.	The line number on which the final print line was presented.				LINE-COUNTER is not affected.

primary index

The primary index of a table is the index designated by the first index-name in the INDEXED BY clause for that table.

See index-name, OCCURS, table.

primary index-name

The primary index-name is the first index-name specified in the INDEXED BY clause of an item.

See index-name, OCCURS.

prime record key

The prime record key is a data item associated with an indexed file. Its contents uniquely identify a record within the file. It is defined in the RECORD KEY clause of the FILE-CONTROL entry for the file. There can be only one prime record key for a file. All the values of the prime record key item in the file's records must be unique.

See indexed file.

printable group

A printable group is a report group that contains at least one print line.

See report group description.

printable item

A printable item is a data item, specified in an elementary report entry, that contains a COLUMN NUMBER clause, a PICTURE clause, and either a SUM, SOURCE, or VALUE clause.

See report group description.

PRINTING

See SUPPRESS.

PROCEDURE

See MERGE, SORT, USE.

procedure

A procedure is a paragraph or group of logically connected paragraphs, or a section or group of logically connected sections, within the Procedure Division. The end of the Procedure Division, which is also the physical end of the program, is that point after which no further procedures appear.

In a given program, if any paragraph belongs to a section, then all paragraphs must belong to some section.

Example:

```
PROCEDURE DIVISION.
PAR-1.
A-1 SECTION.
PAR-2.
PAR-3.
B-1 SECTION.
        ⋮
```

This structure is illegal since paragraph PAR-1 does not belong to a section.

```
PROCEDURE DIVISION.
Z-1 SECTION.
PAR-1.
A-1 SECTION.
PAR-2.
PAR-3.
B-1 SECTION.
        ⋮
```

This structure is legal since all paragraphs belong to a section.
See paragraph, section.

procedure branching statement

A procedure branching statement is a statement that causes an explicit or implicit transfer of control. The procedure branching statements are ALTER, CALL, EXIT, GO TO, PERFORM.

Note that although ALTER is included in this group it does not, in and of itself, cause a transfer of control.

See transfer of control.

PROCEDURE DIVISION

The PROCEDURE DIVISION contains all the procedures associated with a program. It is the last division in the source program. The PROCEDURE DIVISION begins with the procedure division header.

Format 1:

```
PROCEDURE DIVISION [USING {identifier-1}...].
[DECLARATIVES.
{section-name SECTION [segment-number]. declarative sentence
[paragraph-name. [sentence]...]...}...
END DECLARATIVES.]
{section-name SECTION [segment-number].
[paragraph-name. [sentence]...]...}...
```

Format 2:

<u>PROCEDURE DIVISION</u> [<u>USING</u> {identifier-1}...].
{paragraph-name. [sentence]...}...

The USING phrase in the procedure division header is new to 74 COBOL. *See* division header, source program.

procedure-name

Procedure-name is a collective term for a paragraph-name and section-name. A procedure-name names a paragraph or section in the PROCEDURE DIVISION. Procedure-names are equal if and only if they are composed of the same number of characters in the same positions. Thus, 007 and 7 are not considered the same procedure-name. A paragraph-name can be qualified by a section-name.

See paragraph-name, qualification, section-name.

PROCEDURES

See USE FOR DEBUGGING.

PROCEED

See ALTER.

PROCESSING MODE

PROCESSING MODE was formerly a clause in the FILE-CONTROL paragraph.

PROGRAM

See EXIT, OBJECT-COMPUTER.

PROGRAM-ID

The PROGRAM-ID paragraph is the only mandatory entry in the IDENTIFICATION DIVISION. It contains the name of the program being compiled.

Format:

<u>PROGRAM-ID</u>. program-name.

The program-name must conform to the rules for a user-defined word. It must be unique among all other program-names at the installation. If more than one operating system is in use at an installation, the program-name must be unique among all other program-names in the system.

See program-name, user-defined word.

program-name

A program-name is a user-defined word that appears in the PROGRAM-ID paragraph of the IDENTIFICATION DIVISION. The program-name identifies the source program, the object program, and all printed listings pertaining to them.

Within a given installation's library, or within its operating system, if more that one library is used at an installation, all program-names must be unique.

See object program, source program, user-defined word.

program segments

See fixed overlayable segment, fixed permanent segment, independent segment, segmentation.

pseudo-text

Pseudo-text is a sequence of character-strings and/or separators that is bounded by pseudo-text delimiters viz. (==). The pseudo-text delimiters are not part of the pseudo-text.

See character-string, pseudo-text delimiter, separator.

pseudo-text delimiter

The pseudo-text delimiter is two contiguous equal signs (==); it is used to delimit pseudo-text in a COPY statement.

The pseudo-text delimiter is a new feature in 74 COBOL.

punctuation character

A punctuation character is a character that is used to improve readability and/or to delimit an item. The punctuation characters are the comma, period, semicolon, stroke, the left and the right parenthesis, quotation character, and blank (space).

The period is always mandatory wherever it appears in a format and can be used only where shown in the formats. The comma and semicolon are always optional but must be followed by a space.

Parentheses are used to delimit subscripts or indices, to alter the normal evaluation of arithmetic expressions, and to group operands together in conditions.

Any punctuation character appearing in a PICTURE string or literal conforms to the rules for the PICTURE string or literal and is not considered a punctuation character.

See arithmetic expression, condition, identifier, indexing, literal, logical operations, operand, separator, subscript.

Q

qualification

Every user-specified name that defines an element in a source program must be capable of being uniquely referred to. This can be done by ensuring that (1) no other name has the identical spelling or (2) that the name exists within a hierarchy of names so that references to it can be made unique by mentioning one or more of the higher levels of the hierarchy. These higher level names are called *qualifiers*.

Qualification is the process of making a reference to an item unique by the use of qualifiers. It is the same process one uses when saying 'Frederick II of Prussia' to distinguish that ruler from Frederick II of Sicily.

Format 1:

$$\begin{Bmatrix} \text{data-name-1} \\ \text{condition-name} \end{Bmatrix} \left[\begin{Bmatrix} \underline{\text{IN}} \\ \underline{\text{OF}} \end{Bmatrix} \text{data-name-2} \right] \cdots \left[\begin{Bmatrix} \underline{\text{IN}} \\ \underline{\text{OF}} \end{Bmatrix} \begin{Bmatrix} \text{file-name} \\ \text{cd-name} \end{Bmatrix} \right]$$

Format 2:

$$\text{paragraph-name} \left[\begin{Bmatrix} \underline{\text{IN}} \\ \underline{\text{OF}} \end{Bmatrix} \text{section-name} \right]$$

Format 3:

$$\text{text-name} \left[\begin{Bmatrix} \underline{\text{IN}} \\ \underline{\text{OF}} \end{Bmatrix} \text{library-name} \right]$$

A data-name, condition-name, paragraph-name, text-name, or LINAGE-COUNTER can be qualified as shown in the formats. (OF and IN are considered equivalent.)

When a data-name is qualified, names associated with a level-indicator are the most inclusive. This inclusiveness decreases as one moves from level-number 01 down to level-number 48. A procedure can be qualified only by a section-name. A text-name can be qualified only by a library-name.

Qualification is required when any of the following conditions exist:

- Two different sections each contain a paragraph with the same name.
- Within two data structures, elementary or group items have the same name.
- A text-name appears in more than one library.
- Two identical data-names appear in the same group item.
- More than one File Description entry contains a LINAGE clause.

(At least five levels of qualification must be provided.)

Rules for Qualification

- Each qualifier must be of a successively higher level and within the same hierarchy as the name it qualifies.

- The same name must not appear at two *different* levels within a hierarchy. A name can appear twice *at the same level* as long as it can be made unique by qualification. Note that this means that a complete set of qualifiers for one name cannot be the same as a partial set for another.

- The most significant name in a hierarchy must be unique and cannot itself be qualified.

- If a data-name or condition-name is assigned to more than one data-item, it must be qualified each time it is referred to, except in the REDEFINES clause where qualification is expressly forbidden.

- A name can be qualified even if it is already unique.

- Any combination of qualifiers that ensures uniqueness is valid, even if all possible qualifiers are not mentioned.

- A data-name cannot be subscripted when used as a qualifier.

- If more than one library is available during compilation, the text-name must be qualified each time it is referenced.

- Paragraph-names must not be duplicated within a section. When a paragraph-name is qualified by a section-name, the word SECTION is not included in the qualification. A paragraph-name need not be qualified if referred to from within the section in which it resides.

- Qualification may also be used on subscripted or indexed data-names and conditional variables. The name of a conditional variable can be used as a qualifier for any of its condition-names.

- No name can be both a data-name and a procedure-name, regardless of the available qualifiers.

  Examples: Consider the structure:

```
FD   FILE-A ... •
01   ABC
     02   DEF
          03   GHI
          03   JKL
     02   PDQ
          03   GHI
          03   XYZ
```

Here, FILE-A is the most significant name in the hierarchy and thus cannot be qualified. Therefore no other record in FILE-A can be named ABC. Note that

GHI appears at the same level, level 03, twice. It would be incorrect to have, for example, an 04 level item with the name GHI.

One could qualify DEF even though it is not necessary. To refer simply to GHI would create an ambiguity; the proper way of referencing is to refer to GHI OF DEF or GHI OF PDQ, whichever one is intended. Observe that GHI OF ABC does not resolve the ambiguity; however, GHI OF DEF OF ABC is acceptable.

Consider the structure:

```
02  ABC
    88  DEF
02  PDQ
    88  DEF
```

One would qualify a reference to DEF as DEF IN PDQ or DEF OF ABC.

See conditional-name, conditional variable, data-name, elementary item, file description, group item, indexing, level-indicator, level-number, library-name, paragraph, paragraph-name, procedure, section, section-name, source program, subscripting, text-name.

qualified data-name

A qualified data-name consists of a data-name followed by either OF or IN and a data-name qualifier.

See data-name, qualifier, qualification.

qualifier

A qualifier is a name that is used in conjunction with another name to make the latter name a unique reference to a data item, paragraph, or library.

1. A data-name is used to qualify another data-name at a lower level in the same hierarchy.

2. A section-name is used to qualify a paragraph-name that is part of that section.

3. A library-name is used to qualify a text-name that is part of that library.

See data-name, library-name, paragraph-name, qualification, section-name, text-name.

qualifier connective

The qualifier connectives are the words OF and IN.

See qualification.

QUEUE

See communication description entry.

queue

A queue is a logical collection of messages awaiting transmission or processing.

See communication description entry, messages, RECEIVE, SEND.

queue-name

A queue-name is a symbolic name that indicates to the message control system the logical path by which all of or a portion of a completed message can be accessed in a queue.

See message, message control system.

quotation character

The quotation character (″) is used to delimit nonnumeric literals. Quotation characters so used can appear only in balanced pairs, except when the literal is continued. An opening quotation character must be immediately preceded by a space or a left parenthesis, and a closing quotation character must be immediately followed by a space, comma, semicolon, period, or right parenthesis, depending on context.

To represent the quotation character inside a nonnumeric literal, two consecutive quotation characters are used.

Example: To write GRADE ″A″ EGGS as a nonnumeric literal, one would write:

> ″GRADE ″″A″″ EGGS″

Here, the first and last quotation characters are used to delimit the nonnumeric literal and each pair of quotation characters inside of the literal represent one instance of the quotation character. This ability to represent a quotation character in a literal is a new feature of 74 COBOL.

See continuation of lines, nonnumeric literal.

QUOTE, (QUOTES)

QUOTE is a figurative constant that has the value of one or more instances of the quotation character (″). QUOTE cannot be used instead of the quotation character to delimit a nonnumeric literal.

See figurative constant, nonnumeric literal.

R

radix point

The radix point is the actual or assumed symbol that separates the fractional part of a number from the integer part. 'Radix point' is a general term; in decimal arithmetic the radix point is called the decimal point. The symbol for the radix point need not be a period; it could be a comma, for example.

See SPECIAL-NAMES.

RANDOM

See ACCESS MODE, FILE-CONTROL, SELECT.

random access

Random access is an access mode that uses a program-specified value of a key data item to identify the logical record that is accessed in a relative or indexed file.

See ACCESS MODE, indexed i-o, key, relative i-o.

random i-o

The random i-o module has been dropped. Its functions are replaced by indexed i-o.

See indexed i-o.

range of inspection

See INSPECT.

RD

RD is a level indicator, indicating 'report description.'

See CODE, CONTROL, DATA DIVISION, PAGE, REPORT SECTION.

READ

The READ verb moves a record from a file into that file's record area and makes it available for processing. If the file is in the sequential access mode, the next logical record is made available. If the file is being accessed in the random mode, a specified record is made available.

Format 1:

> READ file-name [NEXT] RECORD [INTO identifier-1]
>
> [;AT END imperative-statement-1]

The file being read must be open in the input or i-o mode and must not be a SORT or MERGE file. The READ statement makes a record available to the object program in the file's record area and, optionally, in another specified area. The value of the FILE STATUS item associated with the file is updated.

A format 1 READ must be used for all files in sequential access mode and, with the NEXT[1] option, for files in the dynamic access mode that are being accessed sequentially. When the READ is executed, the record indicated by the current-record pointer is made available. The current-record pointer must have been previously positioned by a START, OPEN, or a previous READ. If positioned by a START or OPEN, the record must still be accessible through the path indicated by the current-record pointer. If a record is no longer accessible, which can be the case if it was deleted or, in the case of indexed files, if there was a change in an alternate record key, the current-record pointer is updated to point to the next existing record in the file, and that record is made available. If the current-record pointer was positioned by a previously successful READ, it is updated to point to the next record in the file, and that record is made available. For sequential files the next record is the record that was written or rewritten after the current one. For relative files the next record is the one that is in the first succeeding record position that contains a record. For indexed files the next record is the one with the smallest key item value that is greater than the current key of reference.

If the current-record pointer is null or undefined when the READ is executed, the READ will be unsuccessful.

If the file has relative organization, a format 1 READ updates the contents of the relative key data item if such an item is defined in the FILE-CONTROL entry for the file. The value placed in this data item is the relative record number of the record that has just been made available.

If the file has indexed organization, a format 1 READ updates the key of reference to contain the value of the key of the record that has just been made available. If an alternate record key is the key of reference, records with the same duplicate value are made available in the same order that they were created by WRITE or REWRITE statements.

If the file has sequential organization and the end of a reel or unit is reached during execution of the READ but the logical end of the file has not been reached, the following operations are executed:

1. The standard ending reel/unit label processing.

2. A reel/unit swap.

3. The standard beginning reel/unit label processing.

4. The first data record of the new reel/unit is made available.

The details of these operations are implementor-defined.

If level 2 of sequential i-o is implemented and if a file that has been designated as OPTIONAL is not present when the file is opened, the first READ executed causes the AT END condition.

---

[1] This is a new feature of 74 COBOL, and is implemented in level 2 of the relative i-o and indexed i-o modules. NEXT cannot be used with sequential files.

The Into Phrase

When the INTO phrase is specified, the record that is made available in the file's record area is also moved to identifier-1, according to the rules for a format 1 MOVE statement. This phrase cannot be used if the file contains records of different sizes; furthermore, the area designated by identifier-1 cannot be the same as the file's record area.

The sequence of operations when INTO is specified are:

1. The record is put into the file's record area.
2. Any subscripting or indexing associated with identifier-1 is evaluated. (This may be important if any items in the record are used in evaluating the subscripts or indices, since it is the values just read in that will be used.)
3. The data is moved to identifier-1.

The data is then available in both the file's record area and identifier-1. This implicit move does not take place if the READ was unsuccessful.

The At End Condition

The AT END condition occurs if no 'next' logical record exists in the file. When the AT END condition is recognized, the READ is unsuccessful and the following actions take place in the order specified:

1. The value '10' is placed into the FILE STATUS data item, if one is specified for this file, to indicate the AT END condition.
2. If the AT END phrase is specified, control passes to imperative-statement-1. Any format 1 USE procedure that is specified is *not* executed. (This is a new feature of 74 COBOL. Previously, the AT END phrase was mandatory.)
3. If the AT END phrase is not specified, in which case a format 1 USE procedure must have been specified, the USE procedure is executed.

When the AT END condition is recognized, in the case of sequential files a READ must not be executed for the file without first executing a successful CLOSE followed by a successful OPEN. In the case of relative or indexed files, a READ must not be executed for the file without first executing one of the following steps:

- A successful CLOSE followed by a successful OPEN.
- A successful START.
- A successful format 2 READ.

(Note that all of the above affect the current-record pointer.)

Unsuccessful Read

If a READ is unsuccessful, the contents of the associated record area and the position of the current-record pointer are undefined. If the INTO phrase was specified, no implicit move takes place, and the contents of identifier-1 are unaffected.

File Status

If a FILE STATUS item is specified, it is updated with the following codes:

Status Key 1	Status Key 2	Meaning
0	0	Successful completion
1	0	At end
3	0	Permanent error
3	4	Boundary violation
9	–	Implementor-defined

Format 2:

>   READ file-name RECORD [INTO identifier-1][KEY IS data-name-1]
>
>   [; INVALID KEY imperative-statement-1]

A format 2 READ is used with files from which records are being retrieved randomly. As such, it can be used only with relative or indexed files.

The file being read must be open in the input or i-o mode and must not be a SORT or a MERGE file. The READ statement makes a record available to the object program in the file's record area and, optionally, in another specified area. The value of the FILE STATUS item associated with the file is updated.

For a file with relative organization, a format 2 READ sets the current-record pointer to the record whose relative record number is contained in the data item named in the RELATIVE KEY clause for the file. The record is then made available. If the record does not exist in the file, the Invalid Key condition exists, and the READ is unsuccessful.

For a file with indexed organization, a format 2 READ sets the current-record pointer to the first record in the file with a key data item value which matches the value in the key of reference. This record is then made available. If no such record exists in the file, the Invalid Key condition exists, and the READ is unsuccessful.

The Into Phrase

The same considerations as described under a format 1 READ hold for a format 2 READ when the INTO phrase is specified.

The Key Is Phrase

The KEY IS phrase can be specified only for indexed files. It is implemented in level 2 of the indexed i-o module. If this phrase is not specified, the prime record key is established as the key of reference for the retrieval. If this phrase is specified, data-name-1 is established as the key of reference for this retrieval. Data-name-1 must be a data item that has been specified as a record key for the file. It can be qualified.

If the file is in the dynamic access mode, then this key of reference is also used for retrievals by subsequent format 1 READ statements which are given for the file until a different key of reference is established for the file.

Invalid Key Condition

When the Invalid Key condition exists, the READ is unsuccessful and the file is not affected. The following actions are taken.

1. The value 2 is put into status key 1; the value 1, 2, 3, or 4 is put into status key 2, depending on the cause of the condition.
2. If the INVALID KEY phrase is specified, control is transferred to imperative-statement-1. Any format 1 USE procedure is *not* executed.
3. If the INVALID KEY phrase is not specified, then a format 1 USE procedure must have been specified. This USE procedure is executed. (This is a new feature of 74 COBOL; previously INVALID KEY was mandatory.)

Unsuccessful Read

If a READ is unsuccessful, the contents of the associated record area and the position of the current-record pointer are undefined. For indexed files the key of reference is also undefined. If the INTO phrase was specified, no implicit move takes place and the contents of identifier-1 are unaffected.

File Status

If a FILE STATUS item is specified, it is updated with the following codes:

Status Key 1	Status Key 2	Meaning
0	0	Successful completion
1	0	At end
2	1	Sequence error
2	2	Duplicate key
2	3	No record found
2	4	Boundary violation
3	0	Permanent error
9	–	Implementor-defined

See current-record pointer, dynamic access, FILE STATUS, indexed i-o, indexing, input mode, Invalid Key condition, I-O mode, key, key of reference, prime record key, random access, RECORD KEY, relative i-o, relative record number, sequential access, sequential i-o, subscripting.

RECEIVE

The RECEIVE verb makes a message, a message segment, or part of a message segment available to the program. This verb is new to 74 COBOL.

Format:

RECEIVE cd-name $\left\{ \begin{array}{l} \text{MESSAGE} \\ \text{SEGMENT} \end{array} \right\}$ INTO identifier-1 [NO DATA imperative-statement-1]

Cd-name must reference an input communication description. Information about the data made available, taken from a queue maintained by the message control system (MCS), is also made available. The queue structure containing the message is defined by the SYMBOLIC QUEUE and the three SYMBOLIC SUB-QUEUE fields in the cd-name's description.

The message, segment, or portion is transferred to identifier-1, left-aligned, without space filling. The data items in the cd-area are updated.

If, as a result of the action of a RECEIVE, data is made available in identifier-1, control then passes to the next executable sentence. When no data is available, if the NO DATA phrase is specified, the RECEIVE operation is terminated with the data items in cd-area updated, and imperative-statement-1 is executed. If the NO DATA phrase is not specified, execution of the object program is suspended until data is available to identifier-1. If one or more queues are unknown to the MCS, control passes to the next executable statement, whether or not the NO DATA phrase is specified. In this case the STATUS KEY, data-name-10 in the description of cd-name, is set to 20.

A single execution of a RECEIVE statement never returns more than a single message or segment to identifier-1. However, the MCS does not pass any part of a message to identifier-1 unless the entire message is available in the input queue, even if the SEGMENT phrase is specified.

Once a RECEIVE has returned a portion of a message, only subsequent RECEIVE statements in the same run unit can cause the remaining portion of the message to be returned. If a STOP RUN statement is executed, the disposition of the remaining portion of a message partially obtained in that run unit is implementor-defined.

The Message Phrase

When the MESSAGE phrase is specified, end-of-segment indicators (ESI) are ignored. If the message size is less than or equal to identifier-1, the message is stored in identifier-1, left-aligned, with no space filling. If the message size is greater than identifier-1, the message fills identifier-1 from left to right until it is full. The remainder of the message will be transferred to identifier-1 by subsequent RECEIVE statements that refer to the same queue and subqueue. This process can be continued until the entire message has been transferred. If only level 1 of the Communication Module is implemented, the disposition of the remainder of the message is undefined.

The Segment Phrase

When the SEGMENT phrase is specified and the message segment is less than or equal to identifier-1, it is stored in identifier-1, left-aligned, with no space filling. If the message is too large for identifier-1, action proceeds as described under MESSAGE except that only the rest of the message *segment* is transferred by subsequent RECEIVE statements, even though the entire message is available to the MCS.

If the text to be received contains an end-of-message or end-of-group indicator, the existence of an end-of-segment indicator is implied, and the text is treated as a message segment.

See cd-name, communication description entry, message, message control system (MCS), message segment, next executable sentence, queue, run unit.

receiving item

The receiving item is the item that receives data as a result of the execution of a statement. For example in the statement, MOVE 100 TO NET-PAY, NET-PAY is the receiving item.

If the receiving item is too small to receive the data, a size error, overflow, or truncation can occur.

See ADD, COMPUTE, DIVIDE, MULTIPLY, overflow condition, ROUNDED, sending item, SUBTRACT, truncation.

RECORD

See DELETE, READ, RETURN.

record

1. A record is a member of a file that is treated as an entity by input and output operations. A file can contain data records and, optionally, label records. There can be more than one type of data record in a file; all data records of a given type in a file must have identical structures as defined by a record description. The structure of label records is specified by the implementor.

2. A record is a group of related information uniquely identifiable and treated as a unit. A record can be specified in the FILE SECTION or in the WORKING-STORAGE section where it is the most inclusive data item and has a level-number of 01.

Example:

```
01  A
    02  B
        03  C
        03  D
    02  E
    02  F
```

Here, 'A' is the name of the record; it is subdivided into B, E, and F. B is further subdivided into C and D. A and B are group items; the others are elementary items.

See elementary item, group item, logical record, record description.

record area

A record area is a storage area that is allocated to contain a record for processing. The size of the storage area depends on the file's record description entry.

See record description.

RECORD CONTAINS

RECORD CONTAINS is a file description clause that specifies the size of data records.

Format:

RECORD CONTAINS [integer-1 TO] integer-2 CHARACTERS

Since the size of each record is completely defined within the record description entry, this clause is never required.

The size of the record is specified in terms of the number of character positions required to store the logical record, regardless of the types of characters used to represent the items in the record. The size is determined by adding together the number of characters in each fixed-length elementary item in the record and the maximum number of characters in each variable-length item in the record. This sum may be different from the actual size of a record.

Integer-2 can be used alone only if all data records in the file have the same size, in which case it represents the exact number of characters in the record. If integer-1 and integer-2 are both shown, they refer to the number of characters in the smallest size record and the number of characters in the largest size record, respectively.

See elementary item, file description, OCCURS, SYNCHRONIZED, USAGE.

record description

A record description is an entry that describes all of the elementary and group items in a record and their relationships.

Format 1:

level-number $\begin{Bmatrix} \text{data-name-1} \\ \underline{\text{FILLER}} \end{Bmatrix}$ [$\underline{\text{REDEFINES}}$ data-name-2]

$$\left[\begin{Bmatrix} \underline{\text{PICTURE}} \\ \underline{\text{PIC}} \end{Bmatrix} \text{ IS character-string} \right] \left[[\underline{\text{USAGE}} \text{ IS}] \begin{Bmatrix} \underline{\text{COMPUTATIONAL}} \\ \underline{\text{COMP}} \\ \underline{\text{DISPLAY}} \\ \underline{\text{INDEX}} \end{Bmatrix} \right]$$

$$\left[[\underline{\text{SIGN}} \text{ IS}] \begin{Bmatrix} \underline{\text{LEADING}} \\ \underline{\text{TRAILING}} \end{Bmatrix} [\underline{\text{SEPARATE}}] \text{ CHARACTER} \right]$$

$$\left[\underline{\text{OCCURS}} \begin{Bmatrix} \text{integer-1 TIMES} \\ \text{integer-2 } \underline{\text{TO}} \text{ integer-1 TIMES } \underline{\text{DEPENDING}} \text{ ON data-name-3} \end{Bmatrix} \right]$$

$$\left[\begin{Bmatrix} \underline{\text{ASCENDING}} \\ \underline{\text{DESCENDING}} \end{Bmatrix} \text{ KEY IS \{data-name-4\}} \dots \right] \left[\underline{\text{INDEXED}} \text{ BY \{index-name-1\}} \dots \right]$$

$$\left[\begin{Bmatrix} \underline{\text{SYNCHRONIZED}} \\ \underline{\text{SYNC}} \end{Bmatrix} \left[\begin{matrix} \underline{\text{LEFT}} \\ \underline{\text{RIGHT}} \end{matrix} \right] \right] \left[\begin{Bmatrix} \underline{\text{JUSTIFIED}} \\ \underline{\text{JUST}} \end{Bmatrix} \text{ RIGHT} \right]$$

[$\underline{\text{BLANK}}$ WHEN $\underline{\text{ZERO}}$]

[$\underline{\text{VALUE}}$ IS literal-1]•

Entries with level-number 01 and 77 must begin in Area A, with the level-number followed by a space. The data-name and associated clauses must begin in Area B. Successive entries can be indented any number of spaces to the right of margin B without affecting the magnitude of the level-number.

The level-number can be from 01 to 49 or 77. If only level 1 of the Nucleus is implemented, level-numbers can range from 01 to 10 and 77. A data-name or FILLER must immediately follow the level-number. If the REDEFINES clause is used, it must immediately follow data-name-1. All other clauses may be written in any order. The PICTURE clause must be specified for all elementary items whose usage is not INDEX.

The SYNCHRONIZED, PICTURE, JUSTIFIED, and BLANK WHEN ZERO clauses can be applied only to elementary items.

Format 2:

66   data-name-1 $\underline{\text{RENAMES}}$ data-name-2 $\left[\begin{Bmatrix} \underline{\text{THROUGH}} \\ \underline{\text{THRU}} \end{Bmatrix} \text{ data-name-3} \right]$•

For information on this entry, see RENAMES.

Format 3:

$$88 \quad \text{condition-name} \left\{ \frac{\underline{\text{VALUE}} \text{ IS}}{\underline{\text{VALUES}} \text{ ARE}} \right\} \left\{ \text{literal-1} \left[\left\{ \frac{\underline{\text{THROUGH}}}{\underline{\text{THRU}}} \right\} \text{literal-2} \right] \right\} \dots \bullet$$

See Area A, Area B, data-name, elementary item, group item, level-number, margin.

RECORD KEY

The RECORD KEY clause specifies the prime record key and alternate record keys for a file. This clause appears in the FILE-CONTROL paragraph and is new to 74 COBOL.

Format:

<u>RECORD</u> KEY IS data-name-1

[<u>ALTERNATE</u> <u>RECORD</u> KEY IS data-name-2 [WITH <u>DUPLICATES</u>]] ...

The RECORD KEY clause can be specified only for indexed files, for which it is mandatory. Data-name-1 specifies the prime record key for the file. The prime record key provides an access path to records in the file. All values of the prime record key data item must be unique within the file.

If the ALTERNATE RECORD KEY clause is specified, data-name-2 specifies an alternate record key for the file. An alternate record key provides an alternate access path to records in an indexed file. The number of alternate record keys specified must be the same as when the file was created. (The alternate record key feature is new to 74 COBOL, and is implemented in level 2 of the indexed i-o module.)

If DUPLICATES is not specified, the values of the alternate record key data item must be unique within the file. If DUPLICATES is specified, these values need not be unique.

The data descriptions for data-name-1 and data-name-2, as well as their relative locations within a record, must be the same as were specified when the file was created. Both data items must be alphanumeric and be defined within a record description entry associated with the file whose file description contains the RECORD KEY clause. Neither data-name-1 nor data-name-2 can describe an item with a variable size. Both data-name-1 and data-name-2 can be qualified.

The left-most character position of data-name-2 cannot correspond to the left-most character position of data-name-1 or of any other alternate record key specified for this file.

See file description, indexed file, prime record key, record description, SELECT.

record key

A record key is either the prime record key or an alternate record key the contents of which identify a record within an indexed file.

See FILE-CONTROL, indexed i-o, prime record key, SELECT.

record-name

A record-name is a user-defined word that names a record. Record-names are found in file description clauses in the DATA RECORD entry wherein they are represented by 'data-name.'

A record-name must have an associated 01 level record description with the same name.

See file description, record description, user-defined word.

RECORDS

See BLOCK CONTAINS, file description, I-O-CONTROL, RERUN.

REDEFINES

The REDEFINES clause allows the same storage area to be described by different data description entries.

Format:

level-number   data-name-1 <u>REDEFINES</u> data-name-2

Note: The level-number and data-name-1 are not, strictly speaking, part of the REDEFINES clause. They are included to give an idea of the context of the REDEFINES clause.

The REDEFINES clause redefines a *storage area*, not the data-items that occupy this area. This clause must immediately follow data-name-1 and cannot be used in level 01 entries in either the FILE or the COMMUNICATION SECTION. The area redefined begins at data-name-2 and ends when a level-number numerically less than or equal to that of data-name-2 is encountered.

When a given character position in a record is defined by more than one data description entry, any of the associated data-names can be used to reference that character position. When the level-number of data-name-1 is anything but 01, data-name-1 must specify the same number of characters as data-name-2. Even if data-name-2 is not unique, it must not be qualified; no ambiguity exists due to the required placement of the REDEFINES clause.

Multiple redefinitions of the same character position are permitted,[1] but they must all use the data-name of the entry that originally defined the area, i.e., if B redefines A, C cannot redefine B. However, C can redefine A. The entries specifying the new descriptions must follow the entries specifying the area being redefined without any intervening entries that define new character positions.

---

[1] This is a new feature of 74 COBOL.

Furthermore, no entry with a level-number numerically lower than the level-number of data-name-2 can occur between the data description entries of data-name-1 and data-name-2.

Entries giving the new description of the storage area must not contain any VALUE clauses, except in level 88 (condition-name) entries.

The data description for data-name-2 cannot contain an OCCURS or REDEFINES clause. If only level 1 of the Nucleus is implemented, data-name-2 cannot be subordinate to an entry that has a REDEFINES or OCCURS clause. If level 2 of the Nucleus is implemented, data-name-2 *can* be subordinate to an entry with a REDEFINES or OCCURS clause.[1] In the latter case the reference to data-name-2 in the REDEFINES clause cannot be subscripted or indexed. The level-numbers of data-name-1 and data-name-2 must be identical but cannot be level 66 or 88.[1] Neither the original definition nor the redefinition can include an item of variable size.

Examples:

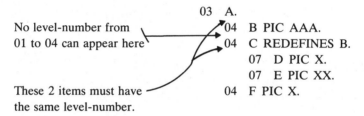

A reference to D will access the same character as the first character of B. A reference to E will access the same characters as the last two characters of B.

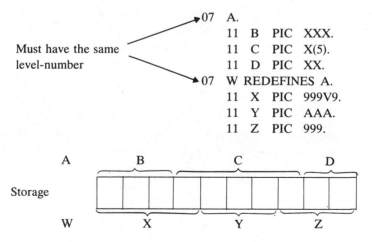

---

[1] This is a new feature of 74 COBOL.

```
01  FILLER.
    02  PC-TABLE.
        03  FILLER PIC V999 VALUE .100.
        03  FILLER PIC V999 VALUE .200.
        03  FILLER PIC V999 VALUE .300.
        03  FILLER PIC V999 VALUE .400.
        03  FILLER PIC V999 VALUE .500.
    02  PERCENT-TABLE REDEFINES PC-TABLE.
        03  PER-CENT PIC V999 OCCURS 5 TIMES.
```

Referencing PER-CENT (1) will access the item whose value is .100; referencing PER-CENT (3) will access the item whose value is .300; etc.

Implicit Redefinition

Multiple level 01 entries subordinate to any given level-indicator represent implicit redefinitions of the same storage area. That is, in

```
FD  ...
    01  GROSS-PAY.
        02  ...
            .
            .
            .
    01  NET-PAY.
        07  ...
```

both GROSS-PAY and NET-PAY refer to the same storage area.

REDEFINES differs from RENAMES in that the former lets the data description of the area be changed, while the latter allows alternative groupings of the elementary items without changing the data description.

See data description entry, indexing, subscripting, variable size item.

REEL

See CLOSE, I-O-CONTROL, RERUN.

reference format

Reference format refers to the character positions in a line for an input or output medium. The reference format for a line is

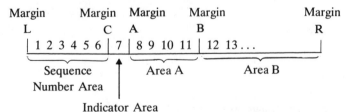

See Area A, Area B, indicator area, margin, sequence number area.

REFERENCES

See USE FOR DEBUGGING.

relation

In COBOL a relation is a logical association between two arithmetic expressions. A relation can be either true or false.

See arithmetic expression, relational operator, relation condition.

relation character

The relation characters are > (greater than), < (less than), and = (equal to). Relation characters are used in relation conditions to define a relationship between two operands. Relation operators must be preceded and followed by at least one space.

See operand, relation, relation condition.

relation condition

A relation condition determines whether or not a specified relationship exists between two operands.

Format:

$$
\left\{ \begin{array}{l} \text{identifier-1} \\ \text{literal-1} \\ \text{arithmetic-expression-1} \end{array} \right\}
\left\{ \begin{array}{l} \text{IS [NOT]} \left\{ \begin{array}{l} \underline{\text{GREATER}}\ \text{THAN} \\ > \end{array} \right\} \\ \text{IS [NOT]} \left\{ \begin{array}{l} \underline{\text{LESS}}\ \text{THAN} \\ < \end{array} \right\} \\ \text{IS [NOT]} \left\{ \begin{array}{l} \underline{\text{EQUAL}}\ \text{TO} \\ = \end{array} \right\} \end{array} \right\}
\left\{ \begin{array}{l} \text{identifier-2} \\ \text{literal-2} \\ \text{arithmetic-expression} \end{array} \right\}
$$

In a relation condition, the operand to the left of the operator is called the 'subject' of the condition; the operand to the right of the operator is called the 'object' of the condition. Each operand can be an identifier, a literal, or an arithmetic expression. However, both operands cannot be literals, and there must be at least one variable in the relation condition. This is a new restriction of 74 COBOL. Each relational operator must be preceded and followed by a space. Depending upon the class of the operands, there are two types of comparison: numeric and nonnumeric.

Numeric Comparison

If both operands have a class of numeric, regardless of their USAGE, a numeric comparison takes place. I.e., the algebraic values of the operands are compared, the number of digits in an operand being inconsequential. Unsigned operands are considered positive in this comparison, and zero is considered a unique value regardless of its sign.

Nonnumeric Comparison

If either operand does not have a class of numeric, or if either operand is a group item, a nonnumeric comparison takes place. In a nonnumeric comparison, both operands must have the same USAGE, and if any operand is numeric, it must be an integer data item or an integer literal. A numeric item is treated as if it were moved to either an elementary or group alphanumeric data item of the same size as the nonnumeric operand, depending upon whether the nonnumeric operand is an elementary or group item.

In a nonnumeric comparison there are two cases depending upon the sizes of the data items involved.

If the operands are of equal size, comparison proceeds by comparing corresponding characters starting at the high-order ends of the operands and proceeding until either the low-order ends are reached or a pair of characters that have the same ordinal position in the two data items are not identical. In the latter case, the relative positions of the two unequal characters in the collating sequence which is being used are determined, and the operand whose character is furthest from the beginning of the collating sequence is considered the greater operand.

If the operands are of unequal size, the shorter operand is treated as if it were extended to the *right* by a sufficient number of spaces to make the operands equal. Then the comparison for equal size operands is performed.

These rules are new to 74 COBOL.

Index Data Items

In relation conditions involving index-names and index data items, tests can be made between:

1. Two index-names; in which case their occurrence numbers are compared.

2. An index-name and an index data item, or two index data items; in this case their actual contents are compared.

3. An index-name and a data item that is not an index data item or a numeric literal; in this case the index-name's occurrence number is compared with the value of the data item or literal.

4. The result of the comparison of an index data item with any data item or literal not specified above is undefined.

N.B. The fact that TO is not required in EQUAL TO is a new feature of 74 COBOL.

See class, elementary item, group item, high-order end, index data item, index-name, low-order end, operator.

relational operator

A relational operator is a set of reserved words and/or relation characters that are used in the construction of a relation condition. The permissible operators are:

OPERATORS

IS GREATER THAN
IS >

IS NOT GREATER THAN
IS NOT >

IS LESS THAN
IS <

IS NOT LESS THAN
IS NOT <

IS EQUAL TO
IS =

IS NOT EQUAL TO
IS NOT =

In formats the operators > , < , and = are always considered keywords. They are not underlined to avoid confusion.

See keyword, relation character, relation condition, reserved word.

RELATIVE

See FILE-CONTROL, ORGANIZATION, SELECT.

relative file

A relative file is a file with relative organization.

See relative i-o.

relative i-o

Relative i-o can be used only with mass storage files. In a relative file, each record is uniquely identified by an integer greater than zero that specifies the logical ordinal position of that record in the file. This integer is called the relative record number. A relative record number can designate an area in the file that does not currently contain a record. If this area is accessed, the Invalid Key condition exists. Relative files can be accessed in the sequential, random, or dynamic access mode.

Sequential Access of Relative Files

In the sequential access mode, when records are being written the first record has a relative record number of 1, the next a relative record of 2, etc. When records are being retrieved, they are accessed in ascending order by relative record number for all records currently existing in the file. If a START was executed that positioned the current-record pointer to record number N, then the first record accessed will be record N; the next record will be record N + 1, etc. If no START was given, the first access will be to the record with the lowest relative record number that currently exists in the file. For example, if records with relative record numbers 2, 4, 5, 7, and 9 are currently in the file, the first access will be to record 2, the next to record 4, etc.

Random Access of Relative Files

In the random access mode the user determines the order in which the records will be accessed by putting the relative record number of the desired record into the RELATIVE KEY data item. If no record exists with the designated relative record number, the access is unsuccessful.

Dynamic Access of Relative Files

In the dynamic access mode the user can change back and forth between sequential and random access mode by using the appropriate verbs.

Level 1

Level 1 provides partial facilities for FILE-CONTROL, I-O-CONTROL, and file description entries, as well as partial capabilities for READ and USE. Full capabilities are provided for CLOSE, DELETE, OPEN, REWRITE, and WRITE.

Level 2

Level 2 provides full facilities for all relative i-o functions, including RESERVE, READ NEXT, SAME RECORD AREA, and Dynamic Access.

Current-Record Pointer

In relative i-o the current-record pointer is affected by OPEN, READ, and START statements.

File Status

The FILE STATUS item, if specified, is updated by relative i-o verbs. Valid combinations are

Status Key 1	Status Key 2	Meaning
0	0	Successful completion
1	0	At end
2	2	Duplicate key
2	3	No record found
2	4	Boundary violation
3	0	Permanent error
9	–	Implementor-defined

The verbs CLOSE, DELETE, OPEN, READ, REWRITE, START, USE and WRITE can be used with relative files.

See current-record pointer, dynamic access, ordinal position, random access, relative record number, sequential access.

Relative I-O Module

See relative i-o.

RELATIVE KEY

The RELATIVE KEY phrase is in the FILE CONTROL entry for a relative file. It specifies a key data item that indicates the record to be accessed in random access mode. If the file is being sequentially accessed, after a READ the key data item will contain the relative record number of the record just read.

This phrase must be specified if the file is to be accessed by a START statement.

The RELATIVE KEY feature is new to 74 COBOL.

See ACCESS MODE, key, random access, relative i-o, SELECT, sequential access.

relative line number

See LINE NUMBER.

relative record number

See relative i-o.

RELEASE

The RELEASE verb transfers records to the first phase of a SORT operation.

Format:

RELEASE record-name [FROM identifier-1]

Execution of a RELEASE causes a record to be released to the initial phase of a SORT operation. A RELEASE can appear only in the input procedure associated with a SORT statement that specifies a file which contains record-name. After the RELEASE has been executed, the logical record is no longer available in the file's record area unless the associated sort-merge file is named in a SAME RECORD AREA clause. In that case the record is available as a record of the other files named in that clause.

When control passes from the input procedure, the file consists of all those records that were placed in it by the execution of RELEASE statements. Record-name must be the name of a logical record in a sort-merge file description entry; it can be qualified.

The From Phrase

If the FROM phrase is specified, the contents of identifier-1, which cannot refer to the same storage area as record-name, are moved to record-name. Then, the

contents of record-name are released to the sort file according to the rules for a
MOVE statement without the CORRESPONDING phrase. After execution of
the RELEASE statement, data is still available in identifier-1 but not in record-
name.

See qualification, record-name, sort-merge file description.

REMAINDER

See DIVIDE.

REMARKS

Formerly a paragraph in the Identification Division, REMARKS has been
replaced by a general comment facility.

See comment line.

REMOVAL

See CLOSE.

RENAMES, level 66

The RENAMES clause permits alternative, possibly overlapping, groupings of
elementary items. It is implemented in level 2 of the Nucleus module.

Format:

$$66 \quad \text{data-name-1} \; \underline{\text{RENAMES}} \; \text{data-name-2} \left[\left\{ \begin{matrix} \underline{\text{THROUGH}} \\ \underline{\text{THRU}} \end{matrix} \right\} \text{data-name-3} \right] \bullet$$

One or more RENAMES entries can be written for a logical record. All of
the RENAMES entries that refer to data items within a given logical record must
immediately follow that record's last data description entry. A level 66 entry
cannot rename another level 66 entry, nor a level 01, 77, or 88 entry.

Data-name-2 and data-name-3 must name elementary items, or groups of
elementary items, and must be in the same logical record. Either or both can be
qualified, but they cannot be the same data-name. The beginning of the area
described by data-name-3 must not be to the left of the beginning of data-name-2
nor can the end of data-name-2 be to the right of the end of data-name-3.
Data-name-3 cannot be subordinate to data-name-2. Neither data-name-2 nor
data-name-3 can have an OCCURS clause in its description nor be subordinate to
an entry that contains an OCCURS clause.

Data-name-1 cannot be used as a qualifier and can only be qualified by the
names of level 01, file description (FD), communication description (CD), or
sort-merge description (SD) entries. None of the elementary items within the
range of data-name-1 can have a format 2 OCCURS clause in its data description.

RENAMES differs from REDEFINES in that there is still only one data description for the area but the area can be known by different names; whereas in REDEFINES, the same area can have different data descriptions.

The THROUGH Clause

If the THROUGH clause is not specified, data-name-2 can be either a group item or an elementary item, and data-name-1 will be considered a group or elementary item accordingly.

If the THROUGH clause is specified, data-name-1 is considered a group item with a range from the first elementary item in data-name-2 to the last elementary item in data-name-3. If either data-name is not a group item, the elementary item itself defines the beginning or end of the range.

Example:

```
            02   A.
                 03   B   PIC XXX.
                 03   C.
                      04   D PIC XX.
                      04   E PIC X.
                 03   F.
                      05   G PIC XXXX.
                      05   H PIC XX.
            02   J PIC XXXX.
            02   K PIC XXXXX.
            66   X RENAMES C.
            66   Y RENAMES D.
            66   Z RENAMES E THROUGH G.
            66   W RENAMES H THROUGH K.
            66   V RENAMES J.
```

The above would be structured:

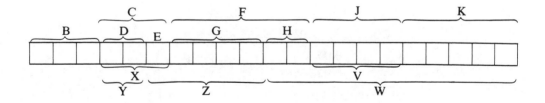

See communication description entry, data description entry, elementary item, file description entry, qualification, REDEFINES, sort-merge file description.

REPLACING

See COPY, INSPECT.

REPORT

The REPORT clause is used in a report description to name the reports that are in a report file.

Format:

$$\left\{ \begin{array}{l} \underline{\text{REPORT}} \text{ IS} \\ \underline{\text{REPORTS}} \text{ ARE} \end{array} \right\} \{\text{report-name-1}\}\dots$$

The REPORT clause specifies the reports in a file. A report-name can appear in only one REPORT clause. Each report-name must be the subject of a report description entry in the REPORT SECTION. A file that has a REPORT clause specified can be referenced only by the OPEN OUTPUT, OPEN EXTENDED, and CLOSE statements.

See report description, TYPE.

report clause

A report clause is a clause that appears in a report description entry or in a report group description entry.

See report description, report group description.

report description

A report description (RD) entry names a report, specifies any identifying characters to be appended to each line of the report, and describes the physical structure and organization of the report.

Format:

RD report-name

[CODE literal-1]

$$\left[\left\{ \begin{array}{l} \underline{\text{CONTROL}} \text{ IS} \\ \underline{\text{CONTROLS}} \text{ ARE} \end{array} \right\} \left\{ \begin{array}{l} \{\text{data-name-1}\}\dots \\ \underline{\text{FINAL}} [\text{data-name-1}]\dots \end{array} \right\} \right]$$

$$\left[\underline{\text{PAGE}} \left[\begin{array}{l} \text{LIMIT IS} \\ \text{LIMITS ARE} \end{array} \right] \text{integer-1} \left[\begin{array}{l} \text{LINE} \\ \text{LINES} \end{array} \right] [\underline{\text{HEADING}} \text{ integer-2}] \right.$$

$$[\underline{\text{FIRST}} \ \underline{\text{DETAIL}} \text{ integer-3}] [\underline{\text{LAST}} \ \underline{\text{DETAIL}} \text{ integer-4}]$$

$$\left. [\underline{\text{FOOTING}} \text{ integer-5}] \right] \bullet$$

The report description entry is in the REPORT SECTION of the DATA DIVISION. A report-name can appear in one and only one REPORT clause in an FD of a report file. The order of the clauses in the report description is immaterial.

Report-name is the highest qualification that can be specified for LINE-COUNTER, PAGE-COUNTER, and all data-names defined within the REPORT SECTION. One or more report group description entries must follow a report description entry. Specification of a report-name automatically creates a LINE-COUNTER and a PAGE-COUNTER for that report.

See report group description, report-name.

report file

A report file is an output file with a file description entry containing the REPORT clause. A report file consists of records that are written by the Report Writer Control System.

A report file must be a sequential file that can have only OPEN OUTPUT, OPEN EXTEND, and CLOSE statements executed for it as far as input-output statements are concerned.

See Report Writer Control System, sequential file.

REPORT FOOTING

A REPORT FOOTING is a report group that is presented only at the end of a report.

See report group, report group description, TYPE.

report group

A report group is an 01 level entry and its subordinate entries, as defined in the REPORT SECTION of the DATA DIVISION.

report group description

A report group description is an entry in the REPORT SECTION that specifies the characteristics of a report group and of the items within that report group.

Format 1:

01 [data-name-1]

$$\left[\underline{\text{LINE}} \text{ NUMBER IS } \begin{cases} \text{integer-1 [ON } \underline{\text{NEXT}} \text{ } \underline{\text{PAGE}}] \\ \underline{\text{PLUS}} \text{ integer-2} \end{cases}\right]$$

$$\left[\underline{\text{NEXT}} \text{ } \underline{\text{GROUP}} \text{ IS } \begin{cases} \text{integer-3} \\ \underline{\text{PLUS}} \text{ integer-4} \\ \underline{\text{NEXT}} \text{ } \underline{\text{PAGE}} \end{cases}\right] \text{ [[USAGE IS] } \underline{\text{DISPLAY}}]$$

$$
\text{TYPE IS}
\begin{Bmatrix}
\begin{Bmatrix} \underline{\text{REPORT HEADING}} \\ \underline{\text{RH}} \end{Bmatrix} \\
\begin{Bmatrix} \underline{\text{PAGE HEADING}} \\ \underline{\text{PH}} \end{Bmatrix} \\
\begin{Bmatrix} \underline{\text{CONTROL HEADING}} \\ \underline{\text{CH}} \end{Bmatrix} \begin{Bmatrix} \text{data-name-2} \\ \underline{\text{FINAL}} \end{Bmatrix} \\
\begin{Bmatrix} \underline{\text{DETAIL}} \\ \underline{\text{DE}} \end{Bmatrix} \\
\begin{Bmatrix} \underline{\text{CONTROL FOOTING}} \\ \underline{\text{CF}} \end{Bmatrix} \begin{Bmatrix} \text{data-name-3} \\ \underline{\text{FINAL}} \end{Bmatrix} \\
\begin{Bmatrix} \underline{\text{PAGE FOOTING}} \\ \underline{\text{PF}} \end{Bmatrix} \\
\begin{Bmatrix} \underline{\text{REPORT FOOTING}} \\ \underline{\text{RF}} \end{Bmatrix}
\end{Bmatrix} \bullet
$$

A format 1 report group description entry must be the first entry in a report group. Except for the data-name, which, if specified must follow the level-number, the clauses can be written in any order.

Data-name-1 is required only (1) when a DETAIL report group is referenced by a GENERATE statement or by the UPON phrase of the SUM clause, (2) when a report group is used in a USE BEFORE REPORTING statement, or (3) when the name of a Control Footing report group is used to qualify a sum counter.

If the USAGE clause is specified, at least one subordinate entry must define a printable item. If an entry has a LINE NUMBER clause, no subordinate entry can have a LINE NUMBER clause.

Format 2:

level-number [data-name-1]

$$
\left[\underline{\text{LINE}} \text{ NUMBER IS } \begin{Bmatrix} \text{integer-1 [ON } \underline{\text{NEXT PAGE}}] \\ \underline{\text{PLUS}} \text{ integer-2} \end{Bmatrix} \right]
$$

[[USAGE IS] DISPLAY]•

A format 2 report group description entry must contain at least one optional clause. The level-number must be within the range 02 to 48, inclusive. If specified, data-name-1 must follow the level-number; otherwise, the clauses can be written in any order. A format 2 entry can be immediately subordinate to a format 1 entry, and at least one format 3 entry must be immediately subordinate to it.

If data-name-1 is specified, it can be used only to qualify a sum counter.

The USAGE clause can be used only with printable items. Therefore, at least one subordinate item must be a printable item.

If a LINE NUMBER clause is specified, no subordinate entry can contain the LINE NUMBER clause.

Format 3:

level-number [data-name-1]

    [BLANK WHEN ZERO]

    [GROUP INDICATE]

$$\left[\left\{\begin{array}{l}\text{JUSTIFIED}\\\text{JUST}\end{array}\right\}\text{ RIGHT}\right]$$

$$\left[\text{LINE NUMBER IS }\left\{\begin{array}{l}\text{integer-1 [ON NEXT PAGE]}\\\text{PLUS integer-2}\end{array}\right\}\right]$$

    [COLUMN NUMBER IS integer-3]

$$\left\{\begin{array}{l}\text{PICTURE}\\\text{PIC}\end{array}\right\}\text{ IS character-string}$$

    [USAGE IS DISPLAY]

$$\left\{\begin{array}{l}\text{SOURCE IS identifier-1}\\\text{VALUE IS literal-1}\\\text{\{SUM \{identifier-1\}}\ldots\text{[UPON \{data-name-2\}}\ldots\text{]\}}\ldots\left[\text{RESET ON }\left\{\begin{array}{l}\text{data-name-3}\\\text{FINAL}\end{array}\right\}\right]\end{array}\right\}$$

A format 3 entry can be immediately subordinate to a format 1 entry, and at least one format 3 entry must be immediately subordinate to a format 2 entry. The rules for a format 3 entry are

- A GROUP INDICATE clause can appear only in a DETAIL report group.

- A SUM clause can appear only in a CONTROL FOOTING report group.

- If an entry contains a COLUMN NUMBER clause but no LINE NUMBER clause, it must be subordinate to an entry that contains a LINE NUMBER clause.

- Data-name-1 can be referenced only if the entry defines a sum counter.

- A LINE NUMBER clause must not be the only clause specified.

- An entry that contains a VALUE clause must also contain a COLUMN NUMBER clause.

- An entry that contains a LINE NUMBER clause must not have a subordinate entry that also contains a LINE NUMBER clause.

- If the USAGE clause is specified, the entry must define a printable item.

The following chart shows the valid combinations of clauses for a format 3 report group description entry. It should be read from top to bottom along the selected column. An 'M' indicates that the clause is mandatory; a 'P' indicates that the clause is optional; no entry indicates that the combination is invalid.

PICTURE	M	M	M	M	M
COLUMN		M	P	P	P
SOURCE			M	M	
SUM	M	M			
VALUE					M
JUSTIFIED			P		P
BLANK WHEN ZERO		P		P	
GROUP INDICATE			P	P	P
USAGE		P	P	P	P
LINE	P	P	P	P	P

See data-name, level-number, report group, sum counter.

REPORT HEADING

A REPORT HEADING is a report group that is presented only at the beginning of a report.

See report group, report group description.

REPORTING

See USE BEFORE REPORTING.

report line

A report line is one line of a page in a report. Report lines are numbered consecutively, starting at the top of the page with line number 1.

report-name

A report-name is a user-defined word that names a report described in a report description entry within the REPORT SECTION of the DATA DIVISION.

See report description, user-defined word.

REPORT SECTION

The REPORT SECTION is that part of the DATA DIVISION that contains one or more report description entries and the associated report group description entries.

See report description, report group description.

Report Writer Control System

The Report Writer Control System (RWCS) is an implementor-supplied object time control system that accomplishes the construction of reports.

report writer logical record

A report writer logical record is a record that consists of the report writer print line and associated control information necessary for its selection and vertical positioning.

Report Writer Module

The Report Writer Module provides the facility for producing reports by specifying their physical appearance. A hierarchy of levels is used in defining the logical organization of a report. Each report is divided into one or more report groups which are, in turn, divided into sequences of items. An explicit reference to a report group can implicitly reference other levels in the hierarchy.

As this model has been completely redefined for 74 COBOL, no discussion of its differences from previous Report Writers will be attempted.

RERUN

The RERUN clause of the I-O CONTROL paragraph specifies when and where rerun information is recorded.

Format:

$$
\left[\underline{\text{RERUN}} \left[\underline{\text{ON}} \left\{ \begin{array}{l} \text{file-name-1} \\ \text{implementor-name} \end{array} \right\} \right] \text{ EVERY} \left\{ \begin{array}{l} \left\{ [\underline{\text{END}}\ \text{OF}] \left\{ \begin{array}{l} \underline{\text{REEL}} \\ \underline{\text{UNIT}} \end{array} \right\} \right\} \text{OF file-name-2} \\ \text{integer-1}\ \underline{\text{RECORDS}} \\ \text{integer-2}\ \underline{\text{CLOCK-UNITS}} \\ \text{condition-name} \end{array} \right\} \right] \ldots
$$

Rerun information is recorded in the following ways. If file-name-1 is specified, the rerun information is written on each reel or unit of an output file. The implementor specifies where, on the reel or unit, the rerun information is recorded. File-name-1 must be a sequentially organized file. If implementor-name is specified, the rerun information is written as a separate file on a device specified by the implementor.

There are seven forms of the RERUN clause that are meaningful. Each one is considered separately below. The implementor must provide at least one of these forms.

1. RERUN EVERY END OF REEL/UNIT
   Rerun information is written on file-name-2, which must be an output file with sequential organization.

2. RERUN ON file-name-1 EVERY END OF REEL/UNIT
   The rerun information is written on file-name-1, which must be an output file. File-name-2 can be an input or output file but must have sequential organization. In addition, normal reel or unit closing functions are performed for file-name-2.

3. RERUN ON implementor-name EVERY END OF REEL/UNIT
   Rerun information is written on a separate rerun unit defined by implementor-name. File-name-2 can be an output or input file and must have sequential organization.

4. RERUN ON implementor-name EVERY integer-1 RECORDS OF file-name-2
   Rerun information is written on the device specified by implementor-name whenever integer-1 records of file-name-2 have been processed. File-name-2 can be an input or output file with any organization or access.

5. RERUN ON implementor-name EVERY integer-2 CLOCK-UNITS
   Rerun information is written on the device specified by implementor-name whenever an interval of time, calculated by an internal clock, has elapsed. Only one RERUN clause containing the CLOCK-UNITS phrase can be specified in a program.

6. RERUN ON file-name-1 EVERY condition-name
   Rerun information is written on file-name-1, which must be an output file, whenever a switch assumes a particular status as specified by condition-name. The associated switch must be defined in the SPECIAL-NAMES paragraph. The implementor specifies when the switch status is to be interrogated.

7. RERUN ON implementor-name EVERY condition-name
   Rerun information is written on the device specified by implementor-name whenever a switch assumes a particular status as specified by condition-name. The associated switch must be defined in the SPECIAL-NAMES paragraph. The implementor specifies when the switch status is to be interrogated.

More than one RERUN clause can be specified in the program for a given file-name-2. In this case, if multiple END OF REEL/UNIT clauses are specified, no two of them can specify the same file-name-2.

RESERVE

The RESERVE clause allows the user to specify the number of input-output areas allocated to a file. It is specified in the FILE-CONTROL paragraph.

Format:

$$\underline{\text{RESERVE}} \text{ integer-1} \begin{bmatrix} \text{AREAS} \\ \text{AREA} \end{bmatrix}$$

If this clause is not specified, the number of input-output areas allocated is implementor-defined. If this clause is specified, the number of input-output areas specified is equal to integer-1.

See SELECT.

reserved word

Following is a list of reserved words in COBOL. Individual implementors will, in general, add to this list, so their literature should be consulted. Note that even if a particular module is not implemented, say, for example, the Debugging Module, one should not use reserved words associated with that module (DEBUG-NAME, etc.). Words marked with an asterisk are new to 74 COBOL.

ACCEPT	CF	DATE-COMPILED	*EGI
ACCESS	CH	DATE-WRITTEN	ELSE
ADD	*CHARACTER	*DAY	*EMI
ADVANCING	CHARACTERS	DE	*ENABLE
AFTER	CLOCK-UNITS	*DEBUG-CONTENTS	END
ALL	CLOSE	*DEBUG-ITEM	END-OF-PAGE
ALPHABETIC	COBOL	*DEBUG-LINE	ENTER
*ALSO	CODE	*DEBUG-NAME	ENVIRONMENT
ALTER	*CODE-SET	*DEBUG-SUB-1	EOP
ALTERNATE	*COLLATING	*DEBUG-SUB-2	EQUAL
AND	COLUMN	*DEBUG-SUB-3	*ERROR
ARE	COMMA	*DEBUGGING	*ESI
AREA	*COMMUNICATION	DECIMAL-POINT	*EVERY
AREAS	COMP	DECLARATIVES	*EXCEPTION
ASCENDING	COMPUTATIONAL	*DELETE	EXIT
ASSIGN	COMPUTE	*DELIMITED	*EXTEND
AT	CONFIGURATION	*DELIMITER	
AUTHOR	CONTAINS	DEPENDING	FD
	CONTROL	DESCENDING	FILE
BEFORE	CONTROLS	*DESTINATION	FILE-CONTROL
BLANK	COPY	DETAIL	FILLER
BLOCK	CORR	DISABLE	FINAL
*BOTTOM	CORRESPONDING	DISPLAY	FIRST
BY	*COUNT	DIVIDE	FOOTING
	CURRENCY	DIVISION	FOR
CALL		DOWN	FROM
CANCEL	DATA	*DUPLICATES	
*CD	*DATE	*DYNAMIC	GENERATE

GIVING
GREATER
GROUP

HEADING
HIGH-VALUE
HIGH-VALUES

I-O
I-O-CONTROL
IDENTIFICATION
INDEX
INDEXED
INDICATE
*INITIAL
INITIATE
INPUT
INPUT-OUTPUT
*INSPECT
INSTALLATION
INTO
INVALID

JUST
JUSTIFIED

KEY

LABEL
LAST
LEADING
LEFT
*LENGTH
LESS
LIMIT
LIMITS
LINAGE
LINAGE-COUNTER
LINE
LINE-COUNTER

LINES
LINKAGE
LOCK
LOW-VALUE
LOW-VALUES

MEMORY
*MERGE
*MESSAGE
MODE
MODULES
MOVE
MULTIPLE
MULTIPLY

*NATIVE
NEGATIVE
NEXT
NOT
NUMBER
NUMERIC

OBJECT-COMPUTER
OCCURS
OMITTED
OPEN
OPTIONAL
*ORGANIZATION
OVERFLOW

PAGE
PAGE-COUNTER
PERFORM
PIC
PICTURE
PLUS

*POINTER
POSITION
POSITIVE
*PRINTING
PROCEDURE
*PROCEDURES
PROCEED
PROGRAM
PROGRAM-ID

*QUEUE
QUOTE
QUOTES

RANDOM
READ
*RECEIVE
RECORD
RECORDS
REDEFINES
REEL
*REFERENCES
*RELATIVE
RELEASE
REMAINDER
*REMOVAL
RENAMES
REPLACING
REPORT
REPORTING
REPORTS
RERUN
RESERVE
RESET
RETURN
REVERSED
REWIND
REWRITE
RIGHT
ROUNDED

RUN

SAME
SEARCH
SECTION
SECURITY
SELECT
*SEND
SENTENCE
*SEPARATE
*SEQUENCE
SEQUENTIAL
SET
SIGN
SIZE
SORT
*SORT-MERGE
SOURCE
SOURCE-COMPUTER
SPACE
SPACES
SPECIAL-NAMES
STANDARD
*STANDARD-1
START
STATUS
*STRING
*SUB-QUEUE-1
*SUB-QUEUE-2
*SUB-QUEUE-3
SUBTRACT
SUM
*SUPPRESS
*SYMBOLIC
SYNC
SYNCHRONIZED

*TABLE
TALLYING
TAPE

*TERMINAL	TYPE	VALUES	ZEROS
TERMINATE	UNIT	VARYING	
*TEXT	*UNSTRING		+
THAN	UNTIL	WHEN	–
THROUGH	UP	WITH	*
THRU	UPON	WORDS	/
*TIME	USAGE	WORKING-STORAGE	**
TIMES	USE	WRITE	>
TO	USING		<
*TOP		ZERO	=
*TRAILING	VALUE	ZEROES	

The following are no longer reserved words:

ACTUAL	NOTE
ADDRESS	OBJECT-PROGRAM
AN	OV
APPLY	PROCESSING
BEGINNING	REMARKS
COMMON	RENAMING
ENDING	SA
EXAMINE	SEEK
FILE-LIMIT	SEQUENCED
FILE-LIMITS	TALLY
KEYS	THEN

RESET

See report group description, SUM.

RETURN

The RETURN verb obtains records from the final phase of a SORT or MERGE operation.

Format:

RETURN file-name RECORD [INTO identifier-1]

; AT END imperative-statement-1

Execution of a RETURN statement causes the next record from a SORT or MERGE operation to be made available for processing in the record area associated with those statements. The order in which records are made available is determined by the keys listed in the SORT or MERGE statement.

A RETURN can appear only in an output procedure associated with a SORT or MERGE statement.

When logical records of a file are described with more than one record description, these records share the same storage area. Thus the contents of any data items in the area that lies beyond the area occupied by the current data record are undefined at the completion of the RETURN.

The Into Phrase

When the INTO phrase is specified, the current record is moved from the input area to the area specified by identifier-1 according to the rules for a MOVE statement without the CORRESPONDING phrase. This move does not occur if there is an AT END condition. Data is available in both the input record area and identifier-1 after the RETURN is executed.

Any subscripting or indexing for identifier-1 is evaluated after the record has been returned and immediately before it is moved to the data item. (This may be important if any elements in the record are used in evaluating the subscripts or indices, since it is the values just read in that will be used.) The storage area defined by identifier-1 and the record area associated with file-name cannot be the same area.

The INTO phrase cannot be used when the input file contains logical records of different sizes.

The At End Condition

The AT END condition occurs if no logical records exist for the file when the RETURN is executed. Once imperative-statement-1 has been executed, no other RETURN statement can be executed during the current execution of the output procedure. The contents of the record areas of the file are undefined when the AT END condition occurs.

See indexing, RELEASE, subscripting.

REVERSED

See OPEN.

REWIND

See CLOSE, OPEN.

REWRITE

The REWRITE verb logically replaces an existing record in a mass storage file. This verb is new to 74 COBOL.

Format:

REWRITE record-name [FROM identifier-1][; INVALID KEY imperative-statement-1]

The REWRITE statement replaces a record that currently exists in the file. Record-name, which can be qualified, must specify a logical record defined in the

FILE SECTION of the DATA DIVISION. The file must be a mass storage file that is open in the I-O mode when the REWRITE is executed. It cannot be a SORT or MERGE file.

When a REWRITE is successfully executed, the logical record is no longer available in the file's record area unless that file is named in a SAME RECORD AREA clause. In this case, the record is still available in the file's record area and it is also available as a record of other files appearing in that SAME RECORD AREA clause. Execution of a REWRITE does not affect the current-record pointer.

Sequential Files

If a file is sequential, the INVALID KEY phrase cannot be specified, and the last input-output statement executed for that file must have been a successful format 1 READ. The record that was accessed by this READ is the one that is rewritten.

Relative Files

If a relative file is in the random or dynamic access mode, the record specified by the RELATIVE KEY data item associated with the file is the one rewritten. If the file is in sequential access mode, the last input-output statement executed for the file must have been a successful READ. The record that was accessed by this READ is the one that is rewritten.

Indexed Files

If an indexed file is in the random or dynamic access mode, the record specified by the prime record key is the one that is rewritten. If the file is in sequential access mode, the prime record key's value must be equal to the value of the prime record key item of the last record read from the file.

The From Phrase

When a REWRITE contains the FROM phrase, execution is the same as if one performed a MOVE identifier-1 TO record-name (where 'identifier-1' and 'record-name' are the same as in the REWRITE) before executing the REWRITE. The move follows the rules for an alphanumeric to alphanumeric move. After successful execution of the REWRITE, the data is no longer available in the file's record area. It is, however, available in identifier-1. Identifier-1 cannot refer to the same storage area as the record-name.

The Invalid Key Condition

The Invalid Key condition exists when any of the following occur:

1. An indexed or relative file is being accessed and the value of the prime record key or relative key does not equal that of any record stored in the file.

2. An indexed file is being accessed in the sequential mode and the value of the prime record key item in the record being replaced is not equal to the value of the prime record key of the last record read from the file.

3. An indexed file is being accessed and the value contained in an alternate record key for which no DUPLICATE phrase has been specified is equal to that of a record already in the file.

When the Invalid Key condition exists, the rewriting does not take place, the record area is not affected, and the REWRITE is unsuccessful.

The Invalid Key Clause

The INVALID KEY clause cannot be specified for a sequentially organized file or for a relative file that has sequential access. In all other cases, it is required unless a format 1 USE procedure is specified.

If the Invalid Key condition occurs and if the INVALID KEY phrase is specified, imperative-statement-1 is executed. If the INVALID KEY phrase is not specified, the format 1 USE procedure is executed. If both the INVALID KEY phrase and a USE procedure are specified, only imperative-statement-1 is executed. If neither the INVALID KEY phrase nor a USE procedure is specified, the results are undefined.

File Status

If a File Status data item is specified, it is updated as follows:

Status Key 1	Status Key 2	Meaning	
0	0	Successful completion	
1	0	At end	
2	2	Duplicate key	(relative and indexed only)
2	3	No record found	(relative and indexed only)
2	4	Boundary violation	(relative and indexed only)
3	0	Permanent error	
3	4	Boundary violation	(sequential only)
9	–	Implementor-defined	

RF

An abbreviation for REPORT FOOTING.
See TYPE.

RH

An abbreviation for REPORT HEADING.
See TYPE.

RIGHT

See JUSTIFIED, SYNCHRONIZED.

rolling forward

   See SUM, TYPE.

ROUNDED

   Sometimes the fractional part of the result of a computation contains more places than can be contained in the receiving item. When this happens, the result is truncated, that is, the fractional part is cut off at whatever point is necessary to make the value fit into the receiving item. The truncated digits are lost. If truncation has occurred and the ROUNDED option is specified, then if the most significant digit of the truncated part is five or more, a one is added to the absolute value of the result, irrespective of where the decimal point is located. If the most significant digit of the truncated part is not five or more, then no action is taken on the result.

   Examples: Assume the receiving item has a PICTURE of 999V99

Actual Result	Part Truncated	Value Stored	Value Stored if ROUNDED
123.459999	9999	123.45	123.46
123.450001	0001	123.45	123.45
−123.459999	9999	−123.45	−123.46

   If the PICTURE of the receiving item contains P's in the low order positions, the result is rounded relative to the right-most position for which storage is allocated.

   Examples: Assume the receiving item has a PICTURE of 999PPP

Actual Result	Part Truncated	Number Stored	Number Stored if ROUNDED
123999	999	123	124
1237	7	123	124
123399	399	123	123

   Note that these numbers represent the values 123,000 and 124,000.

   The ROUNDED option can be used with all arithmetic verbs and is indicated in the formats by ROUNDED.

   See ADD, COMPUTE, DIVIDE, MULTIPLY, SUBTRACT.

routine-name

   A routine-name is a user-defined word that identifies a procedure written in a language other than COBOL.

   See ENTER, user-defined word.

RUN

See STOP.

run unit

A run unit is a set of one or more object programs that functions as a unit at object time to solve a particular problem.

RWCS

'RWCS' is an abbreviation for Report Writer Control System. This is an implementor-supplied object time control system that accomplishes the construction of reports.

S

SAME AREA

The SAME AREA clause specifies that two or more files share the same memory area during processing.

Format:

$$\left[\text{SAME} \begin{bmatrix} \underline{\text{SORT}} \\ \underline{\text{SORT-MERGE}} \\ \underline{\text{RECORD}} \end{bmatrix} \text{AREA FOR } \{\text{file-name-1}\}\dots\right]\dots$$

The SAME AREA clause is an optional entry in the I-O-CONTROL paragraph of the ENVIRONMENT DIVISION. More than one SAME AREA clause can be included in a program. However, a file-name cannot appear in more than one SAME AREA clause or more than one SAME RECORD AREA clause.

Files named in a SAME AREA or SAME RECORD AREA clause cannot be sort-merge files. The files named in any form of this clause need not have the same organization or access.

If one or more files specified in a SAME AREA clause appear in a SAME RECORD AREA clause, all the file-names in that SAME AREA clause must appear in the SAME RECORD AREA clause; the SAME RECORD AREA clause can, however, contain files that are not specified in the SAME AREA clause. In other words, the SAME AREA clause entries must be a subset of the SAME RECORD AREA clause entries.

Same Area Clause

The SAME AREA clause specifies that two or more files are to share the same memory area during processing. The area shared includes all storage areas assigned to the specified files. Consequently, no more than one of the files can be open at any time. This rule takes precedence over the rule that all files in a SAME RECORD AREA clause can be opened at the same time.

Same Record Area Clause

The SAME RECORD AREA clause specifies that two or more files are to use the same memory area for processing the current logical record. All of the files can be open at the same time unless the rule described in the preceding paragraph is applicable.

A logical record in this common area is considered a logical record of each opened output file specified in the clause and of the input file specified in the clause that has most recently had a successful READ statement executed for it. Records are aligned by left-most character position.

Same Sort Area and Same Sort-Merge Area Clause

SAME SORT AREA and SAME SORT-MERGE AREA are identical. If this clause is used, at least one file must be a sort-merge file. Files that are not sort-merge files can also be named in this clause. A sort-merge file cannot appear in more than one SAME SORT AREA clause. If a non-sort-merge file is named in a SAME AREA clause and in one or more SAME SORT AREA clauses, all the files in that SAME AREA clause must be named in the SAME SORT AREA clause or clauses.

Storage is allocated so that an area is made available for use in sorting or merging each sort-merge file named. Storage areas assigned to files that are not sort-merge files may be allocated as needed for sorting or merging the sort-merge files named in this clause. Files that are not sort-merge files do not share the same storage area with each other. To take part in this sharing, the files must be named in a SAME AREA or SAME RECORD AREA clause.

During execution of a SORT or MERGE statement that refers to a sort-merge file named in this clause, no non-sort-merge files named in this clause can be open.

See ACCESS MODE, file-name, file organization.

saved next group integer

The saved next group integer is a data item that is accessible only by the Report Writer Control System (RWCS). When an absolute NEXT GROUP clause specifies a vertical positioning value that cannot be accommodated on the current page, the RWCS stores that value in the saved next group integer.

After page advance processing is completed, the next body group is presented using the stored value.

See Presentation Rules.

scaling (scaling factor)

A data item is said to be scaled or to have a scaling factor if, instead of its actual value being represented in the item, only the significant digits and a scaling factor, which indicates the magnitude, are represented.

The scaling factor is indicated by the character 'P' in the PICTURE clause.

Examples: Assume the characters stored are 654

PICTURE	Value Represented by Item
9V99	6.54
999PPPP	6540000.
PPPP999	.0000654

SD

SD is a level-indicator that is used to designate a sort-merge file.

See level-indicator, merge file, sort file.

SEARCH

The SEARCH verb scans a table for an element that satisfies a specified condition and adjusts an index so that it points to the table element that satisfies the condition. SEARCH is implemented only in level 2 of the Table Handling Module.

Format 1:

$$\underline{\text{SEARCH}} \text{ identifier-1} \left[\underline{\text{VARYING}} \begin{Bmatrix} \text{identifier-2} \\ \text{index-name-1} \end{Bmatrix} \right] [\text{AT} \underline{\text{END}} \text{ imperative-statement-1}]$$

$$\begin{Bmatrix} \underline{\text{WHEN}} \text{ condition-1} \begin{Bmatrix} \text{imperative-statement-2} \\ \underline{\text{NEXT}} \underline{\text{SENTENCE}} \end{Bmatrix} \end{Bmatrix} \cdots$$

A format 1 SEARCH designates a serial search operation that begins with the current index setting. Therefore, before a format 1 SEARCH is executed, the index used must be set to a legal value for the table. This index is then repeatedly incremented so that it references the table elements in a sequential manner. When some element satisfies a condition, the search terminates. Identifier-1 must have an OCCURS clause and an INDEXED BY clause in its data description. In the SEARCH statement, identifier-1 cannot be subscripted or indexed, however. Condition-1 can be any condition.

The Varying Clause

If the VARYING clause is not specified, the index-name that is used for the search operation is the first index-name that appears in identifier-1's INDEXED BY phrase, the primary index. Any other index-names associated with identifier-1 are not changed.

If the VARYING phrase is specified, the search may operate by using an index other than the primary index.

If an index-name is specified and it is associated with identifier-1, then it, instead of the primary index, is used in the search. If the index-name is associated with some other table, the primary index for identifier-1 is used in the search, and index-name-1 is incremented along with the primary index of identifier-1 so that index-name-1 points to the same occurrence number of its table as the primary index does for identifier-1. The incrementing operations on the primary index and on index-name-1 are performed simultaneously as far as the program is concerned.

If identifier-2 is specified, the primary index for identifier-1 is used in the search. Identifier-2 must be either an index data item or an elementary numeric integer. If identifier-2 is an integer, then it is incremented by one each time the primary index is incremented. If identifier-1 is an index data item, its contents are modified by the same amount as the primary index.[1] Note that in either case, unless the initial value of identifier-2 corresponds to the initial value of the primary index, the values of these two items will not necessarily coincide at completion of the search.

Operation of a Format 1 Search

A format 1 SEARCH proceeds as follows:

1. The index used is examined to see if its value is greater than the highest value permitted for the table. If so, the search terminates and action proceeds as in step 4.

2. If the value of the index is not greater than the highest permissible value for the table, then the conditions specified are evaluated in the order in which they are listed in the SEARCH statement. If a condition is satisfied, the associated imperative-statement (or NEXT SENTENCE) is executed, and the search terminates with the index pointing to the element that satisfied the search. Then, unless the imperative-statement ended with a GO TO, the next sentence following the SEARCH is executed.

3. If none of the conditions is satisfied, the index is incremented so that it points to the next element in the table and step 1 is performed again. These steps are iterated until either one of the conditions is fulfilled or the end of the table is reached, terminating the search.

4. In the event that the search terminates without finding an element that satisfied one of the search criteria, if the AT END phrase is specified, imperative-statement-1 is executed, and unless imperative-statement-1 ended with a GO TO statement, the sentence following the SEARCH is executed. If the AT END phrase is not specified, control transfers to the sentence following the SEARCH statement.

---

[1] This is a new feature of 74 COBOL. Previously it would have been incremented by one.

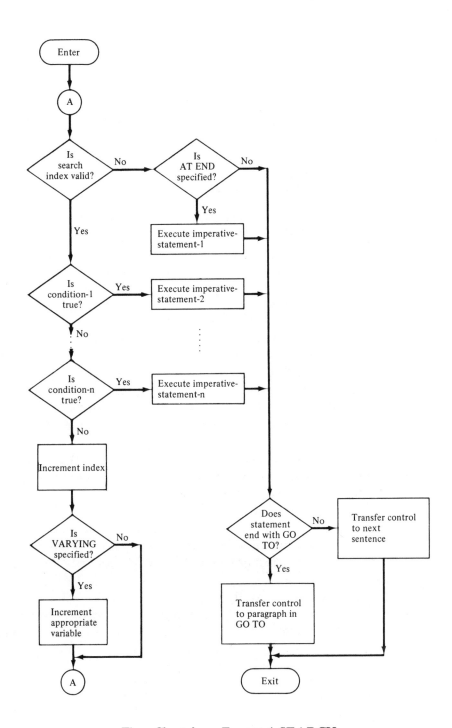

Flow Chart for a Format 1 SEARCH

Format 2:

SEARCH ALL identifier-1 [AT END imperative-statement-1]

$$\text{WHEN} \left\{ \begin{array}{l} \text{data-name-1} \left\{ \begin{array}{l} \text{IS } \underline{\text{EQUAL}} \text{ TO} \\ \text{IS } = \end{array} \right\} \left\{ \begin{array}{l} \text{literal-1} \\ \text{identifier-3} \\ \text{arithmetic-expression-1} \end{array} \right\} \\ \text{condition-name-1} \end{array} \right\}$$

$$\left[\underline{\text{AND}} \left\{ \begin{array}{l} \text{data-name-2} \left\{ \begin{array}{l} \text{IS } \underline{\text{EQUAL}} \text{ TO} \\ \text{IS } = \end{array} \right\} \left\{ \begin{array}{l} \text{literal-2} \\ \text{identifier-4} \\ \text{arithmetic-expression-2} \end{array} \right\} \\ \text{condition-name-2} \end{array} \right\} \right] \ldots$$

$$\left\{ \begin{array}{l} \text{imperative-statement-2} \\ \underline{\text{NEXT}} \text{ } \underline{\text{STATEMENT}} \end{array} \right\}$$

A format 2 search is a nonserial search. Only the primary index is used, and all other indices associated with identifier-1 are unchanged. The initial setting of the primary index is ignored; this index is manipulated in such a way that the entire table is searched but at no time are the contents of the primary index invalid for the table. The results of a format 2 search are predictable only when the data in the table are ordered[1] in the way described in the ASCENDING KEY or DESCENDING KEY clause of identifier-1 and when the contents of the key or keys referenced in the WHEN clause are sufficient to identify a unique table element.

Identifier-1 must contain an OCCURS, an INDEXED BY, and a KEY IS clause in its description. It cannot be subscripted or indexed when it appears in the SEARCH statement, however. Each condition-name must be defined as having only a single value, and the associated conditional variable must appear in the KEY IS clause of identifier-1. Each data-name must appear in the KEY IS clause of identifier-1 and must be indexed by the primary index of identifier-1 along with any other indices or literals that may be required. All data-names can be qualified.

No identifier in the WHEN clause, even if it be part of an arithmetic expression, can appear in the KEY IS clause of identifier-1 nor be indexed by the primary index of identifier-1.[2] When a data-name or associated condition-name in the KEY IS clause of identifier-1 is referenced, all preceding data-names in that KEY IS clause must also be referenced.

---

[1] This is a new restriction of 74 COBOL.
[2] This is a change from 68 COBOL where either the subject (data-name-1) *or* the object could be a data item named in the KEY IS phrase.

A format 2 SEARCH examines the elements of the table in an attempt to find one that satisfies *all* of the conditions in the WHEN clause. If such an element is found, the primary index will be left pointing to that element, and control will pass to imperative-statement-2 or the next sentence, whichever is specified.

If no element in the table is able to satisfy all of the specified conditions, the search terminates and control passes to the next sentence following the SEARCH statement unless the AT END clause is specified in which case control passes to imperative-statement-1. In either case the final setting of the primary index is unpredictable.

Multidimensional Tables

If identifier-1 is subordinate to a data item that contains an OCCURS clause in its data description, an index-name must be defined for each dimension of the table. Only the index-name associated with identifier-1 is modified, however. Therefore, to search completely a multidimensional table, several SEARCH statements must be executed using SET statements prior to each SEARCH to ensure that the index-names have appropriate values.

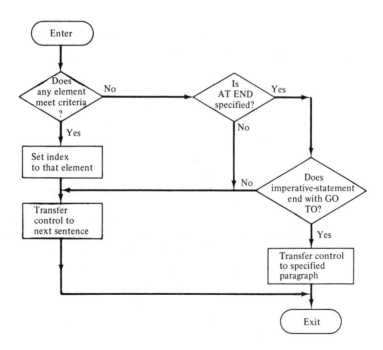

Flow Chart for Format 2 SEARCH

Example: Consider the data description:

```
02  TABLE-A OCCURS 10 TIMES, ASCENDING KEY IS IT-1, IT-2, IT-3,
    INDEXED BY IDEX, JDEX.
    03  IT-1 PIC 99.
        88  BIG-VALUE VALUE IS 9.
    03  IT-2 PIC 9.
        IT-3 PIC 99.
SEARCH ALL TABLE-A AT END GO TO FINITO; WHEN BIG-VALUE(IDEX) AND
IT-2(IDEX) EQUALS 3, AND IT-3(IDEX) EQUALS 7 GO TO FOUND-IT.
```

At the end of the search, if any element of TABLE-A satisfies the following: IT-1 is equal to 9, IT-2 is equal to 3, and IT-3 is equal to 7, then IDEX will point to that element.

The following statement will accomplish the same thing.

```
SET IDEX TO 1. SEARCH TABLE-A AT END GO TO FINITO; WHEN
    BIG-VALUE(IDEX) AND IT-2(IDEX) = 3 AND IT-3(IDEX) = 7
    GO TO FOUND-IT.
```

See arithmetic expression, conditional variable, condition-name, indexing, primary index, qualified data-name, SET, subscripting.

section

A section is a subdivision of a division. In the Procedure Division a section consists of a section-name, the word SECTION, an optional segment-number, a period and space, and optionally, paragraphs or sentences. (In 74 COBOL a section can contain no paragraphs; this is a new feature.)

A section ends either immediately before the next section, at the end of the Procedure Division, or, in the Declaratives part of the Procedure Division, at the words END DECLARATIVES.

In the Environment and Data Divisions, a section is a section header followed by one or more entries.

See division, paragraph, section header, section-name, segment-number.

section header

A section header is a combination of words, followed by a period and space, that indicates the beginning of a section in the Environment, Data, and Procedure Divisions. A section header must begin in Area A and be on a line by itself. After the section header, no text can appear before the following paragraph header or paragraph-name except for COPY or USE sentences.

In the Procedure Division a section header is composed of a section-name, followed by the word SECTION, an optional segment-number, and a period and space.

In the Environment and Data Divisions, the section headers are

Environment Division   Data Division
CONFIGURATION SECTION   FILE SECTION
INPUT-OUTPUT SECTION   WORKING-STORAGE SECTION
          LINKAGE SECTION
          COMMUNICATION SECTION
          REPORT SECTION

See Area A, section-name.

section-name

A section-name is a user-defined word that names a section in the PROCEDURE DIVISION. A section-name must be followed by a period and space. Two section-names are equal if and only if they have the same number of characters in the same positions. Thus, as section-names, 007 and 7 are not equal.

See section, user-defined word.

SECURITY

The SECURITY paragraph is an optional entry in the Identification Division used only for documentation purposes. It does not affect the compilation of the program.

Format:

SECURITY• [comment-entry]...

The comment-entry cannot be continued by using a hyphen in the indicator area; however, the comment can be contained on more than one line. Any character in the computer's character set can appear in a comment-entry.

See comment-entry, continuation of lines, indicator area.

SEEK

SEEK was formerly a verb. It is no longer a reserved word.

SEGMENT

See RECEIVE.

segment

A segment consists of one or more sections of the PROCEDURE DIVISION. All sections having the same segment-number are considered to be in the same segment. Segments can be either fixed or independent.

See fixed overlayable segment, fixed permanent segment, independent segment, segment-number.

segmentation facility

The segmentation facility allows the user to specify object program overlay requirements. Segmentation applies only to procedures, so only the Environment and Procedure Divisions need to be considered in determining segmentation for a program. When using segmentation, the Procedure Division must be in sections, with each section belonging to the fixed portion or to one of the independent segments. When using segmentation, the logical sequence of the program is the same as it would be without segmentation, and control can be transferred to any paragraph within a section. Segmentation in no way affects the need to qualify procedure-names if this is necessary to ensure uniqueness.

When segmentation is used, certain restrictions are placed on the ALTER, PERFORM, SORT, and MERGE statements.

The Alter Statement

A GO TO statement in an independent segment must not be referred to by an ALTER statement in a section with a different segment number.

The Perform Statement

A PERFORM statement in an independent segment can have within its range only sections or paragraphs that are wholly contained in one or more noninde-pendent segments, or sections or paragraphs that are wholly contained in the same independent segment as the PERFORM.

A PERFORM statement in a nonindependent segment can have within its range only sections or paragraphs that are wholly contained in one or more nonindependent segments, or sections and paragraphs that are wholly contained in a single independent segment.

N.B. 68 COBOL had restrictions on the range of PERFORMs involving fixed overlayable segments.

The Sort and Merge Statements

If a SORT or MERGE statement is in a nonindependent segment, then any input or output procedure referenced must be either totally within nonindependent segments or wholly contained in a single independent segment.

If a SORT or MERGE statement is in an independent segment, any input or output procedure referenced must be either totally within nonindependent seg-ments or wholly within the same independent segment as the SORT or MERGE statement.

The constraints on SORT and MERGE statements are new to 74 COBOL.

See fixed position, independent segment.

Segmentation Module

The Segmentation Module provides the capability of specifying object program overlay requirements.

Level 1

Segmentation Level 1 provides a facility for specifying permanent and in-dependent segments. All sections with the same segment-number must be contiguous in the source program, and all permanent segments must be contiguous in the source program.

Level 2

Segmentation Level 2 provides the facility for intermixing sections with different segment-numbers and allows the fixed portion of the program to contain segments that can be overlaid.

See overlay.

SEGMENT-LIMIT

The SEGMENT-LIMIT clause enables the user to vary the number of permanent segments in the program while retaining the logical properties of fixed-portion segments.

Format:

SEGMENT-LIMIT IS segment-number

The SEGMENT-LIMIT clause is used in the OBJECT-COMPUTER paragraph of the ENVIRONMENT DIVISION. Segments are assigned segment-numbers from 00 to 99; those from 00 to 49, are usually part of the fixed portion, and those from 50 to 99 are independent segments.

When insufficient memory space is available to contain all permanent segments in addition to the largest overlayable segment, one must decrease the number of permanent segments. The SEGMENT-LIMIT clause accomplishes this decrease by specifying the highest segment-number that is treated as a permanent segment.

When this clause is specified, segment-number must be from 1 to 49, inclusive. Only segments with segment-numbers from 00 up to but not including the number specified in the clause are considered permanent segments. If this clause is omitted, all segments with numbers from 00 to 49 are considered permanent segments.

Any fixed permanent segment is always made available in its last-used state.
See fixed overlayable segment, fixed permanent segment, fixed portion.

segment-number

A segment-number is a user-defined word that classifies sections in the Procedure Division for purposes of segmentation. Segment-numbers can range from 0 to 99. A segment-number less than 10 can be expressed with or without a leading zero.

Generally, the more frequently a section is referred to, the lower the segment-number. Sections that frequently communicate with one another should be given the same segment-number. If no segment-number is specified, zero is assumed. Although all sections with the same segment-number constitute a single program segment, they need not be contiguous in the source program.

Segments with numbers from 0 through 49, inclusive, belong to the fixed portion of the program. Those with numbers from 50 to 99 are independent segments.

Sections in the DECLARATIVE part of the program must have segment-numbers smaller than 50.

See fixed portion, independent segment, leading character, overlay, user-defined word.

SELECT

The SELECT clause associates a file with a medium.

Format:

SELECT [OPTIONAL] file-name-1 ASSIGN TO{implementor-name-1}...

The SELECT clause must be specified first in the FILE-CONTROL paragraph. The file, specified by file-name-1, is associated with the storage medium specified by implementor-name-1, -2, etc.

The Optional Phrase

The OPTIONAL phrase can be specified only for input files with sequential organization. This phrase indicates that a file is not necessarily present when the object program is run.

See sequential i-o.

semicolon

The semicolon (;) is a separator or series connective. The use of the semicolon is permitted only if level 2 of the Nucleus is implemented. As a separator, the semicolon is used between statements in the Procedure Division or between successive entries in the other divisions. As a series connective, it can be used to link two or more operands.

A semicolon must always be followed by a space, and it cannot appear before the first clause in an entry or paragraph. In general, semicolons are not shown in the formats. Semicolons are interchangeable with commas; this is a new feature of 74 COBOL.

See separator.

SEND

The SEND verb causes a message, a message segment, or part of a message or message segment to be released to one or more output queues maintained by the message control system (MCS). This verb is new to 74 COBOL.

Format 1:

SEND cd-name FROM identifier-1

A format 1 SEND statement releases only a single portion of a message or message segment to the MCS. However, the MCS will not transmit a message until the entire message is placed in the output queue.

During execution of a SEND statement the MCS takes the value of TEXT LENGTH, data-name-2 in the description of cd-name, and uses this value to define the number of left-most characters from identifier-1 that are transmitted. If this field is zero, no characters are transmitted; if it is greater than the number of characters in identifier-1, an error exists, and STATUS KEY, data-name-3 in the description of cd-name, is set to 50. The effect of having special control characters within identifier-1 is undefined.

Once a SEND statement has released a part of a message to the MCS, only subsequent SEND statements within the same run unit can cause the rest of the message to be released.

If a receiving device has a fixed line size, each message or segment will begin at the left-most character position of the line. If the data is smaller than the line, unused character positions are space-filled to the right. If the data is too large to be contained on one line, subsequent SEND statements will cause the surplus to appear on the next line (or lines), left-justified.

If a receiving device can accept variable-length messages, each message or segment will begin at the next available character position of the device.

A format 1 SEND is implemented in level 2 of the Communication Module.

Format 2:

$$\underline{\text{SEND}} \text{ cd-name } [\underline{\text{FROM}} \text{ identifier-1}] \text{ WITH} \begin{Bmatrix} \text{identifier-2} \\ \underline{\text{EMI}} \\ \underline{\text{ESI}} \\ \underline{\text{EGI}} \end{Bmatrix}$$

$$\left[\begin{Bmatrix} \underline{\text{BEFORE}} \\ \underline{\text{AFTER}} \end{Bmatrix} \text{ADVANCING} \begin{Bmatrix} \begin{Bmatrix} \text{identifier-3} \\ \text{integer-1} \end{Bmatrix} \begin{bmatrix} \text{LINE} \\ \text{LINES} \end{bmatrix} \\ \text{mnemonic-name} \\ \underline{\text{PAGE}} \end{Bmatrix} \right]$$

A format 2 SEND releases only one message or segment, as indicated by identifier-2, ESI, EMI, or EGI. However, MCS will not transfer any portion of a message until the entire message is placed in the output queue.

The WITH phrase specifies that identifier-2, ESI, EMI, or EGI is used to notify the MCS that specific conditions exist. ESI indicates that the message segment is complete; EMI indicates that the message is complete; EGI indicates that the group of messages is complete. The precise interpretation given to EGI by the MCS is implementor-defined. ESI and identifier-2 are implemented in level 2 of the Communication Module.

The hierarchy of indicators is EGI, EMI, and ESI; and EGI need not be preceded by an ESI or EMI; an EMI need not be preceded by an ESI. If identifier-2 has a value of 1, an ESI is associated with the message; if it has a value of 2, an EMI is associated with the message; and if it has a value of 3, an EGI is associated with the message. If it has a value of 0, no indicator is associated with the message. Any value of identifier-2 other than 0, 1, 2, or 3 is interpreted as a value of 0. If identifier-2 has a value other than 0, 1, 2, or 3 and identifier-1 is not specified, then an error is indicated, and no data is transferred.

A portion of a message that is not terminated by an EMI or EGI is undefined. Therefore, the message does not logically exist as far as the MCS is concerned and cannot be sent to a destination. After execution of a STOP RUN, any such message portion is lost. Consequently, no portion of the message is sent.

The Advancing Phrase

The ADVANCING phrase allows the vertical positioning of each message or segment. If vertical positioning is not applicable for the device, the MCS ignores any explicit or implicit commands for this positioning. If identifier-2 is specified, but is equal to 0, the ADVANCING phrase is ignored by the MCS.

If vertical positioning is applicable and the ADVANCING phrase is not specified, implicit advancing takes place as if AFTER ADVANCING 1 LINE had been specified.

Any explicit or implicit advancing takes place before or after the message or message segment is output, as specified in the phrase. If integer-1 or identifier-3 is specified, the data is output before or after advancing the specified number of lines.

If PAGE is specified but has no meaning for the output device, advancing occurs as if ADVANCING 1 LINE had been specified. If PAGE has meaning for the device, the data is output before or after the device is positioned at the top of a new page.

If mnemonic-name is specified, the data is output according to the rules specified by the implementor for that device. The mnemonic-name must be defined in the SPECIAL-NAMES paragraph of the ENVIRONMENT DIVISION.

	One character	Integer	No operational sign	Can be = 0
Identifier-2	X	X	X	X
Identifier-3		X		X

See cd-name, Communication Module, destination, message, message control system (MCS), message segment, mnemonic-name, run unit.

sending item

The sending item in a statement is the source of the data that is transferred when the statement is executed. For example, in the statement:

MOVE GROSS-PAY TO LINE-3

GROSS-PAY is the sending item.

See receiving item.

SENTENCE

See IF, SEARCH.

sentence

A sentence is a sequence of one or more statements, the last of which is terminated by a period and space. The three types of sentences are imperative, conditional, and compiler-directing.

See compiler-directing sentence, conditional sentence, imperative sentence.

SEPARATE

See SIGN IS.

separator

A separator is a string of one or more characters used as punctuation. Separators consist of the following characters: the space, comma, semicolon, period, the left and right parentheses, and the quotation character.

A separator can be joined to another separator or a character-string. Separators can appear in a source program only where permitted by formats or by rules governing the particular separator. If a separator appears in a nonnumeric literal, a PICTURE clause, a comment-entry, or a comment line, it is not considered a separator and the rules do not apply.

See comma, comment-entry, comment line, nonnumeric literal, parentheses, period, punctuation character, quotation character, semicolon, space.

SEQUENCE

See MERGE, OBJECT-COMPUTER, SORT.

sequence number

A sequence number consists of six digits located in the sequence number area, between margin L and margin C. A sequence number can be used to label a source program line.

See reference format, sequence number area.

sequence number area

The sequence number area consists of the first six character positions of a line. These positions are located between margin L and margin C.

See reference format.

SEQUENTIAL

See ACCESS MODE, FILE-CONTROL, ORGANIZATION, SELECT.

sequential access

In sequential access mode, records are accessed in a given sequence. For sequential files this sequence is the same sequence as the records were written into the file. For relative files the sequence is in ascending order of relative record numbers of all records currently in the file. For indexed files the sequence is in ascending order of record key values. If duplicate values of a key are allowed, the order within duplicates is the same order as the records were written into the file.

See indexed i-o, RECORD KEY, relative i-o, relative record number, sequential i-o.

sequential file

A sequential file is a file with sequential organization.

See sequential i-o.

sequential i-o

Sequential i-o deals with files which contain records that have a unique predecessor-successor relationship. That is, each record except the first has a unique predecessor, and each record except the last has a unique successor. These relationships are established when the records are written and cannot be changed. However, any record can be updated in place, and records can be added to the end of the file. The sequence of records is logical, not necessarily physical. Sequential organization is device independent.

The only access mode usable with sequential i-o is sequential. In this mode, records are accessed in the order in which they were originally written.

The verbs CLOSE, OPEN, READ, REWRITE, USE, and WRITE can be used with sequential files.

Level 1

Level 1 provides partial facilities for FILE CONTROL, I-O-CONTROL and file description entries, as well as limited capabilities for CLOSE, OPEN, USE, and WRITE. Full capabilities for READ and REWRITE are provided.

Level 2

Level 2 provides full facilities for all sequential i-o verbs and functions, including optional files, multiple file tapes, the RESERVE, SAME AREA, REVERSED, and EXTEND features.

Current-Record Pointer

In sequential i-o the current-record pointer is affected only by OPEN and READ statements.

File Status

The FILE STATUS item, if specified, is updated by sequential i-o verbs. Valid combinations are:

Status Key 1	Status Key 2	Meaning
0	0	Successful completion
1	0	At end
3	0	Permanent error
3	4	Boundary violation
9	–	Implementor-defined

See current-record pointer, file description.

Sequential I-O Module

See sequential i-o.

SET

The SET statement assigns values to or modifies the contents of index-names and index data items and sets data items to values corresponding to occurrence numbers.

Format 1:

$$\underline{SET}\begin{Bmatrix} \text{identifier-1} \\ \text{index-name-1} \end{Bmatrix} \ldots \underline{TO}\begin{Bmatrix} \text{identifier-2} \\ \text{index-name-2} \\ \text{integer-1} \end{Bmatrix}$$

A format 1 SET statement assigns an occurrence number to an index-name or to an index data item, or assigns a value that corresponds to an occurrence number to a data item. Understanding the concept of 'occurrence number' is vital to following the operation of the SET statement. Index-names are related to tables by appearing in the table's INDEXED BY clause. Each of the valid combinations of items in the SET statement will be discussed separately. In all of the following operations, any subscripting or indexing associated with identifier-1 is performed immediately before identifier-1 is changed. In the case of multiple items before the TO phrase, the values that existed for identifier-2 or index-name-2 at the beginning of the execution of the statement are the ones used for all operations.

1.   SET index-name-1 TO integer-1

Index-name-1 is set to the occurrence number corresponding to the value of integer-1. This provides a way of setting an index-name to an initial value.

2.   SET index-name-1 TO identifier-2

If identifier-2 is an integer data item, index-name-1 is set to the occurrence number corresponding to the value of identifier-2. If identifier-2 is an index data item, then index-name-1 is set to the same *contents* as identifier-2 with no conversion of data taking place.

3.   SET index-name-1 TO index-name-2

Index-name-1 is set to the occurrence number designated by index-name-2. Index-name-2 need not refer to the same table as index-name-1.

4.   SET identifier-1 TO identifier-2

For this statement both identifier-1 and identifier-2 must be index data items. Identifier-1 is set equal to the contents of identifier-2 with no conversion of data taking place.

5.   SET identifier-1 TO index-name-2

If identifier-1 is not an index data item, identifier-1 is set to a value corresponding to the occurrence number of index-name-2. If identifier-1 is an index data item, it is set equal to the contents of index-name-2 with no conversion of data taking place.

The following chart shows the valid forms of a format 1 SET.

TO

SET		Integer literal	Integer data item	Index-name	Index data item
Identifier-1	Integer data item			X	
	Index data item			X	X
Index-name-1		X	X	X	X

Format 2:

$$\text{SET} \{\text{index-name-3}\} \ldots \begin{Bmatrix} \underline{\text{UP BY}} \\ \underline{\text{DOWN BY}} \end{Bmatrix} \begin{Bmatrix} \text{identifier-3} \\ \text{integer-2} \end{Bmatrix}$$

A format 2 SET statement causes the contents of index-name-3 to be incremented or decremented by a value that corresponds to the number of occurrences designated by the value of integer-2 or identifier-3.

Both Formats:

	Index data item	Elementary numeric integer	Greater than 0	Optional sign
Identifier-1, -2	X	X		
Integer-1			X	X
Identifier-3		X		
Integer-2				X

Neither form of SET can set an index-name to a value that is less than 1 or greater than the maximum occurrence number of the associated table. The fact that integer-2 can be less than zero is new to 74 COBOL.

See index data item, indexing, index-name, occurrence number, subscripting.

SIGN

See CURRENCY SIGN, SIGN IS.

sign

A sign denotes the algebraic value associated with a numerical quantity. Both operational signs and editing signs are used in COBOL.

See operational sign, PICTURE.

sign condition

The sign condition is a determination of whether the algebraic value of a numeric item or arithmetic expression is less than, equal to, or greater than zero. The sign condition appears in IF statements thus:

$$\underline{\text{IF}} \begin{Bmatrix} \text{identifier} \\ \text{arithmetic expression} \end{Bmatrix} \text{IS } [\underline{\text{NOT}}] \begin{Bmatrix} \underline{\text{POSITIVE}} \\ \underline{\text{NEGATIVE}} \\ \underline{\text{ZERO}} \end{Bmatrix}$$

The arithmetic expression must contain at least one variable; this is a new feature of 74 COBOL.

See arithmetic expression.

SIGN IS

The SIGN IS clause explicitly specifies the position and mode of representation of the operational sign. This is a new feature of 74 COBOL.

Format:

$$[\text{SIGN} \ \text{IS}] \begin{Bmatrix} \underline{\text{LEADING}} \\ \underline{\text{TRAILING}} \end{Bmatrix} [\underline{\text{SEPARATE}} \ \text{CHARACTER}]$$

The SIGN IS clause can be applied only to an elementary numeric data item with a PICTURE containing an S, or to a group item that contains at least one such numeric data item. When used with a group item, SIGN IS applies to each numeric data item in the group.

At most, one SIGN IS clause can apply to any data item, and this data item must be described, implicitly or explicitly, as USAGE IS DISPLAY. This clause must be used for any signed numeric data items with a file description containing the CODE-SET clause.

An S in a PICTURE clause makes the data item signed numeric. However, it indicates only the presence of an operational sign. It does not indicate the representation nor, necessarily, the position of this sign. If the SIGN IS clause is not specified, the position and representation of the operational sign are defined by the implementor.

If the SEPARATE character phrase is present, the operational sign is either the character before the leading digit or after the trailing digit of the data item. The position that holds the sign is not a digit position; the letter S in the PICTURE clause *is* counted in determining the size of the item. The operational signs for positive and negative numbers are the standard data format characters '+' and '−' respectively.

If the SEPARATE CHARACTER phrase is not present, the operational sign is associated with the leading or trailing digit position in the elementary item. The S in the PICTURE is not counted in determining the size of the item. What constitutes a valid sign is implementor-defined.

See data description, elementary item, file description, group item, numeric data item.

simple condition

A simple condition is one that cannot be further reduced into two or more conditions.

See complex condition.

68 COBOL

Following is a compendium of the substantive changes from 68 COBOL to 74 COBOL. For complete details on any particular topic, refer to the appropriate entry.

ACCEPT—this verb can now access DAY, DATE, TIME, and MESSAGE COUNT.

ACCESS MODE—one can now specify DYNAMIC access mode.

ADD—one can now have multiple fields after GIVING.

ALTERNATE RECORD KEY—new feature.

arithmetic expression—can now contain a unary plus.

ASSIGN—the 'integer implementor-name' and 'OR implementor-name' options have been deleted.

B—can be an editing character.

BLANK WHEN ZERO—this cannot be used if an asterisk is used in the PICTURE clause.

CALL—'CALL identifier' and the ON OVERFLOW clause are new.

CANCEL—new verb.

class condition—one cannot use a numeric test with a group item that is composed of elementary items that are described as signed.

CLOSE—'FOR REMOVAL' is new; NO REWIND now applies to all devices that can support the concept of 'rewind.'

CODE-SET—clause added to file description for sequential i-o.

combined conditions—now, if any part of an abbreviated combined condition is enclosed in parentheses, all subjects and operators required for that part's expansion must now be enclosed in the same set of parentheses.

comma—is now interchangeable with the semicolon.

comment-line—now the last line in the program can be a comment-line.

communication module—new feature.

comparison rules—if NOT is immediately followed by a relational operator, it is part of the relational operator; previously, it was a logical operator.

composite of operands—this is now limited to 18 digits for *all* arithmetic operations; previously, it had been limited only for ADD and SUBTRACT.

COMPUTE—this verb can now have multiple receiving fields.

CONTROLS ARE FINAL—this has been deleted.

COPY
    Library-name is new.
    Groups of words can be replaced.
    The COPY statement can appear anywhere in a program.

CURRENCY SIGN—L, /, and = cannot be specified.

debug module—new feature.

debugging line—new feature.

DELETE—new verb.

DISPLAY—if operand is numeric-edited, it must be an unsigned integer.

DIVIDE—multiple receiving fields are now permitted.

dynamic access—new feature.

ENABLE—new feature.

EXIT PROGRAM—new feature.

FILE-CONTROL
    ORGANIZATION IS RELATIVE—new feature.
    RELATIVE KEY clause—new feature.
    ACCESS MODE clause—new feature.
    RESERVE integer AREAS clause—new feature.
    MULTIPLE REEL/UNIT clause—deleted.
    PROCESSING MODE clause—deleted.
    Except for the ASSIGN clause, all other clauses can appear in any order.

file description entry—this clause must now be equivalent to that used when the file was created.

FILE STATUS clause—new feature.

GO TO—the 'TO' is no longer required.

IF—the 'ELSE' is no longer permitted.

indexed i-o
    ORGANIZATION IS INDEXED clause—new feature.
    ACCESS MODE clause—new feature.
    RECORD KEY clause—new feature.

INSPECT—can count or replace groups of characters, whereas EXAMINE only allowed single-character operations.

Inter-Program Communication Module—new feature.

LABEL RECORDS—data-name option deleted; the ability to define and access user-specified labels has been deleted.

level-numbers—except for 01, level-numbers can now appear anywhere to the right of margin A.

level 77—need not precede level 01 items in working storage.

library—one can now have more than one library.

library-name—new feature.

LINAGE—new feature.

LINE NUMBER IS NEXT PAGE—deleted.

LINKAGE SECTION—new feature.

MERGE—new feature.

mnemonic-name—must now have at least one alphanumeric character.

MOVE—an integer item whose right-most PICTURE character is a P can be moved to an alphanumeric or alphanumeric-edited item.

numeric field—cannot be over 18 digits.

OBJECT-COMPUTER—see PROGRAM COLLATING SEQUENCE.

OCCURS . . . DEPENDING ON

The fixed portion of a record must entirely precede the variable portion.
If SYNC is specified for an item, any implicit FILLER generated is generated for each occurrence of that item.

OPEN REVERSED—now positions a file at its end.
—now applies to all devices that can support this function.

OPEN EXTEND—new feature.

OPEN INPUT, OPEN I-O—now make a record area available to the program.

OPEN NO REWIND—applies to all devices that can support the concept of REWIND.

paragraph—now it is possible for a paragraph to contain no entries.

PERFORM

There are now restrictions on the range of a PERFORM that are based on segmentation considerations.
VARYING—identifiers need not be integers; changing the FROM variable during execution can affect the number of times that the procedures are executed if more than one AFTER phrase is specified.
Control is passed only once in a format 2 PERFORM; thus an independent segment will be made available in its initial state only once for each execution of that PERFORM.

PICTURE

Now the number of digit positions described in a numeric item cannot exceed 18.
Now the character-string is limited to 30 *characters*, rather than to 30 symbols.
The stroke (/) and B are now editing characters.

procedure division header—can now have the USING clause.

PROCESSING MODE—dropped from FILE-CONTROL paragraph.

PROGRAM COLLATING SEQUENCE—new feature in OBJECT-COMPUTER paragraph.

pseudo-text delimiter—new feature.

qualifier

Must now be at least five levels deep.

Now a complete set of qualifiers for one name connot be the same as a partial set for another.

QUOTES—now one can represent a quotation character in a nonnumeric literal by two contiguous quotation marks.

random access—this module has been dropped.

READ—the AT END and INVALID KEY phrases are now optional under certain conditions.

READ NEXT—new feature.

RECEIVE—new verb.

REDEFINES—the object of this clause can now be subordinate to a data item described with an OCCURS clause.

relation condition
'TO' is no longer required in EQUAL TO.
There must be reference to at least one variable in the condition.
If 'NOT' is immediately followed by a relational operator, it is part of that operator (formerly it was a logical operator).

REPORT IS—dropped from SPECIAL-NAMES.

Report Writer Module—entirely rewritten; reports need not be presented on a printer.

REWRITE—new verb.

SAME AREA—now SAME SORT-MERGE AREA is possible.

SEARCH ALL
The subject of the condition in the WHEN phrase must be a data item that is named in the KEY phrase of the referenced table.
The object of the condition in the WHEN phrase cannot be a data item that is named in the KEY phrase of the referenced table. (Previously either the subject *or* the object could be such an item.)
Results are predictable only when the data is organized as described by the ASCENDING or DESCENDING KEY clause.
VARYING identifier-2—if identifier-2 is an index data item it is incremented as the associated index is incremented. (Previously it was incremented by the same amount as the occurrence number, viz., one.)

section—now a section need not contain any paragraphs.

segmentation
There is now no logical difference between fixed and fixed overlayable.
New restrictions on the range of a PERFORM and on SORT and MERGE input and output procedures.

semicolon—is now interchangeable with the comma.

SEND—new verb.

SET—an index can now be set up or down by a negative value.

SIGN—the sign can now be specified as leading or trailing and as whether it occupies a separate character position.

sign condition—arithmetic expression must refer to at least one variable.

SORT

Restrictions on input and output procedures based on segmentation considerations.

COLLATING SEQUENCE phrase added.

Multiple file names allowed in USING phrase.

Semicolon no longer mandatory.

No more than one file from a multiple-file reel can appear in a SORT.

spaces—can now precede a comma, period, semicolon, and parenthesis, except in a PICTURE clause.

SPECIAL-NAMES

L, /, and = cannot be specified in the CURRENCY SIGN clause.

Alphabet-name is a new feature.

REPORT IS clause dropped.

START—can position a relative or indexed file for sequential retrieval of records.

STOP—if the operand is a numeric literal, it must be an unsigned integer.

STRING—new verb.

stroke (slash)—is now an editing character.

SUBTRACT—can now have multiple receiving fields.

switch status—switches can now be hardware or software.

table handling

Commas are not required between subscripts or indices.

Literals and index-names can be mixed in a table reference.

UNSTRING—new verb.

USE . . . LABEL—label processing is no longer permitted via the USE verb.

USE . . . ERROR—changed to ERROR/EXCEPTION so that a procedure can be invoked on either an error or an exception condition.

USE procedures—cannot be invoked by other USE procedures.

VALUE IS

The data-item must agree with the literal with respect to sign.

If the data-item is numeric-edited, the literal must be nonnumeric.

VALUE OF—the data name, which was formerly in this clause, must now be an implementor-name; it can no longer be a user-defined field.

WRITE

INVALID KEY phrase deleted from sequential i-o.

PAGE phrase added.

INVALID KEY phrase required in relative and indexed i-o only under certain conditions.

SIZE

See OBJECT-COMPUTER.

size

The size of an elementary or group item is the number of characters the item contains. Synchronization and usage may cause a difference between this size and the actual number of bytes required for internal representation of the item.

See elementary item, group item, SYNCHRONIZED, USAGE.

SIZE ERROR

See ADD, COMPUTE, DIVIDE, MULTIPLY, SUBTRACT.

Size Error condition

The Size Error condition exists when, after execution of an arithmetic statement and subsequent decimal point alignment, the integer portion of the absolute value of the result is too large to fit into the receiving item. The Size Error condition does not apply to intermediate results except in the MULTIPLY and DIVIDE statements. Division by zero always causes the Size Error condition. If ROUNDING is specified, the rounding occurs before the check for the Size Error condition.

When the Size Error condition occurs, subsequent action depends upon whether or not the SIZE ERROR phrase is specified in the statement causing the condition. If the SIZE ERROR phrase is specified, the values of those receiving items affected by size errors are not altered; after execution of the statement is complete, the imperative-statement in the SIZE ERROR phrase is executed. This imperative-statement is executed only once, no matter how many size errors have occurred during execution of the arithmetic statement. If the SIZE ERROR phrase is not specified and a size error occurs, the values of those identifiers affected by size errors are unpredictable. In either case, values of identifiers for which no size errors occur will be correct even though size errors have occurred for other identifiers in the statement.

If an operation causes a Size Error condition, in an ADD or SUBTRACT statement with the CORRESPONDING phrase, the imperative-statement is not executed until all of the operations are completed.

See the arithmetic verbs and receiving item, ROUNDING, truncation.

size of record
> *See* RECORD CONTAINS.

SLASH

> A slash (/) in column 7 will cause the current page to be ejected during compilation. The remainder of the line that contains the slash is treated as a comment.
> *See* PICTURE.

SORT

> The SORT verb creates a sort file by executing input procedures or by transferring records from another file. Using a set of specified keys, it sorts these records and then makes each record available, in sorted order, to one or more output procedures or to an output file.

> *Format:*

$$\underline{SORT} \text{ file-name-1} \left\{ ON \left\{ \frac{\underline{ASCENDING}}{\underline{DESCENDING}} \right\} KEY \{\text{data-name-1}\} \ldots \right\} \ldots$$

$$[COLLATING \ \underline{SEQUENCE} \ IS \ \text{alphabet-name}]$$

$$\left\{ \begin{array}{l} \underline{INPUT} \ \underline{PROCEDURE} \ IS \ \text{section-name-1} \left[\left\{ \frac{\underline{THROUGH}}{\underline{THRU}} \right\} \text{section-name-2} \right] \\ \underline{USING} \ \{\text{file-name-2}\} \ldots \end{array} \right\}$$

$$\left\{ \begin{array}{l} \underline{OUTPUT} \ \underline{PROCEDURE} \ IS \ \text{section-name-3} \left[\left\{ \frac{\underline{THROUGH}}{\underline{THRU}} \right\} \text{section-name-4} \right] \\ \underline{GIVING} \ \text{file-name-3} \end{array} \right\}$$

> A SORT statement has three phases:

1. Records are released to it or obtained from an input file.

2. The records are sorted.

3. Records are returned by the sort so that they can be processed by the program.

If only level 1 of the Sort-Merge Module is implemented, then the Procedure Division of the program can contain only one SORT statement and a STOP RUN statement in the first nondeclarative portion; the USING phrase can contain only one file-name, and the COLLATING SEQUENCE phrase cannot be used. Other sections can consist of only the input and output procedures associated with the SORT statement.

> If level 2 of the Sort-Merge Module is implemented, SORT statements can appear anywhere in the Procedure Division except in the DECLARATIVES portion or in the input and output procedures associated with a SORT or MERGE statement.

File-name-1 must be described in a sort-merge file description in the DATA DIVISION. No more than one file from a multiple file reel can appear in a SORT statement. (This is a new restriction of 74 COBOL.) The data-names following KEY are listed from left to right in order of decreasing significance. If there is more than one KEY phrase, the way in which the data-names are divided among the KEY phrases does not affect this order.

When ASCENDING is specified, the sorted sequence will be from the lowest value of the data items specified in the KEY clause to the highest value, as defined by the rules for comparison of operands in a relation condition.

When DESCENDING is specified, the sorted sequence will be from the highest value of the data item specified in the KEY clause to the lowest value, as defined by the rules for comparison of operands in a relation condition.

The data-names specified in the KEY clause must conform to the rules:

1. They must be described in records associated with file-name-1.

2. They cannot be variable size items, their data description cannot contain an OCCURS clause, nor can they be subordinate to an entry with an OCCURS clause.

3. If file-name-1 has more than one record description, the data items need be described in only one of the record descriptions.

4. They can be qualified.

Input Procedure

If only section-name-1 is specified, it defines the input procedure. If section-name-2 is also specified, the input procedure is from the first statement in section-name-1 to the last statement in section-name-2. The statements comprising the input procedure must be contiguous in the program and not be a part of any output procedure.

The input procedure can contain any statements necessary to select, create, or modify records except

• A SORT or MERGE statement.

• Any statement that causes an explicit transfer of control to points outside the input procedure, e.g., ALTER, GO TO, or PERFORM.

Control cannot be transferred into the input procedure from points outside of it. Control can, however, be transferred implicitly to DECLARATIVES.

If an input procedure is specified, control is transferred to it by the sort mechanism before file-name-1 is sorted. In order to transfer records to file-name-1, the input procedure must contain at least one RELEASE statement. A return mechanism is inserted at the end of the last section of the input procedure and when control passes from the last statement of this procedure, the records that have been released to file-name-1 are sorted.

The Using Phrase

If the USING phrase is specified, all the records in file-name-2 are transferred to file-name-1. This is the implied input procedure. File-name-2 must have sequential organization and must not be open at the time the SORT is executed. The SORT statement uses file-name-2 in such a way that any associated USE procedures are executed. When the SORT statement is through with file-name-2, the terminating function that is performed is equivalent to a CLOSE statement without any optional phrases. (68 COBOL allowed for only one file in this clause; and, if only level 1 of the SORT-MERGE Module is implemented, this is still the case.)

The actual size of a record in file-name-2 must be equal to the actual size of a record in file-name-1. If the data descriptions are not identical, it is up to the user to describe the records so that an equal number of character positions will be allocated for corresponding records.

Output Procedure

If only section-name-3 is specified, it defines the output procedure. If section-name-4 is also specified, the output procedure is from the first statement in section-name-3 to the last statement in section-name-4. The statements comprising the output procedure must be contiguous in the program and not be a part of any input procedure.

The output procedure can include any statements needed to select, create, or modify records except as noted under 'Input Procedure.'

If an output procedure is specified, control passes to it after file-name-1 has been sorted, and the SORT procedure is at a point where it can select the next record in sorted order when requested. In order to make sorted records available for subsequent processing by other parts of the program, the output procedure must include at least one RETURN statement.

A return mechanism is inserted at the end of the last section of the output procedure. When control passes from the last statement of this procedure, the return mechanism terminates the SORT and passes control to the statement following the SORT.

The Giving Phrase

If the GIVING phrase is specified, all the sorted records are written to file-name-3. This is the implied output procedure. File-name-3 must have sequential organization and must not be open at the time the SORT is executed. The SORT statement uses file-name-3 in such a way that any associated USE procedures are executed. When the SORT statement is through with file-name-3, the terminating function that is performed is equivalent to a CLOSE statement without any optional phrases.

The actual size of a record in file-name-3 must be equal to the actual size of a record in file-name-1. If the data descriptions are not identical, it is up to the user to describe the records so that an equal number of character positions will be allocated for corresponding records.

The Collating Sequence Phrase

If the COLLATING SEQUENCE phrase is specified, the collating sequence specified by alphabet-name is used in the sort operation. If this phrase is not specified, the sequence that has been established as the program collating sequence in the OBJECT-COMPUTER paragraph is used. This phrase is a new feature of 74 COBOL, and is implemented in level 2 of the Sort-Merge Module.

Segmentation Considerations

If a SORT statement appears in an independent segment, any input or output procedure referred to by that SORT must be contained wholly within the same independent segment as the SORT statement itself or be contained wholly within nonindependent segments.

If a SORT statement appears in a nonindependent segment, any input or output procedure referred to by that SORT must be contained wholly within a single independent segment or be contained wholly within nonindependent segments.

These constraints are new to 74 COBOL.

See alphabet-name, collating sequence, I-O-CONTROL, MULTIPLE FILE, qualification, relation condition, SAME AREA, sequential i-o, size, variable size item.

sort facility

The sort facility enables the user to put one or more files of records into a desired order according to a set of user-specified keys contained within each record. Furthermore, special processing can be applied before and/or after the records are ordered.

See SORT.

sort file

A sort file is a collection of records to be sorted. It is created when the SORT statement executes input procedures or transfers records from another file or files. A sort file can be accessed only by the SORT statement.

See SORT.

SORT-MERGE

See I-O-CONTROL, SAME AREA.

sort-merge file description

The sort-merge file description, which is indicated by the level-indicator SD, gives information about the size, structure, and names of data records in a sort-merge file.

Format:

SD file-name[RECORD CONTAINS [integer-1 TO] integer-2 CHARACTERS]

$$\left[\text{DATA} \begin{Bmatrix} \underline{\text{RECORD}} \text{ IS} \\ \underline{\text{RECORDS}} \text{ ARE} \end{Bmatrix} \{\text{data-name-1}\} \dots \right] \text{.}$$

The level-indicator, SD, must precede the file name. It identifies the file as a sort-merge file. The two clauses following file-name are optional and can appear in any order. One or more record description entries must follow the SD entry. No input-output statements can be executed for a sort-merge file. Also, there are no label procedures associated with them.

See level-indicator, record description.

Sort-Merge Module

The Sort-Merge Module provides the capability of ordering one or more files of records or combining two or more ordered files of records, according to a set of user-specified keys that are contained within each record. The user can optionally apply special processing to each of the individual records by means of input or output procedures before or after the records are ordered or after the records have been combined.

Level 1

Sort-Merge Level 1 provides the facility for sorting a single file only once within a given execution of a program. Provision for input and output procedures is also provided.

Level 2

Sort-Merge Level 2 provides the facility for sorting one or more files or for merging two or more files one or more times within a given execution of a program.

See MERGE, SORT.

SOURCE

The SOURCE clause identifies the data item that is moved to a printable item.

Format:

SOURCE IS identifier-1

The SOURCE clause appears in a report group description entry. The value of the item specified by identifier-1 is moved to the associated printable item just prior to the presenting of the report group by the Report Writer Control System (RWCS).

Identifier-1 must be defined in such a way that it conforms to the rules for a sending item as described in the MOVE statement. Identifier-1 can be defined in any section of the DATA DIVISION. If identifier-1 is a REPORT SECTION item it can be only PAGE-COUNTER, LINE-COUNTER, or a sum counter associated with the report within which the SOURCE clause appears.

See communication description entry, report group description, Report Writer Control System, sending item, sum counter.

source

A source is the symbolic identification of the originator of a transmission to a queue.

See queue.

SOURCE-COMPUTER

The SOURCE-COMPUTER paragraph is an entry in the CONFIGURATION SECTION of the ENVIRONMENT DIVISION. It describes the computer on which the program is to be compiled.

Format:

SOURCE-COMPUTER• computer-name [WITH DEBUGGING MODE]•

When the DEBUGGING MODE clause is specified, all USE FOR DEBUGGING statements and debugging lines are compiled. If this clause is omitted, USE FOR DEBUGGING statements and their associated sections and debugging lines are treated as comment lines.

Computer-name is specified by the implementor.

See comment line, debugging line.

source item

A source item is an identifier, specified in a SOURCE clause, that provides the value of a printed item.

source program

A source program is a syntactically correct set of COBOL statements including all four divisions: Identification, Environment, Data, and Procedure, in that order.

See object program.

SPACE (SPACES)

SPACE is a figurative constant, representing one or more instances of the space character. The exact number of spaces represented depends on the context in which SPACE appears. The singular and plural forms are considered equivalent, and the choice is generally made for readability.

See figurative constant.

space

The space character is a separator that can immediately precede all separators except a closing quotation character unless prohibited by format rules. A space can immediately follow any separator except an opening quotation character.

A string of contiguous spaces is logically equivalent to a single space; thus anywhere the space character is valid, a string of spaces can be used.

In 68 COBOL a space could not precede a comma, period, semicolon, or parenthesis.

See format, separator.

space fill

Space filling is the process of moving spaces into a receiving item to occupy character positions that would not otherwise be acted upon by an operation. Space filling occurs when the receiving item has more character positions than the sending item.

Example:

    SEND-IT PIC XXX VALUE 'ABC'.

    REC-IT PIC XXXXX VALUE '12345'.

When one executes a

    MOVE SEND-IT TO REC-IT

the resulting contents of REC-IT are ABC△△ not ABC45. REC-IT has been space filled in the two right-most positions that did not correspond to character positions in the sending item.

Note: '△' represents a space.

See alignment rules, JUSTIFIED, MOVE, sending item, receiving item, zero fill.

special character

A special character is any one of the following:

plus sign	+
minus sign, hyphen	−
asterisk	*
stroke	/
period	.
equal sign	=
less than sign	<
greater than sign	>
currency sign	$
comma	,
semicolon	;
quotation character	"
left parenthesis	(
right parenthesis	)

special-character words

Special-character words are the arithmetic operators and relation characters that are considered reserved words. They are

Arithmetic Operators

addition symbol	+
subtraction symbol	−
multiplication symbol	*
division symbol	/
exponentiation symbol	**

Relation Characters

equal sign	=
greater than sign	`>
less than sign	<

Whenever a special-character word appears in a format, it is a keyword. Special-character words are not underlined in the formats so as to avoid confusion.

SPECIAL-NAMES

The SPECIAL-NAMES paragraph relates implementor-names to user-specified mnemonic-names, and alphabet-names to character sets and/or collating sequences.

Format:

SPECIAL-NAMES•

$$\left[\text{implementor-name}\left\{\begin{array}{l}\underline{\text{IS}}\text{ mnemonic-name}\left[\underline{\text{ON}}\text{ STATUS }\underline{\text{IS}}\text{ condition-name-1}\right]\\\quad\left[\underline{\text{OFF}}\text{ STATUS }\underline{\text{IS}}\text{ condition-name-2}\right]\\\left[\underline{\text{ON}}\text{ STATUS }\underline{\text{IS}}\text{ condition-name-1}\right]\left[\underline{\text{OFF}}\text{ STATUS }\underline{\text{IS}}\text{ condition-name-2}\right]\end{array}\right\}\right]\dots$$

$$\left[\left\{\text{alphabet-name IS}\left\{\begin{array}{l}\underline{\text{STANDARD-1}}\\\underline{\text{NATIVE}}\\\text{implementor-name}\\\left\{\text{literal-1}\left[\left\{\begin{array}{l}\underline{\text{THROUGH}}\\\underline{\text{THRU}}\end{array}\right\}\text{literal-2}\\\left\{\underline{\text{ALSO}}\text{ literal-3}\right\}\dots\right]\right\}\end{array}\right\}\right\}\dots\right]\dots$$

[CURRENCY SIGN IS literal-4]

[DECIMAL-POINT IS COMMA]•

Implementor-name

If implementor-name is not a switch, the associated mnemonic-name can be used in ACCEPT, DISPLAY, SEND, and WRITE statements. If implementor-name is a switch, at least one condition-name must be associated with it. For a given implementor-name there can be at most one condition-name for the ON condition and one condition-name for the OFF condition. The condition-name defines the status of the switch, i.e., whether it is on or off. The status of the switch is interrogated by testing the condition-names. The ON STATUS and OFF STATUS clauses can be written in any order.

Currency Sign Clause

The CURRENCY SIGN clause defines the character that is used in the PICTURE clause to represent the currency symbol. Literal-4 must be only one character long and cannot be any of the following: 0 through 9, A, B, C, D, L, P, R, S, V, X, Z, *, +, (, –,), /, =, comma, period, quotation character, or space. (In 68 COBOL, the characters: L, /, and =, could appear in this clause.)

If this clause is not present, the currency sign ($) is used in PICTURE clause to represent the currency symbol.

Decimal-point is Comma Clause

If the DECIMAL-POINT IS COMMA clause is specified, the functions of the period and comma are interchanged in PICTURE clauses and numeric literals.

Alphabet-name Clause

The alphabet-name clause relates an alphabet-name to a specified collating sequence or character code set. If the alphabet-name defined in this clause is referred to in the COLLATING SEQUENCE clause of the OBJECT-COMPUTER paragraph, the SORT statement, or the MERGE statement, it specifies a character code set. This clause is new to 74 COBOL.

Native

If NATIVE is specified, the native collating sequence or native character code set is used. The ordering of characters within native sequences is implementor-defined.

Standard-1

If STANDARD-1 is specified, the ASCII character sequence is used. Each character in the ASCII set is associated with the corresponding character in the native character set. If there is no corresponding character in the native set, the correspondence is implementor-defined.

Implementor-name

If an implementor-name is specified, the character set is defined by the implementor. There can be more than one implementor-name defined in this way and thus more than one ordering of characters. The implementor also defines, for each implementor-name, the correspondence between characters of the set specified by the implementor-name and the characters in the native character set.

Literal

If the literal phrase is specified, the associated alphabet-name cannot be referenced in a CODE-SET clause. A given character cannot be specified more than once in the alphabet-name clause. Use of the literal phrase defines a collating sequence as follows:

1. If the literal is numeric, it specifies the ordinal position of a character within the native character set. The literal must be an unsigned integer and have a value greater than one and not greater than the number of characters in the native character set.

2. If the literal is nonnumeric, it specifies the actual character within the native character set. If the literal contains more than one character, each character, starting with the left-most, is assigned successive ascending positions in the collating sequence being specified.

3. The order in which literals appear in this clause specifies, in ascending sequence, the ordinal number of the character within the collating sequence being specified.

4. Any characters in the native collating sequence that are not specified in this phrase assume a position in the collating sequence being specified that is

greater than any of the specified characters. If more than one character of the native sequence is not specified, the unspecified characters maintain the same relative order as they had within the native collating sequence.

5. If THROUGH or THRU is specified, the set of contiguous characters in the native character set, beginning with the character specified by literal-1 and ending with the character specified by literal-2, is assigned a successive ascending position in the collating sequence being specified. The set of characters specified by the THRU or THROUGH clause can be in ascending or descending sequence in the native character set. All literals must be one character long.

6. If ALSO is specified, the character of the native character set specified by literal-3 is assigned to the same position in the collating sequence being specified. All literals must be one character long.

Effect on Figurative Constants

The figurative constant HIGH-VALUE is associated with the character that has the highest position in the program collating sequence. If more than one character has the highest position, HIGH-VALUE is the last character specified.

The figurative constant LOW-VALUE is associated with the character that has the lowest position in the program collating sequence. If more than one character has the lowest position, LOW-VALUE is the first character specified.

See alphabet-name, collating sequence, condition-name, currency symbol, implementor-name, mnemonic-name, numeric-literal.

special register

Special registers are compiler-generated storage areas that are used to hold information produced in conjunction with specific COBOL features. The special registers are LINAGE-COUNTER, DEBUG-ITEM, LINE-COUNTER, PAGE-COUNTER.

STANDARD

See file description, LABEL RECORDS, USE.

standard alignment rules

See alignment rules.

standard data format

Standard data format refers to the way data would appear on a printed page, rather than the way it is stored internally or on an external storage medium.

STANDARD-1

See SPECIAL-NAMES.

START

The START verb positions the current-record pointer within a relative or indexed file prior to sequential retrieval of records. START is supported only in level 2 of the Relative I-O and Indexed I-O modules and is a new feature of 74 COBOL.

Format 1:

$$
\underline{\text{START}}\text{ file-name}\left[\underline{\text{KEY}}\text{ IS}\left\{\begin{array}{l}\underline{\text{EQUAL}}\text{ TO}\\ =\\ \underline{\text{GREATER}}\text{ THAN}\\ >\\ \underline{\text{NOT}}\ \underline{\text{LESS}}\text{ THAN}\\ \underline{\text{NOT}}\ <\end{array}\right\}\text{data-name-1}\right]
$$

[; <u>INVALID</u> KEY imperative-statement-1]

To position the current-record pointer, the comparison specified in the KEY phrase takes place between a key associated with each record in the file and the key data item of the file. If the KEY phrase is not specified, the operator '=' is used. The current-record pointer is positioned to the first logical record with a key that satisfies the comparison. If no record in the file satisfies the comparison, the START is unsuccessful and the Invalid Key condition exists.

The file referenced by file-name cannot be a SORT or MERGE file. It must have indexed or relative organization and be in the sequential or dynamic access mode. The file must be opened in the input or I-O mode before the START is executed.

Relative Files

If START is to be used with a relative file, the RELATIVE KEY clause must be specified in that file's FILE-CONTROL entry. A comparison is made between the value of the data item specified in this clause and the logical ordinal position of the records in the file, i.e., the relative record numbers. (If the KEY phrase is specified, data-name-1 must be the same data item that is specified in this RELATIVE KEY clause.) The programmer is responsible for putting a value into the RELATIVE KEY item before executing the START.

The current-record pointer is positioned to the first record in the file with a relative record number which satisfied the comparison. In the case of an EQUAL TO comparison, if there is no record in the record position specified by the key, the START is unsuccessful. In the case of a NOT LESS THAN comparison, if there is no record in the position specified by the key nor in any higher position, the START is unsuccessful. In a GREATER THAN comparison, if there is no record in any position higher than the one specified by the key, the START is unsuccessful.

Examples: Assume that in the FILE-CONTROL paragraph of MASTER-FILE the following clause appears:

RELATIVE KEY IS NEW-KEY

Further assume that the current value of NEW-KEY is 50.

1. START MASTER-FILE

1.' START MASTER-FILE KEY IS EQUAL TO NEW-KEY

Both of these statements have the same result. The current-record pointer is positioned to the 50th record area in the file. If this area does not contain a record, the Invalid Key condition exists.

2. START MASTER-FILE KEY IS GREATER THAN NEW-KEY

The current-record pointer is positioned to the first record area after the 50th that contains a record. If there are no records in the 51st through the last record areas in the file, the Invalid Key condition exists.

Indexed Files

If the KEY phrase is not specified, the data item specified in the file's RECORD KEY clause is used in the comparison. The user must place a value into this data item in the file's record area before the START is executed.

If the KEY phrase is specified, data-name-1 is used in the comparison. Data-name-1 must be either the item specified in the file's RECORD KEY clause or an item subordinate to this item. If data-name-1 is subordinate to the RECORD KEY item, then it must be alphanumeric and must extend from the left-most position of the RECORD KEY item.

For example, with the structure:

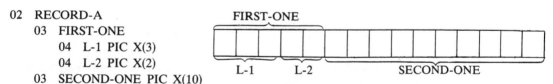

```
02  RECORD-A
    03  FIRST-ONE
        04  L-1 PIC X(3)
        04  L-2 PIC X(2)
    03  SECOND-ONE PIC X(10)
```

and with RECORD KEY IS FIRST-ONE specified in the associated FILE-CONTROL paragraph, a reference in the KEY IS phrase to FIRST-ONE or to L-1 would be correct. A reference to L-2, SECOND-ONE, or RECORD-A would be incorrect.

Key of Reference

If the START has been successfully executed, in addition to positioning the current-record pointer, a key of reference, which will be used in subsequent format 1 READ operations, is established as follows:

If the KEY phrase is not specified, the file's prime record key is the key of reference.

If the KEY phrase is specified and data-name-1 is a record key for the file, then data-name-1 becomes the key of reference.

If the KEY phrase is specified and data-name-1 is not a record key for the file, then that record key which has a left-most character position corresponding to the left-most character position of data-name-1 becomes the key of reference.

If the START was unsuccessful, the key of reference is undefined and must be established before a format 1 READ is given for the file.

Examples: Assume in all the examples that there will be a record found with a key data item that fulfills the criterion. Assume that the structure for RECORD-A is as shown above, and assume that the record key is defined as FIRST-ONE in the FILE-CONTROL paragraph.

1. START MASTER-FILE

1.' START MASTER-FILE KEY IS FIRST-ONE

In both of these cases, the current-record pointer points to the record with a key data item equal to the contents of FIRST-ONE. The key of reference is FIRST-ONE.

2. START MASTER-FILE KEY IS L-1

The current-record pointer points to the record with a key equal to the contents of L-1. The key of reference is FIRST-ONE.

Invalid Key Condition

The Invalid Key condition occurs when no record in the file satisfies the comparison criterion. In this event the current-record pointer and key of reference are both undefined.

A START statement must have either the INVALID KEY phrase specified, a format 1 USE procedure specified, or both.

If the INVALID KEY phrase is specified, then imperative-statement-1 is executed. If this phrase is not specified, then the applicable format 1 USE procedure is executed. If both the INVALID KEY phrase and a USE procedure are specified, only imperative-statement-1 is executed.

File Status

If a File Status item is specified, it is updated with the following codes:

Status Key 1	Status Key 2	Meaning
0	0	Successful completion
0	2	Successful completion, duplicate key
1	0	At end
2	1	Invalid key, sequence error
2	2	Invalid key, duplicate key
2	3	No record found
2	4	Boundary violation
3	0	Permanent error
9	—	Implementor-defined

See current record pointer, indexed file, input mode, key, key of reference, OPEN, open mode, ordinal position, prime record key, relative file, sequential access.

statement

A statement is a syntactically correct combination of words and symbols written in the Procedure Division that begins with a verb. Statements are either conditional, imperative, or compiler directing.

See compiler directing statement, conditional statement, imperative statement.

STATUS

See communication description entry, FILE-CONTROL, SELECT, SPECIAL-NAMES.

Status Key

See FILE STATUS.

STOP

The STOP verb either causes a temporary suspension of the execution of the program or permanently terminates the program.

Format:

$$\text{STOP} \begin{Bmatrix} \underline{\text{RUN}} \\ \text{literal-1} \end{Bmatrix}$$

STOP RUN causes the program to be terminated. If it appears in an imperative sentence, it must be the last statement in the sentence.

STOP literal-1 causes a temporary suspension of the execution of the program, and literal-1 to be output to the computer operator. If literal-1 is a figurative constant, only one instance of it is output. Continuation of the program begins with the next statement following the STOP.

The procedures for resuming a temporarily suspended program and for permanently terminating a program are implementor-defined.

Literal-1 can be numeric, nonnumeric, or any figurative constant except ALL. If numeric, it must be an unsigned integer. This is a new restriction in 74 COBOL.

If a file is in the open mode when a STOP RUN statement is issued, the action taken is implementor-defined.

STRING

The STRING verb concatenates the whole or partial contents of two or more data items into a single data item. This verb is supported only if level 2 of the Nucleus is implemented. It is new to 74 COBOL.

Format 1:

$$\underline{\text{STRING}} \left\{ \begin{Bmatrix} \text{identifier-1} \\ \text{literal-1} \end{Bmatrix} \right\} \dots \underline{\text{DELIMITED}} \text{ BY} \left\{ \begin{Bmatrix} \text{identifier-2} \\ \text{literal-2} \\ \underline{\text{SIZE}} \end{Bmatrix} \right\} \dots \underline{\text{INTO}} \text{ identifier-3}$$

[WITH <u>POINTER</u> identifier-4][ON <u>OVERFLOW</u> imperative-statement-1]

The items before DELIMITED are the sending items; identifier-3 is the receiving item. When a STRING statement is executed, characters from the sending items are transferred into the receiving item in accordance with the rules for alphanumeric-to-alphanumeric data transfer, as defined in the MOVE statement, except that no space filling is provided.

Delimited By Clause

If SIZE is used as the delimiter, all of the contents of the left-most sending item are transferred to the receiving item, then all of the contents of the next sending item are transferred, etc.

If SIZE is not specified, identifier-2 or literal-2 is the *delimiter*. Transfer of data proceeds as in the preceding paragraph beginning with the left-most sending item. However, if at any time the characters specified by the delimiter are encountered in the data being moved, transfer stops before these characters are moved into the receiving item, and the next sending item is then considered. Note that the specified delimiter is applicable to *all* of the sending items before the associated DELIMITED BY.

Data transfer continues until the data in all of the sending items have been transferred or until an overflow condition occurs.

Pointer Clause

When a character is moved from the current sending item, it is placed into the character position of the receiving item that is designated by the current value of identifier-4. Identifier-4 is then incremented by one prior to moving the next character. The programmer is responsible for setting identifier-4 to a value greater than zero prior to the execution of the STRING statement. Identifier-4 must be large enough to contain a value equal to the size of identifier-3 plus one. (If the POINTER phrase is not specified, an implicit pointer with an initial value of one is assumed. This pointer is not accessible by the programmer.)

After execution of the STRING, only that portion of the receiving item referenced by the STRING is changed. In other words any character in the receiving item with an ordinal position greater than the final value of the pointer item is unchanged by action of the STRING. If at any time during execution the value of the pointer item is less than one or greater than the number of character positions in identifier-3, no further data is transferred. If the ON OVERFLOW phrase is specified, imperative-statement-1 is then executed. If not, control passes either to the statement following the STRING or returns to control of a PERFORM or USE.

	Numeric integer	Nonnumeric	Alphanumeric	Usage of DISPLAY	Figurative constant
Literal-1, -2		X			X
Identifier-1, -2, -3	X		X	X	
Identifier-4	X				

Identifier-3 cannot have editing symbols or a JUSTIFIED clause.
Identifier-1, -2, -3 cannot have a 'P' in the PICTURE clause.
Any figurative constant refers to a one-character data item.
'ALL' cannot be used with a figurative constant.

Examples: Assume that ALPHA = A, B, C, . . . Z (26 characters)
VETA = IJK
THIRD = MBLE
TEMP = A, B, C, . . . Z (26 characters)

1. STRING VETA, "XYZ," SPACE, THIRD DELIMITED BY SIZE INTO TEMP

After execution TEMP will contain

I	J	K	X	Y	Z		M	B	L	E	L	M	N	O	P	Q	R	S	T	U	V	W	X	Y	Z

These characters were not altered.

2. MOVE 1 TO HERE•
STRING VETA, "XYZ," SPACE, THIRD DELIMITED BY SIZE; ALPHA DELIMITED BY VETA INTO TEMP WITH POINTER HERE

After execution TEMP will contain

I	J	K	X	Y	Z		M	B	L	E	A	B	C	D	E	F	G	H	T	U	V	W	X	Y	Z

These characters were not altered.

3. MOVE 6 TO HERE•
STRING VETA, "XYZ," SPACE, THIRD DELIMITED BY SIZE; ALPHA DELIMITED BY VETA INTO TEMP WITH POINTER HERE

After execution TEMP will contain

A	B	C	D	E	I	J	K	X	Y	Z		M	B	L	E	A	B	C	D	E	F	G	H	Y	Z

Since the pointer item contained 6, the first character transferred went here.

These characters were not altered.

See delimiter, ordinal position.

stroke

A stroke (/) in column 7 will cause the current page to be ejected during compilation. The remainder of the line that contains the stroke is treated as a comment.

See PICTURE.

structured programming

The following discussion is not intended to be a comprehensive treatment of structured programming. Rather it is a survey of the more important topics in the field.

It is, perhaps, appropriate to begin a discussion of structured programming by stating what it is *not*. Structured programming is not 'top down coding,' 'modular programming,' 'structured design,' the 'chief programmer' concept, 'top down (or bottom up) implementation,' or 'structured walkthroughs.' Structured programming is a technique of writing programs that is based on the theorem (proved by Böhm and Jacopini) that any program's logic, no matter how complex, can be unambiguously represented as a sequence of operations, using only three basic structures, each with only one entrance and one exit point. Furthermore, in implementing these structures, the GO TO statement is not necessary. It is this latter fact that has led some to believe that structured programming is a ruthless drive to purge GO TO's from the face of the earth. As shall be seen, there is still room for GO TO statements within the framework of a structured program.

The three basic structures are the Process, the Loop, and the Decision.

The Process

The process structure is represented by a box. It corresponds to a COBOL imperative statement.

ADD A TO B.

The Loop

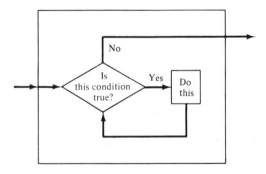

The loop structure, known as a DO WHILE, is a conditional iteration. It executes a process box repeatedly as long as a specified condition is true. The loop structure is implemented in COBOL by a PERFORM... UNTIL NOT statement.

PERFORM PROCESS-BOX UNTIL NOT condition.

The Decision

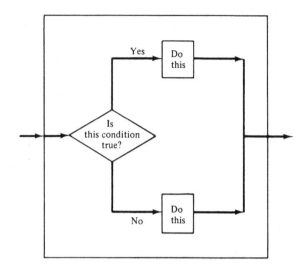

The decision structure, known as an IF THEN ELSE, executes one out of two process boxes based on a test. In COBOL this structure is implemented by an IF statement.

IF condition THEN PROCESS-1 PROCESS-2.

Note that ELSE is no longer a part of the IF statement.

If a process is longer than a sentence it can be written as a paragraph and executed via a PERFORM. For example,

IF condition PERFORM PAR-A ELSE PERFORM PAR-B.

Note that each of these structures, viewed as a totality, has but one entrance point and one exit. The actual code that the compiler generates for any structure may well contain jump instructions, the machine language equivalent of GO TO, but this is of no concern to the programmer. The important thing is that no GO TO statements are required in the source code.

As mentioned, any program can be implemented by a suitable combination of these three basic structures. Furthermore, in diagramming a program, anywhere a process box appears (even within a loop or decision structure) it can be replaced by

- Two or more process boxes in sequence.
- A DO WHILE box.
- An IF THEN ELSE box.

These three replacements can be applied as often as possible, so that in practice a process box can be replaced by any combination of the three basic structures, no matter how complex. It also follows from the first replacement rule, stated just previously, that a process box can represent a series of imperative statements, a paragraph composed entirely of imperative statements, or a series of consecutive paragraphs each composed entirely of imperative statements.

As an example of the above replacements, consider the following:
The process box, a

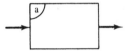

can be expanded to

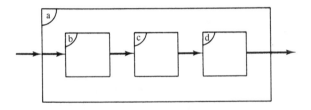

and then to

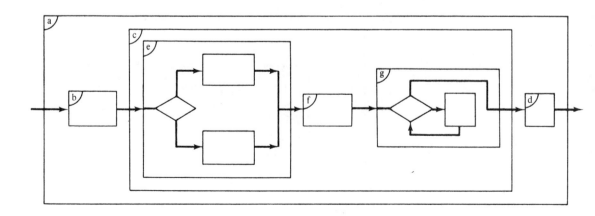

Thus, in a program flow chart, a simple process box may in reality be a very complex process.

To show how these techniques apply to programming, let us consider a few unstructured programs and convert them to structured programs.

Example 1: Put the largest of A, B, and C into BIG.

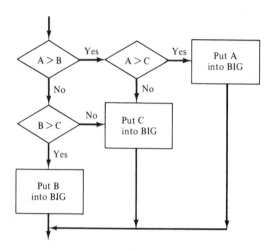

This flow chart does not represent a structured program since, among other reasons, there are two entrance points into the box labelled 'Put C into BIG.' We can redraw this flow chart in structured form as follows. First we consider the entire program as a big IF THEN ELSE. Starting with the test A > B (chosen at random), we generate

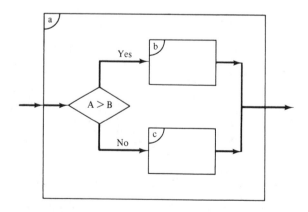

We observe that, if A > B is true, we want to compare A and C, while, if A > B is false, we want to compare B and C. So we can expand boxes b and c thus:

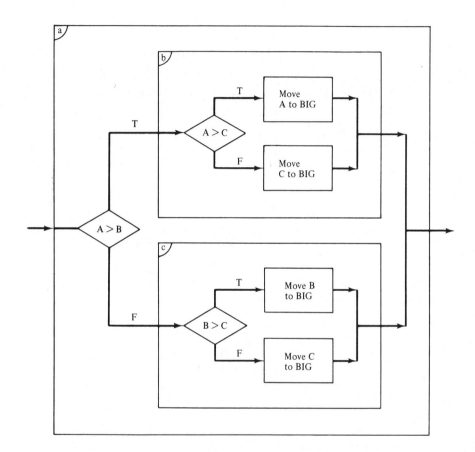

This represents the finished program. Of course, the flow chart could have been drawn from top to bottom instead of from left to right. This program could be coded:

IF A GREATER THAN B, IF A GREATER THAN C MOVE A TO BIG; ELSE MOVE C TO BIG; ELSE IF B GREATER THAN C MOVE B TO BIG; ELSE MOVE C TO BIG.

Now many programmers have an aversion to nested IF statements; fortunately, one need not use nested IF's at all but can implement the above program in this alternate way.

MAIN-ROUTINE.

    IF A GREATER THAN B PERFORM PAR-B ELSE PERFORM PAR-C.
STOP RUN.

PAR-B.

    IF A GREATER THAN C MOVE A TO BIG ELSE MOVE C TO BIG.

PAR-C.

    IF B GREATER THAN C MOVE B TO BIG ELSE MOVE C TO BIG.

Thus, by successively using PERFORM statements to execute paragraphs that themselves contain other PERFORM's, one can avoid nesting IF statements entirely.

Example 2: If at least two of A, B, and C are true, perform paragraph X (where A, B, and C are conditions).

A conventional flow chart might be

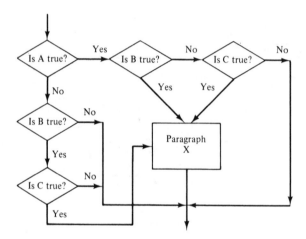

Again, this is not structured. The structured version would be developed thus:

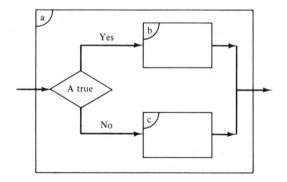

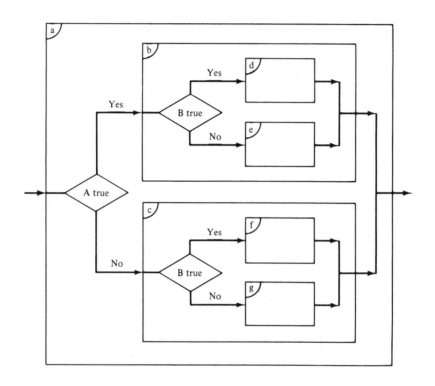

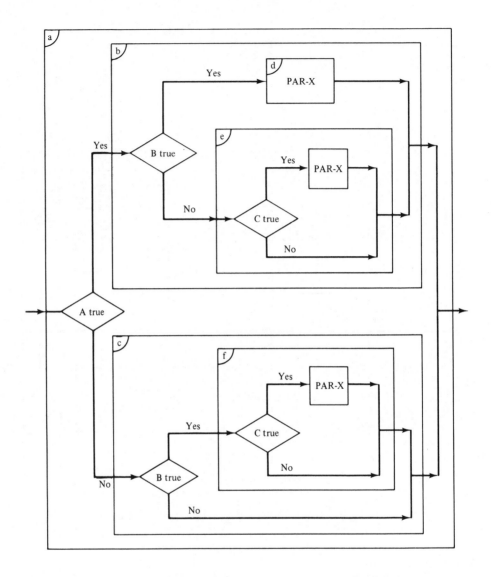

Observe that in boxes c, e, and f there is no process box for one value of the condition. This can be conceptualized, if one so desires, as equivalent to executing a 'do nothing' operation, such as ADD 0 TO A, or the like. It can be implemented by the NEXT SENTENCE option, if desired.

To code this program without using nested IF statements, we write

IF COND-A PERFORM PAR-B ELSE PERFORM PAR-C. STOP RUN.
PAR-B.
    IF COND-B PERFORM PAR-X ELSE PERFORM PAR-E.
PAR-E.
    IF COND-C PERFORM PAR-X ELSE NEXT SENTENCE.
PAR-C.
    IF COND-B PERFORM PAR-E ELSE NEXT SENTENCE.

(Recall that the NEXT SENTENCE phrases are not mandatory.) By observing that boxes e and f are functionally equivalent we need not write an explicit paragraph F. This is one of the powerful features of structured programming.

Example 3. If condition 1 is false, execute procedure 4. If condition 1 is true, execute procedure 1, and then, if condition 2 is true, execute procedure 2, whereas if condition 2 is false execute procedure 3. In any case, then execute process 4. The conventional structure is

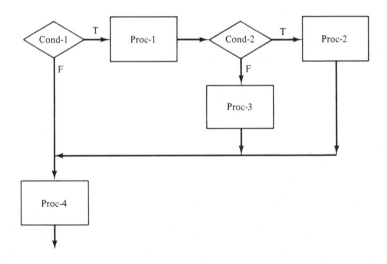

The structured program is developed in this way:

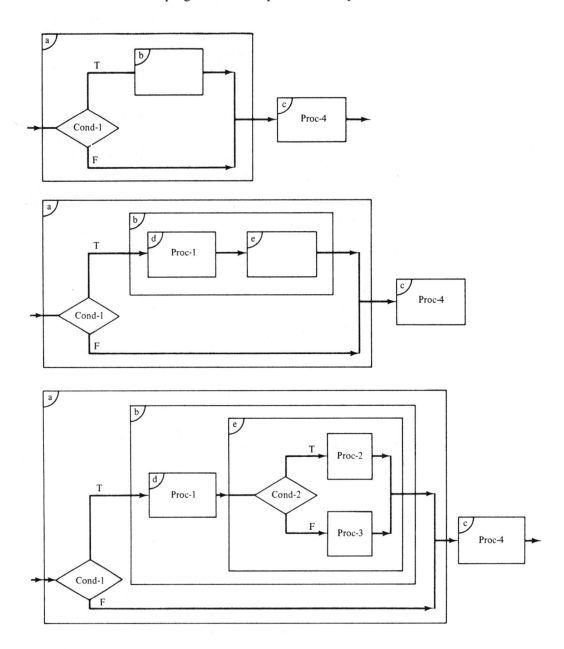

This can now be coded as follows.

MAIN-ROUTINE.
    IF COND-1 PERFORM PAR-B. PERFORM PROC-4.
PAR-B.
    PERFORM PROC-1. IF COND-2 PERFORM PROC-2 ELSE PERFORM PROC-3.

Now consider a slight change in the flow chart of example 3.

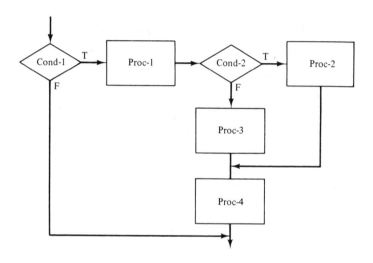

This program can be developed as shown.

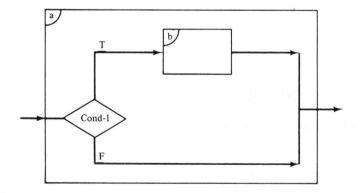

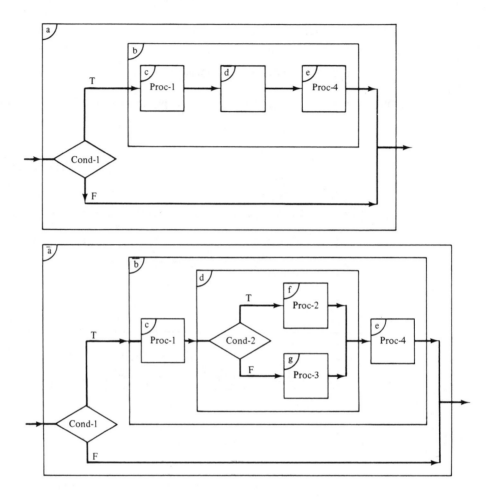

It can be coded thus.

MAIN-ROUTINE.
       IF COND-1 PERFORM PAR-B. STOP RUN.
PAR-B.
       PERFORM PROC-1. IF COND-2 PERFORM PROC-2 ELSE PERFORM PROC-3.
PERFORM PROC-4.

   Notice how simple it was to change the program from one form to another.
   Although not theoretically necessary for a structured program, there are certain other structures that are sometimes useful when writing programs. We will discuss two of them and show how they are equivalent to combinations of the three basic structures.

The Repeat Until

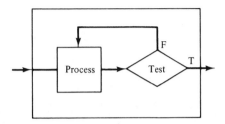

The REPEAT UNTIL construct is a variation of the DO WHILE. It always executes the associated process at least once. Subsequent executions depend upon whether the state of the condition tested is true or not. Obviously, if one negates the condition, one can execute the process until the condition becomes false. The REPEAT UNTIL construct is equivalent to the following:

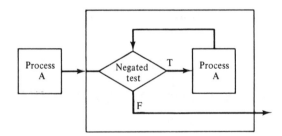

Note that in the DO WHILE box the condition must be negated to correspond to the REPEAT UNTIL box. This structure would be implemented in COBOL by

    PERFORM PROC-A. PERFORM PROC-A UNTIL condition.

The Select Case

The SELECT CASE structure is in vogue mainly, one suspects, because it is easily implemented in PL/I. The idea is that a variable is in one of several mutually exclusive states (or cases). If it is in state 1, procedure 1 is to be executed; if it is in state 2, procedure 2 is to be executed; etc.

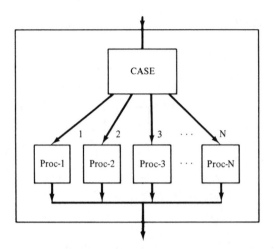

The SELECT CASE structure is equivalent to

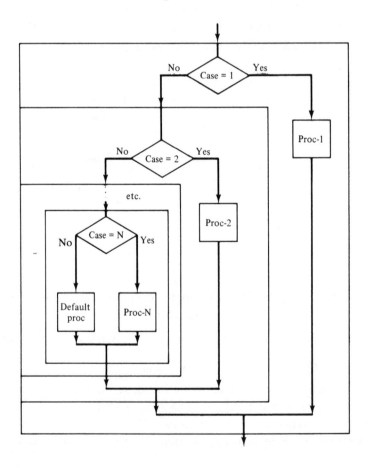

The SELECT CASE structure is implemented by:

```
PERFORM SELECT-CASE.
SELECT-CASE SECTION.
PAR-A.
        GO TO PROC-1, PROC-2,... PROC-N DEPENDING ON CASE.
GO TO DEFAULT-PROC.
PROC-1.
        (procedures) GO TO SEL-CASE-END.
PROC-2.
        (procedures) GO TO SEL-CASE-END.
PROC-N.
        (procedures) GO TO SEL-CASE-END.
DEFAULT-PROC.
        (procedures)
SEL-CASE-END.
        EXIT.
```

Note that besides GO TO statements, this structure contains a GO TO
DEPENDING. The important consideration is that their use is localized to a
certain set of contiguous paragraphs, as opposed to indiscriminate GO TO's
everywhere. In this context there is nothing very insidious about using GO TO
statements. However, GO TO's are not necessary. One could implement the
SELECT CASE structure by

```
IF CASE EQUALS 1 PERFORM PROC-1.
IF CASE EQUALS 2 PERFORM PROC-2.
        .
        .
        .
IF CASE EQUALS N PERFORM PROC-N.
IF CASE IS LESS THAN 1 OR CASE IS GREATER THAN N PERFORM
DEFAULT-PROC.
```

Let us now work our way through a typical, albeit trivial, program. The
program is to read in a card that contains two numeric fields. If both fields are
greater than zero, their sum is to be printed. Otherwise, print zero. Repeat this
process until there are no more cards in the reader.

We start with three process boxes:

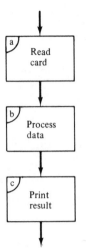

Expanding on the above, we generate

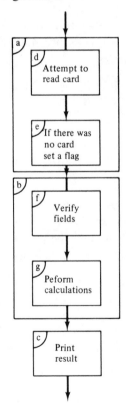

Further expansion:

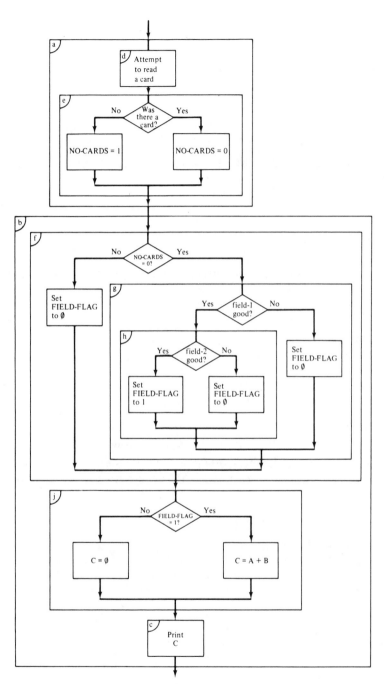

Sordillo structured programming (y)

This program can be implemented as follows:

```
MAIN-PROGRAM.
      MOVE 0 TO NO-CARDS. PERFORM RUN-IT UNTIL NO-CARDS EQUALS 1.
STOP RUN.
RUN-IT SECTION.
PAR-D.
      MOVE 0 TO C-FLAG. READ CARD-RDR AT END MOVE 1 TO C-FLAG.
PAR-E.
      IF C-FLAG EQUALS 0, MOVE 0 TO NO-CARDS; ELSE MOVE 1 TO NO-CARDS.
PAR-B.
      PERFORM PAR-F. PERFORM PAR-J.
PAR-C.
      WRITE C.
OTHER-SECTION SECTION.
PAR-F.
      IF NO-CARDS EQUALS 0, PERFORM PAR-G; ELSE MOVE 0 TO FIELD-FLAG.
PAR-J.
      IF FIELD-FLAG EQUALS 1, ADD A, B GIVING C; ELSE MOVE 0 TO C.
PAR-G.
      IF FIELD-1 IS NUMERIC AND FIELD-1 IS GREATER THAN 0, PERFORM PAR-H;
ELSE MOVE 0 TO FIELD-FLAG.
PAR-H.
      IF FIELD-2 IS NUMERIC AND FIELD-2 IS GREATER THAN 0, MOVE 1 TO
FIELD-FLAG; ELSE MOVE 0 TO FIELD-FLAG.
```

Observe that NO-CARDS must be set to zero in the main program, since the condition is tested before the PERFORM transfers control and cannot be sure of the state of NO-CARDS when we first execute. (Unless we initialize it by the VALUE IS clause.) Also, C-FLAG need not be used. One could write

```
      PAR-D.
            READ CARD-RDR AT END MOVE 1 TO NO-CARDS.
```

and delete PAR-E.

There is another way one might implement this program. Using the chart:

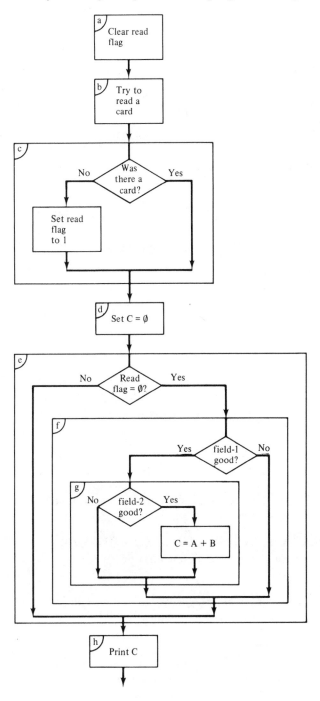

MAIN-PROGRAM.
        MOVE 0 TO READ-FLAG. PERFORM RUN-IT UNTIL READ-FLAG EQUALS 1.
STOP RUN.
RUN-IT SECTION.
PAR-B-AND-C.
        READ CARD-RDR AT END MOVE 1 TO READ-FLAG.
PAR-D.
        MOVE 0 TO C.
PAR-E.
        IF READ-FLAG EQUALS 0 PERFORM PAR-F.
PAR-H.
        WRITE C.
OTHER-SECTION SECTION.
PAR-F.
        IF FIELD-1 IS NUMERIC AND FIELD-1 IS GREATER THAN 0 PERFORM PAR-G.
PAR-G.
        IF FIELD-2 IS NUMERIC AND FIELD-2 IS GREATER THAN 0 ADD A, B
GIVING C.

subject of condition

>   The operand that precedes the operator in a relation class, or sign condition is termed the 'subject' of the condition.
>
>   *See* class condition, object of condition, relation condition, sign condition.

subject of entry

>   The subject of an entry is the operand or reserved word that appears immediately after the level-indicator or level-number in a DATA DIVISION entry.
>
>   *See* level-indicator, level-number, object of entry, operand, reserved word.

subprogram

>   *See* called program.

sub-queue

>   A sub-queue is a logical subdivision of a queue.
>
>   *See* queue.

SUB-QUEUE-1, SUB-QUEUE-2, SUB-QUEUE-3

>   *See* communication description entry.

subscript

>   A subscript is an integer whose value identifies a particular element in a table.
>
>   *See* table, table element.

subscripted data-name

>   A subscripted data-name is a data-name followed by one or more subscripts. All subscripted data-names are identifiers.
>
>   *See* data-name, identifier, subscript.

subscripting

Subscripting allows reference to be made to individual elements within a table when these elements do not have individual data-names.

Format:

$$\begin{Bmatrix} \text{data-name-1} \\ \text{condition-name} \end{Bmatrix} \left[\begin{Bmatrix} \underline{OF} \\ \underline{IN} \end{Bmatrix} \text{data-name-2} \right] \dots (\text{subscript-1 [, subscript-2 [, subscript-3]]})$$

A subscript must be an integer and can be either a data-name or a numeric literal. Data-names used as subscripts can be qualified but cannot themselves be subscripted. The parentheses are required for subscripts.

Up to three subscripts can be used for one item. When more than one subscript is used, they are written in the order of less inclusive dimensions of the data organization.

If a subscript is signed, the sign must be positive. The range of values of a subscript is from one to the maximum number of occurrences of the item as specified in the OCCURS clause. An element of a table is identified by correlating the numeric value of the subscript with the logical ordinal position of that element within the table.

Commas are not necessary between subscripts; this is a new feature of 74 COBOL.

See OCCURS, ordinal position, qualification, table.

subtotalling

See SUM.

SUBTRACT

The SUBTRACT verb subtracts a single data item, or the sum of two or more data items, from one or more data items; and then sets one or more data items equal to the result. The composite of operands must not exceed 18 digits.

Format 1:

$$\underline{\text{SUBTRACT}} \begin{Bmatrix} \text{identifier-1} \\ \text{literal-1} \end{Bmatrix} \dots \underline{\text{FROM}} \{\text{identifier-m } [\underline{\text{ROUNDED}}],\} \dots$$

$$[; \text{ON } \underline{\text{SIZE ERROR}} \text{ imperative-statement-1}]$$

All data items preceding the word FROM are added together; this sum is then subtracted from the current value of each identifier following FROM, and the result is left in that identifier. Thus the new value of each identifier following FROM is equal to its original value minus the sum of all the identifiers preceding FROM. The composite of operands is determined by superimposing all the operands used, aligned by decimal point.

Examples: Assume as initial values: FICA = 20
                                                FEDTAXES = 55
                                                STATE-TAXES = 15
                                                BCBS = 10
                                                GROSS-PAY = 350
                                                ESCROW = 1000

1. SUBTRACT FICA FROM GROSS-PAY
   After execution the value of GROSS-PAY is 330.

2. SUBTRACT FICA, FEDTAXES, STATE-TAXES, BCBS FROM GROSS-PAY
   After execution the value of GROSS-PAY is 250.

3. SUBTRACT FICA FROM GROSS-PAY, ESCROW
   After execution the value of GROSS-PAY is 330, the value of ESCROW is 980.

4. SUBTRACT FICA, FEDTAXES, STATE-TAXES, BCBS FROM GROSS-PAY, ESCROW
   After execution the value of GROSS-PAY is 250, the value of ESCROW is 900.

Format 2:

$$\underline{\text{SUBTRACT}}\begin{Bmatrix}\text{identifier-1}\\\text{literal-1}\end{Bmatrix}\ldots\underline{\text{FROM}}\begin{Bmatrix}\text{identifier-m}\\\text{literal-m}\end{Bmatrix}\underline{\text{GIVING}}\,\{\text{identifier-n}\,[\underline{\text{ROUNDED}}],\}\ldots$$

[; ON <u>SIZE</u> <u>ERROR</u> imperative-statement-1]

All data items preceding the word FROM are added together; this sum is then subtracted from literal-m or identifier-m. The result of this subtraction is stored as the new value of each identifier following GIVING. Thus the new value of each identifier following GIVING is equal to the result of the subtraction. The composite of operands is determined by superimposing all of the operands preceding GIVING, aligned by decimal point. Note that the previous contents of identifiers following GIVING do not participate in the subtraction.

Examples: Assume as initial values: FICA = 20
                                                FEDTAXES = 55
                                                STATE-TAXES = 15
                                                BCBS = 10
                                                GROSS-PAY = 350
                                                NET-PAY = 0
                                                RESULT = 0

1. SUBTRACT FICA FROM GROSS-PAY GIVING RESULT
   After execution the value of RESULT is 330.

2. SUBTRACT FICA, FEDTAXES, STATE-TAXES, BCBS FROM GROSS-PAY GIVING RESULT

After execution the value of RESULT is 250.

3. SUBTRACT FICA, FEDTAXES, STATE-TAXES, BCBS FROM GROSS-PAY GIVING RESULT, NET-PAY

After execution the values of RESULT and NET-PAY are each 250.

N.B. The multiple receiving fields of formats 1 and 2 are a new feature of 74 COBOL, and are implemented in level 2 of the Nucleus Module.

Format 3:

$$\text{SUBTRACT} \left\{ \begin{array}{l} \underline{\text{CORRESPONDING}} \\ \underline{\text{CORR}} \end{array} \right\} \text{identifier-1 } \underline{\text{FROM}} \text{ identifier-2 } [\underline{\text{ROUNDED}}]$$

[; ON $\underline{\text{SIZE ERROR}}$ imperative-statement-1]

Every numeric data item in identifier-1 that has a corresponding data item in identifier-2 is subtracted from its corresponding data item, and the result is stored as the new value of the corresponding data item. Thus the new value of a data item in identifier-2 is its original value minus the value of the corresponding data item in identifier-1. The composite of operands is determined separately for each pair of corresponding data items by superimposing the two items aligned by decimal point. Each identifier must be a group item.

This form of SUBTRACT is implemented only in level 2 of the Nucleus.

Example: Assume the following data structures with initial values in parentheses; assume that all elementary items are numeric:

```
01  ABC                    02  WXY
    02  DEF                    05  DEF
        03  GHI  (7)               06  GHI  (10)
        03  JKL  (20)              06  PDQ  (10)
    02  MNO  (40)             05  STU  (10)
    02  PQR  (15)             05  PQR  (10)
```

1. SUBTRACT CORRESPONDING ABC FROM WXY

After execution the values of WXY will be

```
                02  WXY
                    05  DEF
                        06  GHI  (3)
                        06  PDQ  (10)
                    05  STU  (10)
                    05  PQR  (−5)
```

Format 1:   *Format 2:*

	Numeric
Literal-1	X
Identifier-1	X
Identifier-m	X

	Numeric	Numeric-edited
Literal-1, -m	X	
Identifier-1, -m	X	
Identifier-n	X	X

See arithmetic statements, composite of operands, CORRESPONDING, multiple results in arithmetic statements, overlapping operands, ROUNDED, SIZE ERROR.

SUM

The SUM clause establishes a sum counter and designates the data items to be summed into the counter.

Format:

$$\{\underline{\text{SUM}}\,\{\text{identifier-1}\}\dots[\underline{\text{UPON}}\,\{\text{data-name-1}\}\dots]\}\dots$$

$$\left[\text{RESET ON}\begin{Bmatrix}\text{data-name-2}\\\underline{\text{FINAL}}\end{Bmatrix}\right]$$

The SUM clause is part of a report group description entry; it can appear only in the description of a Control Footing report group. The SUM clause establishes a sum counter, which is a numeric data item with an optional sign. Its size is defined by the associated PICTURE clause. Only one sum counter exists for an elementary report entry, regardless of the number of SUM clauses specified in the elementary report entry. A sum counter can be altered by statements in the program; the highest permissible qualifier for a sum counter is a report-name.

If a data-name appears as the subject of the elementary report entry that contains a SUM clause, that data-name is the name of the sum counter; it is not the name of the printable item that the entry may also define.

If the elementary report entry for a printable item contains a SUM clause, the sum counter serves as the source data item. The Report Writer Control System (RWCS) moves the data contained in the sum counter to the printable item, according to the rules for a MOVE statement.

Using the rules of the ADD statement the RWCS adds the values of all specified identifiers into the sum counter during the execution of GENERATE and TERMINATE statements.

There are three types of operations involving sum counters: subtotalling, crossfooting, and rolling forward.

Subtotalling

Subtotalling occurs when the item added to a sum counter is not itself a sum counter. If the SUM clause contains the UPON phrase, the addends are subtotalled when a GENERATE statement for the designated Detail report group is executed. If the SUM clause does not contain the UPON phrase, these addends are subtotalled when the GENERATE data-name statement is executed for the report but before the Detail report group is processed.

Crossfooting

Crossfooting occurs when the item added to a sum counter is a sum counter that is defined in the same Control Footing report group. Crossfooting takes place when a control break has occurred and the Control Footing report group is being processed. It is performed according to the sequence in which SUM counters are defined within the Control Footing report group: All crossfooting into the first sum counter is completed, all crossfooting into the second sum counter is completed, etc., until all crossfooting operations have been completed.

Rolling Forward

Rolling forward occurs when the item added to a sum counter is a sum counter that is defined in a lower level Control Footing report group. A sum counter is rolled forward when a control break occurs at the time that the lower level Control Footing report group is being processed.

Identifiers

All identifiers must be defined as numeric data items; if any one is defined in the REPORT SECTION it must be a sum counter. If two or more identifiers specify the same addend, it is added into the sum counter as many times as it is specified in the SUM clause. Two or more of the data-names can specify the same Detail group. When a GENERATE data-name statement for such a Detail group is executed, the incrementing occurs as many times as data-name appears in the UPON phrase.

The Upon Phrase

The UPON phrase allows selective subtotalling for the Detail report groups named in the phrase. If this phrase is specified, the addends are subtotalled when a GENERATE statement for the designated Detail report group is executed. In this case the identifiers in the SUM clause cannot be sum counters.

If the UPON phrase is not specified, any identifiers in the SUM clause that are themselves sum counters must be defined either in the same report group that contains this SUM clause or in a report group that is at a lower level in this report's control hierarchy.

All data-names must be the names of Detail report groups that are described in the same report as the Control Footing report group in which the SUM clause appears. Any data-name can be qualified by a report-name.

The Reset Phrase

If the RESET phrase is not specified, the RWCS will set a sum counter to zero when the RWCS is processing the associated Control Footing report group.

If the RESET phrase is specified, the RWCS will set the sum counter to zero when the RWCS is processing the designated level of the control hierarchy.

A sum counter will be set to zero by the RWCS during the execution of the INITIATE statement for the associated report. Data-name-2 must be specified in the associated report's CONTROL clause. It cannot be a lower level control than the associated control for the report group in which the RESET phrase appears. If FINAL is specified, it must also appear in this report's CONTROL clause.

See control break, Control Footing, GENERATE, report group description, report-name, sum counter, TYPE.

sum counter

A sum counter is a signed numeric data item that is established by a SUM clause in the REPORT SECTION of the DATA DIVISION. Sum counters are used by the Report Writer Control System (RWCS) to hold the results of designated summing operations that take place during the production of a report.

See Report Writer Control System.

summary report

A summary report is one in which no DETAIL report group is presented.

See GENERATE, report group description.

SUPPRESS

The SUPPRESS verb causes the Report Writer Control System (RWCS) to inhibit the presentation of a report group.

Format:

SUPPRESS PRINTING

The SUPPRESS statement can appear only in a USE BEFORE REPORTING procedure. It inhibits presentation of the report group named in the USE procedure that contains the SUPPRESS statement.

When the SUPPRESS statement is executed, the RWCS is instructed to inhibit the processing of all LINE clauses and the NEXT GROUP clause in the report group, the adjustment of LINE-COUNTER, and the presentation of the print lines of the report group.

The SUPPRESS statement must be executed each time the presentation of the report group is to be inhibited.

See Report Writer Control System.

switch-status condition

A switch-status condition determines the 'on' or 'off' status of an implementor-defined switch. The implementor-name and the 'on' and 'off' values associated with the condition must be specified in the SPECIAL-NAMES paragraph of the ENVIRONMENT DIVISION.

The result of the test of the switch-status condition is true if the switch is set to the position ('on' or 'off') corresponding to the condition-name. The switch-status condition is used in an IF statement as follows:

IF condition-name

In 74 COBOL a switch can be either hardware or software. Previously, they could only be hardware.

See SPECIAL-NAMES.

SYMBOLIC

See communication description entry.

synchronization

Certain uses of data, such as in arithmetic operations or subscripting, are executed more efficiently if the data is aligned on natural addressing boundaries, e.g., byte, half-word, word, in storage. In fact, additional execution time may be needed if data items appear between the boundaries or if these boundaries split a single data item. Data items aligned on these boundaries in such a way as to avoid additional machine operations are said to be *synchronized*. Synchronization can be accomplished by either the SYNCHRONIZED clause or by recognizing the natural boundaries and organizing the data appropriately without using the clause. This latter method requires considerable mental effort and is worthwhile only when main storage is at a premium.

See alignment rules, JUSTIFIED, SYNCHRONIZED.

SYNCHRONIZED, SYNC

The SYNCHRONIZED clause is one way of providing synchronization of data. It specifies the way in which elementary items are stored within computer storage with respect to natural boundaries.

Format:

The SYNCHRONIZED clause is used to enable more efficient execution of the program. It can be applied only to elementary items. In all contexts, SYNC is equivalent to SYNCHRONIZED. The SYNC clause specifies that the associated data item is to be aligned in memory in such a way that no other data item occupies any of the character positions between the left-most and right-most natural boundaries containing this item.

If the number of character positions needed to store the data item is less than the number of character positions between the delimiting natural boundaries, the unused character positions cannot be used for any other data item. However, these unused positions are included (1) in determining the size of any group item to which the elementary item belongs and (2) in the redefined character positions when this item is the object of a REDEFINES clause.

Left and Right Synchronization

If neither LEFT nor RIGHT is specified, the item is positioned between natural boundaries in such a way as to provide for the most efficient utilization of the item. The specific positioning is implementor-defined.

If LEFT is specified, the item is positioned so that its left-most character position abuts a natural boundary. Depending on the size of the item and the number of character positions between boundaries, the right-most character position may also abut a natural boundary.

If RIGHT is specified, the item is positioned so that its right-most character position abuts a natural boundary. Depending on the size of the item and the number of character positions between boundaries, the left-most character position may also abut a natural boundary.

The boundary for a group item is always the most stringent one that is required for alignment of any item subordinate to the group.

Effect of Occurs Clause

If the SYNC clause is specified for an item with, or subordinate to, an OCCURS clause, each occurrence of the item is synchronized, and implicit FILLER items are generated. These implicit FILLER items cannot be implicitly referenced.

Operational Sign

When the SYNC clause appears in a data description that contains an operational sign, the sign still appears in the normal operational sign position.

Size of a Synchronized Item

When a synchronized item is referenced in the program, the size of the item, as determined by its PICTURE clause, is used in determining any action that depends on size such as truncation, justification, or overflow.

Implementor-Defined Characteristics

Since the SYNC clause is hardware dependent, the implementor must specify how synchronized items are handled with respect to

1. The format on external media.
2. The generation of implicit FILLER if the item preceding the SYNC item does not end on a natural boundary. These filler positions are included in the size of the group item to which the filler item belongs and the number of character positions allocated when the filler is part of an item that is the object of a REDEFINES clause.

The implementor may specify automatic synchronization for any internal data formats except for items within a record with a usage of display. The record itself may be synchronized.

The implementor must specify any synchronization rules for the records in a data file since this could affect the synchronization of elementary items within the record.

Examples: Assume that there are four character positions per word and that the word is the appropriate natural boundary. Also assume that a record always starts at a natural boundary. Let 'W' indicate a word boundary and 'f' indicate a filler character inserted as a result of the synchronization operation.

Consider the record:

```
01  A.
    02  B  PIC XX.
    02  C  PIC XX.
    02  D  PIC XX.
```

This would be allocated in storage thus:

The size of this record is 6.

Now consider the following records with their corresponding storage allocations:

```
01  A.
    02  B  PIC XX SYNC LEFT.
    02  C  PIC XX SYNC LEFT.
    02  D  PIC XX.
```

Size is 10

01 A.
    02 B PIC XX.
    02 C PIC XX SYNC LEFT.
    02 D PIC XX.

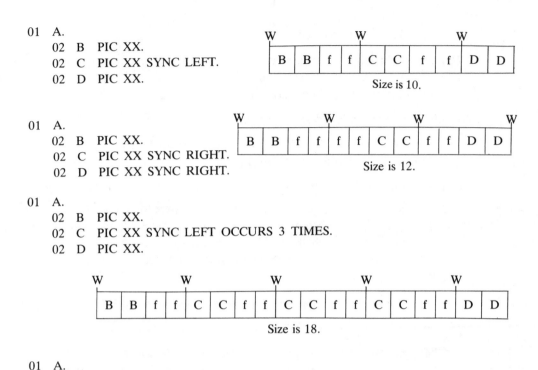

01 A.
    02 B PIC XX.
    02 C PIC XX SYNC RIGHT.
    02 D PIC XX SYNC RIGHT.

01 A.
    02 B PIC XX.
    02 C PIC XX SYNC LEFT OCCURS 3 TIMES.
    02 D PIC XX.

Size is 18.

01 A.
    02 B PIC XX.
    02 C PIC XXXXX SYNCH LEFT OCCURS 2 TIMES.
    02 D PIC XX.

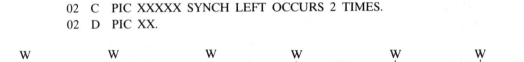

Size is 22.

See elementary item, group item, justification, overflow, truncation.

system-name

A system-name is a COBOL word that is used to communicate with the operating system.

There are three types of system-names: computer-name, implementor-name, and language-name.

See computer-name, implementor-name, language-name, word.

T

TABLE

See communication description entry.

table

A table is a set of logically consecutive data items with a common name that is defined by an OCCURS clause. The elements of a table are referenced either by an index or a subscript. The entry

ABC OCCURS 3 TIMES PICTURE IS XXXXX

defines a table of three elements, each element being five characters long. (N.B. Due to synchronization and other factors the amount of area occupied by the table may be longer than the number of characters in the table.)

Tables of up to three dimensions can be specified in COBOL.

See indexing, occurrence number, OCCURS, subscripting, synchronization, SYNCHRONIZED.

table element

A table element is any one of the data items that is part of a table.

Table Handling Module

The Table Handling Module provides the capability of defining tables of contiguous data items and of accessing an item relative to its position in the table by means of a subscript or an index.

Level 1

Table Handling Level 1 provides the capability of accessing items in fixed-length tables of up to three dimensions. This level also provides the ability to vary the contents of indices by an increment or decrement.

Level 2

In addition to the features enumerated under Level 1, Table Handling Level 2 provides the capability of accessing items in variable-length tables of up to three dimensions. The additional features of specifying ascending or descending keys and searching a table for an item that satisfies a specified condition are also provided.

See INDEX, subscript.

table handling statements

The table handling statements are SET and SEARCH.

TALLY

TALLY was a special register that was used in conjunction with the EXAMINE verb. TALLY is no longer a reserved word.

TALLYING

See INSPECT, UNSTRING.

TERMINAL

See DISABLE, ENABLE.

terminal

A terminal is the originator of a transmission to a queue or the receiver of a transmission from a queue.

See queue.

TERMINATE

The TERMINATE verb causes the Report Writer Control System (RWCS) to complete the processing of a report.

Format:

TERMINATE {report-name-1}...

Each report-name must be defined by a report description entry in the REPORT SECTION. The TERMINATE statement causes the RWCS to produce all the Control Footing report groups, beginning with the minor Control Footing report group. Then the Report Footing report group is produced.

The RWCS will make the prior set of control data item values available to the SOURCE clauses and USE procedures associated with Control Footing and Report Footing as if a control break had been sensed in the major control data-name.

If no GENERATE statements have been executed for a report, the TERMINATE statement does not cause the RWCS to produce any report groups or perform any of the related processing. During report presentation the RWCS will automatically process PAGE HEADING and PAGE FOOTING report groups, where required, if these are defined.

A TERMINATE statement cannot be executed for a report-name unless an INITIATE statement was previously executed for that report-name. The TERMINATE statement does not close the report's file. Therefore a CLOSE statement must be issued for the file. However *every* report in the file that has had an INITIATE statement executed for it must have a TERMINATE statement executed before a CLOSE statement can be executed for that file.

See control break, control data-name, report description, report-name.

TEXT

See communication description entry.

text-name

A text-name is a user-defined word that identifies a text in a library.
See library, user-defined word.

text-word

A text-word is any character-string or separator except space that is in a COBOL library or pseudo-text.
See character-string, library, pseudo-text, separator.

THAN

See relation condition, START.

THROUGH, THRU

THROUGH and THRU are reserved words used in various formats. The two spellings are always interchangeable, and no distinction is made between them by the compiler.
See condition-name, MERGE, PERFORM, RENAMES, SORT, SPECIAL-NAMES.

TIME

See ACCEPT, communication description entry.

TIMES

See OCCURS, PERFORM.

TO

See ADD, ALTER, GO, MOVE, RECORD CONTAINS, relation condition, SEARCH, SELECT, SET, START.

TOP

See file description, LINAGE.

TRAILING

See SIGN IS.

transfer of control

The normal transfer of control in a COBOL program is from statement to statement in the order in which the statements appear in the source program. This type of transfer of control is termed 'implicit,' since it requires no procedure-branching statement to be executed. There are both implicit and explicit ways of altering this normal transfer of control.

Implicit Transfers of Control

1. When a paragraph or section is being executed under control of another statement, e.g., PERFORM, SORT, USE, and that paragraph or section is the last one in the range of the statement, an implicit transfer of control occurs from the last sentence in the paragraph or section to the return mechanism of the controlling statement.

2. If a PERFORM statement causes repetitive execution of a paragraph or section, an implicit transfer of control occurs between that PERFORM and the first statement in the paragraph or section each time that it is executed.

3. When a SORT or MERGE statement is executed, an implicit transfer of control to any associated input or output routine occurs.

4. When a statement is executed that causes the execution of a DECLARA-TIVE, an implicit transfer of control to the declarative section occurs. When the declarative section has been executed, another implicit transfer of control occurs back to the statement following the one that invoked the DECLARA-TIVE.

If, in any of the above transfers, there is no 'next executable statement,' transfer of control is undefined unless control is transferred outside of the COBOL program. There is no 'next executable statement' after the following:

- A STOP RUN or EXIT PROGRAM statement that transfers control outside the COBOL program.

- The last statement in a program unless it is being executed under control of some other COBOL program.

- The last statement in the declarative section, unless it is being executed under control of some other COBOL statement.

Explicit Transfers of Control

An explicit transfer of control is an alteration of the normal sequential transfer of control by the execution of a procedure branching statement or a conditional statement. The EXIT statement causes an explicit transfer of control only when it contains the PROGRAM phrase and is executed in a called program. Executing an ALTER statement does not in and of itself cause an explicit transfer of control.

See conditional statement, next executable statement, procedure branching statement.

truncation

When the fractional part of the result of an arithmetic operation contains more characters than there are positions in the receiving item, truncation—the dropping off of excess digits—occurs so that the result can fit into the receiving item. Thus a result of 56.719999, when truncated to two decimal places, becomes 56.71. To store the value 56.72, the ROUNDED option must be used.

See ROUNDED, Size Error condition.

truth value

The truth value of an expression describes whether the expression is true or false. For an expression to have a truth value it must be able to be evaluated as either 'true' or 'false,' but not both. For example, the expression '4 IS GREATER THAN 1' has a truth value of true. The expression '1 IS GREATER THAN 4' has a truth value of false. The expression '6 - NUM-DEDS' does not have a truth value.

The truth value of an expression need not always be the same over a period of time. For example, the truth value of 'X IS LESS THAN 4' changes as a function of the current value of X, being true when X is negative, 0, 1, 2, or 3, and false when X is 4 or more.

See logical operations.

TYPE

The TYPE clause specifies the particular type of report group that is described by the entry and indicates the time at which the report group is processed by the Report Writer Control System (RWCS).

Format:

```
          ⎧ ⎧REPORT HEADING⎫                        ⎫
          ⎪ ⎩RH            ⎭                        ⎪
          ⎪ ⎧PAGE HEADING⎫                          ⎪
          ⎪ ⎩PH          ⎭                          ⎪
          ⎪ ⎧CONTROL HEADING⎫⎧data-name-1⎫          ⎪
          ⎪ ⎩CH             ⎭⎩FINAL      ⎭          ⎪
TYPE IS   ⎨ ⎧DETAIL⎫                                ⎬
          ⎪ ⎩DE    ⎭                                ⎪
          ⎪ ⎧CONTROL FOOTING⎫⎧data-name-2⎫          ⎪
          ⎪ ⎩CF             ⎭⎩FINAL      ⎭          ⎪
          ⎪ ⎧PAGE FOOTING⎫                          ⎪
          ⎪ ⎩PF          ⎭                          ⎪
          ⎪ ⎧REPORT FOOTING⎫                        ⎪
          ⎩ ⎩RF            ⎭                        ⎭
```

The TYPE clause is part of a report group description entry. Except for a DETAIL report group, the RWCS processes these groups automatically. The action that the RWCS takes is described by type of report in the following paragraphs.

In this discussion, the term 'body group' refers to a Control Heading, Detail, or Control Footing group.

Report Heading

Only one Report Heading group can appear in a report description. Processing of a Report Heading group is done automatically by the RWCS, once per report, as the first group of the report. This group is processed when the first GENERATE statement is executed for the report.

The steps executed in processing a Report Heading report group are:

1. If there is a USE BEFORE REPORTING statement that references the data-name of the report group, it is executed.
2. If a SUPPRESS statement has been executed or if the report group is not printable, there is no further processing of the group.
3. Otherwise, the RWCS presents the group according to the presentation rules for that type of report group.

Page Heading

Only one Page Heading group can appear in a report description and then only if a PAGE clause is specified in the report description. Processing of a Page Heading group is done automatically by the RWCS as the first group on each page of the report unless:

1. A page is to contain only a Report Heading or only a Report Footing group.
2. A Report Heading is not to be presented on a page by itself in which case the Page Heading follows the Report Heading.

Steps one through three specified under Report Heading apply also to Page Heading report groups.

In a Page Heading report group, SOURCE clauses and USE procedures cannot reference control data items, group items containing a control data item, a data item subordinate to a control data item, or any item that redefines or renames any part of a control data item.

Control Heading

A Control Heading group is processed at the beginning of a control group for a designated control data-name or, if FINAL is specified, during the first GENERATE that is executed for the report.

During the execution of any GENERATE statement, if the RWCS detects a control break, any Control Heading report groups associated with the highest control level of the break and all lower levels are processed.

Only one Control Heading FINAL group can appear in a report description.

Steps one through three specified under Report Heading apply also to Control Heading report groups.

Data-name-1 and/or FINAL must be specified in the CONTROL clause of the corresponding report description entry. However, a Control Heading group is not *required* even if a data-name or FINAL is specified in the CONTROL clause of the report description entry. No data-name can have more than one Control Heading clause specified for it.

Detail

A DETAIL report group is processed by the RWCS when a GENERATE data-name or GENERATE report-name statement is executed. When a GENERATE report-name is specified, the corresponding report description entry must have no more than one DETAIL report group. If no GENERATE data-name statements are specified for such a report, a DETAIL report group is not required.

If a GENERATE data-name is executed, all four of the steps listed below are executed. If a GENERATE report-name is executed and the description of the report includes exactly one DETAIL report group, steps one through three are executed; if no DETAIL report group is included only step one is performed.

1. Any subtotalling that has been designated for the DETAIL report group is done.
2. If a USE BEFORE REPORTING procedure is specified for the group, it is executed.
3. If a SUPPRESS statement has been executed or if the report group is not printable, no further processing is done.
4. The RWCS formats the print lines and presents the report group according to the presentation rules for DETAIL report groups.

Control Footing

Only one Control Footing group can appear in a report description. Processing of a Control Footing group is done at the end of a control group for a designated control data-name.

During the execution of any GENERATE statement in which the RWCS detects a control break, any Control Footing report group associated with the highest level of the control break or with any lower level is presented. If there has been at least one GENERATE statement executed for a report, all Control Footing report groups will be presented during execution of a TERMINATE statement for that report.

If Control Footing FINAL is specified, the group is processed only once per report as the last body group of that report. Only one Control Footing FINAL group can be specified in a report description.

In a Control Footing group SOURCE clauses and USE procedures cannot reference a group data item that contains a control data item, a data item subordinate to a control data item, or any item that redefines or renames any part of a control data item.

Data-name-2 or FINAL must be specified in the CONTROL clause of the corresponding report description entry. However, a Control Footing group is not required even if a data-name or FINAL is specified in the CONTROL clause. No data-name can have more than one Control Footing clause specified for it.

The steps executed in processing a Control Footing report group are:

1. All sum counters defined in the report group that are also operands of SUM clauses in the same report group are added to their sum counters. This process is termed 'crossfooting.'

2. All sum counters defined in the report group that are also operands of SUM clauses in higher level Control Footing report groups are added to these higher level sum counters. This process is termed 'rolling forward.'

3. Steps one through three specified under Report Heading are executed.

4. Those sum counters that are to be reset when the RWCS processes this level in the control hierarchy are reset.

When a control break occurs, the RWCS produces the Control Footing report group beginning at the minor level and proceeding upward to the level at which the highest control break was sensed. Consequently, even if a Control Footing group has not been defined for a given control data-name the RWCS will still execute step four if a RESET phrase within the report description specifies that control data-name.

Any reference to a control data item in a SOURCE clause or a USE procedure uses those values of the control data items that were present when the RWCS detected the control break. When a TERMINATE statement is executed, the RWCS makes these prior values available to SOURCE clause or USE procedure references as if a control break had been detected in the highest control data-name.

Page Footing

Only one Page Footing group can appear in a report description and then only if a PAGE clause is specified in the report description. Processing of a Page Footing group is done by the RWCS as the last group on each page unless:

1. A page is to contain only a Report Heading or only a Report Footing group.

2. A Report Footing group is not to be presented on a page by itself in which case the Page Footing is the next-to-last group on the page.

Steps one through three specified under Report Heading apply also to Page Footing groups.

In a Page Footing report group, SOURCE clauses and USE procedures cannot reference control data items, group data items containing control data items, a data item subordinate to a control data item, or any item that redefines or renames any part of a control data item.

Report Footing

Only one Report Footing group can appear in a report description. Processing of a Report Footing group is done once per report as the last group of the report. The Report Footing group is processed during execution of a TERMINATE statement if there has been at least one GENERATE statement executed for the report.

In a Report Footing group, SOURCE clauses and USE procedures cannot reference group data items that contain a control data item, a data item that is subordinate to a control data item, or any item that redefines or renames any part of a control data item.

Steps one through three specified under Report Heading apply also to Report Footing groups.

When a TERMINATE statement is executed, the RWCS makes the prior values of control data items available to SOURCE clauses or USE procedures as if a control break had been detected in the highest control data-name.

Body Groups

When the RWCS is processing a Control Heading, Control Footing, or Detail group, it may, after determining that the body group is to be presented, have to interrupt the processing of that body group and execute a page advance (possibly processing Page Footing and Page Heading report groups) before presenting the body group.

See control break, control data item, group item, report description, report group description, REDEFINES, RENAMES, sum counter.

U

unary operator

A unary operator is one that requires only one operand. The minus sign and the logical NOT are unary operators.

See binary operator.

UNIT

See CLOSE, I-O-CONTROL, RERUN.

unit

A unit is a module of mass storage with implementor-defined dimensions.

UNSTRING

The UNSTRING verb separates data in an item and moves it to one or more receiving fields. This verb is new to 74 COBOL and is implemented only in level 2 of the Nucleus.

Format 1:

UNSTRING identifier-1 $\left[\underline{\text{DELIMITED}} \text{ BY } [\underline{\text{ALL}}] \begin{Bmatrix} \text{identifier-2} \\ \text{literal-1} \end{Bmatrix} \left[\underline{\text{OR}} \text{ } [\underline{\text{ALL}}] \begin{Bmatrix} \text{identifier-3} \\ \text{literal-2} \end{Bmatrix} \right] \dots \right]$

INTO {identifier-4 [$\underline{\text{DELIMITER}}$ IN identifier-5][$\underline{\text{COUNT}}$ IN identifier-6]} ...

[WITH $\underline{\text{POINTER}}$ identifier-7][$\underline{\text{TALLYING}}$ IN identifier-8]

[ON $\underline{\text{OVERFLOW}}$ imperative-statement-1]

Identifier-1 is the sending item, identifier-4 the receiving item, and identifier-5 the *delimiter receiving item*. Literal-1 or identifier-2 is the *delimiter*. The UNSTRING statement transfers data from the sending item to the receiving item(s) according to the following rules:

1. Transfer of data in identifier-1 proceeds from left to right in accordance with the MOVE statement rules for elementary alphanumeric data. If the DELIMITED BY phrase is not specified, the number of characters transferred is equal to the size of the receiving item. However, if the receiving item is numeric with its sign occupying a separate position, then the number of characters transferred is one fewer than the size of the receiving item. If DELIMITED BY is specified, transfer of data stops when the delimiter is encountered in identifier-1. If the end of identifier-1 is reached without encountering the delimiter, the UNSTRING operation terminates.

2. A delimiter can contain any character in the computer's character set. If a figurative constant is used as the delimiter, it stands for a single instance of the character considered as a nonnumeric literal. When a delimiter contains

more than one character, all of them must be present in the sending item in the same order as specified by the delimiter before they are, together, considered a delimiter. When two contiguous delimiters are encountered, the receiving item involved with the second delimiter is either space-filled or zero-filled, depending upon its description. However, if ALL is specified, all contiguous occurrences of the delimiter are treated as only one occurrence.

3. When two or more delimiters are specified, by using the OR connective, each nonoverlapping occurrence of any one of the delimiters is considered a delimiter. No character can be part of more than one delimiter. Testing for delimiters is done in the same order as they appear in the UNSTRING statement.

4. The DELIMITER IN phrase can be specified only if the DELIMITED BY phrase is specified. If the DELIMITER IN phrase is specified, the delimiting characters are considered to be elementary alphanumeric data items and are moved into the delimiter receiving item (identifier-5) according to the rules for a MOVE. If the delimiting condition was the end of the sending item, i.e., no instance of the delimiter was found, or if there were two contiguous delimiters, then the delimiter receiving item is space-filled or zero-filled, depending upon its description. However, if ALL was specified, then two or more contiguous delimiters are considered as one, and the delimiter receiving item is not necessarily space- or zero-filled.

5. If the POINTER phrase is specified, transfer of data begins with that character with an ordinal position within the sending item equal to the value of the pointer item (identifier-7). If POINTER is not specified, transfer begins at the left-most character position. The contents of identifier-7 are incremented by one for each character of identifier-1 that is examined, including delimiters. Thus the final contents of identifier-7 are its initial value plus the number of characters in the sending item examined by the statement. The user is responsible for initializing identifier-7 to a value greater than zero.

6. After the data have been transferred to the receiving item, if further receiving items are specified in subsequent INTO clauses, transfer of data from the sending item begins with the first character to the right of the last character transferred or to the right of the delimiter, depending upon whether or not the DELIMITED BY phrase was specified in the previous clause. In either case, the pointer item indicates the next character to be examined. This procedure continues until all the characters in the sending item have been inspected or until there are no more receiving items.

7. When the COUNT IN phrase is specified, a count equal to the number of characters within identifier-1 that were examined is placed in identifier-6. This count does not include delimiter characters.

8. When the TALLYING phrase is specified, identifier-8 is incremented by one for each *receiving item* acted upon. The programmer must be aware of the initial value of identifier-8.

9. An overflow condition occurs if during execution of an UNSTRING the value of the pointer item (identifier-7) becomes less than one or greater than the number of characters in the sending item or if all of the receiving items have been acted upon and the sending item still contains data characters that have not been examined. When the overflow condition occurs, the UNSTRING operation is terminated. If the ON OVERFLOW phrase is specified, imperative-statement-1 is executed. Otherwise control passes to the statement following the UNSTRING (or to a PERFORM or USE statement).

10. Any subscripting or indexing associated with identifier-1, -7, or -8, is evaluated only once, just before data is to be transferred. For identifiers-2 through -6, evaluation takes place immediately before the transfer of data into the respective data item.

	Numeric	Numeric integer	Alphanumeric	Usage DISPLAY	Alphabetic	Figurative constant w/o ALL	Nonnumeric
Identifier-1, -2, -3, -5			X				
Identifier-4	X			X	X		
Identifier-6, -7, -8		X					
Literal-1, -2						X	X

Examples: Assume that ID-1 = ABCDZEFGZZHZIJKL, that the size of ITEM-C is 4, and the size of all other identifiers is 5.

1. UNSTRING ID-1 INTO ITEM-A, ITEM-B, ITEM-C, ITEM-D

2. UNSTRING ID-1 DELIMITED BY "Z" INTO ITEM-A, ITEM-B, ITEM-C

3. UNSTRING ID-1 DELIMITED BY ALL "Z" INTO ITEM-A, ITEM-B, ITEM-C

4. UNSTRING ID-1 DELIMITED BY "Z" OR "D" INTO ITEM-A, ITEM-B, ITEM-C

After execution the contents of the receiving items are as follows:

Statement	ITEM-A					ITEM-B					ITEM-C				ITEM-D				
1	A	B	C	D	Z	E	F	G	Z	Z	H	Z	I	J	K	L			
2	A	B	C	D		E	F	G											
3	A	B	C	D		E	F	G			H								
4	A	B	C								E	F	G						

5. MOVE 1 TO TEMP-1.
UNSTRING ID-1 DELIMITED BY "Z" INTO ITEM-A DELIMITER IN TEMP-A COUNT IN TEMP-AA; ITEM-B DELIMITER IN TEMP-B COUNT IN TEMP-BB; ITEM-C DELIMITER IN TEMP-C COUNT IN TEMP-CC; POINTER TEMP-1, TALLYING IN TEMP-2

After execution the contents of the identifiers involved are

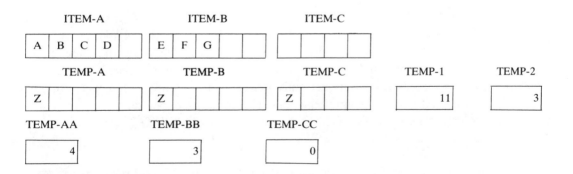

ITEM-A					ITEM-B				ITEM-C			
A	B	C	D		E	F	G					

TEMP-A				TEMP-B				TEMP-C				TEMP-1	TEMP-2
Z				Z				Z				11	3

TEMP-AA	TEMP-BB	TEMP-CC
4	3	0

See delimiter, indexing, ordinal position, subscripting.

unstructured data item

An unstructured data item is a level 77 (WORKING-STORAGE) data item or a level 01 data item that is not further subdivided.

See elementary item, group item, level 77, WORKING-STORAGE.

UNTIL

> *See* PERFORM.

UP BY

> *See* SET.

UPON

> *See* DISPLAY, SUM.

USAGE

> The USAGE clause specifies the way in which a data item is represented in storage.

> *Format:*

$$\text{\underline{USAGE} IS} \begin{Bmatrix} \underline{\text{COMPUTATIONAL}} \\ \underline{\text{COMP}} \\ \underline{\text{DISPLAY}} \\ \underline{\text{INDEX}} \end{Bmatrix}$$

> The USAGE clause does not affect the use of the data item in the program, but it does define the way in which the data is represented in storage. Usually the predominant use of the data determines the USAGE entry, but some statements in the Procedure Division may restrict the USAGE of some operands.

> The USAGE clause can be written at any level. If it is at the group level, it applies to each elementary item in the group; consequently the USAGE of an elementary item cannot contradict the USAGE of its group. Items that do not have the USAGE clause have an implicit USAGE of DISPLAY.

Computational Items

An item with a USAGE of COMPUTATIONAL is one that is used in arithmetic operations and must therefore be numeric. The PICTURE of a computational item can contain only the characters 9, S, V, P, and parentheses. If a group item is described as computational, only the elementary items within that group are considered to be computational since the group item, per se, cannot be used in numeric computations. (COMP is equivalent to COMPUTATIONAL.)

Display Items

A usage of DISPLAY indicates that the format of the data is an implementor-defined standard data format.

Index Items

An item with a usage of INDEX is called an index data item. It can be referred to explicitly only in a SEARCH or SET statement, a relation condition, the USING phrase of a procedure division header, or the USING phrase of a CALL statement. The SYNCHRONIZED, JUSTIFIED, PICTURE, VALUE IS, and BLANK WHEN ZERO clauses cannot be used with items with a usage of INDEX.

An index data item's value must always correspond to an occurrence number of a table element, and it cannot be a conditional variable. For a group item with a usage of INDEX, all elementary items in the group are index data items. The group item, per se, is not an index data item and cannot be used in SEARCH or SET statements or in relation conditions.

If an index data item is part of a group that is referred to in a MOVE or in an input-output statement, it is moved as a string of bytes with no conversion of data taking place. The format of an index data item, both internal and external, is specified by the implementor.

See arithmetic operator, conditional variable, division header, elementary item, group item, index data item, level-indicator, occurrence number, relation condition.

USE AFTER ERROR

The USE verb specifies user procedures for error handling that are executed in addition to the standard procedures provided by the input-output control system.

Format 1:

$$\underline{\text{USE}}\ \underline{\text{AFTER}}\ \text{STANDARD} \begin{Bmatrix} \underline{\text{EXCEPTION}} \\ \underline{\text{ERROR}} \end{Bmatrix} \underline{\text{PROCEDURE}}\ \text{ON} \begin{Bmatrix} \{\text{file-name-1}\}\ldots \\ \underline{\text{INPUT}} \\ \underline{\text{OUTPUT}} \\ \underline{\text{I-O}} \\ \underline{\text{EXTEND}} \end{Bmatrix} \bullet$$

A USE statement, when specified, must immediately follow a section header in the DECLARATIVES Section and must be terminated by a period and space. Only paragraphs that define the procedures to be used can be in this section. The USE statement itself is never executed—rather it defines the conditions under which the associated procedural statements are executed.

A USE procedure cannot reference a nondeclarative procedure. Also, in the declarative portion of the program, no reference can be made to declarative procedures except that a PERFORM statement can refer to a USE statement or to the procedures associated with a USE statement.

The procedures specified are executed by the input-output control system after completing the standard input-output error routine or upon recognition of the Invalid Key condition or At End condition when the INVALID KEY or AT END phrases have not been specified in the associated input-output statement. When the USE procedures are finished, control implicitly returns to the routine that caused the USE procedures to be invoked.

A USE procedure cannot cause the execution of another USE procedure that has been invoked but has not yet returned control to the invoking routine. (This is a new feature of 74 COBOL.) A USE statement cannot reference a SORT or MERGE file. A file-name in a USE statement must not cause the simultaneous request for execution of more than one USE procedure. The files referenced in a USE statement need not all have the same organization or access mode. ERROR and EXCEPTION are considered identical and can be used interchangeably. The EXTEND phrase can be used only with sequential files.

The feature 'EXCEPTION' is new to 74 COBOL. It allows the USE procedure to be invoked for either an error (e.g., boundary violation) or an exception (e.g., AT END condition).

See ACCESS MODE, ORGANIZATION, section header.

USE BEFORE REPORTING

The USE BEFORE REPORTING statement specifies Procedure Division statements that are executed just before a report group is presented.

Format:

USE BEFORE REPORTING identifier-1

The USE statement immediately follows a section header in the DECLARATIVES section. The procedures specified in the section are executed just before the report group, represented by identifier-1, is produced. The rest of the section consists of the procedures to be used. The USE statement itself is not executed; it merely defines the conditions calling for the execution of the USE procedures. The procedures in the USE section must not alter the value of any control data item; nor can they contain a GENERATE, INITIATE, or TERMINATE statement. Identifier-1 must not appear in more than one USE statement.

Within a USE procedure there cannot be any reference to a nondeclarative procedure. In the nondeclarative portion of the Procedure Division there can be no reference to procedure-names that appear in the declarative portion except that a PERFORM statement can refer to a USE BEFORE REPORTING statement or to the associated procedures.

See control data item, report group, section header.

USE FOR DEBUGGING

The USE FOR DEBUGGING statement identifies those user items that are to be monitored by the associated debugging section.

Format:

$$\text{\underline{USE} FOR \underline{DEBUGGING} ON} \left\{ \begin{array}{l} \text{cd-name-1} \\ \text{[\underline{ALL} REFERENCES OF] identifier-1} \\ \text{file-name-1} \\ \text{procedure-name-1} \\ \text{\underline{ALL} \underline{PROCEDURES}} \end{array} \right\} \dots \bullet$$

A section that contains a USE FOR DEBUGGING statement and one or more sentences is a debugging section. All debugging sections must appear together immediately following the declarative header. Except for the USE statement itself, a debugging section cannot contain a reference to a nondeclarative procedure nor can a statement outside a debugging section reference a procedure-name within a debugging section.

Statements within a given debugging section can reference procedure-names defined within a different USE procedure only by means of a PERFORM statement. A procedure-name defined within a debugging section cannot appear within a USE FOR DEBUGGING statement. A debugging section statement will not cause the execution of another debugging section.

Debug-item: Whenever a debugging section is executed, a special register called DEBUG-ITEM is filled with information about the condition that caused the execution of the debugging section. DEBUG-ITEM has the following implicit description:

```
01  DEBUG-ITEM.
    02  DEBUG-LINE       PIC X(6).
    02  FILLER           PIC X VALUE SPACE.
    02  DEBUG-NAME       PIC X(30).
    02  FILLER           PIC X VALUE SPACE.
    02  DEBUG-SUB-1      PIC S9999 SIGN IS LEADING SEPARATE CHARACTER.
    02  FILLER           PIC X VALUE SPACE.
    02  DEBUG-SUB-2      PIC S9999 SIGN LEADING SEPARATE CHARACTER.
    02  FILLER           PIC X VALUE SPACE.
    02  DEBUG-SUB-3      PIC S9999 SIGN LEADING SEPARATE CHARACTER.
    02  FILLER           PIC X VALUE SPACE.
    02  DEBUG-CONTENTS   PIC X(n).
```

In this description 'n' denotes a size large enough to hold the information described below. Prior to each execution of a debugging section, DEBUG-ITEM is space-filled. Then, the subordinate items are updated as described below. Any item not updated remains filled with spaces. Updating is done according to the rules for a MOVE statement.

DEBUG-ITEM can be referenced only from within a debugging section. It contains an implementor-defined way of identifying a source statement.

DEBUG-NAME contains the first 30 characters of the name as defined below. Any qualifiers are separated by OF or IN. Any subscripts and/or indices are not entered in DEBUG-NAME; however, the occurrence number of each level of the table element is entered in DEBUG-SUB-1 through DEBUG-SUB-3, respectively.

DEBUG-CONTENTS is a data item large enough to contain the data specified under each heading, below. Any move to DEBUG-CONTENTS is an alphanumeric-to-alphanumeric move with no conversion of data.

Cd-name-1

If cd-name-1 is specified, the associated debugging section is executed after the execution of any ENABLE, DISABLE, SEND, or ACCEPT MESSAGE COUNT statement that references cd-name-1 and after the execution of a RECEIVE statement that references cd-name-1 if the imperative-statement in the NO DATA clause was not executed.

A cd-name can appear in only one USE FOR DEBUGGING statement, and within that statement, it can appear only once. A reference to cd-name-1 as a qualifier does not cause the debugging section to be executed.

DEBUG-ITEM is updated as follows:

DEBUG-LINE identifies the source statement that referenced cd-name-1.

DEBUG-NAME contains the name of cd-name-1.

DEBUG-CONTENTS contains the contents of the area associated with cd-name.

File-name-1

If file-name-1 is specified, the associated debugging section is executed after the execution of any OPEN, CLOSE, DELETE, or START statement that references file-name-1 and after the execution of any READ that references file-name-1 if the imperative-statement associated with the AT END or INVALID KEY clause was not executed. The debugging section is executed after any other specified USE procedure. A reference to file-name-1 as a qualifier does not cause the debugging section to be executed. A file-name can appear in only one USE FOR DEBUGGING statement and within that statement can appear only once.

DEBUG-ITEM is updated as follows:

DEBUG-LINE identifies the source statement that referenced file-name-1.

DEBUG-NAME contains the name of file-name-1.

DEBUG-CONTENTS contains the entire record read if a READ caused execution of the debugging section. Otherwise, the contents are blank.

Identifier-1

If identifier-1 is specified without the ALL REFERENCES OF phrase, the associated debugging section is executed:

1. Immediately before the execution of a WRITE or REWRITE statement that explicitly references identifier-1, and after the execution of any implicit move resulting from the presence of the FROM phrase in the WRITE or REWRITE statement.

2. Immediately after initialization, modification, or evaluation of identifier-1 by a PERFORM statement that references identifier-1 in a VARYING, AFTER, or UNTIL phrase.

3. Immediately after the execution of any other statement that explicitly references identifier-1 and causes its contents to be changed.

4. If identifier-1 is specified in a phrase that is not executed or evaluated, the associated debugging section is not executed.

   If ALL REFERENCES OF identifier-1 is specified, the associated debugging section is executed:

1. Immediately before the execution of a WRITE or REWRITE statement that references identifier-1 and after the execution of any implicit move resulting from the presence of the FROM phrase in the WRITE or REWRITE statement.

2. Immediately after initialization, modification, or evaluation of identifier-1 by a PERFORM statement that references identifier-1 in a VARYING, AFTER, or UNTIL phrase.

3. Immediately before control is transferred by a GO TO statement with the DEPENDING ON phrase. This takes place prior to the execution of any debugging section that may be associated with the procedure-name to which control is transferred.

4. Immediately after execution of any other statement that implicitly or explicitly references identifier-1. If identifier-1 is specified in a phrase that is not executed or evaluated, the associated debugging section is not executed.

5. A reference to identifier-1 as a qualifier does not cause the debugging section to be executed.

   DEBUG-ITEM is updated as follows:

DEBUG-LINE identifies the source statement that referenced identifier-1.

DEBUG-NAME contains the name of identifier-1.

DEBUG-CONTENTS contains the contents of identifier-1 at the time control passes to the debugging section.

Any identifier can appear in only one USE FOR DEBUGGING statement, and within that statement, it can appear only once. Identifier-1 cannot reference any data item, with the exception of a sum counter, that appears in the Report Section. If identifier-1 contains an OCCURS clause or is subordinate to an entry that contains an OCCURS clause, identifier-1 must be specified without subscripting or indexing.

Procedure-name-1

If procedure-name-1 is specified, the associated debugging section is executed immediately before each execution of procedure-name-1 and immediately after the execution of an ALTER statement that references procedure-name-1.

If the first execution of the first nondeclarative procedure in the program causes the debugging section to be executed, DEBUG-ITEM is updated as follows:

DEBUG-LINE identifies the first statement of the procedure.

DEBUG-NAME contains the name of the procedure.

DEBUG-CONTENTS contains 'START PROGRAM.'

If a reference to procedure-name-1 in an ALTER statement causes the debugging section to be executed, DEBUG-ITEM is updated as follows:

DEBUG-LINE identifies the ALTER statement.

DEBUG-NAME contains the name of procedure-name-1.

DEBUG-CONTENTS contains the procedure-name associated with the TO phrase of the ALTER statement.

If execution of a GO TO statement causes the debugging section to be executed, DEBUG-ITEM is updated as follows:

DEBUG-LINE identifies the GO TO statement.

DEBUG-NAME contains the name of procedure-name-1.

If execution of a SORT or MERGE with the INPUT or OUTPUT phrase causes the debugging section to be executed, DEBUG-ITEM is updated as follows:

DEBUG-LINE identifies that SORT or MERGE statement.

DEBUG-NAME contains the name of procedure-name-1.

DEBUG-CONTENTS contains

'SORT INPUT' if procedure-name-1 is referenced in the INPUT phrase of a SORT statement.

'SORT OUTPUT' if procedure-name-1 is referenced in the OUTPUT phrase of a SORT statement.

'MERGE OUTPUT' if procedure-name-1 is referenced in the OUTPUT phrase of a MERGE statement.

If a PERFORM statement's implicit transfer of control causes the debugging section to be executed, DEBUG-ITEM is updated as follows:

DEBUG-LINE identifies that PERFORM statement.

DEBUG-NAME contains the name of procedure-name-1.

DEBUG-CONTENTS contains 'PERFORM LOOP.'

If a USE procedure causes the debugging section to be executed, DEBUG-ITEM is updated as follows:

DEBUG-LINE identifies the statement that caused execution of the USE procedure.

DEBUG-NAME contains the name of procedure-name-1.

DEBUG-CONTENTS contains 'USE PROCEDURE.'

If an implicit transfer of control from the previous paragraph causes the debugging section to be executed, DEBUG-ITEM is updated as follows:

DEBUG-LINE identifies the previous statement.

DEBUG-NAME contains the name of procedure-name-1.

DEBUG-CONTENTS contains 'FALL THROUGH.'

A reference to procedure-name-1 as a qualifier does not cause the debugging section to be executed. A procedure-name can appear in only one USE FOR DEBUGGING statement, and within that statement, it can appear only once.

A debugging section is executed no more than once as the result of the execution of a single statement. If a PERFORM statement causes iterative execution of a procedure, the associated debugging section is executed once for each iteration.

Within an imperative statement, each individual occurrence of an imperative verb identifies a separate statement for purposes of invoking the debugging section.

All Procedures

The ALL PROCEDURES phrase causes the action described for procedure-name-1 to occur for every procedure-name in the program except those that are within a debugging section.

The ALL PROCEDURES phrase can appear only once in a program. When used, an individual procedure-name cannot be specified in *any* USE FOR DEBUGGING statement.

See indexing, qualifier, subscripting, sum counter.

USE . . . LABEL

Label processing via the USE statement is no longer permitted.

user-defined word

A user-defined word is a word that must be supplied by the user to satisfy a format requirement. The valid characters for making a user-defined word are A through Z, 0 through 9, and the hyphen.

A user-defined word cannot exceed 30 characters in length and cannot begin or end with a hyphen.

There are 17 types of user-defined words:

alphabet-name	paragraph-name
cd-name	program-name
condition-name	record-name
data-name	report-name
file-name	routine-name
index-name	section-name
level-number	segment-number
library-name	text-name
mnemonic-name	

Except for paragraph-names, section-names, level-numbers, and segment-numbers, all user-defined words must have at least one alphabetic character. Except for segment-numbers and level-numbers, all user-defined words must be unique or be able to be made unique within a program. Condition-names, data-names, and record-names can be made unique by qualification.

See the individual entries for details; also qualification, word.

user-name

See user-defined word.

USING

1. USING is a phrase in the SORT and MERGE statements. For its use, see the respective entries.

2. USING is a phrase in the CALL statement; see the entry for details.

3. USING is a phrase used in the Procedure Division header when the object program is to function under control of a CALL statement that also contains a USING phrase.

Format:

PROCEDURE DIVISION [USING {data-name-1} . . .].

The object program behaves as if data-name-1 of the Procedure Division header and data-name-1 of the CALL statement were identical; that is, they both are considered to refer to the same data item. This relationship holds for each and every subsequent pair of data-names occupying the same ordinal position in the CALL statement and Procedure Division header. Each pair of corresponding data-names must describe items with the same number of characters.

Each data-name must be defined as a data item in the LINKAGE SECTION and must have a level-number of 01 or 77. No data item in the LINKAGE SECTION can be referenced in the Procedure Division unless it is an unstructured data item (level 77) or part of a record area referenced by data-name-1. No index-name or condition-name defined in the LINKAGE SECTION can be referenced in the Procedure Division unless it is associated with an unstructured data item or a record referenced by data-name-1.

A data-name cannot appear more than once in the same USING phrase of a Procedure Division header; it can, however, appear more than once in the USING phrase of a CALL statement.

Within a called program, LINKAGE SECTION data items are treated according to the data descriptions in the calling program, not the data descriptions of the corresponding data items in the CALL statement.

If USING is specified, the INITIAL clause must not be present in any CD entry.

See communication description entry, condition-name, index-name, level-number, ordinal position.

V

VALUE IS

The VALUE IS clause defines the value of constants, the initial value of data items in the WORKING-STORAGE, REPORT, and COMMUNICATION SECTIONS, and the values associated with condition-names.

Format 1:

VALUE IS literal-1

The VALUE IS clause cannot be used:

1. In a data description that contains an OCCURS or a REDEFINES clause or that is subordinate to an OCCURS or REDEFINES clause.
2. With a group item that contains items with descriptions having JUSTIFIED or SYNCHRONIZED clauses, or a USAGE other than DISPLAY.
3. With any item with a variable size.

Furthermore, the VALUE IS clause must not conflict with other clauses in the data description of its item or with the data description of an item to which it is subordinate.

Group Items

If the VALUE IS clause is used in an entry for a group item, any literal must be a figurative constant or nonnumeric literal. The group item will be initialized to this value without regard for the way in which the group is divided into elementary or other group items. Also, if a group item has a VALUE IS clause in its data description, no item subordinate to it can contain a VALUE IS clause.

Example:

```
02  ALFABET VALUE IS "ABC△DEF△GHI△JKL".
03  S-1 PIC XXX.
03  S-2 PIC X(5).
03  S-3 PIC X(7).
```

This would result in the following initial values:

S-1 $\boxed{\text{A B C}}$ S-2 $\boxed{\text{△ D E F △}}$ S-3 $\boxed{\text{G H I △ J K L}}$

Furthermore, none of the data-names, S-1, S-2, or S-3 could have a VALUE IS clause associated with it.

Elementary Items: If the data item is not numeric, in particular if it is numeric-edited, literal-1 must be nonnumeric.[1] The literal is aligned in the item as if the item were described as alphanumeric. Editing characters in the PICTURE clause are included in determining the size of the item, but they do not affect the initialization of the item. Therefore the value for an edited item should be in the edited form. For example:

> 02 A PIC IS $999.99, VALUE IS "$123.45"

is correct; whereas,

> 02 A PIC IS $999.99, VALUE IS "12345"

is incorrect. Similarly,

> 02 B PIC IS XX/XX/XX VALUE IS "07/04/76"

is the proper way to initialize an alphanumeric-edited variable.

If the data item is numeric, the literal must be numeric and have a value that is consonant with the PICTURE clause. In particular, if the PICTURE clause contains P's, they must be expressed as zeroes in the VALUE IS clause. If the PICTURE contains a sign, the literal in the VALUE IS clause can be signed; otherwise it must be unsigned. The literal in the VALUE IS clause will be aligned by the standard rules for alignment. For example, the following are all valid uses of the VALUE IS clause:

> 04 A PIC 999PPP VALUE IS 123000.
> 04 B PIC PPP999 VALUE IS .000123.
> 04 C PIC 999V99 VALUE IS 123.45.
> 04 D PIC S999V99 VALUE IS −123.45.

Initialization will always take place irrespective of any BLANK WHEN ZERO or JUSTIFIED clauses that may be specified. These clauses are ignored for the purpose of setting up an initial value. After this initial value is established, these clauses will be considered where applicable.

Linkage and File Sections

In the LINKAGE and FILE SECTIONS, the VALUE IS clause can be used only in condition-name entries, where it is required.

Working-storage and Communication Sections

In the WORKING-STORAGE and COMMUNICATION SECTIONS, the VALUE IS clause must be used in condition-name entries. It can also be used to specify the initial value of any data item. If so used, the data item assumes the

---

[1] This is a new feature of 74 COBOL.

specified value at object time. If this clause is not used, the initial value is undefined.

Report Section

In the REPORT SECTION, if an elementary report entry that contains a VALUE IS clause does not contain a GROUP INDICATE clause, the item will assume the specified value and be presented each time the report group is printed. If the GROUP INDICATE clause is present, although the item still assumes the specified value, it is presented only when certain object time criteria are met.

Format 2:

$$\begin{Bmatrix} \underline{\text{VALUE}} \text{ IS} \\ \underline{\text{VALUES}} \text{ ARE} \end{Bmatrix} \left[\text{literal-1} \left[\begin{Bmatrix} \underline{\text{THROUGH}} \\ \underline{\text{THRU}} \end{Bmatrix} \text{literal-2} \right] \right] \dots$$

The format 2 VALUE IS clause can be used only with condition-name entries. If the THROUGH phrase is used, literal-2 must be greater than or equal to literal-1. The VALUE IS clause and the condition-name are the only two items permitted in a condition-name entry. The characteristics of a condition-name are implicitly those of its conditional variable.

Examples:

```
02  ABC PIC 99.
    88 UNDER-AGE VALUE IS 35.
    88 MIDDLE-RANGE VALUES ARE 01 THRU 34.
    88 OVER-AGE VALUE IS 36 THROUGH 99.
```

In both formats, any literal can be a figurative constant.

See figurative constant, group item, OCCURS, variable size item.

VALUE OF

The VALUE OF clause gives a particular value to an item in a file's label record.

Format:

$$\underline{\text{VALUE}} \ \underline{\text{OF}} \ \text{implementor-name-IS} \begin{Bmatrix} \text{literal-1} \\ \text{data-name-1} \end{Bmatrix}$$

The VALUE OF clause appears in a file description (FD) entry. When VALUE OF is specified for an input file, the appropriate label routine checks whether the value of implementor-name-1 is equal to the value of literal-1 or data-name-1. For an output file the value of implementor-name-1 is set equal to literal-1 or data-name-1 at the appropriate time in the program.

Data-name-1 must be in WORKING-STORAGE and can be qualified, but not subscripted or indexed. It cannot have a usage of INDEX. Literal-1 can be a figurative constant.

The mandatory use of implementor-name is a new requirement of 74 COBOL.

See figurative constant, indexing, qualification, subscripting, USAGE.

variable

A variable is a data item with a value that can be changed by the object program. A variable used in an arithmetic statement must be a numeric elementary item.

variable size item

A variable size item is one that contains an OCCURS clause with the DEPEND-ING option. Each element of a variable size item is of a fixed length; it is the number of *occurrences* of the element that varies and thus makes the item's size variable.

Example:

```
02  ABC.
    03  DEF PIC XXX OCCURS 1 TO 10 TIMES DEPENDING ON PDQ.
```

ABC is a variable size item. Its size can range from 3 to 30 characters, depending on the value of PDQ. However, DEF is a fixed length of three characters.

VARYING

See PERFORM, SEARCH.

verb

A verb is a reserved word that causes an operation to take place.

See execution of object program.

W

WHEN

See SEARCH.

WITH

See CLOSE, DISABLE, ENABLE, OPEN, RECORD KEY, SEND, SOURCE-COMPUTER, STRING, UNSTRING.

word

A word is a character-string of not more than 30 characters. A word is either a reserved word, a user-defined word, or a system-name. A given word can belong to only one of these classes.

See character-string, reserved words, system-name, user-defined word.

WORDS

See MEMORY-SIZE, OBJECT-COMPUTER.

WORKING-STORAGE

The WORKING-STORAGE section of the DATA DIVISION contains descriptions of records not associated with input-output media and descriptions of noncontiguous data. It also contains descriptions of those data items that have preassigned values.

Items in working storage that have a hierarchical relationship to one another must be grouped into records according to the rules for record descriptions. All clauses used in record descriptions in the FILE SECTION can also be used in working storage. All data-names in this section must be unique or be able to be made unique by qualification.

Items that do not have this hierarchical relationship are called noncontiguous data. Each piece of noncontiguous data is described by an entry that must contain the level-number 77, a data-name, and a PICTURE clause. Other data description clauses are optional.

The initial value of any item in the WORKING-STORAGE section, except for an index data item, can be specified by the VALUE IS clause.

In 68 COBOL, level 77 items had to precede level 01 items in working storage.

See index data item, level-number, level 77, qualification.

WRITE

The WRITE verb releases a record to a file.

Format 1:

$$\text{\underline{WRITE} record-name [\underline{FROM} identifier-1]}$$

$$\left[\left\{ \begin{matrix} \underline{BEFORE} \\ \underline{AFTER} \end{matrix} \right\} \text{ADVANCING} \left\{ \begin{matrix} \left\{ \begin{matrix} identifier\text{-}2 \\ integer \end{matrix} \right\} \left[\begin{matrix} LINE \\ LINES \end{matrix} \right] \\ \left\{ \begin{matrix} mnemonic\text{-}name \\ \underline{PAGE} \end{matrix} \right\} \end{matrix} \right\} \right]$$

$$\left[; AT \left\{ \begin{matrix} \underline{END\text{-}OF\text{-}PAGE} \\ \underline{EOP} \end{matrix} \right\} \text{ imperative-statement-1} \right]$$

A format 1 WRITE is used with sequential files.[1] The file must be open in the output or extend mode when the WRITE is executed. If the file is in the output mode, the first WRITE creates the file and establishes its maximum record size. This size cannot subsequently be changed. The WRITE statement can also be used for vertical positioning of lines written within a page.

Record-name, which can be qualified, must name a record that is described in the FILE SECTION of the DATA DIVISION. The file must not be a SORT or MERGE file, however.

Once the WRITE has been successfully executed, the record that was released is no longer available in the file's record area unless that file is named in a SAME RECORD AREA clause. In this case, the record is still available in the record area and is also available as a record of other files appearing in that SAME RECORD AREA clause. Execution of the WRITE does not affect the current record pointer. If a FILE STATUS data item exists for the file, it is updated by the WRITE statement.

If an attempt is made to write beyond the externally defined boundaries of the file, an exception condition exists, the WRITE is unsuccessful, and the contents of the record area are unaffected. The File Status data item, if specified, is set to a value to indicate this condition. If a format 1 USE procedure is specified, it is executed. If no format 1 USE procedure is specified, the results are undefined.

If a file is contained on more than one reel or unit, when an end of reel/unit is recognized, the following actions take place:

The standard ending reel/unit label procedure.

A reel/unit swap.

The standard beginning reel/unit label procedure on the new reel.

---

[1] The INVALID KEY phrase has been dropped from 74 COBOL.

The From Phrase

Execution of a WRITE with the FROM phrase is equivalent to performing

MOVE identifier-1 TO record-name

before executing the write. The MOVE follows the rules for moving group items, that is, it is an alphanumeric-to-alphanumeric move. After successful execution of the WRITE, the data is still available in identifier-1 although it may not be available in the record area. Identifier-1 cannot refer to the same storage area as that defined by record-name.

The Advancing Clause

The ADVANCING clause controls the vertical positioning of lines. An understanding of the function of the parameters in the LINAGE clause is helpful in understanding the mechanism of advancing and its limits. If the ADVANCING clause is specified, advancing takes place as follows:

If identifier-2 is specified, the number of lines advanced is determined by the current value of identifier-2.

If integer-1 is specified, the value of integer-1 determines how many lines are advanced.

In both of the above cases, the advancing takes place before or after the writing, depending upon what is specified.

If mnemonic-name is specified, the advancing takes place according to the rules specified by the implementor for that hardware device designated. This option cannot be used if the file has a LINAGE clause specified in its file description.

If PAGE is specified, the record is written before or after the device is positioned to the next logical page. If a LINAGE clause is specified in the file description, positioning is to the first line that can be written on the next logical page. If LINAGE is not specified, positioning is implementor-defined.

If PAGE has no meaning for a device, advancing occurs as if ADVANCING 1 LINE had been specified. The advancing occurs before or after the writing, whichever is specified. (PAGE is a new feature of 74 COBOL.)

If the ADVANCING clause is not specified, advancing takes place as if AFTER ADVANCING 1 LINE had been specified.

The EOP Clause

If the END-OF-PAGE (EOP) clause is specified, the LINAGE clause must be specified for the file. If either the end-of-page condition or page overflow occurs, imperative-statement-1 is executed. This clause is new to 74 COBOL and is implemented in level 2 of the sequential i-o module.

The End-of-Page Condition

The end-of-page condition occurs whenever a WRITE statement with the END-OF-PAGE clause specified causes writing or spacing within the footing area of a page body. When the end-of-page condition is reached, imperative-statement-1 is executed when the writing is completed. If the associated LINAGE clause has no FOOTING specified, the end-of-page condition occurs simultaneously with the page overflow condition.

The Page Overflow Condition

The page overflow condition occurs whenever the execution of a WRITE statement would cause the LINAGE-COUNTER to equal or exceed the size of the page as specified in the LINAGE clause. If execution of a WRITE statement would cause the page overflow condition and the end-of page condition to occur simultaneously, then the page overflow condition takes precedence and it alone is recognized by the system.

When the page overflow condition occurs, the record is written on the logical page. This is done before or after the device is repositioned to the first line that can be written on the next logical page as specified in the LINAGE clause. If imperative-statement-1 is specified, it is executed.

Examples: Assume that the file description contains the clause

LINAGE IS 50 LINES WITH FOOTING AT 46

This defines a logical page as follows:

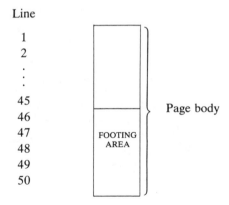

Now assume the following sequence of statements is executed:

1. WRITE HD1 AFTER ADVANCING 1 LINE; AT EOP imperative-statement-1.

2. WRITE HD2 AFTER ADVANCING 1 LINE; AT EOP imperative-statement-2.

3. WRITE HD3 AFTER ADVANCING 4 LINES; AT EOP imperative-statement-3.

4. WRITE HD4 AFTER ADVANCING 2 LINES; AT EOP imperative-statement-4.

Assuming that the associated LINAGE-COUNTER, whose current value designates the line where the device is currently positioned, is at 44 the following actions occur.

Executing statement 1 causes LINAGE-COUNTER to be incremented to 45 and HD1 written. Since line 45 is outside of the footing area and is not the last line on the page, neither the page overflow nor the end-of-page condition occurs.

When statement 2 is executed, LINAGE-COUNTER is increased to 46 and HD2 is written. Now the value of LINAGE-COUNTER indicates that the device is positioned within the footing area, so the end-of-page condition occurs. Since the device is not at the last line of the page, page overflow does not occur. Because of the end-of-page condition, imperative-statement-2 is executed. We will assume that it does not affect the current value of LINAGE-COUNTER.

Upon executing statement 3, LINAGE-COUNTER is increased to 50, which is the last line of the page. HD3 is written, and then, since the line is within the footing area, the end-of-page condition occurs. As a result, imperative-statement-3 is executed.

Now when statement 4 is executed, LINAGE-COUNTER is increased to 52, which exceeds the value of the page. Both the end-of-page and page overflow condition occur simultaneously, but only the page overflow condition is recognized. HD4 is not written on line 52. Rather, the device is positioned to the first line of the next page, and LINAGE-COUNTER is reset to the value one. Then HD4 is written. Imperative-statement-4 is executed only once, as a function of the page overflow condition. The result of this series of WRITE statements is

Current Page		Next Page	
Line		Line	
45	HD1	1	HD4
46	HD2	2	
47		3	
48			
49			
50	HD3		

Assuming the same LINAGE clause and initial value of LINAGE-COUNTER (44) as in the last example, consider the series of statements:

1. WRITE HD1 BEFORE ADVANCING 1 LINE; AT EOP imperative-statement-1.

2. WRITE HD2 BEFORE ADVANCING 1 LINE; AT EOP imperative-statement-2.

3. WRITE HD3 BEFORE ADVANCING 4 LINES; AT EOP imperative-statement-3.

4. WRITE HD4 BEFORE ADVANCING 2 LINES; AT EOP imperative-statement-4.

When statement 1 is executed, HD1 is written on line 44 and LINAGE-COUNTER is increased to 45. Since this is outside of the footing area, no end-of-page condition occurs.

Upon executing statement 2, HD2 is written on line 45, and LINAGE-COUNTER is increased to 46, which is inside the footing area. The end-of-page condition occurs, and imperative-statement-2 is executed. Assume imperative-statement-2 does not affect the value of LINAGE-COUNTER.

When statement 3 is executed, HD3 is written on line 46, and LINAGE-COUNTER is increased to 50. Again, only the end-of-page condition occurs, and imperative-statement-3 is executed.

Now when statement 4 is executed, HD4 is written on line 50. LINAGE-COUNTER is increased to 52, which exceeds the page limit and causes the page overflow condition. (The end-of-page condition also occurs, since this is within the footing area, but only the page overflow condition is recognized.) The device is positioned to the next page, LINAGE-COUNTER is reset to one, and because of the page overflow condition, imperative-statement-4 is executed. The result of executing this sequence of WRITE statements is

Current Page	
Line	
44	HD1
45	HD2
46	HD3
47	
48	
49	
50	HD4

N.B. These examples show the external effects of the WRITE statement; the internal mechanism may be quite different. Furthermore, they do not represent the highest style of programming.

Format 2:

<u>WRITE</u> record-name [<u>FROM</u> identifier-1][<u>INVALID</u> KEY imperative-statement-1]

The format 2 WRITE is used for files with relative or indexed organization. The file must not be a SORT or MERGE file and must be open in the output or I-O mode. Record-name, which can be qualified, must name a record that is described in the FILE SECTION of the DATA DIVISION. The maximum size of a record is established when the file is created and cannot be subsequently changed.

Once the WRITE is successfully executed, the record is no longer available in the file's record area unless that file is named in a SAME RECORD AREA clause. In this case, the logical record is still available in the record area and is also available as a record of other files appearing in that SAME RECORD AREA clause. Execution of the WRITE statement does not affect the current-record pointer.

Relative Files

When a relative file is being sequentially accessed, it must be open in the output mode before a WRITE is executed. The first record to be released will have a relative record number of one; subsequent records will have relative record numbers of two, three, four, etc. If a RELATIVE KEY data item is specified in the associated FILE CONTROL entry, the relative record number or address of the record just released is placed into the RELATIVE KEY data item.

A relative file that is being randomly or dynamically accessed must be open in the output or I-O mode before a WRITE is executed. At the time the WRITE is executed the RELATIVE KEY data item must contain the relative record number of the record being written.

Indexed Files

For indexed files, the prime record key data item must be set to the value of the record to be written before executing the WRITE statement. The prime record key data item values must all be unique within the records in the file. For sequential access, records must be written with prime record key values in monotonically ascending—but not necessarily consecutive—order. For random and dynamic access, records can be written in any order.

If the file has alternate record keys specified with the DUPLICATES phrase, the values of these key data items need not be unique. If that is the case, when records are accessed sequentially, those with the same value of alternate record key are obtained in the order in which they were written.

The From Clause

The operation of this clause is the same as described for a format 1 WRITE.

Invalid Key Condition

For all files the Invalid Key condition occurs if an attempt is made to write beyond the file's limits.

For relative files the Invalid Key condition occurs whenever the file is in the random or dynamic access mode and the RELATIVE KEY data item specifies a record that already exists in the file.

For indexed files the Invalid Key condition occurs whenever:

1. A file is open in the output mode, is being sequentially accessed, and the value of the prime record key is not greater than the value of the prime record key data item of the last record that was written.

2. A value of the prime record key is equal to the value of the prime record key of some record already in the file.

3. A file with an alternate record key for which the DUPLICATES phrase is *not* specified already contains a record with an alternate key data item value equal to the value of the alternate key item of the record being written.

When the Invalid Key condition occurs, the WRITE is unsuccessful, the contents of the record area are unaffected, and the File Status data item, if specified, is set to a value which indicates this condition.

Invalid Key Phrase

The INVALID KEY phrase must be specified if no format 1 USE procedure is specified for the file. (This is a new feature of 74 COBOL; previously this phrase was required.) When the Invalid Key condition occurs, if this phrase is specified, imperative-statement-1 is executed. If this phrase is not specified, the associated format 1 USE procedure is executed. If both the INVALID KEY phrase and a format 1 USE procedure are specified, only imperative-statement-1 is executed. If neither is specified, the results are undefined.

File Status

If a FILE STATUS data item is specified, execution of the WRITE causes it to be updated as follows:

Status Key 1	Status Key 2	Meaning
0	0	Successful completion
0	2	Successful completion; duplicate key
2	2	Duplicate key
2	4	Boundary violation
3	0	Permanent error
9	–	Implementor-defined

	Elementary integer	Zero
Identifier-2	X	X
Integer-1		X

See current-record pointer, dynamic access, extend mode, group item, in-dexed file, I-O mode, mnemonic name, monotonically, open mode, output mode, prime record key, qualification, random access, RECORD KEY, relative file, relative record number, sequential access, sequential file.

Z

ZERO, ZEROS, ZEROES

ZERO is a figurative constant that represents either the *value* zero or one or more instances of the character 0, depending upon the context in which it appears.

If level 2 of the Nucleus is implemented, the plural forms ZEROS and ZEROES can be used. They are equivalent to the singular form and serve only to improve readability.

See BLANK WHEN ZERO, figurative constant, sign condition.

zero fill

Zero filling is the process of moving zeroes into a receiving item to occupy character positions that would not otherwise have been acted upon by an operation. Zero filling occurs when the sending item has fewer positions than the receiving item in either the integral or the fractional part, or both.

Example:

SEND-IT PIC 99.9 VALUE 12.3.

REC-IT PIC 9999.99 VALUE 1234.56.

When one executes

MOVE SEND-IT TO REC-IT

the resulting contents of REC-IT are 0012.30. Zeroes have been placed in the two left-most and in the right-most character position. These positions, then, are said to have been zero filled.

See alignment rules, JUSTIFIED, MOVE, receiving item, space fill.

GENERAL FORMATS

General Format For Identification Division

$$
\begin{aligned}
&\underline{\text{IDENTIFICATION}}\ \ \underline{\text{DIVISION}}\bullet\\
&\underline{\text{PROGRAM-ID}}\bullet\ \text{program-name}\bullet\\
&[\underline{\text{AUTHOR}}\bullet\ [\text{comment-entry}]\dots]\\
&[\underline{\text{INSTALLATION}}\bullet\ [\text{comment-entry}]\dots]\\
&[\underline{\text{DATE-WRITTEN}}\bullet\ [\text{comment-entry}]\dots]\\
&[\underline{\text{DATE-COMPILED}}\bullet\ [\text{comment-entry}]\dots]\\
&[\underline{\text{SECURITY}}\bullet\ [\text{comment-entry}]\dots]
\end{aligned}
$$

General Format For Environment Division

ENVIRONMENT DIVISION•
CONFIGURATION SECTION•
SOURCE-COMPUTER• computer-name [WITH DEBUGGING MODE]•
OBJECT-COMPUTER• computer-name

$$
\left[\ \underline{\text{MEMORY}}\ \text{SIZE integer}
\left\{\begin{array}{l}
\underline{\text{WORDS}}\\
\underline{\text{CHARACTERS}}\\
\underline{\text{MODULES}}
\end{array}\right\}\ \right]
$$

[PROGRAM COLLATING SEQUENCE IS alphabet-name]
[SEGMENT-LIMIT IS segment-number]•
[a][SPECIAL-NAMES• [implementor-name

$$
\left\{\begin{array}{l}
\underline{\text{IS}}\ \text{mnemonic-name}\ [\underline{\text{ON}}\ \text{STATUS}\ \underline{\text{IS}}\ \text{condition-name-1}\ [\underline{\text{OFF}}\ \text{STATUS}\ \underline{\text{IS}}\ \text{condition-name-2}]]\\
\underline{\text{IS}}\ \text{mnemonic-name}\ [\underline{\text{OFF}}\ \text{STATUS}\ \underline{\text{IS}}\ \text{condition-name-2}\ [\underline{\text{ON}}\ \text{STATUS}\ \underline{\text{IS}}\ \text{condition-name-1}]]\\
\underline{\text{ON}}\ \text{STATUS}\ \underline{\text{IS}}\ \text{condition-name-1}\ [\underline{\text{OFF}}\ \text{STATUS}\ \underline{\text{IS}}\ \text{condition-name-2}]\\
\underline{\text{OFF}}\ \text{STATUS}\ \underline{\text{IS}}\ \text{condition-name-2}\ [\underline{\text{ON}}\ \text{STATUS}\ \underline{\text{IS}}\ \text{condition-name-1}]
\end{array}\right\}\ \dots
$$

$$
\left[\ \text{alphabet-name IS}
\left\{\begin{array}{l}
\underline{\text{STANDARD-1}}\\
\underline{\text{NATIVE}}\\
\text{implementor-name}\\
\left\{\text{literal-1}\left[\begin{array}{l}\underline{\text{THROUGH}}\\\underline{\text{THRU}}\end{array}\right\}\text{literal-2}\right.\\
\qquad \underline{\text{ALSO}}\ \text{literal-3}\ [\underline{\text{ALSO}}\ \text{literal-4}]\dots\right\}
\end{array}\right\}\ \right]\ \dots
$$

[CURRENCY SIGN IS literal-9]
[DECIMAL-POINT IS COMMA]•][a]

[a][INPUT-OUTPUT SECTION•
FILE-CONTROL•
    {file-control-entry}...
[b][I-O-CONTROL•

$$\text{[c]}\left[\underline{\text{RERUN}}\left[\underline{\text{ON}}\left\{\begin{array}{l}\text{file-name-1}\\\text{implementor-name}\end{array}\right\}\right]\right]\ \underline{\text{EVERY}}\left\{\begin{array}{l}\left\{\begin{array}{l}\text{[END OF]}\ \left\{\begin{array}{l}\underline{\text{REEL}}\\\underline{\text{UNIT}}\end{array}\right\}\\\text{integer-1}\ \underline{\text{RECORDS}}\end{array}\right\}\ \text{OF file-name-2}\\\text{integer-2}\ \underline{\text{CLOCK-UNITS}}\\\text{condition-name}\end{array}\right\}\text{[c]}\right]...$$

$$\left[\underline{\text{SAME}}\left[\begin{array}{l}\underline{\text{RECORD}}\\\underline{\text{SORT}}\\\underline{\text{SORT-MERGE}}\end{array}\right]\text{AREA FOR \{file-name-3\}}...\right]...$$

[MULTIPLE FILE TAPE CONTAINS {file-name-5 [POSITION integer-3]}...]...•][b]][a]
    N.B. The superscripts above the brackets are to indicate matching sets; they are not part of
    the COBOL language.

General Format for File Control Entry

Format 1

SELECT [OPTIONAL] file-name
    ASSIGN TO {implementor-name-1}...
    $$\left[\underline{\text{RESERVE}}\ \text{integer-1}\left[\begin{array}{l}\text{AREA}\\\text{AREAS}\end{array}\right]\right]$$
    [ORGANIZATION IS SEQUENTIAL]
    [ACCESS MODE IS SEQUENTIAL]
    [FILE STATUS IS data-name-1]•

Format 2

SELECT file-name
    ASSIGN TO {implementor-name-1}...
    $$\left[\underline{\text{RESERVE}}\ \text{integer-1}\left[\begin{array}{l}\text{AREA}\\\text{AREAS}\end{array}\right]\right]$$
    ORGANIZATION IS RELATIVE

$$\left[\underline{\text{ACCESS}}\ \text{MODE IS}\left\{\begin{array}{l}\underline{\text{SEQUENTIAL}}\ \text{[RELATIVE KEY IS data-name-1]}\\\left\{\begin{array}{l}\underline{\text{RANDOM}}\\\underline{\text{DYNAMIC}}\end{array}\right\}\ \underline{\text{RELATIVE}}\ \text{KEY IS data-name-1}\end{array}\right\}\right]$$

    [FILE STATUS IS data-name-2]•

Format 3

SELECT file-name
   ASSIGN TO {implementor-name-1} . . .
   $\begin{bmatrix} \underline{RESERVE}\ integer\text{-}1\ \begin{bmatrix} AREA \\ AREAS \end{bmatrix} \end{bmatrix}$
   ORGANIZATION IS INDEXED

   $\begin{bmatrix} \underline{ACCESS}\ MODE\ IS \begin{cases} \underline{SEQUENTIAL} \\ \underline{RANDOM} \\ \underline{DYNAMIC} \end{cases} \end{bmatrix}$

   RECORD KEY IS data-name-1
   [ALTERNATE RECORD KEY IS data-name-2 [WITH DUPLICATES]] . . .
   [FILE STATUS IS data-name-3]•

Format 4

SELECT file-name ASSIGN TO {implementor-name-1} . . .

General Format For Data Division

DATA DIVISION•
FILE SECTION•
[a][FD file-name

   $\begin{bmatrix} \underline{BLOCK}\ CONTAINS\ [integer\text{-}1\ \underline{TO}]\ integer\text{-}2 \begin{cases} \underline{RECORDS} \\ CHARACTERS \end{cases} \end{bmatrix}$

   [RECORD CONTAINS [integer-3 TO] integer-4 CHARACTERS]

   $\underline{LABEL} \begin{cases} \underline{RECORD}\ IS \\ \underline{RECORDS}\ ARE \end{cases} \begin{cases} \underline{STANDARD} \\ \underline{OMITTED} \end{cases}$

   $\begin{bmatrix} VALUE\ \underline{OF} \begin{cases} implementor\text{-}name\text{-}1\ IS \begin{cases} data\text{-}name\text{-}1 \\ literal\text{-}1 \end{cases} \end{cases} \dots \end{bmatrix}$

   $\begin{bmatrix} \underline{DATA} \begin{cases} \underline{RECORD}\ IS \\ \underline{RECORDS}\ ARE \end{cases} \{data\text{-}name\text{-}3\} \dots \end{bmatrix}$

   $\begin{bmatrix} \underline{LINAGE}\ IS \begin{cases} data\text{-}name\text{-}5 \\ integer\text{-}5 \end{cases} LINES \begin{bmatrix} WITH\ \underline{FOOTING}\ AT \begin{cases} data\text{-}name\text{-}6 \\ integer\text{-}6 \end{cases} \end{bmatrix} \end{bmatrix}$

   $\begin{bmatrix} LINES\ AT\ \underline{TOP} \begin{cases} data\text{-}name\text{-}7 \\ integer\text{-}7 \end{cases} \end{bmatrix} \begin{bmatrix} LINES\ AT\ \underline{BOTTOM} \begin{cases} data\text{-}name\text{-}8 \\ integer\text{-}8 \end{cases} \end{bmatrix}$

   [CODE-SET IS alphabet-name]
   $\begin{bmatrix} \begin{cases} \underline{REPORT}\ IS \\ \underline{REPORTS}\ ARE \end{cases} \{report\text{-}name\text{-}1\} \dots \end{bmatrix}$•

[record-description-entry] . . .][a] . . .
[SD file-name

[RECORD CONTAINS [integer-1 TO] integer-2 CHARACTERS]

$$\left[DATA \begin{Bmatrix} \underline{RECORD} \ IS \\ \underline{RECORDS} \ ARE \end{Bmatrix} \{data\text{-}name\text{-}1\} \right]\bullet$$

{record-description-entry}...]...

[WORKING-STORAGE SECTION•

$$\left[\begin{matrix} 77\text{-level-description-entry} \\ record\text{-description-entry} \end{matrix} \right] \ldots \ ]$$

[LINKAGE SECTION•

$$\left[\begin{matrix} 77\text{-level-description-entry} \\ record\text{-description-entry} \end{matrix} \right] \ldots \ ]$$

[COMMUNICATION SECTION•

[communication-description-entry

[record-description-entry]...]...]

[a][REPORT SECTION•

[b][RD report-name

[CODE literal-1]

$$\left[\begin{bmatrix} \begin{Bmatrix} \underline{CONTROL} \ IS \\ \underline{CONTROLS} \ ARE \end{Bmatrix} \begin{Bmatrix} \{data\text{-}name\text{-}1\}\ldots \\ \underline{FINAL} \ [data\text{-}name\text{-}1]\ldots \end{Bmatrix} \end{bmatrix} \right]$$

$$[c]\left[\underline{PAGE} \begin{bmatrix} \underline{LIMIT} \ IS \\ \underline{LIMITS} \ ARE \end{bmatrix} integer\text{-}1 \begin{bmatrix} \underline{LINE} \\ \underline{LINES} \end{bmatrix} [\underline{HEADING} \ integer\text{-}2] \right.$$

[FIRST DETAIL integer-3][LAST DETAIL integer-4]

[FOOTING integer-5]][c]•

{report-group-description-entry}...][b]...][a]

N.B. The superscripts above the brackets are to indicate matching sets; they are not part of the COBOL language.

General Format For Data Description Entry

Format 1

$$level\text{-}number \begin{Bmatrix} data\text{-}name\text{-}1 \\ \underline{FILLER} \end{Bmatrix}$$

[REDEFINES data-name-2]

$$\left[\begin{Bmatrix} \underline{PICTURE} \\ \underline{PIC} \end{Bmatrix} IS \ character\text{-}string \right]$$

$$\left[[\underline{USAGE} \ IS] \begin{Bmatrix} \underline{COMPUTATIONAL} \\ \underline{COMP} \\ \underline{DISPLAY} \\ \underline{INDEX} \end{Bmatrix} \right]$$

$$\left[[\underline{SIGN} \ IS] \begin{Bmatrix} \underline{LEADING} \\ \underline{TRAILING} \end{Bmatrix} [\underline{SEPARATE} \ CHARACTER] \right]$$

$$\left[\underline{OCCURS} \begin{Bmatrix} integer\text{-}1 \ \underline{TO} \ integer\text{-}2 \ TIMES \ \underline{DEPENDING} \ ON \ data\text{-}name\text{-}3 \\ integer\text{-}2 \ TIMES \end{Bmatrix} \right.$$

$$\left[\left\{ \begin{matrix}\underline{\text{ASCENDING}}\\\underline{\text{DESCENDING}}\end{matrix}\right\}\text{ KEY IS }\{\text{data-name-4}\}\ldots\right]\ldots$$

[<u>INDEXED</u> BY {index-name-1} ...]

$$\left[\left\{ \begin{matrix}\underline{\text{SYNCHRONIZED}}\\\underline{\text{SYNC}}\end{matrix}\right\}\left[\begin{matrix}\underline{\text{LEFT}}\\\underline{\text{RIGHT}}\end{matrix}\right]\right]$$

$$\left[\left\{ \begin{matrix}\underline{\text{JUSTIFIED}}\\\underline{\text{JUST}}\end{matrix}\right\}\text{ RIGHT}\right]$$

[<u>BLANK</u> WHEN <u>ZERO</u>]

[<u>VALUE</u> IS literal]•

Format 2

$$66\text{ data-name-1 }\underline{\text{RENAMES}}\text{ data-name-2 }\left[\left\{\begin{matrix}\underline{\text{THROUGH}}\\\underline{\text{THRU}}\end{matrix}\right\}\text{ data-name-3}\right]•$$

Format 3

$$88\text{ condition-name }\left\{\begin{matrix}\underline{\text{VALUE}}\text{ IS}\\\underline{\text{VALUES}}\text{ ARE}\end{matrix}\right\}\left\{\text{literal-1 }\left[\left\{\begin{matrix}\underline{\text{THROUGH}}\\\underline{\text{THRU}}\end{matrix}\right\}\text{ literal-2}\right]\right\}\ldots•$$

General Format For Communication Description Entry

Format 1

<u>CD</u> cd-name

FOR [<u>INITIAL</u>] <u>INPUT</u>

$$\left[^{\text{a}}\begin{bmatrix}\text{[SYMBOLIC }\underline{\text{QUEUE}}\text{ IS data-name-1]}\\\text{[SYMBOLIC }\underline{\text{SUB-QUEUE-1}}\text{ IS data-name-2]}\\\text{[SYMBOLIC }\underline{\text{SUB-QUEUE-2}}\text{ IS data-name-3]}\\\text{[SYMBOLIC }\underline{\text{SUB-QUEUE-3}}\text{ IS data-name-4]}\\\text{[}\underline{\text{MESSAGE}}\ \underline{\text{DATE}}\text{ IS data-name-5]}\\\text{[}\underline{\text{MESSAGE}}\ \underline{\text{TIME}}\text{ IS data-name-6]}\\\text{[SYMBOLIC }\underline{\text{SOURCE}}\text{ IS data-name-7]}\\\text{[}\underline{\text{TEXT}}\ \underline{\text{LENGTH}}\text{ IS data-name-8]}\\\text{[}\underline{\text{END}}\ \underline{\text{KEY}}\text{ IS data-name-9]}\\\text{[}\underline{\text{STATUS}}\ \underline{\text{KEY}}\text{ IS data-name-10]}\\\text{[}\underline{\text{MESSAGE}}\ \underline{\text{COUNT}}\text{ IS data-name-11]]}^{\text{a}}\end{bmatrix}\right.$$
[data-name-1, data-name-2, . . . , data-name-11] •

N.B. The superscripts above the brackets are to indicate matching sets; they are not part of the COBOL language.

Format 2

<u>CD</u> cd-name FOR <u>OUTPUT</u>

[<u>DESTINATION</u> <u>COUNT</u> IS data-name-1]

[<u>TEXT</u> <u>LENGTH</u> IS data-name-2]

[<u>STATUS</u> <u>KEY</u> IS data-name-3]

[<u>DESTINATION</u> <u>TABLE</u> <u>OCCURS</u> integer-2 TIMES [<u>INDEXED</u> BY {index-name-1} . . .]]

[<u>ERROR</u> <u>KEY</u> IS data-name-4]

[SYMBOLIC <u>DESTINATION</u> IS data-name-5]•

General Format For Report Group Description Entry

Format 1

01 [data-name-1]

$$\left[\text{\underline{LINE}} \text{ NUMBER IS } \left\{ \begin{array}{l} \text{integer-1 [ON \underline{NEXT} \underline{PAGE}]} \\ \text{\underline{PLUS} integer-2} \end{array} \right\} \right]$$

$$\left[\text{\underline{NEXT} \underline{GROUP} IS} \left\{ \begin{array}{l} \text{integer-3} \\ \text{\underline{PLUS} integer-4} \\ \text{\underline{NEXT} \underline{PAGE}} \end{array} \right\} \right]$$

$$\text{\underline{TYPE} IS} \left\{ \begin{array}{l} \left\{ \begin{array}{l} \text{\underline{REPORT} \underline{HEADING}} \\ \text{\underline{RH}} \end{array} \right\} \\ \left\{ \begin{array}{l} \text{\underline{PAGE} \underline{HEADING}} \\ \text{\underline{PH}} \end{array} \right\} \\ \left\{ \begin{array}{l} \text{\underline{CONTROL} \underline{HEADING}} \\ \text{\underline{CH}} \end{array} \right\} \left\{ \begin{array}{l} \text{data-name-2} \\ \text{\underline{FINAL}} \end{array} \right\} \\ \left\{ \begin{array}{l} \text{\underline{DETAIL}} \\ \text{\underline{DE}} \end{array} \right\} \\ \left\{ \begin{array}{l} \text{\underline{CONTROL} \underline{FOOTING}} \\ \text{\underline{CF}} \end{array} \right\} \left\{ \begin{array}{l} \text{data-name-3} \\ \text{\underline{FINAL}} \end{array} \right\} \\ \left\{ \begin{array}{l} \text{\underline{PAGE} \underline{FOOTING}} \\ \text{\underline{PF}} \end{array} \right\} \\ \left\{ \begin{array}{l} \text{\underline{REPORT} \underline{FOOTING}} \\ \text{\underline{RF}} \end{array} \right\} \end{array} \right\}$$

[[<u>USAGE</u> IS] <u>DISPLAY</u>].

Format 2

level-number [data-name-1]

$$\left[\text{\underline{LINE}} \text{ NUMBER IS } \left\{ \begin{array}{l} \text{integer-1 [ON \underline{NEXT} \underline{PAGE}]} \\ \text{\underline{PLUS} integer-2} \end{array} \right\} \right]$$

[[<u>USAGE</u> IS] <u>DISPLAY</u>].

Format 3

level-number [data-name-1]

[<u>BLANK</u> WHEN <u>ZERO</u>]

[<u>GROUP</u> INDICATE]

$$\left[\left\{ \begin{array}{l} \text{\underline{JUSTIFIED}} \\ \text{\underline{JUST}} \end{array} \right\} \text{RIGHT} \right]$$

$$\left[\text{\underline{LINE}} \text{ NUMBER IS } \left\{ \begin{array}{l} \text{integer-1 [ON \underline{NEXT} \underline{PAGE}]} \\ \text{\underline{PLUS} integer-2} \end{array} \right\} \right]$$

[<u>COLUMN</u> NUMBER IS integer-3]

$$\left\{ \begin{array}{l} \text{\underline{PICTURE}} \\ \text{\underline{PIC}} \end{array} \right\} \text{IS character-string}$$

$$\left\{ \begin{array}{l} \underline{\text{SOURCE}} \text{ IS identifier-1} \\ \underline{\text{VALUE}} \text{ IS literal} \\ \{\underline{\text{SUM}} \text{ \{identifier-2\}} \dots [\underline{\text{UPON}} \text{ \{data-name-2\}} \dots]\} \dots \\ \left[\underline{\text{RESET}} \text{ ON} \left\{ \begin{array}{l} \text{data-name-4} \\ \underline{\text{FINAL}} \end{array} \right\} \right] \end{array} \right\}$$

[[USAGE IS] DISPLAY]•

General Format For Procedure Division

Format 1

PROCEDURE DIVISION [USING {data-name-1} . . .]•
[DECLARATIVES•
{section-name SECTION [segment-number]• declarative-sentence
[paragraph-name• [sentence] . . .] . . .} . . .
  END DECLARATIVES•]
{section-name SECTION [segment-number]•
[paragraph-name• [sentence] . . .] . . .} . . .

Format 2

PROCEDURE DIVISION [USING {data-name-1} . . .]•
{paragraph-name• [sentence] . . .} . . .

General Format For Verbs

ACCEPT identifier [FROM mnemonic-name]

$$\text{ACCEPT identifier } \underline{\text{FROM}} \left\{ \begin{array}{l} \underline{\text{DATE}} \\ \underline{\text{DAY}} \\ \underline{\text{TIME}} \end{array} \right\}$$

ACCEPT cd-name MESSAGE COUNT

$$\underline{\text{ADD}} \left\{ \begin{array}{l} \text{identifier-1} \\ \text{literal-1} \end{array} \right\} \dots \underline{\text{TO}} \text{ \{identifier-m [\underline{ROUNDED}]\}} \dots$$

  [ON SIZE ERROR imperative-statement]

$$\underline{\text{ADD}} \left\{ \begin{array}{l} \text{identifier-1} \\ \text{literal-1} \end{array} \right\} \left\{ \begin{array}{l} \text{identifier-2} \\ \text{literal-2} \end{array} \right\} \dots \underline{\text{GIVING}} \text{ \{identifier-m [\underline{ROUNDED}]\}} \dots$$

  [ON SIZE ERROR imperative-statement]

$$\underline{\text{ADD}} \left\{ \begin{array}{l} \underline{\text{CORRESPONDING}} \\ \underline{\text{CORR}} \end{array} \right\} \text{identifier-1 } \underline{\text{TO}} \text{ identifier-2 [\underline{ROUNDED}]}$$

  [ON SIZE ERROR imperative-statement]

ALTER {procedure-name-1 TO [PROCEED TO] procedure-name-2} . . .

$$\underline{\text{CALL}} \left\{ \begin{array}{l} \text{identifier-1} \\ \text{literal-1} \end{array} \right\} [\underline{\text{USING}} \text{ \{data-name-1\}} \dots]$$

  [ON OVERFLOW imperative-statement]

$$\underline{\text{CANCEL}} \left\{ \begin{array}{l} \text{identifier-1} \\ \text{literal-1} \end{array} \right\} \dots$$

$$\text{CLOSE} \left\{ \text{file-name-1} \left[\begin{array}{l} \left[\begin{Bmatrix} \text{REEL} \\ \text{UNIT} \end{Bmatrix} \right] \left[\begin{array}{l} \text{WITH } \underline{\text{NO REWIND}} \\ \text{FOR } \underline{\text{REMOVAL}} \end{array} \right] \\ \text{WITH } \begin{Bmatrix} \underline{\text{NO REWIND}} \\ \underline{\text{LOCK}} \end{Bmatrix} \end{array} \right] \right\} \dots$$

CLOSE {file-name-1 [WITH LOCK]} . . .

COMPUTE {identifier-1 [ROUNDED]} . . . = arithmetic-expression
[ON SIZE ERROR imperative-statement]

$$\text{COPY text-name} \left[\begin{Bmatrix} \text{OF} \\ \text{IN} \end{Bmatrix} \text{library-name} \right]$$

$$\left[\text{REPLACING} \begin{Bmatrix} \begin{Bmatrix} ==\text{pseudo-text-1}== \\ \text{identifier-1} \\ \text{literal-1} \\ \text{word-1} \end{Bmatrix} \underline{\text{BY}} \begin{Bmatrix} ==\text{pseudo-text-2}== \\ \text{identifier-2} \\ \text{literal-2} \\ \text{word-2} \end{Bmatrix} \end{Bmatrix} \dots \right]$$

DELETE file-name RECORD [INVALID KEY imperative-statement]

$$\text{DISABLE} \begin{Bmatrix} \underline{\text{INPUT}} \text{ [TERMINAL]} \\ \underline{\text{OUTPUT}} \end{Bmatrix} \text{cd-name WITH } \underline{\text{KEY}} \begin{Bmatrix} \text{identifier-1} \\ \text{literal-1} \end{Bmatrix}$$

$$\text{DISPLAY} \begin{Bmatrix} \text{identifier-1} \\ \text{literal-1} \end{Bmatrix} \dots \text{[\underline{UPON} mnemonic-name]}$$

$$\text{DIVIDE} \begin{Bmatrix} \text{identifier-1} \\ \text{literal-1} \end{Bmatrix} \underline{\text{INTO}} \text{ {identifier-2 [\underline{ROUNDED}]}} \dots$$
[ON SIZE ERROR imperative-statement]

$$\text{DIVIDE} \begin{Bmatrix} \text{identifier-1} \\ \text{literal-1} \end{Bmatrix} \underline{\text{INTO}} \begin{Bmatrix} \text{identifier-2} \\ \text{literal-2} \end{Bmatrix} \underline{\text{GIVING}} \text{ {identifier-3 [\underline{ROUNDED}]}} \dots$$
[ON SIZE ERROR imperative-statement]

$$\text{DIVIDE} \begin{Bmatrix} \text{identifier-1} \\ \text{literal-1} \end{Bmatrix} \underline{\text{BY}} \begin{Bmatrix} \text{identifier-2} \\ \text{literal-2} \end{Bmatrix} \underline{\text{GIVING}} \text{ {identifier-3 [\underline{ROUNDED}]}} \dots$$
[ON SIZE ERROR imperative-statement]

$$\text{DIVIDE} \begin{Bmatrix} \text{identifier-1} \\ \text{literal-1} \end{Bmatrix} \underline{\text{INTO}} \begin{Bmatrix} \text{identifier-2} \\ \text{literal-2} \end{Bmatrix} \underline{\text{GIVING}} \text{ identifier-3 [\underline{ROUNDED}]}$$
REMAINDER identifier-4 [ON SIZE ERROR imperative-statement]

$$\text{DIVIDE} \begin{Bmatrix} \text{identifier-1} \\ \text{literal-1} \end{Bmatrix} \underline{\text{BY}} \begin{Bmatrix} \text{identifier-2} \\ \text{literal-2} \end{Bmatrix} \underline{\text{GIVING}} \text{ identifier-3 [\underline{ROUNDED}]}$$
REMAINDER identifier-4 [ON SIZE ERROR imperative-statement]

$$\text{ENABLE} \begin{Bmatrix} \underline{\text{INPUT}} \text{ [TERMINAL]} \\ \underline{\text{OUTPUT}} \end{Bmatrix} \text{cd-name WITH } \underline{\text{KEY}} \begin{Bmatrix} \text{identifier-1} \\ \text{literal-1} \end{Bmatrix}$$

ENTER language-name [routine-name].

EXIT [PROGRAM].

$$\text{GENERATE} \begin{Bmatrix} \text{data-name} \\ \text{report-name} \end{Bmatrix}$$

GO TO [procedure-name-1]

GO TO {procedure-name-1} . . . procedure-name-n
    DEPENDING ON identifier

$$\underline{\text{IF}} \text{ condition} \begin{Bmatrix} \text{statement-1} \\ \underline{\text{NEXT}} \ \underline{\text{SENTENCE}} \end{Bmatrix} \begin{Bmatrix} \underline{\text{ELSE}} \text{ statement-2} \\ \underline{\text{ELSE}} \ \underline{\text{NEXT}} \ \underline{\text{SENTENCE}} \end{Bmatrix}$$

$\underline{\text{INITIATE}} \ \{\text{report-name-1}\}\ldots$

$\underline{\text{INSPECT}} \text{ identifier-1} \ \underline{\text{TALLYING}}$

$$\begin{Bmatrix} \text{identifier-2} \ \underline{\text{FOR}} \begin{Bmatrix} \begin{Bmatrix} \underline{\text{ALL}} \\ \underline{\text{LEADING}} \end{Bmatrix} \begin{Bmatrix} \text{identifier-3} \\ \text{literal-1} \end{Bmatrix} \\ \underline{\text{CHARACTERS}} \end{Bmatrix} \left[\begin{Bmatrix} \underline{\text{BEFORE}} \\ \underline{\text{AFTER}} \end{Bmatrix} \text{INITIAL} \begin{Bmatrix} \text{identifier-4} \\ \text{literal-2} \end{Bmatrix} \right]\ldots \end{Bmatrix} \ldots$$

$\underline{\text{INSPECT}} \text{ identifier-1} \ \underline{\text{REPLACING}}$

$$\begin{Bmatrix} \underline{\text{CHARACTERS}} \ \underline{\text{BY}} \begin{Bmatrix} \text{identifier-6} \\ \text{literal-4} \end{Bmatrix} \left[\begin{Bmatrix} \underline{\text{BEFORE}} \\ \underline{\text{AFTER}} \end{Bmatrix} \text{INITIAL} \begin{Bmatrix} \text{identifier-7} \\ \text{literal-5} \end{Bmatrix} \right] \\ \begin{Bmatrix} \begin{Bmatrix} \underline{\text{ALL}} \\ \underline{\text{LEADING}} \\ \underline{\text{FIRST}} \end{Bmatrix} \end{Bmatrix} \begin{Bmatrix} \text{identifier-5} \\ \text{literal-3} \end{Bmatrix} \ \underline{\text{BY}} \begin{Bmatrix} \text{identifier-6} \\ \text{literal-4} \end{Bmatrix} \left[\begin{Bmatrix} \underline{\text{BEFORE}} \\ \underline{\text{AFTER}} \end{Bmatrix} \text{INITIAL} \begin{Bmatrix} \text{identifier-7} \\ \text{literal-5} \end{Bmatrix} \right]\ldots \end{Bmatrix} \ldots$$

$\underline{\text{INSPECT}} \text{ identifier-1} \ \underline{\text{TALLYING}}$

$$\begin{Bmatrix} \text{identifier-2} \ \underline{\text{FOR}} \begin{Bmatrix} \begin{Bmatrix} \underline{\text{ALL}} \\ \underline{\text{LEADING}} \end{Bmatrix} \begin{Bmatrix} \text{identifier-3} \\ \text{literal-1} \end{Bmatrix} \\ \underline{\text{CHARACTERS}} \end{Bmatrix} \left[\begin{Bmatrix} \underline{\text{BEFORE}} \\ \underline{\text{AFTER}} \end{Bmatrix} \text{INITIAL} \begin{Bmatrix} \text{identifier-4} \\ \text{literal-2} \end{Bmatrix} \right]\ldots \end{Bmatrix} \ldots$$

$\underline{\text{REPLACING}}$

$$\begin{Bmatrix} \underline{\text{CHARACTERS}} \ \underline{\text{BY}} \begin{Bmatrix} \text{identifier-6} \\ \text{literal-4} \end{Bmatrix} \left[\begin{Bmatrix} \underline{\text{BEFORE}} \\ \underline{\text{AFTER}} \end{Bmatrix} \text{INITIAL} \begin{Bmatrix} \text{identifier-7} \\ \text{literal-5} \end{Bmatrix} \right] \\ \begin{Bmatrix} \begin{Bmatrix} \underline{\text{ALL}} \\ \underline{\text{LEADING}} \\ \underline{\text{FIRST}} \end{Bmatrix} \end{Bmatrix} \begin{Bmatrix} \text{identifier-5} \\ \text{literal-3} \end{Bmatrix} \ \underline{\text{BY}} \begin{Bmatrix} \text{identifier-6} \\ \text{literal-4} \end{Bmatrix} \left[\begin{Bmatrix} \underline{\text{BEFORE}} \\ \underline{\text{AFTER}} \end{Bmatrix} \text{INITIAL} \begin{Bmatrix} \text{identifier-7} \\ \text{literal-5} \end{Bmatrix} \right] \end{Bmatrix}\ldots \end{Bmatrix} \ldots$$

$$\underline{\text{MERGE}} \text{ file-name-1} \begin{Bmatrix} \text{ON} \begin{Bmatrix} \underline{\text{ASCENDING}} \\ \underline{\text{DESCENDING}} \end{Bmatrix} \text{KEY} \ \{\text{data-name-1}\}\ldots \end{Bmatrix} \ldots$$

$[\underline{\text{COLLATING}} \ \underline{\text{SEQUENCE}} \text{ IS alphabet-name}]$

$\underline{\text{USING}} \text{ file-name-2} \ \{\text{file-name-3}\}\ldots$

$$\begin{Bmatrix} \underline{\text{OUTPUT}} \ \underline{\text{PROCEDURE}} \text{ IS section-name-1} \left[\begin{Bmatrix} \underline{\text{THROUGH}} \\ \underline{\text{THRU}} \end{Bmatrix} \text{ section-name-2} \right] \\ \underline{\text{GIVING}} \text{ file-name-5} \end{Bmatrix}$$

$$\underline{\text{MOVE}} \begin{Bmatrix} \text{identifier-1} \\ \text{literal} \end{Bmatrix} \ \underline{\text{TO}} \ \{\text{identifier-2}\}\ldots$$

$$\underline{\text{MOVE}} \begin{Bmatrix} \underline{\text{CORRESPONDING}} \\ \underline{\text{CORR}} \end{Bmatrix} \cdot \text{identifier-1} \ \underline{\text{TO}} \text{ identifier-2}$$

$$\underline{\text{MULTIPLY}} \begin{Bmatrix} \text{identifier-1} \\ \text{literal-1} \end{Bmatrix} \ \underline{\text{BY}} \ \{\text{identifier-2} \ [\underline{\text{ROUNDED}}]\}\ldots$$

$[\text{ON} \ \underline{\text{SIZE}} \ \underline{\text{ERROR}} \text{ imperative-statement}]$

373

MULTIPLY $\begin{Bmatrix} \text{identifier-1} \\ \text{literal-1} \end{Bmatrix}$ BY $\begin{Bmatrix} \text{identifier-2} \\ \text{literal-2} \end{Bmatrix}$ GIVING {identifier-3 [ROUNDED]} . . .

    [ON SIZE ERROR imperative-statement]

OPEN $\begin{Bmatrix} \text{INPUT} \Big\{ \text{file-name-1} \begin{bmatrix} \text{REVERSED} \\ \text{WITH NO REWIND} \end{bmatrix} \Big\} \cdots \\ \text{OUTPUT \{file-name-3 [WITH NO REWIND]\} . . .} \\ \text{I-O \{file-name-5\} . . .} \\ \text{EXTEND \{file-name-7\} . . .} \end{Bmatrix}$

PERFORM procedure-name-1 $\left[\begin{Bmatrix} \text{THROUGH} \\ \text{THRU} \end{Bmatrix} \text{procedure-name-2} \right]$

PERFORM procedure-name-1 $\left[\begin{Bmatrix} \text{THROUGH} \\ \text{THRU} \end{Bmatrix} \text{procedure-name-2} \right] \begin{Bmatrix} \text{identifier-1} \\ \text{integer-1} \end{Bmatrix}$ TIMES

PERFORM procedure-name-1 $\left[\begin{Bmatrix} \text{THROUGH} \\ \text{THRU} \end{Bmatrix} \text{procedure-name-2} \right]$ UNTIL condition-1

PERFORM procedure-name-1 $\left[\begin{Bmatrix} \text{THROUGH} \\ \text{THRU} \end{Bmatrix} \text{procedure-name-2} \right]$

    VARYING $\begin{Bmatrix} \text{identifier-2} \\ \text{index-name-1} \end{Bmatrix}$ FROM $\begin{Bmatrix} \text{identifier-3} \\ \text{index-name-2} \\ \text{literal-1} \end{Bmatrix}$

    BY $\begin{Bmatrix} \text{identifier-4} \\ \text{literal-3} \end{Bmatrix}$ UNTIL condition-1

$\left[\text{AFTER} \begin{Bmatrix} \text{identifier-5} \\ \text{index-name-3} \end{Bmatrix} \text{FROM} \begin{Bmatrix} \text{identifier-6} \\ \text{index-name-4} \\ \text{literal-3} \end{Bmatrix} \right.$

    $\left. \text{BY} \begin{Bmatrix} \text{identifier-7} \\ \text{literal-4} \end{Bmatrix} \text{UNTIL condition-2} \right]$

$\left[\text{AFTER} \begin{Bmatrix} \text{identifier-8} \\ \text{index-name-5} \end{Bmatrix} \text{FROM} \begin{Bmatrix} \text{identifier-9} \\ \text{index-name-6} \\ \text{literal-5} \end{Bmatrix} \right.$

    $\left. \text{BY} \begin{Bmatrix} \text{identifier-10} \\ \text{literal-6} \end{Bmatrix} \text{UNTIL condition-3} \right]$

READ file-name [NEXT] RECORD [INTO identifier][AT END imperative-statement]
READ file-name RECORD [INTO identifier] [KEY IS data-name]

    [INVALID KEY imperative-statement]

RECEIVE cd-name $\begin{Bmatrix} \text{MESSAGE} \\ \text{SEGMENT} \end{Bmatrix}$ INTO identifier-1 [NO DATA imperative-statement]

RELEASE record-name [FROM identifier]

RETURN file-name RECORD [INTO identifier] AT END imperative-statement

REWRITE record-name [FROM identifier][INVALID KEY imperative-statement]

SEARCH identifier-1 $\left[\underline{\text{VARYING}} \left\{ \begin{array}{l} \text{identifier-2} \\ \text{index-name-1} \end{array} \right\} \right]$ [AT END imperative-statement-1]

$\left\{ \underline{\text{WHEN}} \text{ condition-1} \left\{ \begin{array}{l} \text{imperative-statement-2} \\ \underline{\text{NEXT}} \ \underline{\text{SENTENCE}} \end{array} \right\} \right\} \dots$

SEARCH ALL identifier-1 [AT END imperative-statement-1]

$\underline{\text{WHEN}} \left\{ \begin{array}{l} \text{data-name-1} \left\{ \begin{array}{l} \text{IS} \ \underline{\text{EQUAL}} \ \text{TO} \\ \text{IS} \ = \end{array} \right\} \left\{ \begin{array}{l} \text{identifier-3} \\ \text{literal-1} \\ \text{arithmetic-expression-1} \end{array} \right\} \\ \text{condition-name-1} \end{array} \right\}$

$\left[\underline{\text{AND}} \left\{ \begin{array}{l} \text{data-name-2} \left\{ \begin{array}{l} \text{IS} \ \underline{\text{EQUAL}} \ \text{TO} \\ \text{IS} \ = \end{array} \right\} \left\{ \begin{array}{l} \text{identifier-4} \\ \text{literal-2} \\ \text{arithmetic-expression-2} \end{array} \right\} \\ \text{condition-name-2} \end{array} \right\} \right] \dots$

$\left\{ \begin{array}{l} \text{imperative-statement-2} \\ \underline{\text{NEXT}} \ \underline{\text{SENTENCE}} \end{array} \right\}$

SEND cd-name FROM identifier-1

SEND cd-name [FROM identifier-1] $\left\{ \begin{array}{l} \text{WITH identifier-2} \\ \text{WITH } \underline{\text{ESI}} \\ \text{WITH } \underline{\text{EMI}} \\ \text{WITH } \underline{\text{EGI}} \end{array} \right\}$

$\left[\left\{ \begin{array}{l} \underline{\text{BEFORE}} \\ \underline{\text{AFTER}} \end{array} \right\} \text{ADVANCING} \left\{ \begin{array}{l} \left\{ \left\{ \begin{array}{l} \text{identifier-3} \\ \text{integer} \end{array} \right\} \left[\begin{array}{l} \text{LINE} \\ \text{LINES} \end{array} \right] \right\} \\ \left\{ \begin{array}{l} \text{mnemonic-name} \\ \underline{\text{PAGE}} \end{array} \right\} \end{array} \right\} \right]$

SET $\left\{ \begin{array}{l} \text{identifier-1} \\ \text{index-name-1} \end{array} \right\} \dots \underline{\text{TO}} \left\{ \begin{array}{l} \text{identifier-3} \\ \text{index-name-3} \\ \text{integer-1} \end{array} \right\}$

SET {index-name-4} $\dots \left\{ \begin{array}{l} \underline{\text{UP}} \ \underline{\text{BY}} \\ \underline{\text{DOWN}} \ \underline{\text{BY}} \end{array} \right\} \left\{ \begin{array}{l} \text{identifier-4} \\ \text{integer-2} \end{array} \right\}$

SORT file-name-1 $\left\{ \text{ON} \left\{ \begin{array}{l} \underline{\text{ASCENDING}} \\ \underline{\text{DESCENDING}} \end{array} \right\} \text{KEY \{data-name-1\}} \dots \right\} \dots$

[COLLATING SEQUENCE IS alphabet-name]

$\left\{ \begin{array}{l} \underline{\text{INPUT}} \ \underline{\text{PROCEDURE}} \text{ IS section-name-1} \left[\left\{ \begin{array}{l} \underline{\text{THROUGH}} \\ \underline{\text{THRU}} \end{array} \right\} \text{section-name-2} \right] \\ \underline{\text{USING}} \text{ \{file-name-2\}} \dots \end{array} \right\}$

$\left\{ \begin{array}{l} \underline{\text{OUTPUT}} \ \underline{\text{PROCEDURE}} \text{ IS section-name-3} \left[\left\{ \begin{array}{l} \underline{\text{THROUGH}} \\ \underline{\text{THRU}} \end{array} \right\} \text{section-name-4} \right] \\ \underline{\text{GIVING}} \text{ file-name-4} \end{array} \right\}$

$$\underline{\text{START}} \text{ file-name} \left[\underline{\text{KEY}} \left\{ \begin{array}{l} \text{IS } \underline{\text{EQUAL}} \text{ TO} \\ \text{IS } = \\ \text{IS } \underline{\text{GREATER}} \text{ THAN} \\ \text{IS } > \\ \text{IS } \underline{\text{NOT}} \text{ LESS THAN} \\ \text{IS } \underline{\text{NOT}} < \end{array} \right\} \text{data-name} \right]$$

[INVALID KEY imperative-statement]

$$\underline{\text{STOP}} \left\{ \begin{array}{l} \underline{\text{RUN}} \\ \text{literal} \end{array} \right\}$$

$$\underline{\text{STRING}} \left\{ \begin{array}{l} \text{identifier-1} \\ \text{literal-1} \end{array} \right\} \dots \underline{\text{DELIMITED}} \text{ BY} \left\{ \begin{array}{l} \text{identifier-3} \\ \text{literal-3} \\ \underline{\text{SIZE}} \end{array} \right\} \dots$$

   INTO identifier-7 [WITH POINTER identifier-8]
   [ON OVERFLOW imperative-statement]

$$\underline{\text{SUBTRACT}} \left\{ \begin{array}{l} \text{identifier-1} \\ \text{literal-1} \end{array} \right\} \dots \underline{\text{FROM}} \{\text{identifier-m } [\underline{\text{ROUNDED}}]\} \dots$$

   [ON SIZE ERROR imperative-statement]

$$\underline{\text{SUBTRACT}} \left\{ \begin{array}{l} \text{identifier-1} \\ \text{literal-1} \end{array} \right\} \dots \underline{\text{FROM}} \left\{ \begin{array}{l} \text{identifier-m} \\ \text{literal-m} \end{array} \right\}$$

   GIVING {identifier-n [ROUNDED]} ...
   [ON SIZE ERROR imperative-statement]

$$\underline{\text{SUBTRACT}} \left\{ \begin{array}{l} \underline{\text{CORRESPONDING}} \\ \underline{\text{CORR}} \end{array} \right\} \text{identifier-1 } \underline{\text{FROM}} \text{ identifier-2 } [\underline{\text{ROUNDED}}]$$

   [ON SIZE ERROR imperative-statement]

SUPPRESS PRINTING

TERMINATE {report-name-1} ...

UNSTRING identifier-1

$$\left[\underline{\text{DELIMITED}} \text{ BY } [\underline{\text{ALL}}] \left\{ \begin{array}{l} \text{identifier-2} \\ \text{literal-1} \end{array} \right\} \left[\underline{\text{OR}} \text{ } [\underline{\text{ALL}}] \left\{ \begin{array}{l} \text{identifier-3} \\ \text{literal-2} \end{array} \right\} \right] \dots \right]$$

   INTO {identifier-4 [DELIMITER IN identifier-5][COUNT IN identifier-6]} ...
   [WITH POINTER identifier-10][TALLYING IN identifier-11]
   [ON OVERFLOW imperative-statement]

$$\underline{\text{USE}} \text{ } \underline{\text{AFTER}} \text{ STANDARD} \left\{ \begin{array}{l} \underline{\text{EXCEPTION}} \\ \underline{\text{ERROR}} \end{array} \right\} \underline{\text{PROCEDURE}} \text{ ON} \left\{ \begin{array}{l} \{\text{file-name-1}\} \dots \\ \text{INPUT} \\ \underline{\text{OUTPUT}} \\ \text{I-O} \\ \text{EXTEND} \end{array} \right\}.$$

USE BEFORE REPORTING identifier.

$$\underline{\text{USE}} \text{ FOR } \underline{\text{DEBUGGING}} \text{ ON} \left\{ \begin{array}{l} \text{cd-name-1} \\ [\underline{\text{ALL}} \text{ REFERENCES OF}] \text{ identifier-1} \\ \text{file-name-1} \\ \text{procedure-name-1} \\ \underline{\text{ALL}} \text{ } \underline{\text{PROCEDURES}} \end{array} \right\} \dots .$$

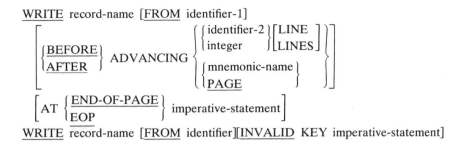

WRITE record-name [FROM identifier][INVALID KEY imperative-statement]

General Format For Conditions

Relation Condition

$$\begin{Bmatrix} \text{identifier-1} \\ \text{literal-1} \\ \text{arithmetic-expression-1} \\ \text{index-name-1} \end{Bmatrix} \begin{Bmatrix} \text{IS [NOT] GREATER THAN} \\ \text{IS [NOT] LESS THAN} \\ \text{IS [NOT] EQUAL TO} \\ \text{IS [NOT]} > \\ \text{IS [NOT]} < \\ \text{IS [NOT]} = \end{Bmatrix} \begin{Bmatrix} \text{identifier-2} \\ \text{literal-2} \\ \text{arithmetic-expression-2} \\ \text{index-name-2} \end{Bmatrix}$$

Class condition

$$\text{identifier IS [NOT]} \begin{Bmatrix} \text{NUMERIC} \\ \text{ALPHABETIC} \end{Bmatrix}$$

Sign condition

$$\text{arithmetic-expression [NOT]} \begin{Bmatrix} \text{POSITIVE} \\ \text{NEGATIVE} \\ \text{ZERO} \end{Bmatrix}$$

Condition-name condition

condition-name

Switch-status condition

condition-name

Negated simple condition

NOT simple-condition

Combined condition

$$\text{condition} \left\{ \begin{Bmatrix} \text{AND} \\ \text{OR} \end{Bmatrix} \text{condition} \right\} \ldots$$

Abbreviated combined relation condition

$$\text{relation-condition} \left\{ \begin{Bmatrix} \text{AND} \\ \text{OR} \end{Bmatrix} \text{[NOT] [relational-operator] object} \right\} \ldots$$

Miscellaneous Formats

Qualification

$$\left\{ \begin{array}{l} \text{data-name-1} \\ \text{condition-name} \end{array} \right\} \left[\left\{ \begin{array}{l} \underline{OF} \\ \underline{IN} \end{array} \right\} \text{data-name-2} \right] \ldots$$

$$\text{paragraph-name} \left[\left\{ \begin{array}{l} \underline{OF} \\ \underline{IN} \end{array} \right\} \text{section-name} \right]$$

$$\text{text-name} \left[\left\{ \begin{array}{l} \underline{OF} \\ \underline{IN} \end{array} \right\} \text{library-name} \right]$$

Subscripting

$$\left\{ \begin{array}{l} \text{data-name} \\ \text{condition-name} \end{array} \right\} (\text{subscript-1} \; [\, , \text{subscript-2} \; [\, , \text{subscript-3}]])$$

Indexing

$$\left\{ \begin{array}{l} \text{data-name} \\ \text{condition-name} \end{array} \right\} \left(\left\{ \begin{array}{l} \text{index-name-1} \; [\{\pm\} \; \text{literal-2}] \\ \text{literal-1} \end{array} \right\} \right.$$

$$\left[\, , \left\{ \begin{array}{l} \text{index-name-2} \; [\{\pm\} \; \text{literal-4}] \\ \text{literal-3} \end{array} \right\} \right] \left[\, , \left\{ \begin{array}{l} \text{index-name-3} \; [\{\pm\} \; \text{literal-6}] \\ \text{literal-5} \end{array} \right\} \right] \right)$$

Identifier Format 1

$$\text{data-name-1} \left[\left\{ \begin{array}{l} \underline{OF} \\ \underline{IN} \end{array} \right\} \text{data-name-2} \right] \ldots [(\text{subscript-1} \; [\, , \text{subscript-2}$$
$$[\, , \text{subscript-3}]])]$$

Identifier Format 2

$$\text{data-name-1} \left[\left\{ \begin{array}{l} \underline{OF} \\ \underline{IN} \end{array} \right\} \text{data-name-2} \right] \ldots \left[\left(\left\{ \begin{array}{l} \text{index-name-1} \; [\{\pm\} \; \text{literal-2}] \\ \text{literal-1} \end{array} \right\} \right. \right.$$

$$\left[\, , \left\{ \begin{array}{l} \text{index-name-2} \; [\{\pm\} \; \text{literal-4}] \\ \text{literal-3} \end{array} \right\} \right] \left[\, , \left\{ \begin{array}{l} \text{index-name-3} \; [\{\pm\} \; \text{literal-6}] \\ \text{literal-5} \end{array} \right\} \right] \right) \right]$$